SPEAKING OF MUSIC

Speaking of Music

Addressing the Sonorous

Edited by

Keith Chapin and Andrew H. Clark

FORDHAM UNIVERSITY PRESS

New York 2013

Library of Congress Cataloging-in-Publication Data

Speaking of music : addressing the sonorous / edited by Keith Chapin and Andrew H. Clark. — First edition.
pages cm
Includes bibliographical references and index.
ISBN 978-0-8232-5138-4 (cloth : alk. paper) —
ISBN 978–0-8232-5139-1 (pbk. : alk. paper)
1. Music—Philosophy and aesthetics.   2. Musical criticism.   3. Music and literature.   I. Chapin, Keith Moore, editor.   II. Clark, Andrew Herrick, 1973–, editor.
ML3800.S69 2013
781—dc23
2013002553

Printed in the United States of America
15 14 13   5 4 3 2 1
First edition

To our parents

CONTENTS

ILLUSTRATIONS

ACKNOWLEDGMENTS

This book results from a series of faculty reading groups on issues of music and language led by the editors at Fordham University from 2002 through 2007, generously supported by the Mellon Foundation in conjunction with the Deans of Fordham College. We thank the other participants in these discussions for their intellectual contributions, especially Chris GoGwilt, Michael Puri, Alexander Rehding, and Philip Rupprecht. The book itself owes much to Sophie Ivory, who assisted in the editing of the manuscript before submission; to Dan Bickerton, who set one of the musical examples; to Cardiff University, Fordham University, and Victoria University Wellington, each of which provided financial and institutional support at various stages; and finally to Helen Tartar, Thomas Lay, Eric Newman, and Andrew Katz of Fordham University Press, who were invaluable in turning an unfinished manuscript into a finished book.

Speaking of Music:
A View across Disciplines
and a Lexicon of Topoi

Keith Chapin and Andrew H. Clark

It is impossible not to speak of music, for language and music are inextricably linked. The ways and means of this linkage are diverse. They run the gamut from the musicality of speech to speech about music. One speaks music even as one writes, as Jean-Luc Nancy notes in his homage to the musical philosopher Philippe Lacoue-Labarthe in this collection. Sonic acts underpin all utterances, and behind every narrative (or *récit*) lies a recitation and behind every recitation a recitative, that paradigmatic marriage of music and language. At the other end of the spectrum, as Lawrence Kramer notes in this volume, "Speaking of music is obviously no problem. We speak about music all the time; we speak about it incessantly. Speaking of music is a normal part of music making and music loving. We listen, we play, we hum, we sing, we talk." The title of this book pays homage, on the one hand, to the performative element involved in all thought about music and emblematized by the act of speaking and, on the other, to the fact that engagement with music returns to speech, a fact betokened in the offhand remark "speaking of music."

If speaking of music happens all the time, it happens in many ways. Music and language are not constants but rather change with changing times and vary depending on the perspectives of their practitioners and theoreticians. The collection of essays in this volume thus arises from three impulses and so is dedicated to the issue of speaking of music on three fronts.

First, this collection addresses the question of how one speaks of music today, especially but not exclusively within the Western tradition. The question of how one speaks about music is an age-old question, but its venerable age in no way superannuates it. It must be readdressed as each generation reforms and rethinks both practices and theories of music and language. Indeed, one of the recurring arguments made in this collection of essays is that music, so often thought in the nineteenth and twentieth centuries as the medium that picks up where language leaves off or as the aureate art toward which other arts aspires, can rather be perceived as the foundation of language. The authors who claim this, and not all do, arrive at their conclusion by different routes, but they have in common their willingness to give up on the fixity of *logos* and the concept as the defining feature of language and rather to insist on its processuality. As a result, the flux and transience of music ceases to be a problem, as they are when judged from the standpoint of *logos*, and become rather a source of insight. Some argue that all arts share the condition of music, that is, its temporality, its embodiment, its dissemination within a community.

Second, this collection arises from the desire to examine how writers in different disciplines in the humanities speak about music. Interdisciplinarity is easy to preach but difficult to practice, as all those dedicated to its ideals well know. At the same time, interdisciplinarity happens all the time. The authors here all speak regularly about music, but each does so from the perspective of his or her discipline. The disciplines represented here include musicology and music theory, literary studies, cognitive science, philosophy, and political science. Although the range could have been expanded further, the selection is enough to achieve insights into music and its processes today, indeed insights that might be difficult to grasp were a discipline to speak alone. There are, in other words, topoi that recur across disciplines. Thus, even as most of the authors here focus on the task at hand—they speak of music, its representations, and its institutions and practices, not of methodology or disciplinary self-reflection—they provide the stuff for such reflection.

Third, there has been a marked shift in studies of music away from the notated music that comprises much of the Western art tradition and toward the panoply of activities that involve music: composing and performing, certainly, but also listening, dancing, humming as one washes the dishes—in short anything involving music. Christopher Small has coined the term "musicking" to address this range of activities.[1] The relationship between music and language looks different once one turns from the idealized reification of music into musical works toward an emphasis placed on practice and process. While sound and body art such as that of Henri Chopin, discussed by Kiene Brillenburg Wurth in this volume, may not fit traditional approaches to the study of music, it makes eminent sense in this context.

The insights gained and the issues raised by the participants in the collection through their discussions can be summarized by naming some of the important topoi that recur and the questions that punctuate them.

Music and Language: Together or Apart

Do language and music work in similar ways, or is music an art apart? Any answer to the question will depend in large part on how one defines one's terms. In any case, most answers will aim for nuanced middle positions between similarity and difference, and the authors here present a variety of such positions, not all of them in agreement with each other.

Since the eighteenth century, as Downing Thomas and Andrew Bowie have noted, philosophers and critics have remarked on the filial relationship between music and language: they are intimately related, but they often quarrel.[2] The family relationship between music and language can be predicated on many levels, from the practical and social to the theoretical and philosophical. Kramer notes in his chapter that people speak about music just as often and as easily as they do about language, or indeed about anything at all. Similarly, Peter Szendy notes that music inescapably opens up a space for words. Per Aage Brandt, by contrast, proposes that the relationship between music and language can be described as a semiotic metalanguage of strong and weak codes. The codes bring music and language together as means of communication but differentiate between their modalities.

Other authors here emphasize differences that make music particular among the arts. As Keith Chapin and Matthew Gelbart examine the aesthetic ideals and institutional practices that underpin any art, they note that musicians worked under conditions that were emphatically their own. Chapin argues that professional musicians engage with their medium in ways that make it difficult for them to enter fully into the ideal humanistic community of the arts: the technical training that enables close attention to minute details is more obscure to the nonspecialist than that involved in language, a medium after all learned and used by all. By contrast, Gelbart proposes that the way that music fills space makes it inherently more physical and even functional than literature. Because of music's strong roots in place and space, Romantic writers on music gave great attention to the issue of genre as a way to situate music, even when they also celebrated the individual genius who trumped all convention.

Limit

Even those writers who emphasize the commonalities between music and language will note that the two are not the same. Thus, a constant topos of discussions about music and language is the limit, gap, or *difference* between them. It is often a gap in which speaking of music occurs. The authors in this volume refer to this point or space with different words: "limit," "gap" (Peter Szendy), a dialectic of "ensnarement" and "withholding" (Kramer), a "hinge" (Jairo Moreno), *difference*, "dissonance" (Andrew H. Clark), and so forth. As this variety suggests, music and language can be seen to relate in many ways. "Music overflows the limits of language and of reason," Moreno writes in his chapter. Kramer notes that "although all the posts in this relay [of music, the stories we tell about it, and their interpretation], including the verbal ones, *withhold* something from language, there is no post that language leaves wholly untouched." "Vocal production," Nancy writes, "puts into play a *resonance* of the body by which inside and outside separate, then respond to each other." Szendy also uses Nancy's musical term: music opens a "gap" or "an in-between in which music, so to speak, speaks about itself, in which words, more and more words, *resonate*." According to Moreno, the unspeakable lies at the heart of both language and music, and thus there is a limit implicit in both. Such limits "mark 'speaking of music' as a particular kind of linguistic *trespassing*." (Emphases added.) These nuances are not a mere matter of words but rather are informed by the different disciplinary concerns of the authors.

The issue of the limit can be seen from at least two angles. There is the invocation of music to evoke the limits of language, and there is the invocation of language to evoke the limits of music. The two limits are of course related, but they are not the same. In many ways, to use music as a metaphor in language is at once to create a limit or gap but also to articulate or delineate it. The metaphor of music appears to enable what mere words are represented as only approximating. Dissonance, for instance, as Clark argues, was for many eighteenth-century writers a metaphor to think about different forms of political and physical engagement, but one that could not be fully articulated or prescribed in language and one that was frequently at odds with the practice of dissonance use in music. In this case, dissonance becomes a metaphor that at once creates and articulates a gap. It becomes a stand-in for that which overflows the limit.

The authors collected here draw different practical and ethical implications from their ways of viewing the limits of both language and music. For Kramer, as mentioned before, speaking of music is "no problem at all." Those who construe a problem mystify music, cordon it into a sanitized "absolute" realm in which meaning seems an imposition. Whereas Kramer would argue that both music and language flourish in the gap that separates them—this has been a leading theme in his work—Laura Odello, analyzing Ulysses's resistance to the Sirens by limiting his own power, suggests that the gap or limit might consume music's alterity altogether by surrendering it and its function to the *logos*. Speaking of music, in other words, is dangerous. "And music?" she writes, "What about music in this *other* song that the narrative becomes? What remains of music in this gap between real song and imaginary song?" Her response is that music is muted. How do we preserve the limit or gap between music and words? And how do we (or can we or should we) prevent the gap from being filled with more words: *parole, parole, parole*. That is, how do we prevent the limit or gap from benefiting words at the cost of music?

Whereas some of the authors in this collection deal with the issue of speaking of music at a theoretical level, if often by reading the implicit theory behind the actions or statements of protagonists in literature or music, others examine either the practices of speaking of music or the proposals for practice. In such cases, it often appears that the gap or limit between music and language has a function of its own. As Tracy B. Strong notes, building on Jean-Jacques Rousseau's musical and political theory, it is when words are lacking or have not been formed that music takes its strongest hold and helps us find our commonality. In Moreno's examination of the political protests by illegal immigrants in 2006, he finds that music, through its testing of limits, allowed protesters to build a community that confounded the U.S. government's claim to represent both *logos* and the authority that goes with it.

To many practitioners, music has existential or even metaphysical significance, and such is the significance that they cannot help talking about it. Yet the limits between music and language take on new modalities when these situations occur. Very frequently, the experience of a limit on language occurs at the point that one feels a limit on one's own individual identity. Yet the significance of this existential experience can be spun at times toward the communal, at times toward the metaphysical. Whereas Rousseau portrays individuals as fully human only insofar as they communicate and commune through music, Olivier Messiaen, Sander van Maas argues in this volume, views music as sketching the limit not only of the speakable but also of the experience of time. Messiaen's music takes the form of a "proclamation" or "*annonce*," to use Nancy's term, of things to come.

Speaking of Music is in many respects our collective attempt at both recognizing and articulating the gap or limit between language and music. It seeks to preserve the difference and specificity of music and language but also to establish a collaborative space between the two, in which the limit is at once established, transgressed, and deterritorialized. This collaborative space is at once the point at which meaningful discussion between the disciplines can take place and also the point at which disagreements have occurred and will continue to occur.

Logos

The definition of the limit between language and music has often been accomplished by an appeal to *logos*—a Greek word that originally meant "reason," "word," "discourse," and "speech." The definition has social, political, and metaphysical implications for the various ways that human beings use sound to act in their world. More often than not, music has suffered.

For the philosophers of ancient Greece and for the Christian theologians and contemporary writers who have explicitly or implicitly borrowed their words, to have reason is to control the word. The metaphysical hegemony of *logos* has tended to privilege the theoretical discussion of music over the production of sound, to subsume sounding music into language, or to ban music altogether. As Boethius wrote in the sixth century in his translation and paraphrase of Greek writers, "For it is far greater and nobler to know what someone does than to accomplish oneself what someone else knows, for physical skill obeys like a handmaid while reason rules like a mistress. . . . How much more admirable, then, is the science of music in apprehending by reason than in accomplishing by work and deed!"[3] For the Greeks, to speak was a means to power in which, as Moreno notes, *logos* was viewed as being "inscribed into the very core of Being." Being is made manifest by speech. Christian theologians followed their lead and made *logos* or the *word* a designation of the second person of the Trinity—Jesus, the *word* of God.[4] Odello in this volume notes a similar tendency among philosophers: "The philosopher does not want to know anything about listening; hearing is of no use to the philosopher because the end as well as the beginning of all philosophizing resides in the intellectual understanding: sonorities are superfluous, secondary, unnecessary for the silent vision of the *logos*, of the idea, of the ideal signified, which alone serves to grasp the truth."

While the traditional invocation of *logos* distinguishes speaking from musicking, it is also possible to conceive of *logos* such that it is not defined through the rejection of something else, such as emotion or sensation. This is the strategy of several of the writers in this volume, and for good reason. According to Odello and Moreno, making music subservient to *logos* comes at a linguistic and political cost: music becomes mute, and political actions based on communal actions or sentiments are undermined.

Rather, it may be possible to conceive of a more equal dynamic between the two. This can be done by shifting the emphasis in definitions of *logos* toward speech acts and performance, that is, away from the fixity of a rational concept, a point of origin, a commanding directive. As soon as the sonic medium and the temporal and physical embodiment that goes with it are not opposed to *logos*, then it becomes much easier to overcome the oppositions between *logos* and its various potential opposites, *aesthesis*, emotion, sensation, or narrative. There are different ways to construe *logos* or its performance. The philosopher and cognitive scientist Brandt sets out distinctions between different types and uses of words: words related to space have a particular affinity with music, he argues. In other words, if one articulates and nuances *logos* itself, it is easier to avoid oppositions between *logos* and music. For Nancy, who investigates the sonic qualities of narration, the opening and reconceiving of *logos* occurs around narrative. "For *narration is knowledge* (*gnarus, co-gnosco, ignoro*); it is knowledge that reports, that relates what has taken place, that it took place and how it took place, how the order and succession of things occurred and then modified, modulated, altered." Kramer, less focused on discourse alone than Nancy is, also emphasizes the process by which individuals tell stories about their words and about their music. Once again, the fixity of *logos* is replaced by a constant, if at times tempestuous, process of narration.

In short, the political and philosophical position of *logos* has often given it a false sense of constancy. Once this constancy is taken away, one is left with many opportunities for reconceiving the relationship between music and language.

Supplement

If a medium limits another, it also can supplement it. The *supplement* is thus a recurrent topos in discussions of music. Jacques Derrida established the term in modern scholarship,[5] though the issues he raised go back to a critique of language that gained force in the eighteenth century. At this time, the *logos* lost its pride of place among certain philosophers: its control no longer seemed to provide an access to Being, to guarantee that spoken language could legitimately and immediately represent the world. In the beginning, Rousseau speculated, singing and speech were one. After the Fall, however, language lost its purchase on immediacy. Music offered a *supplement* to language.

In many ways, however, Rousseau simply reversed the then-traditional privilege given to words, whose potential for accuracy was thought to offer a supplement to the vagaries of music. As the writers collected here demonstrate, speaking of music permits the bidirectionality of the process of supplementation. In most accounts of music and language, music has acted as a supplement of language. For Rousseau, as for many Romantics after him, music offered a nostalgic reminder of lost origins, a supplement that offset the alienation proper to modernity and paradigmatically represented by the opacity of language. This process was not always experienced as a good thing. In Odello's study of Plato and in her analysis of Ulysses's encounter with the Sirens, she notes that music disobediently supplements the aporia of philosophy, of *logos*: "music shamelessly and disobediently returns as the very disorder that the Greek philosopher spent his life trying to contain, to neutralize, giving it a deaf ear."

But language may also complete music. For example, Hamilton argues in his reading of Balzac's *Massimilla Doni* that music and the Absolute that it evokes are finally redeemed in words, but only when the music performed within the novella is over, when it has been lost. "The desired goal [of reaching the Absolute] has been attained; impotence has been cured, but only after the music is over, only after sound has been definitively exchanged for written prose, only after the opera has *taken place*." However, despite this process of posthumous completion, the musical method still permeates Balzac's discourse and provides counterpoint to the text's realism.

If each medium—music and language—can supplement the other, it may be that it is the very gap between them that offers a supplement. Strong rereads Rousseau's arguments about the supplementary nature of music. Music may not so much complete language as open up a space in which the quest to know, express, and communicate might take place. "Music can/should establish a space between that for which one has words and that for which one would wish to find one's own words, words to which one would have right, even if, in the end, they are words that will always be insufficient." One could imagine that this space might work to the advantage of either medium.

Ineffability/Absolute

Historically, a strong topos in discussions of the relationship between music and language is that of ineffability. Because music does not seem to signify in quite the same way as language—because it does not seem to work with concepts—its meaning and sense seem to eschew designation, even to intimate things about which one cannot speak. Music seems to laugh at language, or at least at concrete uses of language in everyday human affairs. Loath to remain silent about the ineffable, some writers—Balzac, for instance, or Hoffmann, Balzac's source of inspiration—posed music as a token of that which transcends human laws and limits: the Absolute or some other vision of holistic totality, dogmatic or nondogmatic, confessional or unconventional. A deep chasm may separate the rhetorical topos of ineffability from beliefs or hopes in metaphysics, but many have made a short step of it.

One recent musician who undoubtedly and explicitly made such a step was Messiaen, but Messiaen made the step by going beyond avian, not human, language. As van Maas argues in this volume, drawing on Gilles Deleuze, Messiaen did not aim at an ornithographic depiction of birds and nature. Nor, for that matter, did he envisage other mimetic relationships, say, between musical time and the linear and cyclical time of natural and human events. Rather, Messiaen transcribed bird songs and at the same time transformed them: the musical stasis that ensconces them has the form of a "proclamation," an instantiation of the end of time even at the moment of its beginning. To go briefly beyond van Maas's argument, it may even be that the apparent fixity and immobility of human words and concepts take on new meaning in such a musical context. Messiaen's titles to his works are doctrinally precise: *Méditations sur le mystère de la Sainte Trinité* (1969). They seem to denote what the music is supposed to connote: Catholic theology, liberally understood. Yet if they too are understood as proclamations, then the tension between the "to come" of the end of time as forever held present (on the one hand) and the present and its passing (on the other) is held forever open within them.

If the writers collected here generally avoid enthusiasm for the Absolute and its brethren, just as they question the ineffability of music, they find the issue alive in the texts they study and in the traditions with which they are in dialogue. Kramer takes a strong stance against those who would avoid speaking of music, as well as those who would restrict the types of language they would use to speak about it. Ineffability is a "bugbear," he writes. Hamilton is similarly skeptical about ineffability and the Absolute in his study of Balzac, though he notes the crucial importance of the idea for Balzac. Hamilton argues that the Absolute is attained only when music is absorbed into literature. Precisely because a literary depiction of musical performances renders music mute—the sounds can exist only in the imagination—literature best preserves the ideal of music's ineffability, but only by robbing music of its sound.

Physicality, Process, and Performance

Despite the close attention to differences between music and language, the authors in this volume join in their careful regard for the physical presence and temporal process involved in music's production, action, and effects. Sound is performed into the world and subsequently reels through the body. It inflects the fixity and fixations of linguistic concepts. As noted earlier, the venerable question of the relationship between music and language loses some of its point when physicality and temporality are taken as the fundamental strata of human existence.

But the forces of time and the processes of embodiment affect the ways one speaks through and about music in many ways. At times, it is music's power to mediate the physical relationships between individuals that allows it its particular power. In Strong's study of Rousseau, he highlights the power of music to further social interaction. One becomes fully human only when one is integrated—sonically rather than linguistically—into a community. Hamilton also focuses on the ability of music to form and rule a very different community, the erotic love square that exists between the principal characters of Balzac's novella *Massimilla Doni*.

In dialogue with Nancy's *Listening*, Lawrence M. Zbikowski argues that while Nancy is right to point to the need to listen to music listening to itself, to think of sound-as-sense rather than sound-as-signification, what Nancy leaves out is the embodiment of music, by not addressing the body that listens to music. For Zbikowski, cognitive categories, with their reliance on analogical rather than symbolic reference, provide a more expansive and flexible mode with which to address the dynamic qualities of music and its embodiment. "Analogical reference—as a mode of representation that cuts across perceptual channels and that offers a way to explain the role of the body in the construction of meaning"—he writes, "points to a different kind of knowledge from that on which philosophy has concentrated." According to Zbikowski, cognitive categories also enable one to think about commonalities between musics that have been traditionally seen by Western musicologists as having absolutely nothing in common. One might be able to speak then, as Zbikowski does in his chapter, about the mourning practices in Fernando Sor's *Fantaisie élégiaque* in connection to West African Akpafu's dirges if one looks at the embodiment of this music and not to categories organized around conceptual models. Cognitive categories enable Zbikowski to think about how one can understand and speak of music's embodiment in experiences and events beyond language.

Such a potential for music's embodiment is also noted in Clark's reading of the eighteenth-century vitalist doctor Joseph-Louis Roger, who proposed musical cures for a number of ills weakening the individual and social body. For Roger, we have a kind of musical instinct that predisposes the body to be embodied by music, to exist, respond, and communicate beyond language.

In Wurth's study of the uses of technology to present the voice in music—through the real instruments that Henri Chopin uses to turn the sounds of his body into music—she also notes that bodies disrupt any idealized process by which a listener hears a disembodied work. "This, perhaps, is how bodies come to tamper and interfere with regulated, instrumental music: they make listening—linear, focused listening—nearby impossible. They make noise."

Music and Space

Traditional discussions of music and language often operated as if space was inconsequential. Either music and language were classed together by virtue of their sonic medium as opposed to the visual or plastic arts, or they were rated in terms of their ability to allow people to escape space, to access the Absolute. However, the topos of space has moved toward the center of discussion of music and language. At times, it functions as a metaphor to capture particularities of music and language. At times, it serves to emphasize the physicality of music and speech or the contexts that determine speaking about music. No matter whether "space" designates a physical environment or serves as a metaphor in another domain, however, it serves to rescue speaking of music from models of unilinearity and certitude. Space stands for the complexity of the task of speaking of music, for the many directions that it can move and for the difficulty and even undesirability of pinning it down.

The turn away from unilinearity can be seen at the cognitive level, argues Brandt, in the way that people mentally "see spaces" when they hear music. In other words, their cognition of the world gains in amplitude and dimension as they hear music. According to van Maas, people are to experience a new sense of space through Messiaen's music, to open up a play between a sense of the finite (delimited space) and the infinite (open space).

This mental space can unwork physical space, as Hamilton describes in his analysis of *Massimilla Doni*: the voice evokes the loss of self and of a specific articulate space. "The voice that intrudes on Massimilla's consciousness," he writes, "is incorporeal and compelling, not dissimilar to Socrates's *daimonion* or Kant's 'voice of reason'—a voice that arrests, a voice that overtakes one's subjective position. It is a voice, most importantly, that cannot be located. Emilio, too, is overmastered by a voice, the voice of his beloved, that is, a voice whose master source may be identified but whose efficacy lies in its capacity to dislocate and confuse sources." For Balzac, according to Hamilton, music erodes clearly defined spaces and even one's own subjective position. Space is dislocated. Space does not ground our understanding, nor is it stable.

While music may undo physical space or create a parallel mental space, the physical space in which it occurs can also ground music's ability to destabilize the lines along which speaking of music occurs. Nancy emphasizes the body cavities without which no speech is possible, while Wurth examines the music made by the sound artist Chopin through the amplification of his own bodily sounds. Nancy emphasizes the musical aspect of speech (whether devoted to music or not), while Wurth describes how Chopin forces us to reconsider both what music is and how it relates to the constitution of human identity and autonomy. In both cases, the physicality of music poses questions about the nature of genres and institutions of language, music, and human identity.

Genre and institution themselves pose questions about the space—not (only) the bodily spaces that allow one to speak or produce music but also the physical and contextual environments within which speaking takes place. As studied by Gelbart, because genre involves a contract between composers, performers, and listeners about expectations that certain types of music are appropriate to certain times, places, and people, it necessarily involves a consideration of the physical spaces in which music is heard and the mental spaces. "In music," he writes, "genre is almost inalienably linked to types of rooms, types of movement, times of day, membership in a particular kind of audience, and so forth." Similarly, Chapin looks at the institutional spaces that determine different approaches to speaking about music.

If the universality of music as a language persists as a topos of music aesthetics—music can seem to force space to disappear—many people who speak about music also use the topos of space to emphasize the particular and the contingent: music can mark regional identities and can remind one of particular places.

Loss or Maintenance of Self

Insofar as music fills space, relating people to each other and to the physical worlds that surround them, it erodes or qualifies the processes of individuation that have traditionally been seen to constitute the "self," the subjectivity that underpins a person's actions and motions in the world. At the same time, music can be seen to help individuals constitute themselves, to crystallize their identities in the groove of a good tune or through their participation in musical activities. There is no question that music plays into processes of identity formation, but it does so in many and at times contradictory ways. Music is now the self's nemesis, now its strength and support.

No matter whether the authors here focus on the production or the reception of music, they tend to question the autonomy of the self—to note the ways that individual agency is impeded or dependent, as well as the ways that the maintenance of self through self-consciousness and memory is elusive or illusory. As an ideal, however, autonomy seems to remain intact in many of the discussions, even if this autonomy can never fully be achieved.

On the side of production—singing, playing, speaking, or any other sonic emission—the authors note the ways that the physicality and processuality of music inhibits the attainment of a stable self, long conceived as an incorporeal, noumenal, or otherwise metaphysical entity. Wurth notes that the voice emitted by Chopin's body in his *L'Énergie du sommeil* would seem to negate the humanist ideal of autonomy. Nancy emphasizes the dissociation between a narrator and his narration. One may hope to become a self by speaking, but because language and culture are inherited and thus interpersonal, one also gives up one's self as one speaks. An aspiration is also an expiration. The aporia is unavoidable. The musical aspects of narrative lie in the gap between the narrator and the narration—in the voice of the recitation—and there lies both the hope and the death of the self.

On the side of reception, music disturbs dreams of autonomous agency and selfhood in a diametrically opposed way. If the physicality of sound production makes the dream of autonomy but a dream, the relative incorporeality of received sound destabilizes whatever constancy and freedom a person has in fact managed to achieve. Hamilton argues that the voices trouble both Massimila and her lover, Emilio. It is precisely the seeming lack of origin of heard music that tears them both from their senses and from their sense of themselves. According to Odello, this incorporeality is given figurative form by the Sirens who sing sailors to their graves. While the Sirens who sing to Ulysses and other mariners in the ancient myth, have bodies, it is again their sound that destabilizes as it seduces, not their bodies. Following Adorno, Odello notes that Ulysses can only constitute himself as a free agent by opposing his rational self-control to the destabilizing power of the voice. Yet such destabilization is ironically an integral part of the process of self-formation, Odello argues. Only by undergoing the trial does Odysseus establish himself, and indeed the self requires its own destabilization to attain its constancy. The process, one imagines, is never ending. Only by selfishly making use of "music"—which serves Odello as an elusive metaphor for all that is elusive—does a person become a self.

Musical Communities and Discourse Traditions

If music tends to destabilize the autonomous self in its potential disruption of rationality, it has a great role in giving life substantive content. That is, music may often impede free will and free choice, but it can powerfully set forth the options of what one wills and what one chooses. One way to conceive of the options from which a person can or cannot choose is in terms of the communities with which a person identifies. As one plays the various roles of one's life—as one performs one's various identities—one acts within a mobile and shifting field of communities and subcommunities, each grouped around certain ideals of identity and sustained through certain institutions, practices, and goals. Such networks are often determined in terms of shared languages—shared systems of code that allow interlocutors to communicate—as well as shared practices. Music, at times at one with language, at times opposed to it, helps form identities and communities, just as it can also subvert them.

In part, music and language participate together to foster communities. For Rousseau, Strong notes, expression, through its origins in song, "thus actualized the fact of participation in a particular musico-linguistic community." Brandt describes a system of codes that allows him to posit music and language as different within a shared discursive space.

In part, music and language form communities in different ways and thus have quite distinct political and social roles to play. In 2006, undocumented immigrants to the United States marched in protest of restrictions placed on them. Song played a prominent part in their protests, as it does in almost all protest movements. Moreno argues that music was much more than a source of inspiration or a means of solidarity for the marchers, however. As political norms tend to be defined through positive rational laws, formulated through language, music's political and ethical power lies precisely in its aesthetic nature: its ability to resist the defining power of language and the singular definitions of politics but also its inability to render any positive politics beyond the event of appearance of people in the public arena.

Chapin turns his attention to the community of musicians in eighteenth-century Germany and notes that there were at least two different identities to which the musically skilled could adhere, each supported by its own institutions. Musicians could define themselves as members of a broad intellectual group bound together by their use of language—the Republic of Letters—or they could define themselves as members of a narrower group of professional musicians more specifically directed toward the combination of tones. Musicians could adhere to both, and they certainly could define themselves in many other ways as well, but frequently they listed to one side or the other.

The tensions between the two identities are perhaps perennial. Kramer challenges the sophisticated linguistic codes developed by professional musicians to speak about music as well as the vision of ineffability which seemed to deliver them from the necessity of addressing broader concerns. At the same time, the language of ineffability, Gelbart argues, was one aspect of a genre system through which musicians defined their art and thereby their relationships with their audience. To speak of music is to speak through the various contracts and codes of genre.

Musical ekphrasis

The Greek word *ekphrasis* (*ekphrazein*: "to recount, to describe"; from *ex-*: "out" and *phrazein*: "to speak") has traditionally been coopted by the visual arts to speak of the verbal representation of visual representation, such as we find in W. J. T. Mitchell's informative chapter "Ekphrasis and the Other."[6] The *locus classicus* of ekphrasis is the description of Achilles's shield in Homer's *Illiad*. The term brings up three closely interrelated issues— the specificity and uniqueness of different artistic media, the possibilities and pitfalls of secondary representations of an artwork in a different artistic medium, and, finally, the complex issues involved in the use of "artificial" signs (namely, words) to represent what were long thought of as "natural" signs (visual signs but also, as we argue, sonic ones). In other words, ekphrasis brings up the issue of whether it is possible to bridge between an abstract sign system (language) and one rooted to a greater extent in the physicality of the world.

As this list of issues suggests, ekphrasis need not be limited to visual representation. In antiquity, ekphrasis referred to the verbal description of anything (whether a person, a thing, music, etc.). Ekphrasis can thus also refer to the verbal representation of musical representation, that is, musical ekphrasis.[7] Musical ekphrasis is by definition a speaking (out) of music. Like its sister in the visual arts, it hopes to make us hear, as it wishes to make us see, to suture word and music. Its fear, to borrow Mitchell's terminology again, is that somehow the difference between musical representation and verbal representation will collapse, leaving no autonomy or specificity to one or the other.

Balzac was certainly aware of this issue, and he made frequent use of both traditional ekphrasis and musical ekphrasis. But as Hamilton has shown in his chapter in this volume, traditional ekphrasis and musical ekphrasis do not function in the same way for Balzac. Whereas ekphrasis as traditionally understood (the verbal representation of a visual representation) encourages us to look again and to decipher the iconography, music silences this activity. "With music," Hamilton writes, "the silencing appears to be more definitive and therefore more fatal, insofar as the verbalization strives to finalize a meaning, in an analogously iconological fashion, for an art that is presented as fundamentally aniconological." Verbal accounts of music function thus quite differently from verbal accounts of painting. "The consequence," Hamilton argues, "is that any verbal reformulation should be taken as heterogeneous to the sound and movement of performed music."

The alleged nonrepresentational quality of music makes musical ekphrasis all the more problematic. How do we make representational that which is nonrepresentational? How do we speak music? For Szendy, following Carl Dahlhaus's arguments about the literary-philosophical discussion that gave rise to the idea of absolute music, ekphrasis is the nature of all literature about music, with literature understood in its widest sense. "Literature about music," he writes, "is constitutive not only of its reception but also, if we agree to trust provisionally such a distinction, of its production." Szendy takes ekphrasis as the condition of all music. Music produces a gap in which music "speaks about itself." While the specialist discourse of music theory provides one such mode of ekphrasis, others exist as well.

The language traditionally used in program notes and reviews provides one alternative example. Curious about what happens cognitively and linguistically when people describe music, Brandt looks at various descriptions of music all linked around meteorological metaphors and tries to analyze the referential difference between music and language. Music, he argues, lacks the "referentializing elements." But this lack of referential precision, he continues, opens up music to the imagination; it creates a temporal space. Mentally seeing and evoking spaces is something that musicians and those who describe music both do (see "Music and Space" section). For Brandt, music and musical ekphrasis are defined by weak codes and by shared mental spaces, ones in which the affective emotional communication is privileged over the functionally communicative. Music is what gives language its imaginative affective space. It is what allows us, as Brandt concludes, to "transcend the immediate."

But if different types of language may provide different approaches to musical ekphrasis, musical ekphrasis nonetheless posits or proposes music far more than it describes it. In Odello's examination of Maurice Blanchot's interpretation of Ulysses and the Sirens, she suggests that for Blanchot the song of the Sirens is an encounter that can only occur in the tale, in narrative, not in music. She writes that "only when it is written into the narrative, as the opening of the infinite movement toward the song to come, does the encounter happen. It happens when constituting itself as narrative." Of course, this encounter is an impossibility. Musical ekphrasis does not describe something that has been heard. It cannot. For Odello, as for Hamilton, the writing that inscribes the music, that brings it into being, can only occur once the music is lost.

A special subcategory of musical ekphrasis involves those moments when music itself refers to other music. Van Maas highlights the transformation that takes place through such musical referentiality in his consideration of Messiaen's birdsong. The transformation wrought by the musical depiction of music is of a particular type. It suspends "all determinations" and "loosens the nuts and bolts of the perceptual world, beginning with its temporal structure." In Messiaen's case, this transformation is given a particular significance—the musical birdsong represents a "song to come" and thus suggests the eventual renewal of life "in and through Christ"—but it seems to us that van Maas's point is generalizable beyond the religious context. Musical representations of music create a kind of imaginative and sonorous space in which the represented music receives as its supplement new fluidity and physicality.

A Note on Methodology

This collection is born of the conviction that insight is won from methodological pluralism, even as the ability to speak with insight springs from specialization and intradisciplinary debate. Thus, each author brings the methodology of his or her discipline (and, in some cases, disciplines) to bear on the issue of speaking of music. At the same time, each author transcends the strict boundary of his or her discipline, learning much from other scholars and their approaches. Some authors read texts (both verbal and musical) closely, others define historical contexts, others philosophically illuminate presuppositions to arguments, and so forth. Within this diversity, as the review of topoi in this introduction suggests, the authors recur to common questions, though they do not necessarily arrive at common positions.

From the standpoint of methodology, the collection speaks modestly in two senses. First, the collection does not represent all the disciplines in which scholars speak about music. The collection identifies points of contact between disciplines through triangulation, not through exhaustive coverage. Second, the collection does not speak of all types of music. The writers predominantly speak of music (or they speak of speaking of music) in the Western tradition, though of course with the full awareness of the cultural boundaries to this tradition. Moreno studies the way that a political culture that prides itself on its Western roots is musically challenged by an immigrant culture that it hopes to exclude yet that is a part of it. Zbikowski examines the foundations on which one might propose to study the significance of musical mourning in both nineteenth-century France (Fernando Sor's *Fantaisie élégiaque*) and in twentieth-century Africa (the Akpafu of Ghana). It is certain that this collection would look different were it written by scholars within a different cultural tradition.

Speaking of Music

Lawrence Kramer

Speaking of music is obviously no problem. We speak about music all the time; we speak about it incessantly. Speaking of music is a normal part of music making and music loving. We listen, we play, we hum, we sing, we talk.

Speaking of music is obviously a problem. Otherwise the contributors to the book now in your hands (or on your screen) would not have convened on a pair of wintry afternoons to speak about speaking of music. They—we—would not have been vexed by the unspoken worry that speaking about music is lying about music. We would not have been saddled with a tradition that tells us to enjoy communicating with music but to distrust communicating about it.

All right, then: what's the problem? And why is it no problem? Because that is what I want to claim: that speaking of music is no problem at all. It is no problem because the problem of speaking of music is the same problem as the problem of speaking of anything. It is the same problem as the problem of speaking at all, which is not a problem that has ever caused anyone in normal circumstances to stop speaking.

Speaking of music is beset by two bugbears. These seem to be as old as speaking of music itself, but they are actually chimeras of more recent birth, specters of the antithesis between music and language, or more broadly between music and representation, that followed the anointing of music as a fine art in the mid-eighteenth century.

Bugbear number one is the myth of ineffability. This is a myth strongly upheld by cliché and conventional wisdom, a seemingly obvious observation that is actually a prescription meant to reinforce the antirepresentational, hence expressively full, hence transcendental status allocated to music in the modern West. Everyone knows the drill: musical expression begins where words leave off, music expresses what words can't, no description can do justice to the way music affects us. It is of course possible to describe musical technique using a certain specialized vocabulary, but it is impossible to say what music expresses or what it means. Music eludes our description, what we can say about its content is not what matters most about it, and no two people will agree about the content, anyway, except at the level of crude terms like *sad* or *cheerful*, and not always then. So really, it would be better if we just said nothing. We should enjoy the music we like, give ourselves the scholarly pleasure of compiling its history, and be content.

This position has had its scholarly champions of late, some more thoughtful than others.[1] But it has needed the champions because it has been subject to serious critique for over twenty years. Agree with it or not, the myth of ineffability can no longer be trotted out as an obvious, irrefutable truth. For some of us, in any but the most trivial respect, it is obviously and irrefutably false.[2]

The second bugbear is the myth of a private language, or at any rate a coterie language that excludes most people from speaking of music, at least if they want to speak credibly. The nub of the matter was embedded in the account of bugbear number one: the only indisputably valid way to speak of music is with the specialist vocabulary of musical technique, up to and including the various languages of music theory and analysis. This technical language is sometimes used to support claims about expressive content, but there is little comfort in that fact. Those who make the claims are hard put to explain how technique translates into expressive content, even of the limited sort usually allowed in this context, and those not conversant with the languages are barred from making expressive claims even if their own musical experience strongly impels them to. It is a fine mess.

It's a mess, moreover, that no one can clean up fully in a single essay and that in all likelihood will keep reinventing itself as a kind of selective deafness. As Keith Chapin observed to me in an editorial communication, music, "at the very least, is a placeholder for issues of ineffability and private language." Those issues "remain important enough to people that . . .

if for no other reason than habit and adherence to platitudes about music, they will probably still turn to music as a way to address [them]." There is a certain weight of history here that cannot be wished or whisked away. What can be wished, however, is a reflective awareness of when and why speaking of music is invoked to confound us and what each of us may find to say when we venture to speak of music nonetheless.

So I will not try here to do anything comprehensive.[3] What I can try to do instead is, first, sketch the reasons why each bugbear by which speaking of music is vexed is just that, a mere chimera and, second, suggest how working through the conceptual difficulties of the two bugbears can help clear the way for speaking of music without tears. The bugbear of ineffability is really a worry about truth and interpretation; the bugbear of technical language is a worry about competence. The first worries about being wrong, the second about looking foolish. To deal with them, and relieve ourselves of the worry, we first need to investigate the assumptions about music, language, and meaning that typically underlie both of these phantasms—the alligators under the bed of speaking of music.

If music can be spoken of, music can be interpreted. Or, put more strongly, if music can be spoken of *at all*, all of music can be interpreted. Interpretation is a topic that literary theory, which once made a special province of it, has largely abandoned. Old debates over topics like authorial intention seem dated, even quaint, and nothing has taken their place; instead, a generalized hermeneutics of suspicion, perhaps more politically than theoretically motivated, has become the default position. The true area of advance in hermeneutics is music—thinking about it, writing about it, speaking of it—because, as I've suggested elsewhere, music exposes the position of the interpreter with ruthless clarity. Music refers to the world weakly or not at all; the same music may express a multitude of different things to different listeners, at different times, or in different circumstances; any safety net one brings to the interpretation of music has holes in it. What these things do *not* do is show that music cannot be interpreted credibly or deeply. What they do instead is render transparent both the conditions of possibility for interpretation and the character of interpretation as act and experience. One of these conditions is that interpretation is always a risk, a venture or adventure. Another is a venturesome claim of, or more properly a claim on, truth.

The truth claims of language are part of the linguistic medium. As Derrida observes, to speak to another is to promise the truth, a promise, then, that is part of the illocutionary force of every locution.[4] Every utterance is accompanied by a tacit "believe me": believe what I'm saying, believe that I believe it, believe that what I say is a true speech act. All statements, even lies, call truth to witness; all speech acts gather force from unspoken truths.[5] The relative force of the truth claim, the impression of veracity, is one of the qualities of the statement qua statement.

For Kant, human society could not operate without a general grant of the claim of language on truth.[6] But what Derrida calls the history of the lie compels the recognition that neither the claim nor the grant can be unequivocal except in a purely formal sense.[7] There are many instances in which it is not clear what it would mean for a given utterance to be true and many others in which the truth of a statement depends on its recognition as a lie. Perhaps the most universal instance, which can fall into either category, or neither, is the statement "I love you." We would usually like to believe that the meaning of this statement is perfectly transparent, even as we repeatedly find ourselves having to ask what it might mean. We try to get into the city and some sphinx blocks our way with a riddle we have to interpret—or else.

Interpretations are statements that simultaneously emphasize the promise of truth and render it questionable. An interpretation promises to reveal something about what the object of interpretation means, but in order to make this revelation it has to leave the safe ground of verifiable description. Any hermeneutics that wants to disengage from the mystical underpinnings that run through the tradition of philosophical hermeneutics from Schleiermacher through Gadamer has to begin with the understanding that interpretations can be neither true nor false in a simple, unequivocal sense. Interpretation is the supplement of truth; it becomes both possible and mandatory (though perhaps not both at once) precisely where fact, however determined, must be incorporated into the sphere of choice, discourse, human significance, the arena of contending values. This is not to deny that fact is always already impregnated with value but to mark out a sphere of determination, priority, and authority.

What interpretations can be in place of simply true is be true *to* their object, to have the verbal equivalent of verisimilitude—literally likeness to truth—in relation to what they represent. In taking verisimilitude as a model, one also takes over the understanding that it is not an either/or relationship. Dramatic or pictorial depictions are verisimilar, "lifelike" or "realistic," in a certain sense and not in others, and the judgment of verisimilitude must demonstrate (in order to validate itself) just what sense that is in the given instance. The same burden falls to interpretation, on which it is incumbent to demonstrate, implicitly or explicitly, the sense in which it forms and maintains truth to its object and may therefore claim to be credible: not unequivocally true, but imaginable as true were a truth available and even, in the best of cases, indispensable to establishing the range of imaginable truths that come to surround anything we describe and redescribe, perceive and reperceive, so that its interpretation becomes a part of our history and culture.

If truth in its worldly sense is primarily virtual and promissory, and if truth in its metaphysical sense is for most of us, or many of us anyway, a fiction, no longer credible in itself although eminently worthy of interpretation; if truth is now smaller and less rigid than we used to think, or than it used to be, then interpretation may be more important than truth. Should we interpret—not just music, of course, but anything; music just makes the stakes of interpretation abundantly clear—should we interpret when we cannot verify? Of course we should. That is exactly when we should interpret. And must interpret, unless we are to live in an impoverished world devoid of the richness that the lost fictions of truth used to provide in such ample measure.

The moment we do commit ourselves to interpretation, we insert ourselves in a multimedia communications network involving continual movement through a continually evolving network of posts, relays, and positions, a movement that, again continually, changes its content as it moves. According to what Derrida called the postal principle—the principle that a letter may always fail to reach its destination[8]—the message that passes along this relay does not consist of an item that is neatly packaged and transmitted. Instead, the message is the precipitate of a complex communicative act that is constitutively subject to interpretation, transformation, and transposition in the course of its movement from post to post. Messages are instruments of performance.

Of course, in saying all this, I might just as well be describing the Internet. But the Internet is only the latest technological realization of a historical series of networks, including the telephonic, the telegraphic, and the postal.

The only limit on a communications network is the requirement that it be answerable, at least in part, to a symbolic order. To constitute a communicative act, a performative relay must assume the agency of a symbolically constructed reality that as such lies outside the communicative circuit but is at the same time recognized as enclosing, limiting, and shaping the circuit, which in turn threads through the reality it addresses. The communicative act proceeds from an intersection between the characteristic form of that effective reality (its role as world) and a contingent formation of it (its role as event).

The outline of a mature critical hermeneutics emerges from a recognition of the complex nonlinearity of the communications network. Applying this recognition specifically to music enables us to take the restricted content of the musical message as a property, not a problem: part of a general mapping of the circulation of musical meaning, not a bar shutting off musical meaning (except as trivial or "subjective") from discourse.

But this is just a first step. The real implication of the network model is that music becomes the paradigmatic medium of communicative action itself—music, not words, not images, not the word-image nexus or *imagetext* that is the defining grid of representation in Western culture.[9] Music, that is, becomes the medium in which the performative force of all meaning, the power of any message, utterance, text, or expression to do something in being transmitted, becomes most fully apparent.

This is the point at which the specific difference between music and the imagetext becomes freshly pertinent to the problem of speaking about music. What raises the problem is not that music is uniquely ineffable. Music is ineffable in exactly the way everything else is—and isn't. What raises the problem, rather, is music's characteristic lack of the referential automatism of language and images, a lack that has traditionally been confused with the lack of meaning. But that very lack is also what raises the solution to the problem or, rather, dissolves the problem. It does so by making apparent that the source of meaning and participation in any circumstance is precisely the surplus over and above referential automatism. Music does not demand more of that surplus than anything else. But it makes the surplus explicit, and for some people disconcerting, by standing apart from the imagetext-derived illusion that meaning and participation are "covered" (in all senses of the term) by the referential umbrella. In standing apart from assured or extended reference while still "communicating" effectively to its listeners, music both embodies the independent performativity of meaning and accommodates itself, extends itself, to the performative force of utterance for those whose venture it is to be speaking of music.

Just think of the short musical phrases that epitomize any number of famous pieces, from "Silent Night" to "Eine kleine Nachtmusik," "The Ride of the Valkyries" to "Take the A Train," "Vesti la giubba" to "Send in the Clowns," not to mention the obvious archetype for this sort of synoptic compression, the motto of Beethoven's Fifth Symphony. The history of music is replete with such phrases; they are endemic to musical memory and musical pleasure; and they are the tiles of a semantic mosaic continually being reshuffled into new forms. If you hear one of these phrases without knowing what it is, you have not really heard it at all. The phrase may once have been just a handful of notes, but for a long time it has been something else, something inescapable within a certain cultural sphere and there as solid as a block of granite. On the other hand, if you do know what the phrase is, what the notes have become, you cannot hear it outside the web of allusion, citation, association, travesty, prestige, interpretation, and application that has been spun around the notes and is continually being respun. Each new use or recognition of this music, like each rehearing of the whole piece into which the music flows or radiates, adds a new thread to the shimmering ensemble. Peel away one set of meanings and all you get is another. No one has ever heard this music as mere sound. Every phrase, every piece, is a promise of the truth.

When we speak of music, we absorb that promise into the general promise of truth that is rooted in language as such. But just because we do that, we also commit ourselves to the famous motto of Emily Dickinson: "Tell all the truth but tell it slant—/ Success in Circuit lies."[10] For language can keep its promise only by indirection. The moment language is involved at all, its inevitably hermeneutic and tropological nature is involved as well. Language is always caught in a relay between one post and another. So is music. The aim of speaking of music is not to achieve a state of impossible fixity but to show that, in the particular case at hand, music and language share some of the same detours.

One of those detours, moreover, is language itself. As Peter Szendy observes in his contribution to this volume the separation of music from words is itself the work of words—"other words," as he calls them (always *other* words). This verbal ensnarement exemplifies the broader principle that all interpretation *in* words is an interpretation *of* words. When we address nonverbal forms in order to interpret them, we are obliged to describe them both before we start and as we go along; we interpret what we address by interpreting the descriptions. We only interpret music, as we only interpret dreams or the past, by interpreting the stories we tell about it. In so doing, we do not distance ourselves from what we address but involve ourselves with it. And although all the posts in this relay, including the verbal ones, withhold something from language, there is no post that language leaves wholly untouched. We can address the nonverbal forms, say the music, only "under a description," that is, as potentially subject to a certain range of designations and classifications.[11] In a sense, without speaking of music there *is* no music, and we are free to speak of music by seeking to share its detours because music has always already begun that process for us.

Consider a simple example, which will also facilitate a transition to the second bugbear. The example is from a classical piece, which is customary for me, but since the normative status of classical music can no longer be taken for granted, it is important to note two points in passing. First, the sorts of thematic and rhythmic relationship I will be talking about in Beethoven are found in virtually all genres of Western music, though the uses to which they are put vary widely. Second, the classical score normally presumes the relative independence of the musical "work" from its performance. This condition is not absolute even with classical music, and other kinds of music, especially popular song, commonly dispense with it. But the degree to which something called "the" music is identifiable with specific acts of performance does not change the fundamental suppositions that music, as such, is ineffable and, except in a technical sense, indescribable. Beethoven, accordingly, can plausibly be given license to represent "music" here—which should be no problem for him; he's used to it.

Beethoven's Piano Sonata no. 12 in A-flat, op. 26, is unusual in several respects, two of which will concern us here: it opens not with the usual fast movement but with a slow theme-and-variations movement in 3/8 time, and the third of its four movements is a funeral march from which the sonata derives its familiar nickname. These two movements are connected by an easily perceptible device that nonetheless requires some effort to describe and that demands interpretation, in both musical senses of the term: the performer must realize the device, and the listener must understand it.

The theme of the first movement opens with even eighth notes. The second measure, however, doubles the pace of the theme and breaks up the even flow with a pair of consecutive figures in dotted rhythm, little twinges of impulse that start on the same note (example 1.1). This rhythmic signature gives the theme much of its character; the double fillip returns twice in full, and echoes of it, isolated dotted figures, lightly punctuate the theme throughout. What is most notable about the dotted rhythm, however, is that it virtually disappears during the five variations. Its presence recedes in Variation 1, and nothing is heard of it thereafter until it takes a fleeting curtain call near the end of Variation 5. By that time, though, the figure is really the ghost of its former self, which Variation 5 has explicitly smoothed out into even sixteenth notes (example 1.2).

But the dotted rhythm nonetheless turns out to have been a portent. It returns in force as the chief melodic signature of the funeral march, exactly

Ex. 1.1. Beethoven, "Funeral March" Sonata, first movement, mm. 1–4

Ex. 1.2. Beethoven, "Funeral March" Sonata, first movement, Variation 5, mm. 26–29, 34–37

Ex. 1.3. Beethoven, "Funeral March" Sonata, openings of first and third movements

as the genre of the march would dictate. Although the march is in common time, the two movements are close enough in pace and their figures
in consecutive dotted rhythms are close enough in contour to underline
the connection. The funeral march simply drags out the original rhythm
a little and lets itself be permeated by it. The opening of the march even
forms a minor-mode counterpart to the opening of the earlier theme: in
both, a pickup octave on E♭, the fifth scale degree, leads quasi-cadentially
to a downbeat on the root-position tonic chord, which leads in turn to a
downbeat on the dominant seventh (example 1.3). In the second iteration
of the variations theme, the pickup, originally a lone eighth note, breaks
into the dotted rhythm that its counterpart will have in the march, as if to
secrete a warning, as yet barely audible, of what is to come. The registers
are the same in both passages, and in both, the dominant seventh arrives
with a major-second dissonance, D♭-E♭, in the same registral location.
Mode aside, the main difference is that the march solemnizes its occasion
by filling out the lower octave.

So much we can say for sure; these are technical facts. But what do they
have to do with the expressive quality of the music? How can we speak
about their content? And my answer again will be, the same way we speak
about the content of anything that confronts us: by mobilizing our language, accepting and crossing the gap between phenomenon and signifi-

cance, choosing our tropes well rather than trying to avoid them. My technical description has already started to do that; it is unapologetically and obviously full of metaphors at the same time as it is technically explicit.

In that light, consider the following three statements and the relations among them:

1. The variations of the first movement continually animate and transfigure the theme but avoid or suppress its dotted rhythms. Variations 1 through 4 revel in rhythmic displacements, consistently phrasing off the beat and pulsing with syncopated accents; Variation 5 assimilates both features into a texture that quickens the theme with murmurous figuration above and below. Heard in relation to the third movement, the variation process suggests the vitality and open-endedness of life as opposed to the fixity and finality of death. The march identifies death with the petrifaction of this transformational vitality in, and as, the repetition of the one element in the theme that the variation process neglects.

2. The cross-reference between movements threatens to extend a chain of negations back, retrospectively, to anchor in the variations: threatens, especially, because the only broad melodic motion in the march, a rising triadic bass figure, comes to grief—but cannot contain it—as the march comes to a close on both its iterations. The figure originates as an answer to the level footfalls that begin the march theme, whose dotted rhythms it echoes. It ends by splitting off as the theme returns to round off the march. Three successive statements carry the figure from the deep bass to the midtreble on the heels of a thick chord that climbs higher, and becomes shriller, with each statement. The first time we hear the march, what follows is a blunt cadence. The second time, the sequel is the coda, which fills the void that the flight of the rising figure has left in the bass. But the replacement is itself a kind of void. It is a reduced and simplified form of the funereal tread that begins the march theme: the pure oblique motion of a single note in dotted rhythm (example 1.4).

The tread has so far failed to penetrate the bass as an independent figure, but once there it becomes insistent and, in the end, cavernous as it drops an octave for its last two statements. The dotted-rhythm profile that the tread and the rising figure share gives the final turn of events an extra weight of gloom. It is as if the tread were undoing the figure in the act of replacing it, stripping the rising contour of its melodic expressiveness and reducing it to the bare, now almost meaningless rhythm for which, it the end, it was no more than a pretext. Once again dynamism gives way to fixity—so to speak, to a kind of rigor mortis. Emptied of its ceremonial character, which was in any case already compromised by its dark echoes of the first-

Ex. 1.4. Beethoven, "Funeral March" Sonata, third movement, mm. 63–69

movement theme, the tread becomes at once visceral and disembodied, the
pace of a haunting memory or of a shade in the underworld.

The relationship between the march and the variations is exactly the
reverse of its counterpart in the *Eroica* Symphony, composed in 1804, two
years later than the sonata. The variations-finale of the symphony answers
the work's massive funeral march with a heroic transformative power identified as Promethean; the laconic march of the sonata marks the blockage
of any such power by the death of the hero, the event identified by the sub-
title appended to "Marcia Funebre": "sulla morte d'un eroe." The sonata
movement does not attempt anything like the breadth and intensity of the
symphonic dirge, but it also, unlike the latter, offers no hint of consolation
even in passing.[12]

3. The ripple effect of the march's entropic close is linked to anxieties
over the state of war omnipresent in the Europe of 1802, when the para-
mount fact of life was already Napoleon's long shadow. Austria was especially beset, having been spectacularly routed by Napoleon at the Battle
of Marengo in 1800. The sonata's funeral march is specifically military
in character, as its central episode, an imitation trumpet-and-drum fan-
fare with firearms salute, makes explicit. The figures in consecutive dotted
rhythms impel both the inexorable tread of the march and the free fantasy
of the earlier variations, the one by inclusion, the other by exclusion. The
dotted figures thus form an ambiguous and symbolically invested presence
hovering uneasily between war and peace. Each figure becomes a particle

of sense that does not so much signify anything in particular as embody a certain irreducible vulnerability. What in a world of peace one has the luxury to spare becomes what in the world of war binds one to unsparing loss.

And please note that I haven't said that the funeral march is sad. I have, however, said that its technique is thus and so, and there is obviously much more of the kind I could have said. But should I have? And how should we think about the connection between musical technique and musical meaning?

The short answer is that in many cases it is not necessary to speak of technique, at least in any depth; speaking of musical experience in more intuitive terms is often not far removed from speaking of technique or may readily be supplemented by it. To be sure, no one with an intimate working of knowledge of music is likely to want to forget the practical devices by which music works. But to speak of more than technique alone requires that we keep open the possibility of paraphrasing musical events in a vocabulary that music, if it could really speak, could understand. The depth of detail to which such a paraphrase should or might or sometimes must reach cannot be fixed in advance and may well require a degree of musical expertise to observe. But it is nonetheless the case, and not by accident, that the depth involved will in all likelihood fall far short of the deeper reaches of musical analysis. For if the analyst's latter-day credo is that analysis helps enhance the experience of music, one still has to ask whose experience. And the raw fact is that most who play or listen do not do so in full-bore analytical terms either during or after the event; even composers don't, than whom no one could be more concerned with musical detail.

The reason is not lack of interest or capacity but lack of language. The vocabulary of significant experience and the vocabulary of musical analysis have very little in common; their familiar forms tend to be mutually exclusive. These vocabularies occupy different regions of the symbolic order; they promise divergent kinds of truth.[13] To bring them together requires not a compromise but a fundamental realignment.

It is a basic point of understanding human experience qua human that it is permeated by what Heidegger called care or concern (*Sorge*), a condition of involvement that organizes our experience of time and endows it with qualitatively distinct textures. Care arises from the inescapable condition of our being "thrown" into a historical world that we must come to inhabit meaningfully.[14] For Paul Ricoeur, the articulation of this process is the basic principle of narrative. Regardless of its content, narrative in its form rises above the "abstraction" of clock time to embody the richness of "within-time-ness," the experience of giving or having, taking or making "time *for*" or " time *to*" or "time *with*," something that for Heidegger is the medium of an "authentic," more than merely utilitarian relation to care. Ricoeur's observation applies even more readily to music than to narrative. For music palpably depends on, indeed consists of, the qualitative organization of time.[15] Music is a flowing or unfolding in time that invites care at every moment and, in so doing, gives time a palpable form in which care can flourish. But the technical vocabulary for analyzing music resists permeation by the language of care, except minimally. In that respect, it impoverishes the perception of music itself as a vehicle of care. If in speaking about music we want to echo its general rather than a special interest, we need to avoid confusing musical understanding with the construction of a comprehensive analysis. Both analytically and otherwise, we need to let care for and care through music guide what we say.

When needed, such care can reach a fine technical level; when needed, it may refrain from doing so with equal tact. The fundamental question is what is needed and when. Contrary to a claim often advanced in defense of musical analysis, it is not unproblematically the case that the pursuit of analytic detail brings one closer to the musical work, much less to the performance or event, unless one defines such closeness in circular terms as analytic awareness.[16] As Nietzsche might have suggested, a certain creative forgetting may be involved when what is at stake is genuine experience, *Erfahrung* in German, experience that resonates beyond the moment in which it is lived.[17] Both performance and composition are receptive to, even demanding of, such forgetting. What creative forgetting forgets is not knowledge or know-how but an action, as one forgets an errand or an appointment because something of more importance has come up.

Consider two ways of accounting for the tonal design of the funeral march in Beethoven's op. 26, one of them sparing of technical detail and one of them liberal with it (though still far short of the kind of analytic detail possible with this music). The preservation in the second account of the language of the first is part of the point:

1. As a tonic, A-flat minor, the key of the march, is bizarre. A key signature of seven flats is very far outside the realm of normal practice at the end of the eighteenth century.[18] It is clearly chosen over the four flats of the relative F minor so as to refer back specifically to the A-flat-major variations, the *minore* of which goes, conventionally, to the parallel minor mode. The convention establishes the context in which the extra flats are tolerable. The key of the march is thus a peculiar echo or uncanny repetition of a normal move. Its weirdness will be confirmed when its simple

beginning—itself a peculiar echo of the earlier movement—gives way to a tortured series of harmonies. The harmonic contortions lead to a passage of extended dissonance that, though excruciating, does finally find a way back to the tonic. But the strangeness of the key is if anything enhanced by the process.

Against this bemusement, the literalness of the military middle section sounds particularly rigid and inadequate; one hears the military ritual emptying itself of meaning. That the harmony in this section is all primitive tonic-and-dominant in A-flat major adds to the depreciation of its apparent normality and perhaps, retrospectively, to that of the variations movement as well. The normal/normative return of the march that follows thus becomes a confession of defeat, and one confirmed, it will turn out, by the coda.

The march movement as a whole is a paradox. It begins with and reiterates an essentially cadential statement of the tonic, but it defers a real cadence until the close of the second A section. The ensuing coda ends in A-flat major, but the change of mode is anything but comforting. It arrives mixed with pathos-laden harmonies from which it offers no escape. There is no sense at all of a turn back to the key of the life-affirming variations.

2. As a tonic, A-flat minor, the key of the march, is bizarre. A key signature of seven flats is very far outside the realm of normal practice at the end of the eighteenth century. Add the minor mode to the flats on every scale degree, and A-flat minor is the most remote of all keys from C major—the fixed point of normative reference, the so-called key of nature. The almost unheard-of key is clearly chosen over the alternative, the relative F minor with its four flats, so as to refer back specifically to the A-flat-major variations, the *minore* of which goes, conventionally, to the parallel minor mode. The convention establishes the context in which the extra flats are tolerable. The key of the march is thus a peculiar echo or uncanny repetition of a normal move.

The tonal weirdness will be confirmed when the simple beginning of the march—itself a peculiar echo of the earlier movement—gives way to a tortured series of harmonies. As if to extend its esoteric distance from C, the march emphasizes the key furthest from C in point of tonal axis, F-sharp major, here understood as the dominant of B, which is to say, of C-flat, the relative major. Once established, B rotates the wrong way through the cycle of fifths to E, A, and D, the enharmonic spellings of the strange, not to say chimerical, regions of F-flat, B-double flat, and E-double flat, the tritone of A-flat. All this happens quite quickly, as if the music were hurtling to a fatal destination despite its solemn tempo.

After a faux-cadence on the tone D/E♭♭, the music dwells excruciatingly on the diminished seventh chord built on that tone until, after a climax, the tone leads back to the tonic, already strange enough and now perhaps even stranger, by becoming the leading tone to the dominant, E-flat. The march thus dwells in a sphere of alienation and unreality, the latter not in a sense of fictitiousness but, on the one hand, in a willed sense of denial, a tonal encrypting of death itself, and, on the other hand, in a Greek-classical sense that the world of death is the world of shades, oddly resembling the world of the living but insubstantial.

Against this bemusement, the literalness of the military middle section sounds particularly rigid and inadequate; one hears the military ritual emptying itself of meaning. That the harmony in this section is all primitive tonic-and-dominant in A-flat major adds to the depreciation of its apparent normality and perhaps, retrospectively, to that of the variations movement as well. The normal/normative return of the march that follows thus becomes a confession of defeat, and one confirmed, it will turn out, by the coda.

The march movement as a whole is a paradox. It begins with and re-iterates an essentially cadential statement of the tonic, but it defers a real cadence until the close of the second A section. The ensuing coda is an extended Picardy third but not at all a source of comfort or demystification. On the contrary, it is a demonstration of convention, or ceremony, under the aspect of its artifice and ineffectuality. The major mode is reached first through modal mixture with the minor subdominant and thereafter through the traditionally pathetic Neapolitan sixth, B♭♭. This A-flat major is a ghost. There is no sense at all of a turn back to the key of the life-affirming variations.

What is the relationship between these two descriptions and of either to the music of which it speaks? And what does either one do when it speaks "of" the music? Of "the" music?

The answer will be clearest if it starts in the negative. The description with less technical detail is not a watered-down version of the one with more, a kind of low-resolution image that conveys meaning only by diluting it. If anything, the relation leans to the contrary; the less technical description acts as an implicit curb on its more technical sibling. It is mindful of a certain economy that scholarly speaking of music too often forgets: a surplus of detail fosters a deficit of meaning. The problem comes not when the resolution is too low but when it is too high. There is of course no formula to determine when the pursuit of technical refinement leaves care behind—becomes careless in a double sense. But the question should be kept in play. At least it should if our aim in speaking of music is to bring it more openly into the network of concerns that have drawn us to it in the first place.

If that is indeed the aim, then the relation of either description to the music should be understood as a positioning: not as an approximation of some fixed musical form or meaning but as a *proximation*, a coming near, to a possible musical experience. What speaking of music does, understood in these terms, is to make available an informed framework in which re-alizations of the music may be heard as extensions of care. "The" music emerges as a sonorous image within that framework. The speech opens the music to possibilities of performance, listening, and recollection in which certain affective and conceptual values resonate. How long and how often they do so is up to those who enter the conversation.

All speech about music works toward or against this outcome. One implication of this deceptively simple principle is that neither music nor speaking of music can be disengaged from the problem of care, even when the work of speech runs "against" it. Another is that the condition of pos-sibility for speaking of music, again regardless of whether the speech is transparent or opaque to care, is the music's participation in a more inclu-sive process in which speech is also implicated. (Implicated: folded in; shar-ing responsibility for—the word is offered as exact. As Heidegger notes, language acts even when we are not speaking.)

Both of our descriptions, for example, understand Beethoven's music as a refusal to maintain the validating link between artistic genre and social ritual. Both accounts depend on animating the contrast between the picto-rial or, as it were, auditory literalism of the middle section and the more generic topicality of the surrounding march sections. The ceremonial middle exerts a mimetic pull on the march, drawing its broadly funereal character into the depiction of a military funeral. But the bizarre harmony of the march pulls the other way. Completely out of bounds for any mili-tary band, the harmony not only estranges the march from the supposed funeral rites but even estranges it from its own generic identity. The music does its generic duty, but with a resolute withdrawal of credibility. It is heroic only because it proceeds to the end while proposing all along that the end is only emptiness and mortification. Both of our descriptions speak of this without exactly saying it, and because they do, it is possible to say it here.

But speaking of this music cannot stop here. The only heroism in Beethoven's march may be its going through to the end, but through to the end it goes. It even breaks through; its coda may be dark, but it is also a stay against nihilism, something that Beethoven was often willing to confront but never to accept. Unlike the famous funeral march from Chopin's Sonata in B-flat Minor, a piece that almost surely alludes to it, Beethoven's march does not just stop with a handful of grief. It goes on to achieve something like acquiescence, short of reconciliation but short, too, of despair. In an earlier account of this music, in the context of its link to Chopin's, I observed that "in the coda (mm. 68–74) the melodic line elaborates on the [march] theme's dotted rhythms to achieve an unwonted suppleness and also to find its registral peak, while the march rhythm gradually dissipates in the bass. Gloom gives way to the *gravitas* of sublimation."[19] This outcome may not be "redemptive" (as I called it then), but the contrast to Chopin might make the exaggeration pardonable.

The preceding paragraph might form an appropriate coda to either of the two accounts it follows. It might even intimate an alternative to them. Which aspect to emphasize when speaking of Beethoven's march depends on what one is speaking of. The focal points of the observation I quoted are melody and register; the focal points of the twin accounts in this chapter are melody and harmony. At one level, this difference suggests that grappling with the more esoteric dimension of harmony, however lightly, fosters a deeper understanding. But at another, more challenging level, the difference suggests that the alternative possibilities are inscribed in the music, which harbors a latent tension, even an antagonism, between its registral passage and its harmonic impasse. There is no question of "depth" here. Or rather what is "deepest," if we must have that metaphor, is the chance, which is also the need, to decide how the music should be played or heard on a particular occasion. Even if neither the player nor the listener says a word, the decision acts as if to meet an obligation to speak. Speaking of music may have a troubled history in part because music, at least in the classical genres, has regularly been asked both to bring us to the threshold of speech and to excuse us for holding our tongues.

But this is not the place to stop either. We can still go a step further in following this march that moves at a ceremonial pace to which no one ever paces. How metaphorical would it be to say that this music is speaking: speaking as music, of music? Do the descriptions I have offered of it have the first word (for certainly they don't have the last)? No matter which description one prefers, does either do more than repeat, or more exactly speak as if it were repeating, something like a speech act, a disengagement from ceremony, that the music has already made, no matter when it is made? And isn't this an act that the music can make good on only by making it again, and then again, insofar as this music, any music, can find a hearing only in being learned, practiced, rehearsed, recorded, repeated? How metaphorical would it be to say that the experience built up by and around this music is, whatever else it is, a circulation of something like speech acts?

Perhaps these questions are themselves most "happy" when left to their interrogative form, as if to open but not force a decision. But one of them, formed only in passing, invites a more definite treatment.

Asked which of these descriptions should be preferred, I would say neither. The second gets further hermeneutically, but its claims are already implicit in the first; and the observations of the first can serve as the basis for the second. What the two descriptions have in common, moreover, as the use of the same language in both should help convey, is more significant than what distinguishes them from each other. Both pointedly decline to separate the language in which they speak technically about music from the language ordinarily used to form descriptions of matters felt to have a rich burden of concern. Both understand that understanding music is inevitably a verbal as a well as an acoustic enterprise.

But the differences between the two descriptions still need to be accounted for constructively. The most demanding passage of the second, where enharmonic relationships come up, does enable the interpretation to elicit a more specific sense than the first can of the alienation that pervades the movement. There is something to be gained by paying close musical attention, if you can. Even the first statement requires some musical knowledge. But even hermeneutically, the difference is relatively modest and not necessarily unbridgeable. Knowing the enharmonic relations allows one to name and to some degree explain their effect, but if one does not know them, or does not bother to identify them except via an intuitive sense of strangeness, their effect is undiminished and perhaps even enhanced: the effect, that is, of being tilted out of focus, sundered from one's own perceptions, dipped in perplexity. The second statement has its advantages, but the first is related to it not as a defective version but as a suggestive condensation.

That fact is good news. Those who have a large analytical vocabulary need not worry; they are not being asked to abandon what they know, just to use their knowledge selectively. And those who have a limited analytical vocabulary need not worry, either; it is often quite sufficient to reach the point where technical paraphrase becomes possible without the paraphrase necessarily having to be carried out there and then. Like one of those mu-

sical phrases I alluded to earlier, the point is a threshold already laden
with the meanings to which it leads. That threshold is the essential place
for speaking about music whether or not we cross it. And in reaching it,
we find ourselves back at the original claim of this chapter, which can be
compressed into a simple antiphony: How should we speak about music?
The same way we speak about everything else.

Waiting for the Death Knell:
Speaking of Music (So to Speak)

Laura Odello

I would like to start out with a quote from Vladimir Jankélévitch about music, words, Socrates, and above all a certain quandary:

> The ineffable . . . cannot be expressed [*est inexprimable*] because there are infinite and interminable things to be said of it. . . . Ineffability provokes bewilderment, which, like Socrates's quandary, is a fertile aporia. . . . There will be things to be said (or sung) about the ineffable until the end of time. Who can possibly say, Now, everything is said? No. No one, ever, will be done with this Charm, which interminable words and innumerable musics will not exhaust, where there is so much to do, to contemplate, to say—so much to say, and in short, and again and again, of which there is everything to say.[1]

So much can be said, indeed, beginning with what interests us here, that is, "Socrates' quandary."

However, before speaking of Socrates and music, let us follow a song, a song that might mislead, a song that is going to make us drift and deviate—let us allow the Sirens to lead us astray with their song. Provided that, whenever one speaks about music, it is not already, almost always, in the form of a certain deviation, turn, or trope that is suggested or required by the constitutive ambivalence of music itself, the ambiguity or uncertainty of the musical *ipseity*[2] lends itself to all possible appropriations or reappropriations. It lends itself, it gives itself to all, like a prostitute (from the Latin *prostituta, prostituere*, from *pro*, meaning "before" and *stituere* or *statuere*, meaning "to put, pose, place," that is to say, "to expose to dealing or trade"). We might thus handle music like a prostitute, like a hooker hooking every possible meaning.

Here, metaphors begin. And they are only just beginning. Precisely because we do not know what music is, we speak of it, we keep moving it from here to there, transferring it around, constraining it endlessly into metaphor, exactly as I myself am doing right now, by calling music a prostitute. We exploit it, we force it, we do violence to it, we rape it, for we desire it, it arouses our desire: we push it, we urge it into prostitution or substitution, putting it to good use (to our good use) by trading it, by selling it in the exchange of speech. And as Jankélévitch reminds us, it lets itself be handled this way, obediently, "lending itself willingly to innumerable associations."[3] For whatever happens, music cannot be grasped; the more it resists the claims of speech—any speech that claims to be proper or appropriate—the more we speak about it by multiplying metaphors, by constraining it into metaphor, indeed into the constrained metaphor, into what has been called a catachresis, that is to say, an irreducible metaphor (for example, the wings of a building, the legs of a table, etc.), since the figurative meaning cannot be grafted onto the literal meaning, which does not exist. Catachresis is an incomplete metaphor, in a way. It is an abuse, such as the one I am committing here with regard to music, such as has always been perpetrated with respect to music.

So let us abuse our power of speech, let us speak of music, so to speak.

Since the Sirens appeared in the twelfth book of the *Odyssey*, they have dwelled in the margins, on the outer borders of the Western stage of speech, which they endlessly haunt with their song, with a bewitching and seductive music: that famous song that, according to Ovid, is born to captivate, flatter, delight the ears (*ille canor mulcendas natus ad aures*).[4]

Beginning with Plato, this speaking scene, as we know, will be understood as a deaf representation, as a visual theater, a great logocentric show offered to eyes which are and which will remain hard of hearing. Indeed, the dimension of listening was put out of bounds precisely by Plato; it was neutralized in favor of a logical understanding. In the *Cratylus*, while speaking of the act of naming, Plato distinguishes between musical imitation—capable of imitating mere qualities such as voice (*phone*), shape (*skhema*), and timbre (that is to say, color, *khroma*)[5] and of imitating the essence of things—the only one able to guarantee their true nomination. The timbre and the voice—that is to say, the sonority—are subordinated to the logical ideality of things: the Platonic gesture is as obvious as it is decisive for philosophy. The philosopher does not want to know anything about listening; hearing is of no use to the philosopher because the end as well as the beginning of all philosophizing resides in the intellectual understanding: sonorities are superfluous, secondary, unnecessary for the silent vision of the *logos*, of the idea, of the ideal signified, which alone serves to grasp the truth.

The Sirens' song seems to be banished; music is liquidated, repressed. In fact, the Platonic gesture is not so simple: music does not disappear; it remains present by becoming silent. This is the great imprisonment of sound carried out by philosophy. Music remains present so that it can be banished, exhausted, dismissed, tamed; in this Platonic operation of subjugation, it is put in the service of philosophy itself, becoming the silent sound track of metaphysics, its tolling bell, the almost inaudible ringing of a death knell.

But let us return to the Sirens. In the *Phaedrus*, their song can be heard in the sonority of the cicadas. I am referring here to the famous myth that Plato seems to have made up himself: under the bright and blinding light of noon, Socrates says to Phaedrus that if the cicadas singing above their heads saw them sleeping, as all those who sleep at that time of day, they would make fun of them. Indeed, they would think that the philosophers had allowed themselves to be charmed by their song (in Greek, *keléo* can mean "bewitched, seduced, fascinated" as well as "calmed") and had given up their discourse (*dialegein*, meaning "to speak, discuss, reason," in the sense of to choose, select, distinguish, thus to engage in dialectics). On the other hand, if the cicadas saw them philosophizing, discussing philosophically and "sailing past them [*paraplein*], as past the Sirens, without letting themselves be charmed [*kelein*]," perhaps, says Socrates, they would admiringly intercede with the gods to ask them to grant Socrates and Phaedrus the same divine gift as has been given the cicadas. Once upon a time—and here begins Socrates's mythical narrative—the cicadas were men who were so passionate about song that they did nothing else; they neither ate nor drank; all they did was sing. And so they died; they died of music. The Muses turned them into cicadas, granting them the gift of being able to live life without eating, only singing, feeding themselves solely on music. After death, the cicadas return to the Muses to tell them who, among men, honor them. In particular, says Socrates, the cicadas give an account to Calliope and Urania (the Muses with the most beautiful voices, who rule over the sky as well as over divine and human speech) of who, among the philosophers (among those that live out their lives in philosophy, *tous en philosophie diagontas*), most honor their music.[6]

How many songs are announced here? How many musics? One must not let oneself be charmed by the cicadas' song, nor by that of the Sirens; but it is fitting to honor singing. Music has begun to split; the singing cicadas, protected by the Muses, admire he who does not let himself be fooled by music. So there is music and music; there is music which fools, which leads us into error, and there is music which is true, which is able to see and have clear ideas. The Platonic text announces a music suitable to philosophy, a music which does not distract from discourse and dialectical reasoning; it is enough to lower the sound, to turn down the volume and to continue to speak. In fact, Socrates concludes: "So for many reasons we ought to talk and not sleep in the noontime." And Phaedrus: "Yes, we ought to talk."[7]

So, let us talk. Let us speak of music.

Nothing new under the sun. On the speaking scene (on the scene of speech, *parole*), we could say, it is always the same music, always the same song, the same theme muffled by the visually blinding noon. Ulysses too resists the Sirens' song under the scorching sun of noon, at that moment when the sun lights things up with almost no shadow: in absolute visibility, Ulysses is sailing, and in the middle of the day (in the midday, which also means the South in Italian, the *mezzogiorno*), he reaches Li Galli, the island opposite Positano, which Strabo the geographer has identified as the Sirens' home.

The story is well known: having been warned by Circe, Ulysses orders his men to plug their ears with wax and has himself bound to the mast so as to be able to listen to the Sirens' seductive song. Ulysses will resist, and his heroic resistance will become a narrative, it will become speech, the *Odyssey* itself, the Sirens' grave, as Blanchot writes, where their song urges Ulysses toward another voyage, that of the narrative in which the song is no longer real and immediate but imaginary and enigmatic. It will be told, to be exact. According to Blanchot, it is here that Ulysses becomes Homer; by resisting and surviving the Sirens' song, the hero becomes Homer, who can tell it. The song of the Sirens is a song to come, in that it has never been present and will never be presentable: in fact, only in the song-tale (of Ulysses become Homer) does the encounter with the Sirens' song take place; only when it is written into the narrative, as the opening of the infinite movement toward the song to come, does the encounter happen. It happens when constituting itself as narrative. But the encounter produced by the narrative is a failed encounter, one that is always missed and takes place as the very impossibility of the encounter. This narrative, Blanchot says, as all narratives, does not render the event of the encounter present; rather, it is the opening of the infinite movement toward the encounter itself: the song is to come; it is distant, it is distance itself, an otherness impossible to appropriate, an alterity that the narrative has to cross, "a space to travel" that the words desperately seek to fill without ever succeeding, the place where the song leads "as the point where singing can stop being a lure."[8]

In the struggle with the Sirens (which Blanchot compares to that of Ahab with Moby Dick, in that in both cases two opposing forces, two powers, want to be everything, want to be the absolute world), Ulysses comes out victorious; he resists their song, whereas Ahab ends up swallowed by the sea and by his obsession. Ulysses knows that he can aspire to everything; he knows that "he will be everything, if he keeps a limit, a gap between the real and the imaginary, precisely the gap that the song of the Sirens invites him to cross."[9] The Sirens' song will cease being a lure and will thus become the song of Ulysses.

And music? What about music in this *other* song that the narrative becomes? What remains of music in this gap between real song and imaginary song?

What we would like to highlight here is the unheard-of power of Ulysses's tenacity, a "premeditated tenacity,"[10] capable of measuring his own power against the other power. Blanchot writes that "between Ahab and Ulysses, the one who has the greatest wish for power is not the most out of control":[11] Ulysses wins out because his strength, his cunning, consists in the illusion that he is limiting his power; and it is precisely this apparently unpowerful strength that neutralizes the Sirens' song. What appears to be at stake is a confrontation between powers, a power conflict in which the prize is the very sovereignty of the subject. Music will bear the cost.

In *Dialectic of Enlightenment*, Theodor Adorno and Max Horkheimer seem to confirm this aspect which we wished to underline in Blanchot's text. Ulysses bows down to the song, Adorno and Horkheimer argue, because he knows nobody can resist it. He thus recognizes the power of the song; he recognizes it "insofar as, technically enlightened [*technisch aufgeklärt*], Odysseus acknowledges the archaic supremacy of the song by having himself bound";[12] the temptation of the Sirens jeopardizes "the effort [of the ego] to hold itself together," but, on the other hand, "the temptation to be rid of the ego has always gone hand-in-hand with the blind determination to preserve it" (*mit der blinden Entschlossenheit zu seiner Erhaltung gepaart*).[13]

Without going into the details of Adorno and Horkheimer's critique of rationalization and the bourgeois system embodied by Ulysses's cunning, which enables man's self-preservation within relations of domination, what must be underlined here is the fact that Ulysses (the Self, as Adorno says) does not simply oppose the power of the song, but it is precisely by resisting that he constitutes himself as a subject. His power consists precisely in his resistance to the Sirens' song, in that he does not "succumb to them" (*ihnen nicht verfällt*).[14]

In this scene, which lends itself to an interpretation in terms of power and sovereignty, music seems to get lost, to fade into silence, and to become ill (*erkrankt*).

> Since the happily hapless meeting of Odysseus with the Sirens, all songs have ailed [*erkrankt*]; the whole of western music suffers from the absurdity [*Widersinn*] of song in civilization, yet the motive force [*bewegende Kraft*] of all art-music [*Kunstmusik*] is song.[15]

Since Ulysses's failed encounter with the Sirens, all the songs have become sick. But what is this sickness of music? What has made it feel indisposed? Or better still, what is this metaphor of sickness about?

In order to expand this metaphor, we could hypothesize that music's sickness is the unfortunate result of an intense philosophical therapy, the side effects of the excessive administration of words that crippled it without damaging it irreparably. Here is what the true sickness of music really consists of: a nosocomial infection, an illness contracted during its forced hospitalization that did not reduce it to silence but rather muted it.

The paradox here, however, lies in the fact that music starts to get sick insofar as the word tries to cure it; in other words, the *logos* tries to neutralize the musical pathology that the *logos* itself caused in order to eliminate it by reestablishing itself, phantasmatically, as being originally unharmed.

This results in a split between good and bad music, a split which the *logos* itself produces while denying it; in fact, the *logos* becomes the *logos* that it is only by maintaining its own purity through the sacrificial movement that excludes music. This sacrificial movement is also what happens to writing, as Derrida has demonstrated in important texts.[16]

Music, as we have already said, is not so much reduced to silence as it is muted. Like a political prisoner, she has been deprived of her freedom without being destroyed, for she alone holds the precious military secrets fundamental to the survival of the State. Here, of course, we are alluding to the Platonic scene in the *Republic*, it being the first to warn against music, the first, in Western history, to be both a philosophical and political scene. Plato speaks of music in strictly philosophical and political terms but not at all in musical ones.[17] What interests Plato, more than the musical effects of the modes, are their moral effects.

Music is put to the service of education because it allows "rhythm and harmony [to] find their way to the inmost soul."[18] The politics of the *polis* are based above all on harmonic attunement, on being attuned to each other and to the law; music seems to be indispensable to the *polis* as the vital and sovereign unity of the political community. But we must not let music bewitch us, for music is also toxic; it is a *pharmakon*, one might say, a drug, a remedy, a cure, a medicine, but also a poison, a danger, a contamination. A certain sound regimen or diet is called for, under the control of a *logos* that gives the measure of which music is deprived.

He who has been educated in music must be "a good guardian of himself and of the music which he has received,"[19] the best guardian (*phulax:* "he who protects") being a mix, a conjunction, a blend of *logos* and music ("*logos* blended with *mousike*").[20]

To protect and preserve the *polis*, then, music is essential. Or, better still, as Plato says, "it is . . . in music . . . that our guardians must build their guardhouse and post of watch" (*to de phulakterion entautha pou oikodometeon tois phulaxin, en mousikei*).[21] Literally, *phulakterion*, the guardhouse, the guardians' body, the defense of the defenders, must be built on music (*oikodometeon*, from *oikodomeo*, "to construct, edify, put down the base": *oikodometikes techne* means "architecture"). *Phulakterion* is a means of defense, something that guards, protects, and preserves; it is a protective measure, a sheath, in short, a prophylactic.

Music helps the city to preserve itself, to guarantee and protect itself, to keep its life, integrity, and immunity safe and whole. When Aristotle says that song is "a harmless joy" (*charan ablabe*), the platonic gesture has already been absorbed and digested; music purifies the soul even when it is a game; it can harm no one, for it is first and foremost a form of knowledge, and as such, it is incorporated into the sovereign immunizing process of the *polis*.

Music thus saves. It immunizes. Once the sound has been lowered, once music has been reduced to logical understanding, it resonates in politics and philosophy—in the philosophico-political that the *polis* inaugurates—as a hymn to salvation or safety, measured, contained, and moderate. In the *Phaedo*, at the moment of Socrates's sacrifice—that decisive moment for the subsequent history of philosophy—while he waits for death, refusing to avoid it, we find a definition of philosophy as the greatest, the highest music (*philosophias ouses meghistes mousikes*).[22] At that moment, then, when Socrates gives himself death so as to save himself, in that self-immunizing gesture which will mark the future of philosophy and which consists in the exercise of death as the sacrifice of life, music suddenly appears as a trope for philosophy. Socrates dreams that he is ordered to compose music in honor of Apollo: *O Sokrates, mousiken poiei kai ergazou*—literally, "compose, make music, work at it."[23] And Socrates explains that the music his dream urges him to compose is none other than the music he has always composed: "the dream was encouraging me to do what I was doing, that is, to make music [*mousiken poiein*], as if philosophy were the greatest music [*hos philosophias ouses meghistes mousikes*]."[24]

In composing music in honor of the god Apollo—whose feast day, as we know, delays Socrates's execution—Socrates feels the need to obey the dream: "But now, after the trial and while the festival of the god delayed my execution, I thought, in case the repeated dream really meant to tell me to make this which is ordinarily called music, I ought to do so and not to disobey."[25] Obeying the dream would mean composing sacrificial music while waiting for his death, a death through which Socrates thinks he can save himself.

The Sirens seem to have disappeared indeed; all that remains of them is the death knell, funereal, gloomy, and sinister. What is music, as it so strangely appears in *Phaedo*, if not the knell of philosophy itself, as a preparation for death, as a learning to die? The Sirens no longer sing (as Kafka imagined in an ingenious little tale).[26] The Sirens no longer sing because the philosopher speaks: and such will be his music. Sacrificial music, music to accompany death; the tempo of death, a philosophical music that announces salvation and death, salvation as death. Music, so to speak.

However, we could perhaps try to give another reading of this episode of Socrates's musical dream in which music seems to give way to the philosophical *logos* and to its powerful economy of reappropriation, this time a reading *sub specie philosophiae*. If music, as we said in the beginning, lends itself willingly to all metaphors, to all narratives, to all rhetorical devices of speech—be they subtle or heavy—we should ask ourselves about that metaphor (philosophy as the highest music) from the point of view of philosophy itself, that is to say, from the point of view of the literal meaning of the metaphor. This time philosophy translates itself, it transfers itself into the place of music. What does philosophy want to hear from music?

What does music have to say to philosophy? Music, as we know, expresses nothing, means nothing; it has no discursive power.

But why does Plato use such a metaphor at the very moment when Socrates is about to die and speaks to his disciples. Why this metaphor precisely when Socrates is discoursing on philosophy as preparation for death, urging us toward sacrifice in the name of the *logos* and its truth? Why does Plato have recourse precisely to music when producing one of the most powerful discourses, among those which constitute the very foundation of Western philosophy?

What does philosophy need music for, at the culminating point of its self-celebration as an exercise in the preparation for death? Why does Plato insert that trope just here? Plato, who exorcized music in all possible ways, tells us that Socrates, when about to die, had nothing better to do than to compose music. To celebrate the deaf discourse of philosophy, let us make some music, that which, says Socrates, we have always been making while philosophizing.

Did we? Really? But what kind of music are we talking about, then?

All of Plato's discourse about music seeks to warn us: music is a *pharmakon;* it must be educated. Could it be that music, when cured by *logos*, would be equal to *logos* in philosophical dignity? Could it be that philosophy is not self-sufficient? What was the need to add music?

Unless we assume we are dealing here with a *lapsus*, with a return of the repressed, that is to say, of that music Plato strived to keep quiet: that excessive music which the platonic text seeks to reduce to silence, that music which lends itself to all and any transport, to all and any emotion, to anything which exceeds the *logos* and its ideal present. We could then think that the metaphor indicates a sort of black hole, the place in which the power of speech is lacking. It is no longer music that becomes philosophical; it is philosophy that turns into music: excessive and immoderate like music, philosophy here exposes itself to its own excess, the excess of an uncertain, lacking, or impertinent speech.

In dying, Socrates says to us that philosophy prepares us to die. And Plato indulges in a metaphor, a metaphor that escapes him, as if it were a catachresis in which music is called on to fill the space of the missing proper sense of philosophy itself, an irreducible metaphor in which music shamelessly and disobediently returns as the very disorder that the Greek philosopher spent his life trying to contain, to neutralize, giving it a deaf ear. In neutralizing music as the otherness that must be excluded in order to keep the *logos* unharmed, the *logos* not only loses music, but it jeopardizes its own integrity, since it loses the constitutive alterity that lies at the heart of its very *ipseity*. And Socrates almost seems to admit as much for an instant; for the time of a metaphor, he seems to suspect that life, as absolute immunity, might be the death of *ipseity*: such would be his *lapsus* on the threshold of death, a hesitation, a puzzlement, a quandary, as we said at the beginning, a last doubt before honoring philosophy with his sacrifice, before closing it tight on its injunction to immunize itself against the other.

Nietzsche had already focused, though briefly, on Socrates's dream by underlining in his way what we suggest to call a *lapsus* of philosophy on the threshold of its sacrifice:

> These words heard by Socrates in his dream are the only indication [*Zeichen*] that he ever experienced any uneasiness [*Bedenklichkeit*] about the limits [*Grenzen*] of logic. He may have asked himself: Have I been too ready to view what was unintelligible to me [*das mir Nichtverständliche*] as being devoid of meaning [*Unverständige*]? Perhaps there is a realm of wisdom, after all, from which the logician is excluded? Perhaps art must be seen as the necessary complement and supplement [*Korrelativum und Supplement*] of science [*Wissenschaft*]?[27]

We have abused and we continue to abuse music as we have done here, by prostituting it to every speech, to every discourse. But we can wonder for whom the bell tolls. We can wonder if the death knell does not toll, in the end, in the very realm of the speech we believe to own and dominate and to have at our disposal—a speech that, in the end or already since the beginning, is elusive, uncertain, and illicit.

Exactly like music, so to speak.

Bach's Silence, Mattheson's Words: Professional and Humanist Ways of Speaking of Music

Keith Chapin

In 1719, the Hamburg music journalist Johann Mattheson (1681–1764) wrote a pointed reminder to Johann Sebastian Bach (1685–1750), among other German-speaking musicians: Mattheson was still awaiting their contributions to a collection of biographies. Bach never did furnish a biography, and Mattheson eventually published his patriotic *Grundlage einer Ehrenpforte* (Foundation of an Arch of Tribute) in 1740 with contributions from many other prominent German musicians of past and present, including Georg Philipp Telemann, George Frideric Handel (Mattheson insisted on the composer's German heritage and the German form of his name), and, of course and at great length, Mattheson himself, but with no entry on Johann Sebastian Bach.

No editor's prod to a delinquent contributor on a collaborative project, Mattheson's reminder in 1719 owed its sharpness to several facts. First, Mattheson disseminated his reminder in a highly public fashion: in print. Bach's name appeared in upper-case letters toward the end of a meandering and far-ranging "theoretical preface" to Mattheson's first handbook on thoroughbass for organists, the *Exemplarische Organisten-Probe im Artikel vom General-Bass* (1719).[1] Second, Bach probably never agreed to furnish a biography in the first place. Mattheson had sent out the call for musicians to provide biographies in 1713 in *Das Beschützte Orchestre* and simply expected musicians to comply.[2] Some did, as Mattheson's list of thirty-one biographies received attests. Many did not, as Mattheson's list of fifty "desiderantur in specie" shows, though none of the others were typographically singled out through upper-case letters, as Bach was.[3] Third, the public forum of print that Mattheson had made his own was yet a novelty in musical circles.[4] Through Mattheson's pen, it had become synonymous with a challenge to the strong North German tradition of organists and cantors, and, as the scion of an already illustrious family of musicians, Bach had every reason to identify himself with this particular tradition of practicing professionals.

When taken in context, Mattheson's zeal and Bach's reticence can be interpreted not just as aspects of the personal relationship between two musicians, as George Stauffer has noted in an excellent survey of contacts between the two men, but also as a token of a conflict between two notions of the expert: the musical humanist and the practicing musician, as they might be called. The musical humanist is a connoisseur and man of letters with an extensive, humanistic breadth of education. The practicing musician, on the other hand, is devoted to the production of music and has intensive and authoritative knowledge of discipline-specific techniques and practices.[5] Practicing musicians participated in the larger community of the humanities at times centrally and at times tangentially. And at times one finds individuals who are both humanists and practicing musicians, participating in both traditions with versatility and virtuosity. Thus, these two identities are not mutually exclusive but rather should be understood as ideal types. All individuals involved in music, no matter their level of specialization, not only participate in the humanist discussion of music, the arts, and the world generally but also have some degree of specialized knowledge of musical styles, performance practices, and other discipline-specific matters. Nonetheless, individuals will often tend toward one pole or the other, and, as they tread the path of specialization, they must often choose, if for no other reason than that specialization encourages different ways of speaking of music and is supported by different institutions.

This chapter interprets the words of Johann Mattheson and the silence of Johann Sebastian Bach as tokens of the ideal types of the musical humanist and the practicing musician, respectively. I first discuss the two types in a history of realignment: if the musical humanists and practicing musicians found common ground in seventeenth-century practices and institutions of music, the accord was broken in the eighteenth century with the opening of relatively closed discourse communities to a large and ideally open public sphere. Mattheson was both herald and instigator of this change. Second, I argue that some aspects of Mattheson's humanistic approach to music—one characteristic of the *"galant homme"* of the early eighteenth century—were actually well prepared in the seventeenth century. If Mattheson and other journalists spoke of a sharp break between old and new practices, it was because they wished not only to portray themselves as proponents of the newest style but also because they had to break professional musicians' relative monopoly on the discourse around their subject. To do so, they needed to cast some professionals as conservative, even if these professionals had also been innovators in their own right. The up-to-date musician, in short, was not just one in command of the most recent styles from France and Italy but was also one who could communicate both as humanist and as professional musician, one who professed to speak of music from the point of view of a broad public. Third, I argue that specialist practical discourses on music had their own internal dynamic: if they opened out constantly toward the broad, humanistic discussions of music, they also tended to fall back on themselves, perhaps a tendency of all disciplinary discourses within the humanities. Even humanist musicians such as Mattheson had difficulties maintaining his appeal to a broad public and tended to slip back into specialist terms and debates. Finally, I look at Bach's maintenance of distance from Mattheson as a token of a professional musician's skepticism toward Mattheson and other musical humanists.

Some qualifications are necessary. Mattheson and Bach are not pure examples of the types of the humanist and the practicing musician. Mattheson may have owed his fame to his quasi-literary publications on music and his fortune to his secretarial service to a diplomat, but he knew the specialized practices of performance and composition firsthand. Bach, for his part, found his own fame as a performer on the organ and as a composer and teacher, but he engaged musically with theological, philosophical, and social debates of the time.[6] Second, as we will see, words and silence are not exclusively linked to humanists and musicians, respectively. Practicing, professional musicians did write, even if they lacked Mattheson's verbal virtuosity and verbosity. Mattheson's words and Bach's silence with respect to the *Grundlage einer Ehrenpforte* are thus tokens of the relative place of words—written or spoken—in the specialized practices of the humanist and the practitioner. Third, Mattheson receives greater attention in the discussion below than Bach, an imbalance called for by Mattheson's position as the most preeminent of his type in Germany during the early eighteenth century. Bach, by contrast, was one of many, and his fellows among the caste of professional organists and cantors stand up frequently in the following pages.

Although the subject of this study is historical, its stakes are entirely contemporary. These two ideals of musical expertise continue to inform discussions of music today and have found different institutional homes, especially the modern research university and conservatory. Indeed, in modern institutions of higher learning, one finds a gamut of ways that practical specialization and humanist specialization are transmitted. Conservatories and schools of music can exist as their own entities; they can be separate but equal to other schools underneath the larger umbrella of the research universities; and their functions can be taught within music departments fully integrated into faculties of arts, humanities, and sciences. To look at how Mattheson and Bach construed their fields is to examine the processes that still inform speaking about music today. This chapter is thus about a tension that is symptomatic and illustrative of the variety of positions in this book. While all the authors collected here desire to overcome the mythic autonomy or isolation of music, they do so from a variety of different standpoints.

Disciplinary Practices in and out of Synch

All musicians, no matter their allegiances, depend on words to formulate and propagate goals, methods, and values. Within the European tradition of art music, beginning at the very least as early as the fifteenth century,[7] musicians have developed their own ways of speaking about music proper to the production of music, and the sophistication of their ways of speaking has kept pace with the sophistication of the music itself, even to the point of esoteric exclusivity. Musicians have developed these ways of speaking in practices of performance and composition above all, but the centripetal impulse toward disciplinary independence is represented best and paradigmatically by the specialist terms of music theory and performance practice. But even as musicians constitute their own specialist discipline, they also participate within the larger community of people engaged in the arts and sciences. As humanists, musicians participate in a cross-disciplinary discourse with a vocabulary drawn from the component disciplines, though often at the price of the nuances associated with the terms in their original disciplines. Furthermore, disciplines that depend on words as their primary means or field of action—for example, philosophy and literature—have always tended to have primacy in the interdisciplinary exchange, a primacy that was qualified but hardly lost when nineteenth-century intellectuals made music the model of all the arts.

Humanist musicians and the practicing musicians, as the two ideal types might be called, each had their own institutional supports. Up through the end of the eighteenth century, art musicians depended on sinecures in church and court jobs above all, and later they depended on specialized music publishers, concert halls and societies, and conservatories. In turn, the larger community in the early modern period developed its own modes of specialization and institutions of supports over the centuries: the Republic of Letters; the public spheres of Parisian salons, English coffee houses, and German literary clubs; the university; and so forth.[8]

The relationship between the humanist musician and the practicing musician is complex. As in other arts that do not use the word as their primary media, there has often been tension between these two types of specialization. Professional musicians have scorned the "dilettante" man of letters, just as men of letters have sneered at "philistine" musicians, interested only in their craft.[9] Yet the types can also find relative peace with each other, as was the case in Germany during the seventeenth century: music had an important place in the grammar and Latin schools in which most burghers were educated, while professional musicians had excellent and at times even advanced educations in rhetoric, theology, and other academic subjects. Indeed, the communities of letters and music had achieved a striking synthesis during the seventeenth century. J. S. Bach's predecessor as cantor at the church of St. Thomas in Leipzig, Johann Kuhnau (1660–1722), exemplifies the synthesis. Kuhnau practiced professionally both as a lawyer and as musician. His versatility in music and letters allowed him to publish a novel on a musical subject, *Der musicalische Quacksalber* (The Musical Charlatan, 1700), and a musical work that exemplified biblical stories, the *Musicalische Vorstellung einiger Biblischer Historien* (The Musical Representation of Several Biblical Histories, 1700). But versatility in multiple areas did not eradicate the specialization that occurred in each discipline. In a biographical entry on Kuhnau, the eighteenth-century historian and lexicographer Jacob Adlung later noted that Kuhnau had his feet in two camps, suggesting that other learned men, despite their own specializations in various areas of the arts and sciences, had perhaps more in common among themselves than did musicians with the rest: "I do not know if he brought more honor to the order of musicians or to other learned men. He was learned in theology, law, rhetoric, poetry, mathematics, foreign languages, and music."[10]

It is at moments of striking change in the broad humanist sphere or in the specialized musical sphere that the tensions turn to cracks and ruptures, and one finds such a moment at the beginning of the eighteenth century. (*Speaking of Music* is itself symptomatic of the reorganizing and rethinking of the humanities that is currently visible in universities around the world.) When Johann Mattheson wielded print against learned musicians, he disseminated a new type of behavior that had already done much to transform the way that erudite discussions took place in Germany. The new habitus was that of the "*galant homme,*" the relaxed, socially conscious, cosmopolitan, and ethically correct bearing of the man of the world. This model changed the way learned discussion operated.

Like other intellectuals who gathered at the opera in Hamburg, Mattheson had formed himself as a *galant homme* in part in response to the teachings and writings of Christian Thomasius (1655–1728), a professor of law first in Leipzig and then later in Halle who did much to reorient German erudite discourse toward French models. Although trained in jurisprudence in traditional German academic style, Thomasius turned in 1687 to criticize the scholastic positions and rigid traditions of his university colleagues. He dropped the severe robes of the university academic and donned instead the fashionable garb of the cavalier. The change of clothing was a token of a change in both outlook and manner of speaking. He lectured in German rather than Latin and recommended French salon writers to his students, among them Dominique Bouhours and Madeleine de Scudéry. In Thomasius's reading, the French aristocratic salon was to provide the German burgher with a model of *galant* behavior: a cultured *je ne sais quoi* would trump erudition, and eclecticism would put dogmatism to rout in matters of philosophy, theology, and statecraft.[11] He disseminated this approach to the world in his university lectures, which were subsequently published, as well as in a series of "monthly conversations" on life and literature, the *Monats-Gespräche* (1688–90).

The *Monats-Gespräche* themselves indicate a shift in the way sophisticated discussion occurred in Germany. Good education had long been a centerpiece for German burghers and aristocrats. If aristocrats aspired to the cosmopolitan culture idealized, for example, by Baldassare Castiglione in his book on the ideal courtier, German burghers followed the humanist programs of education set forth by Martin Luther and Philipp Melanchthon and ingrained in the excellent compulsory school system in Lutheran lands. Nonetheless, the community of the lettered had its hierarchies. Poets often depended on their proximity to aristocratic academies (modeled on Italian ones) for support, and erudition had clear seats of power in the schools and the universities.

Thomasius sought to modify this system. One of his chosen genres, the fictional "discussion," was well known to German men of letters in the seventeenth century. It had illustrious precedents in classical antiquity (e.g., Cicero's *De oratore*) and in Italian Renaissance literature (e.g., the frame story to Bocaccio's *Decamerone*), and German writers used it to edify and entertain their readers. But whereas Georg Philipp Harsdörffer ("Frauenzimmer-Gesprächspiele," 1641–49) and Sigmund von Birken ("Die Betrübte Pegnesis," 1684) tended to stage discussions that occurred in a fictional time and space of a written narrative, were dominated by a single person, and promulgated a certain point of view, Thomasius made his works a point of crystallization for a large and ideally inclusive public. First, he promised to deliver his "monthly" discussions every month, thus binding his words to the calendar.[12] As the fictional time of the staged discussions was linked to the real time of a regularly appearing periodical, the real readership was invited more emphatically into the discussions. The narrative time became in part the time of the readers. Second, Thomasius allowed the characters to expound a variety of viewpoints, which in turn allowed readers great latitude to form their own opinions. He thus invited his readers to continue the discussions begun in print.

In all, Thomasius worked to soften the hierarchical and exclusive nature of German literary culture, to expand discussion out of the institutional frameworks of school, university, and aristocratic "academy" and into a larger and more chaotic (if still relatively reserved) public sphere. Later journal writers did not necessarily imitate the relativism or latitude allowed for debate by Thomasius. Mattheson, for example, often presented his own decided opinions as self-evident truths. Yet the public sphere had opened, for the debate in private progressively became a debate in print.

Thomasius's personal example was important for a generation of artists and intellectuals born in the 1680s, including Johann Mattheson and other prominent writers in Hamburg, such as Barthold Heinrich Brockes and Christian Friedrich Hunold.[13] Indeed, Thomasius's teachings entered into various behavior handbooks that circulated in the early decades of the eighteenth century.[14] Thomasius was not alone in his attempt to open a discourse community. For instance, Christian Weise (1642–1708), professor at a Gymnasium in Weißenfels and then later rector at the Gymnasium in Zittau, was another who strove to open discourse communities. In *Der politische Redner* (1679) and other books, he gave instructions to the new class of burghers who had taken up administrative positions of importance in German courts. Through his handbooks, they learned to speak well, to act practically, and to move between the civic worlds of the burgher and the courtly worlds of the nobleman.[15] Thomsiusis's *galant* man and woman of letters and Weise's politic man at court could be one and the same person.

In addition, the discourse community opened because Thomasius's successors could draw on a variety of English and French models to suit the particularities of their interests and audiences. England provided further models of print journalism. Joseph Addison's and Richard Steele's newspapers, the *Spectator* and the *Tattler*, provided models for the first moral weekly in Germany, *Der Vernünfftler*, published in Hamburg in 1713–14 and edited by Johann Mattheson. The public sphere of the French salon, on the other hand, was a more exclusive social environment than the one formed of newspaper-reading commoners in the English coffee house, but the salon also opened the sphere of intellectual discussion beyond private libraries, academies, and universities. Although fewer records exist of the doings of German aristocrats, they did imitate their French counterparts, just as they had imitated Italian aristocratic "academies" earlier in the seventeenth century. In Hamburg, for instance, Mattheson and other musicians associated with the opera depended on the aristocratic patrons who circulated in and around Hamburg both for financial support and for inspiration and models of aristocratic "good" taste.[16]

Opera played a special role in the expansion of the public sphere in Germany. Whereas English journalists such as Addison and Steele patriotically criticized the genre as an extravagant and foreign import, early German writers tended to see it as a civilizing force, as a way for burghers to form themselves according to an aristocratic model.[17] The first stage of Germany's assimilation of opera took place in courts, where Italian and French operas were performed and some German musicians wrote operas that depended heavily on foreign models. In a second stage, however, opera houses were founded in merchant cities, especially Hamburg. Yet it would be a mistake to see opera in Germany as a burgher pastime. In Hamburg, it was the large group of aristocratic foreign residents and ambassadors who were particularly important in supporting the opera, along with certain nonnoble members of the patrician class that controlled Hamburg's city council. Because opera provided a degree of common ground between aristocrats and well-to-do burghers, it served as a powerful symbol of social reorientation in German culture. It showed what the burgher could learn from aristocratic codes of behavior. Because opera had this formative function, many opposed it for sociopolitical reasons. They defended the traditional structures and hierarchies of German society.

Mattheson participated fully in the reorientation of German culture and the introduction of new forms of writing and publicness. Although he devoted himself to music early in life, first as a singer at the Hamburg opera (as of 1690) and later as a harpsichordist, composer, and conductor as well, he grounded his existence after 1704 in his role as a cosmopolitan *galant homme* and man of letters.[18] He earned his fortune (and a sizable one at that) as secretary to the English residents and pursued composition when time permitted. The experience in the opera prepared him well for this career. Already in 1693 he had been briefly inscribed as a page boy to Count von Güldenlöw, the "Vice-King" of Norway and brother of the king of Denmark, and there Mattheson learned a life of luxury. He later wrote fondly of the "white plume in his hat, the elaborate velvet clothes, and the silver sword" on which he prided himself but which his father, opposed to this courtly life, had obliged him to quit. In 1704, he became tutor to the son of the English resident (or ambassador) in Hamburg, Sir Cyril Wich, and in 1706, he took on the position of secretary to Sir Cyril and, after Sir Cyril's death, to his son John, who had acceded to his father's post. Mattheson devoted himself seriously to this and related positions until the early 1750s, when old age and ill health diminished but did not stop his activities. Through his close and friendly contacts with the members of the aristocracy, Mattheson managed to acquire many mostly honorary positions and titles that attested to his worldly success. His epitaph notes his titles, not his musical activities: "The Chamber of Rest unto Days Eternal for Herr Johann Mattheson, once Legation Counselor of the Grand Duchy of Holstein, and his Partner in Marriage."[19] If he attained great fame as a critic and theorist of music, he wrote always from the secure position of the educated and cosmopolitan man of letters.

Mattheson's literary activities were diverse, and only a portion of them were devoted to music. They were dictated in part by his position as secretary to Cyril and John Wich. He sent official diplomatic and trade reports to the English government and translated various propagandistic English texts on diplomatic affairs into German.[20] The signs of the high esteem in which he was held are many. In 1720, for example, Sir John Wich entrusted him with the delivery of an English subsidy to Count Flemming in Leipzig, a general in the Saxon army. Flemming received him with high honors, Mattheson reported. Mattheson's literary activities were also devoted to the dissemination of English thought and letters. His moral weekly, as noted, was composed primarily of translations of Addison and Steele. In

1723 and 1742–43, he published the first German translations of Daniel Defoe's *Moll Flanders* and Samuel Richardson's *Pamela*. An extensive but not complete list of Mattheson's literary doings is included in Beekman Cannon's biography, and it tells the story of a man of many interests.

Mattheson, of course, always regarded himself as a musician as well as a man of letters, but he self-consciously avoided some of the paths of traditional German musicians and struggled self-consciously for recognition as a musician. While many musicians before Mattheson worked in courts and produced operas, Mattheson seems to have avoided traditional church jobs with special care. This opposition came from his advocacy for opera and dramatic music in all musical spheres. Thus, he wrote church music that made use of operatic styles (as did many of his compatriots, including Buxtehude, Handel, and Bach) and made use of women as singers in the church. On both points, he faced opposition from the Pietists in Hamburg who controlled the parish churches, the spiritual ministry of the city, and to a large extent the city councils (but not the city senate) and from theologians around North Germany. When Mattheson did take on a church job, it was that of the Hamburg Cathedral, which was not part of the city's system of parishes and rather had ties to the aristocratic network that existed within and around Hamburg. The Swedish envoy supported Mattheson's application for the job of director of music at the cathedral, and the influence was important.

Mattheson's Words I: Preaching to the Partially Converted

Mattheson and his fellow early journalists earned their fame as critics of tradition. Because they hoped to form and speak to a public sphere, they often framed their discussions through simple oppositions between old and new. Yet the polemical language masks the complexity of the situation. The critique of antiquity was itself a rhetorical figure of sorts that could be used to defend a moderate conversation with the past, a tradition without pedantry.[21] More importantly, the "traditionalists" in the debates had themselves been "progressives" in the past; as their biographies show, some of them had cultivated opera and thus had full rights to claim the mantle of the *galant homme*. As for the journalists, they all were also professional musicians. Johann Adolph Scheibe, for instance, critiqued Bach for his "bombastic" style in 1737 but later served as music director to the Danish court in Copenhagen.

In part, Mattheson's criticisms of older musicians exemplify generational change: each new generation criticizes the last for its conservatism, only to be in turn branded as old iron twenty years later.[22] But the criticisms are also a token of a multilateral movement between musicians playing at one point the role of the man of letters, at another the role of the professional musician. Mattheson launched his critique from the vantage point of the man of letters. His primary respondents, Johann Heinrich Buttstett (1666–1727) and Johann Bokemeyer (1679–1751), by contrast, defended the ways of specialist musicians.

The history of Mattheson's critiques of the musical establishment has been documented in good detail.[23] In the *Neu-Eröffnetes Orchestre* (1713), a pamphlet that professed to "open" the "orchestra" to the *galant homme*, that is, to invite amateurs to join professional musicians on the floor of a virtual opera house and to decrease the traditional distance that had separated the professional from the amateur, Mattheson addressed a variety of issues that he hoped would be of value to his aristocratic and burgher public: basic terminology, compositional theory, judgment, and religious and aesthetic issues. The title page announces its intent clearly: "The Newly Opened Orchestra, or universal and thorough introduction as to how a *galant homme* should acquire a perfect idea of the height and dignity of noble music, form his taste accordingly, understand the technical terms, and skillfully reason on this excellent science."

One of the passages in the book that inspired controversy was buried in a discussion of key characteristics (C minor, in this case). After noting that the "quite lovely, if also sad" key could not be found in various traditional modes, Mattheson found himself inspired to pen a lengthy diatribe against conservative approaches to music (which would have permitted the old church modes but not this delicate key). The passage deserves quotation at length, for if professional musicians responded most vociferously to Mattheson, it was because Mattheson challenged not only the principles and practices of North German organists and cantors but also their cherished monopoly on knowledge and criteria within their discipline. Traditionalists, Mattheson argued, held on to that which had been superseded (and thus showed that they were dedicatees of tradition for its own sake rather than of music itself). They also supported their preferences by arguments that were more proper to other professions than they were to music. By attributing the criticisms of new musical trends to people outside the musical profession, Mattheson implied that anyone who did not see things his way was not really a musician at all.

In my true and honest devotion to the beautiful music of today, I sometimes cannot avoid writing "praise God!" when now and then a fantas-

tic lament arises in books that the music of the ancients is now among
the lost things. It seems to me almost as if a theologian among us
would regret that the burnt offerings of the Old Testament have been
extinguished or that the gold has fallen off an old image of Mary in a
Catholic peasants' church. People who speak and write thus—may they
be ever so learned otherwise—make a stalk for a louse and reveal their
great simplicity. It shines forth all the more when a person speaks as a
professional and writes that he is a theologian or philosopher, lawyer
or doctor, historian, orator, poet or the like, and knows all grammatical, rhetorical, logical, physical, metaphysical, mathematical, and other
rules, but does not think about the rules of music and of the musicians.
It is as if a musician [*Musicus*] or music were such despised things that
they earned no place in the world but were merely shadows.[24]

The sly force of Mattheson's polemical "defense" of music can best be
judged by the outraged responses he received. Given Mattheson's criticism of those who judge music from outside the profession, one might
expect musicians to applaud his words. Some did, and Mattheson prefaced
his subsequent books with encomiums from his supporters. Yet striking
responses also came from capable, professional musicians.

Mattheson's *Neu-Eröffnetes Orchestre* attracted one of its most notable
responses from Heinrich Buttstett. In *Ut, mi, sol, re, fa, la, tota musica et
harmonia aeterna* (1716), Buttstett criticized Mattheson's treatment of various music-theoretical issues and argued more broadly that the Hamburg
journalist did not respect antiquity enough. Buttstett was an excellent example of the type of professional musician that formed the core of the
professional corps of North German musicians. Buttstett lived almost his
entire life in Erfurt, the town in Thuringia where Bach was born. There
he held a series of church organist jobs, composed organ and vocal music,
and also taught Latin at a school associated with one of his churches—all
activities that marked him as following the traditional path of the learned
musician. A student of Johann Pachelbel (1653–1706), he took up a tradition of counterpoint that was particularly important to North German
musicians and in turn passed it on to his own students, including Johann
Walther (1684–1748), a cousin of J. S. Bach and an important organist
and scholar of music. For Buttstett, as for Pachelbel and for Walther, music possessed metaphysical significance due to the mathematical nature of
its basic material: consonances and dissonances. They were the sonorous
manifestation of divine harmony, a position with explicit links to Pythagorean ideals of a common rational harmony to world, soul, and sound. The
position underpinned a preference for replete musical textures, careful and

exacting resolutions of dissonances into consonance, and music oriented around the Lutheran chorale as its cantus firmus. In each case, musicians sought solidity or, as their critics saw it, stolidity.

Yet not all of Mattheson's critics so perfectly exemplified the traditional German musician. Heinrich Bokemeyer (1679–1751) also entered the lists against Mattheson. Although he shared some of Buttstett's convictions, such as a belief in Pythagorean principles, he focused in his response on a music-theoretical point on which up-to-date musicians did not necessarily fully agree with Mattheson. Whereas Mattheson had argued that each melody needed clear statement with no competition, Bokemeyer hoped to show that the canon—the contrapuntal weaving of two or more melodies, each imitating the others—was the true symbol of musical perfection. Again, the music-theoretical discussion crystallized differences about aesthetics and metaphysics. As a contrapuntal technique and thus one that required careful negotiation of consonances and dissonances, the canon had long been associated with the Pythagorean worldview and religious metaphysics. Melody, by contrast, needed little theoretical knowledge for its development. Mattheson printed Bokemeyer's objections in his short-lived journal *Critica musica*, along with further installments in a debate that ended with Bokemeyer's capitulation.

Bokemeyer's response to Mattheson was at least as much that of the professional musician defending his territory as it was that of the conservative opposing innovation or change. Mattheson used an opposition between melody and harmony that had been borrowed primarily from early eighteenth-century French debates about national style. The French excelled in melody, the Italians in harmony.[25] However, even as they divided the musical sphere sharply in two, they only talked about one part of it: opera. French "melody" referred to the simple, suave lines of French recitatives and airs; Italian "harmony" referred to the vibrant, virtuosic lines of Italian arias. Both, in other words, were in essence talking about species of what musicians would normally call melody. When German musicians and burgher men of letters took up debates, they needed to adapt the prestigious categories to their own concerns. As the French dichotomy between French melody and Italian harmony did not easily fit the German plurality of traditions, Mattheson and others adapted. Later writers posited the German as a "mixed style," but such mixture presupposed that fusion had already taken place. What was one to do with the traditional German preference for counterpoint? Mattheson associated canon with "harmony," emphasizing the multiplicity of parts sounding at once and the rules that governed their relation. But Bokemeyer defended canon as a combination of melodies, emphasizing rather the mellifluous nature of sophisticated part-writing.

Details from Bokemeyer's biography show him as a full member of the German professional sphere. Like Buttstett, he was trained at a church school, though in Brunswick, and, like Buttstett, he eventually took on a church job, though as cantor. Furthermore, Bokemeyer was firmly integrated into the network of professional, amical, and family relations that governed the professional sphere in North Germany. He was a good friend to Johann Walther, J. S. Bach's cousin, and Bokemeyer had close enough ties to his own teacher, Georg Österreich (1664–1735), to receive the latter's impressive collection of music as an inheritance.[26] Later Bokemeyer became a member of a corresponding Society of Musical Science begun by Lorenz Mizler and joined by Telemann, Bach, and other learned musicians.[27]

But Bokemeyer does not fit Mattheson's mold of the died-in-the-wool conservative. While working as a cantor at the church of St. Martin in Braunschweig, he took music lessons from Österreich, cantor and music director to the court of Braunschweig-Lüneburg. While working as cantor in Schleswig, he studied "the manner of singing *alla siciliana*" with the Italian music director Bartolomeo Bernhardi and even sung some of the latter's cantatas for the king of Denmark. Österreich himself had cultivated church music in a traditional seventeenth-century style but had also been closely associated with opera productions at the courts of Brunswick and Schleswig-Holstein.[28]

In other words, when Mattheson criticized traditionalists, he struck out at musicians who had long been open to the cosmopolitan influences associated with opera and Italian music generally. Toward the end of the seventeenth century, opera (the symbol of the new) and counterpoint (the symbol of tradition) were by no means mutually exclusive. Johann Theile (1646–1724), for instance, is famous for his compendium of counterpoint, the *Musikalisches Kunstbuch* (Musical Book of Art). It was one of the models for Bach's later systematic essays in fugue, the *Well-Tempered Clavier*, the *Art of the Fugue*, and the *Musical Offering*. But Theile also produced the first opera in Hamburg as Capellmeister to Duke Christian Albrecht of Schleswig-Holstein-Gottorp (then in exile in Hamburg).

Thus, to defend the canon, whether the musical genre or the body of received models, was not to take a simple conservative position. It was rather to fashion oneself as a professional composer. Georg Philipp Telemann, the very model of a modern *galant* musician in the early decades of the century, sided with Mattheson on many issues but defended the canon as a flower of compositional craft.[29] In the end, Mattheson won his debate with Bokemeyer: Bokemeyer sent a letter admitting defeat and professing conversion to Mattheson's way of seeing things.[30] However, Mattheson's victory was in some measure that of the practiced wordsmith, the man of letters. He argued his point well and at times viciously, and his opponents could neither match his élan nor muster his mastery of a public, confrontational mode of writing. Bokemeyer wrote toward the beginning of the debate that he preferred calm discussion to sharp disputation, a preference that shows his ties to the more intimate modes of communication proper to circles of friends, like-minded colleagues, and other types of small, chosen communities.[31]

If seventeenth-century professional musicians had found ways to negotiate the demands of traditional German church jobs, on the one hand, and the attractions of foreign opera and the German courts that produced them, on the other, those who lived into the eighteenth century, whether in fact or in histories, found themselves branded as conservatives in the public arenas opened up by the journals. Wolfgang Caspar Printz toured Italy as a young man and had jobs as both church cantor and court music director over his career. For the latter, if the titles of his compositions are anything to go by, he composed Italianate vocal works. Yet in an autobiography written for Mattheson's *Ehrenpforte* (1740), Telemann called Printz a Heraclitus to his own Democritus: "For he bitterly lamented the extravagances of current melodic composers just as I laughed at the unmelodic artifices of the ancients."[32] Other "ancients" had been moderns in the not-so-distant past. Johann Kuhnau, mentioned earlier for his multivalence, may have acted a traditional role as cantor of St. Thomas in Leipzig, but he also wrote an Orpheus opera and other dramatic music early in his career. Furthermore, he was closely associated with Christian Weise, one of the agents of social and intellectual change discussed earlier. Kuhnau too, however, comes in for branding. Telemann says that while a student of law at the University of Leipzig, he learned much of counterpoint from Kuhnau but studied melody by himself.[33]

Such remarks show Telemann's sense of generational superiority. But they must be balanced against Telemann's defense of canon in his response to Mattheson, his intention (never realized) to publish a translation of one of the best treatises on counterpoint of the age (Johann Joseph Fux's *Gradus ad parnassum*), and his willingness to write appropriate music for all occasions: melodies for the theater (his operas, thirty in number), counterpoint for the church (his *XX kleine Fugen* of 1731, among other compositions), and canons and other full-voiced compositions for the chamber (*XIIX canons mélodieux, ou VI sonates en duo* of 1738, written for fashionable Paris). Differences of musical taste and of generation divided Mattheson and other *galant* musicians from their critics. But professional identity was also at stake.

Mattheson's Words II: The Fall into Discipline

As Mattheson's arguments with professional musicians dragged on, he himself shifted his role ever more to that of the professional musician. Even champions of change such as Mattheson tended to fall from *galant* grace into specialist detail, in essence to continue ongoing debates within the profession about minute facets of theory and practice. This move toward specialization can be seen in the three volumes of his *Orchestre* series. If, in the first, he explicitly appealed to the *galant homme*, by the last he argued with other specialist musicians. The loquacious titles of the three volumes tell the story well. In *Das Neu-Eröffnete Orchestre* [*sic*] (1713), Mattheson addressed his book primarily to the *galant homme*: "The Newly Opened Orchestra, or universal and thorough introduction as to how a *galant homme* should acquire a perfect idea of the height and dignity of noble music, form his taste accordingly, understand the technical terms, and skillfully reason on this excellent science."[34]

In *Das Beschützte Orchestre* (1717), Mattheson addressed the *galant homme* but moved quickly on to joust with the metaphysical claims of Johann Buttstett, whose promise to address "music in its totality" (*tota musica*) Mattheson lampooned with an untranslatable pun. The complete title reads,

> The Defended Orchestra, or its second opening, in which not only an actual man of taste (who bears no relation to the profession) but even some musicians themselves will be given the most honest and clear idea of the musical sciences as they actually and truly are, well cleaned of all scholastic dust; [and in which] all repellent interpretations and mucky accretions are fully and bluntly dismissed; [and in which] finally the long exiled ut—mi—sol / re—fa—la dead [*todte*] (not *tota*) *musica* are buried in their grave and honored with a monument for their everlasting memory, magnificently accompanied by the twelve Greek modes, their noble relations and mourners.[35]

In the course of this volume, Mattheson took on his critics squarely, and as he did so, he moved away from the general topics and general presentation that graced the first volume. The first part contains replies to each of Buttstett's criticisms, the second a critique of the system of solmisation.

Finally, in the third volume of the series, *Das Forschende Orchestre* (1721), Mattheson claimed victory over his specialist opponent and gave up all pretension of addressing the *galant homme*, though he continued to write on the latter's behalf. "The Probing Orchestra, or its third opening, in which *sensus vindiciae et quartae blanditiae*, that is, the vindicated position of the senses and the flattering sound of the fourth are presented to all impartial *Syntechnitis* [craftsmen] for their use and consideration; though [they are] investigated *sana ratione & autoritate* [with pure reason and authority] and to the disadvantage to no one, and presumably put in their proper light."[36] The subsequent pages bear out the title. Mattheson first grounds the study of music in the senses, drawing on John Locke's empiricist theories to legitimate his stance in an age-old debate, and then goes on to address the nature of the perfect fourth as a dissonance. These are technical issues, not necessarily appropriate for the evening reading of a *galant homme*.

As Mattheson sought truth, he spoke less and less to the *galant homme* and more and more to the "impartial" person with a firm knowledge of musical techniques. He may have spoken on behalf of "*gens de lecture*" (the reading public), as he wrote in the introduction "*ad lectorem*" (to the reader) to *Das Forschende Orchestre*, but he had a narrower ideal public for the volume firmly in mind: "I wish not only that my reader be a capable musician, but also that he should at the same time be a learned one equipped with a sharp power of judgment."[37] Arno Forchert has noted that Mattheson used polemical discussions in his journals as a way to gain insights into musical issues.[38] A side effect of the method was that Mattheson turned away from his broad audience and toward the very writers with whom he carried on polemical debates.

All told, Mattheson wrote for a variety of audiences throughout his career and never turned entirely away from the lay audience. Nonetheless, he also gave increasingly more attention to solidifying his position as a professional musician. His claim to professionalism is emblematized in two texts that were published in 1739 and 1740, respectively, *Der vollkommene Capellmeister* (The Perfect Music Director) and the *Grundlage einer Ehrenpforte*. In the first, he laid out his prescriptions (and many proscriptions) for performance, composition, and indeed all that would be needed by the musician who aspired to perfection.[39] As the first practical handbook (rather than encyclopedic collection) that professed to cover so many areas, Mattheson's text claimed much. He claimed not just the place of a senior member of the profession—a teacher who taught disciples—but the position of senior master in the profession. The *Grundlage* followed up on this move. In it, Mattheson defined the German sphere of professional musicians and, through his extensive and self-congratulatory autobiography, his own crucial place in this sphere.

It should, of course, be remembered that Mattheson had rights to the claim to be a professional, for he continued to compose music, even as he increasingly went deaf. The role of the humanist, lettered musician and that of the specialist, learned musician were not mutually exclusive. He also seems to have had at least some success as a composer. Bach, for example, probably performed a Magnificat by Mattheson in Leipzig in 1725.[40] Yet it was undoubtedly as a writer of words, not notes, that his contemporaries knew him best. Bach pursued a different path.

Bach's Silence: The Professional Resists

Johann Sebastian Bach wrote many words over the course of his life, but he tended to write only when professional or personal obligations required it. Bach wrote attestations of the organs whose construction he had been asked to judge, letters of reference for students and colleagues, proposals and missives to his various employers about the requirements and the details of his positions, and finally letters to friends and colleagues about both personal and professional matters. If he was willing to send his music into the public sphere, even in print, he specifically avoided sending his words there. It should be noted at the outset that Bach had reasons for disgruntlement that went beyond the institutional. In *Critica musica* (1725), Mattheson criticized Bach's repetition of words in the Cantata No. 21: "Ich, ich, ich, ich hatte viel Bekümmerniß ‖ in meinem Hertzen ‖ in meinem Hertzen ‖ ‖ [etc.]." Such word repetition destroyed the cogency of the statement, Mattheson argued. Elsewhere Mattheson also cast aspersions on Bach's conservatism and on the difficulty of his music, though Mattheson also recognized the organist and composer as one of the best at his particular art of composition.[41]

There are a number of indications that Bach's avoidance of public words was a studied one. First, as noted at the outset of this chapter, Bach provided Mattheson with no biography, and Mattheson gave Bach's reluctance a high profile in the *Exemplarische Organisten-Probe* (1719). Bach, it should be noted, was not the only one to leave Mattheson's call unanswered. Of the fifty names mentioned by Mattheson in 1719, thirty find no place in the *Grundlage*, including other luminaries such as Dieterich Buxtehude and Johann Joseph Fux.[42] However, Bach did provide biographical details to the competition, namely, to Johann Gottfried Walther's *Musikalisches Lexikon* (1732), a dictionary that also gives biographical information on many German musicians. Walther, who was Bach's friend and cousin, included an entry with Bach's personal history and even noted a personal communication from the author.

If one is willing to walk the tightrope of informed speculation, it is even possible to see the lack of biography in the *Grundlage* as a sign of Mattheson's conscious or unconscious ire at Bach's slight of silence. At the most basic level, Mattheson surely excluded the composer because he had received no materials directly from him. Mattheson specifically noted that he only included biographical information that was either new or that came from manuscripts and thus was not otherwise available to the public.[43] It may be that Mattheson thought that the biography in Walther's *Lexikon* was sufficient. However, this biography is sparse and in no way matches the extensive entries on other prominent musicians that Mattheson printed in the *Grundlage*. Bach certainly counted as a prominent musician for Mattheson, if one may judge by the various comments in Mattheson's writings, and Mattheson was not averse to supplementing a composer's biography from his personal knowledge, as he did extensively for Handel. No certainty can be found on the whys and wherefores of the lack of a Bach biography in the *Grundlage*. The very lack nonetheless hangs like a cloud over Bach's silence in the printed debates.

A second indication of Bach's distance from Mattheson's enterprise can be seen in the oblique response he offered to Mattheson's critique of traditional compositional practice. As David Ledbetter has noted, in the title to the first volume of the *Well-Tempered Clavier* (1722), Bach chose to designate the distinction between major and minor keys with traditional and even antiquated terminology. He referred to key distinctions by naming the solmisation syllables underpinning the initial tones of major and minor scales, following the standard practice of naming the ancient modal hexachords, even though the cleaner and simpler "major" (*dur*) and "minor" (*moll*) were available to him. The title page begins, "The *Well-Tempered Clavier*. Or *Preludes* and *Fugues* through *all the tones and semitones*, both with the major 3rd, or Ut Re Mi and with the minor 3rd, or Re Mi Fa." Thereby Bach paid homage to Johann Kuhnau's *Clavier-Übungen* (two series of suites in seven major and seven minor keys published in 1689 and 1692, respectively), and he also offered support for Buttstett and an implicit critique of Mattheson. Buttstett, after all, had inscribed the designation of major and minor with solmisation syllables into his title and title page: *Ut, mi, sol, re, fa, la, tota musica et harmonia aeterna*. Rather than emphasizing the break with the past, as Mattheson did, Bach emphasized the continuity between the Guidonian system of solmisation and the modern system of major-minor tonality. By emphasizing the continuity in terminology, he also highlighted the continuity of the profession.[44]

A third sign of Bach's opposition to the habitus represented by Mattheson involves his most famous silence: his learned presence behind a penned and published response to the journalist Johann Adolph Scheibe. As a student in Leipzig, Scheibe had studied music with Bach and had followed the courses and publications of the literary critic Johann Christoph Gottsched (1700–1766). By the time he moved to Hamburg in 1736, at the latest, Scheibe had taken his distance from Bach. There he began publication of the journal *Critischer Musikus* in 1737. The journal, which Scheibe began at Telemann's urging, was inspired by Mattheson's journals and by Gottsched's *Versuch einer critischen Dichtkunst für die Deutschen* (An Attempt at a Critical Poetics for Germans, 1730). In his journal, Scheibe celebrated Telemann and Carl Heinrich Graun above all—*galant* musicians both—though he distributed praise, advice, and criticism where he felt it due. In 1737, there is a report from an "anonymous traveling musician," most likely Scheibe himself, that describes the activities of various musicians in Germany. A certain organist and composer easily recognizable as Bach came in for scolding for his "turgid" (*schwulstig*) writing for voices and for his lack of "agreeableness" (*Annehmlichkeit*), among other musical sins.[45]

Although Bach offered no direct response, a Leipzig professor of law named Johann Abraham Birnbaum published a lengthy, point-by-point response to Scheibe.[46] The response is a token of the professional musician's silence toward the literary world. Birnbaum insists on Bach's status as a professional musician of high class (he is a royal Capellmeister) and on his thorough knowledge of the art of harmony. More importantly, as Christoph Wolff has shown, Birnbaum acted directly as spokesperson for Bach. Birnbaum discusses musicians known to Bach as a specialist musician but not to the general public in Germany, the French organist Marchand, for instance, with whom Bach competed at the organ during a visit to Dresden in 1717.

The conflict between Scheibe and Bach became something of a cause célèbre among professional musicians in Germany, even though Bach never uttered a word. Others jumped into the breach for him. After Birnbaum, there was Lorenz Mizler, another journalist-musician, though one who tried to update the seventeenth-century metaphysics of music by translating it into the philosophy of Christian Wolff. Much later, in 1746, Christoph Gottlieb Schröter summarized the stages of the debate and noted that since Bach "was not in a position, on account of the piling up of his official duties, to answer the Critical Musician properly, Magister Birnbaum undertook the task."[47]

There are other indications that Bach followed closely what Mattheson published but replied to the man only in music. It is probable that one of the inspirations for Bach's *Art of the Fugue* (begun in 1740) was a challenge issued by Mattheson in *Der vollkommene Capellmeister* (1739): Mattheson "modestly" did not recommend his own *Die wol-klingende Fingersprache* (The Well-Sounding Finger Language, 1735) as a model of fugal writing with three subjects, noted the lack of other such models, and finally suggested that Bach would be the person to compose such a work. Numerous musical parallels between the two works indicate that Bach did indeed wish his work to be placed next to Mattheson's.[48] He surely believed that he would fare well in the comparison.

Conclusion

Mattheson straddled the fence between specialist spheres of his day—the Republic of Letters and the world of music. Bach represented the more seasoned professional, at least by North German standards. Yet even as Mattheson attacked the self-understandings of professional organists and cantors that had allowed them to sit comfortably within the stratified and regimented intellectual world of seventeenth-century Germany, he envisioned a new rapprochement of the professional musician and the man of letters, one based less on erudition and more on the habitus of the relaxed man of letters. Indeed, he did contribute to a new accord between the spheres of learned notes and learned letters. This accord developed most strongly in Germany in the nineteenth century, when the new metagenre of art music sketched by Gelbart in this volume allowed musicians, poets, painters, and others to find common ground and common cause in their pursuit of art and the Absolute.

In the centuries between then and now, the two approaches to music have moved in and out of synch. The tension is a productive one, though it is one that necessitates continuing discussion as the conditions change under which musicians of different stamps operate and as goals and interests of humanists and professionals change. And as the examples of Mattheson and Bach show, the approaches always mix in practice. The man of letters can stop speaking. The silence of the musician is never perfect.

Making Music Speak

Andrew H. Clark

In this chapter, I am interested in the manner in which music was seen in the eighteenth century as a common good and imagined strategically, not just in religious communities but in secular ones as well, as a means to effect and potentially control the public (usually through its effect on a listening body) and to create a sense of shared sentiment, purpose, and citizenship. To this effect, I examine the ways in which three well-known eighteenth-century Europeans who wrote on music and its effects—Denis Diderot (1713–84), Johann Mattheson (1681–1764), and Jean-Jacques Rousseau (1712–78)—theorize dissonance in their social therapies and make music speak for specific sociopolitical goals or cures. For each, bodies possess a certain kind of musical instinct that makes them particularly responsive to music. This understanding of musical instinct is deeply informed by eighteenth-century empirical theories of the body and sound. I am interested in how certain music metaphors, such as that of dissonance, were harnessed to articulate and potentially control unspeakable forces and relations visible in animal and social bodies. I argue that whereas writers such as Mattheson and Rousseau tried to minimize dissonance in their social therapies, others such as Diderot saw it as important.

As Laura Odello writes in her chapter in this book, when one writes about music, the metaphors begin, and we abuse music as if it were a "prostitute." Music "lends itself, it gives itself to all, like a prostitute." This chapter is similarly abusive, and it is not only abusive to music; it is abusive to history. I have selected a few characters or actors to tell a tale of musical effects and their potential consequences. While all of these actors were prominent figures of the Enlightenment in Europe and while all "prostituted" or talked about music for their own purposes, they were not necessarily closely connected. Nor did they have the same social, epistemological, and theoretical concerns. However, they did make use of similar music metaphors to articulate their positions. They did all also believe that music has a place in questions of philosophy, power, public utility, and sovereignty. They also represent various currents and discussions in their respective countries and in Europe more generally. I am interested in the metaphors they used, in the purported effects of music from their observations and conjectures, and in the way in which alternative forms were imagined to make music speak.

In antiquity, music and the arts in general had been used to the benefit of the state, a use that Odello convincingly argues subordinates music to the *logos*.[1] Examples abound in the works of Plato, Aristotle, and Boethius of music's intimate and necessary relation to the state and the health of its citizens. Many eighteenth-century thinkers saw as much and wished to resurrect the place of music in order to address the various political, aesthetic, and social concerns and changes taking place in their homeland. As the eighteenth-century musician, music theorist, musical historian, translator, diplomat, businessman, and general polymath Mattheson observed in his seminal work *Der vollkommene Capellmeister* (1739), "Plato knew very well that even in music there is something useful for the preservation of the state."[2] The importance of the arts in stimulating and preserving civic virtue is a recurrent theme in eighteenth-century aesthetic and moral treatises, and antiquity frequently serves as the model for a new ideal unity of citizenship and the arts.[3] In Diderot's *Entretiens sur le fils naturel* (1757), for instance, Dorval discusses a new dramatic aesthetics and the desire to animate the public with the sentiment of virtue. The character uses the metaphor of a large musical instrument to refer to the theater in antiquity and its relation to the public and its ability to resonate their voices. "There are no longer, to speak accurately, public performances," Diderot writes to advocate his program of theatrical reform. "What relationship is there between our gatherings at the theater on the days with the greatest number of spectators and those of the people of Athens and Rome? The ancient theaters would seat up to 80,000 citizens. In the construction of these buildings, one employed all the means available in order to enhance the voices and instruments. One had the idea of [the theater as] a large instrument."[4] From the fifteenth century on, the musical instrument (a stringed instrument, as wind instruments were negatively connoted in the writings of antiquity) was perhaps the most common metaphor used to discuss this new communication of aesthetic and civic virtue and was perhaps most characteristic in the eighteenth century in the neo-Platonist philosophy of Anthony Ashley Cooper, 3rd Earl of Shaftesbury. Bernard Mandeville, Adam Smith, Laurence Sterne, and Pierre Jean Georges Cabanis, among others, continued to use the metaphor frequently throughout the eighteenth century.[5] Building, for instance, on the idea of each being's unique order and its corresponding relation or *rapport* to a universal harmony, a relation essential for aesthetic appreciation and virtue, Shaftesbury compares the passions in animal constitution with musical strings:

> Upon the whole, it may be said properly to be the same with the affections or passions in an animal constitution as with the cords or strings of a musical instrument. If these, though in ever so just proportion one to another, are strained beyond a certain degree, 'tis more than the instrument will bear: the lute or lyre is abused, and its effect lost. On the other hand, if while some of the strings are duly strained, others are not wound up to their due proportion, then is the instrument still in disorder, and its part ill performed. The several species of creatures are like different sorts of instruments; and even in the same species of creatures (as in the same sort of instrument) one is not entirely like the other, nor will the same strings fit each. The same degree of strength which winds up one, and fits the several strings to a just harmony and consort, may in another burst both the strings and instrument itself. Thus men who have the liveliest sense, and are the easiest affected with pain or pleasure, have need of the strongest influence or force of other affections, such as tenderness, love, sociableness, compassion, in order to preserve a right balance within, and to maintain them in their duty, and in the just performance of their part, whilst others, who are of a cooler blood, or lower key, need not the same allay or counter part, nor are made of Nature to feel those tender and endearing affections in so exquisite a degree. It might be agreeable, one would think, to inquire thus into the different tunings of the passions, the various mixtures and alloys by which men become so different from one another.[6]

According to Shaftesbury, one could orchestrate with careful tuning a society in which all the various individuals would be in universal harmony if one could merely determine each individual's timbre. Music's ineffability and supposedly universal appreciation made it a convenient metaphor to describe forms of union and communication that could not otherwise be conjectured or explained. Most theories of sympathy and sociability during the eighteenth century relied on musical metaphors of harmony and concord to speak of man's natural sociability and the necessary and involuntary movement of like matter and beings to one another.

But while seventeenth- and eighteenth-century philosophers, scientists, medical doctors, and theologians made frequent reference to musical metaphors to articulate their own metaphysical theories on the movement of the spheres, the communications between body and soul, the resonances between nature and God, and the instinctive sociability of all, musicians and music theorists also saw the importance of using music as a public good.[7] Aligning music with the public and public utility could only serve to protect music from being further marginalized in the increasingly modernized and centralized states of Europe. Like other trades/disciplines such as medicine that were becoming professionalized in the eighteenth century, musicians sought to be at the forefront of social debates and reforms. The public venue of musical performances, in particular, the opera house, provided a space in which political connections and ideas could be negotiated. Furthermore, in aligning music with the common good, many of these musicians and music theorists led the way in separating music from metaphysics as well as in imagining the place of the general public or "masses" in the appreciation and judgment of music.[8] Implicit in substantiating the social benefits of music seemed to be the new need to criticize those reigning theories on the harmonies of the sphere that mixed philosophical and mathematical concepts and to encourage more empirical thinking.[9]

I would like to focus on Mattheson as one of the actors in this change. His eclectic sources and pragmatic writing and active involvement with the state bring together and summarize many of the positions articulated at the time and also show how Mattheson attempted to use music treatises, reforms, and journals as a way of fashioning civic engagement and the state.[10] Mattheson emphasized experiences (sensations), observations, and so on over "measuring" tones as the essential ingredients for good music and dismissed preconceptions of musical sounds:

> It is not so much good *proportion*, but rather the apt *usage* of the intervals and keys, which establishes the beautiful, moving and natural quality in melody and harmony. Sounds, in themselves, are neither good nor bad; but they become good or bad according to the way in which they are used. No measuring or calculating art teaches this. If propor-

tion is also to please the hearing, then mathematical exactness must always yield. What good is it?[11]

Mattheson insisted that music is a natural science and not a mathematical tool: "Hence the prime, established bases of music lie in physics or natural science. One advocate of mathematics even admits *that music derives certain fundamentals from nature. . . . Music draws its water from the spring of nature; and not from the puddles of arithmetic.*"[12]

In making these empirical assertions, ones that were not uncommon in eighteenth-century discussions of music, Mattheson called into question the assumptions of Cartesian music theorists such as Jean-Philippe Rameau (1683–1764).[13] In his *Traité de l'harmonie* (1722), published seventeen years before *Der vollkommene Capellmeister* (1739), Rameau argued,

> Music is a science which must have rules which are certain; these rules must be derived from a self-evident principle, and this principle cannot be known to us without the use of mathematics. I must confess that despite all the experience that I could acquire in music, having practiced it for such a long time, it is nevertheless only with the use of mathematics that my ideas have taken shape, and that light has followed darkness which I did not perceive in the past.[14]

However, even Rameau, as critics have argued, moved to a more empirical understanding of music theory despite his Cartesian leanings, but his text was not easily intelligible to its readers, a fact which became evident as other musicians and scholars attempted to translate his ideas for a more general public.[15] While Mattheson kept abreast of theories and ideas in England and the European continent, the majority of his own theories and treatises were articulated around local concerns and debates in German music, not as a response specifically to Rameau or French music. He did criticize Rameau's theory of harmony, but he was hardly in dialogue with him. As Beekman Cannon remarks, Rameau "presumably remained happily unconcerned with Mattheson's attacks on his harmonic theories."[16] Nonetheless, their two positions underline an important empirical shift occurring across the European continent that was by no means limited to music and that Mattheson willfully participated in.

Music in the Service of the General Public

In this empirical vein, Mattheson devotes the fifth chapter of his *Der vollkommene Capellmeister*, "On the Use of Music in the General Public," to the potential benefits of music in the public sphere. As noted in the introduction to this chapter, arguments about the utility of music had been commonplace since antiquity. But philosophers, musicians, doctors, and others in eighteenth-century Enlightenment Europe seemed to be interested in making increasingly emphatic claims about music's pivotal role and utility. Examples abound among writers both well known and less well known. For Rousseau or the Parisian doctor Louis Joseph-Marie Robert (1771–1846), music was at the very origin and heart of civilization. Rousseau made music central to his life and philosophical vision, and as Tracy Strong argues in this volume, music for Rousseau "offers us the vision of the possibility of a human world."[17] It underlines our essential commonality. In *De la musique, considérée sous les rapports de son influence sur les mœurs, les passions et la santé*, Robert argued that music is a universal cure-all and the very food of the soul. It was an essential part of the health, vitality, and moral propriety of every being. Louis Sébastien Mercier (1740–1814) saw music, particularly ambulatory or street music performed for the people, as having the potential to "change in large part the morals of the masses and attach them more strongly to their government."[18] Mattheson participates in a similar ethos in which music is not peripheral but central to the health of the state and to our very physical and moral being. As one considerably influenced by Lutheran views of music in addition to those writings of antiquity, Mattheson, like Luther, assigned music an important role in the health of society. Situating his argument, as noted earlier, by describing the intimate connection between music and the republic in antiquity and basing most of his argument on what was allegedly Plutarch's *De Musica*, Mattheson adumbrates a "politico-musical theory,"[19] but unlike the ancients, he does so through empirical science. He divides this politico-musical theory into three major points. First, he illustrates the importance of music in disciplining the state's subjects. Quoting an anonymous French author, he writes, "music tames the wild spirits; softens the hard and coarse nature of emotions; polishes manners; makes people more capable of being cultivated; unites hearts with one another in a pleasant and agreeable manner, and produces aversion to all vices which lead to severity, inhumanity, and insolence" (123). Because of music's salubrious and cultivating effects on the public and its ability to dissipate passions and vices, Mattheson believed that statesmen should consider music when making political calculations. Most important, he believed the statesman had to stress the primacy of unity and harmony (124–25).

> Is this [harmony] not which unites the citizenry in loving union, which
> sets it in order, reconciles it, and brings it under the laws of a pleasant

society? In it all is peaceful, happy and in good harmony; in it one hears
neither the voice of discord, the noise of the mob, the stormy academic
rubble, the unrestrained yelling from the teachers, nor the cries of the
courtrooms; but only *delightful conformity and quiet consent*. (124, my
emphasis)

Mattheson's polemical language targets his enemies. As Cannon writes,
these included "the pedantic scholars, musicians, and performers who
devoted all their efforts to learned discussion and analysis of antiquated
musical theories," as well as "ill-educated, narrow-minded teachers, parsi-
monious patrons, and frivolous patrons."[20] But the statement also sketches
out a political vision in which music plays an integral part and in which
Mattheson criticizes any form of civic disorder. This primary and effective role of music in affairs of the *polis*—to produce "conformity and quiet
consent"—is not surprising considering the conservative Mattheson's activities in Hamburg's political and international affairs: he was the trusted
secretary to two successive English Residents in the city and carried out
both diplomatic and business tasks.[21] Nor is it surprising that he believed
that dissonant or troublesome voices should be controlled or squelched.
Just as he wished to control dissonance in the musical sphere in the interest
of a "light" and "flowing" melody, he wished to control it in the political sphere, even to the point of avoiding it or banning it altogether. Mattheson's example of the anonymous author who uses musical paradigms to
think politically gives ample proof for him of the efficacy of musical models
that have their origins in natural phenomena and can be used effectively in
the service of the public good.

Mattheson also believed, as part of his politico-musical theory, that
there should be a governing body that administrated the application of
music and made sure that it was used solely for the good (DVC, 126).[22]
Mattheson's principal complaint is that his current government no longer had an interest in music and its promotion and that the state (not to
mention the musicians) was consequently in danger. As Cannon argues,
Mattheson had aspirations of a state modeled on the worldliness, magnifi-
cence, and entrenched hierarchy of Louis XIV, and he was frustrated by the
provincial thought of the Pietist pastors who exercised so much influence
on the politics of the Lutheran city-state.[23] Mattheson believed, moreover, that this musical supervision and reform were particularly necessary
in churches (the reform church) as an important part of public religious
service (DVC, 127). For unlike his French Enlightenment counterparts,
Mattheson was deeply religious. "But how is a clergyman to judge these

matters if he knows nothing of music himself?" Music must be learned and taught for ideological purposes. Just as it was a statesman's obligation to know music when making political calculations, it became a holy duty to know music if you were a clergyman and believer. For the devout Mattheson, as for his church's spiritual father, Martin Luther, music was "the noblest gift of God to man, next only to theology."[24] "For, on the authority of St. Augustine," Mattheson writes, "ignorance of music is an obstacle to true comprehension in interpretation of the Holy Writ" (VC, 128). In *Der vollkommene Capellmeister*, Mattheson outlines the reform for the whole institutional structure of the church in which new Capellmeisters, conductors, cantors, organists, choir boys, and so on would be selected and administered with respect to these musical aims.[25]

But while knowledge of religious music is of primary importance, knowledge of secular music is also vitally important to the larger social project and reform and constitutes the second major point of Mattheson's politico-musical theory. "The second aspect of this theory deals with public, secular music, which certainly and truly requires much official supervision if it is to produce good citizens and virtuous inhabitants rather than give cause for all sorts of scandal, sensuality, impious gallantry and wastefulness. Our pens are insufficient; the long arm of the law must do this" (VC, 128). While it is not explicitly stated, it appears that the order in the secular world that would arise from music would come from music's physiological control and the analogies made between the physical body and the political one: "The last aspect of this theory," writes Mattheson, "is really the most important because it is not only concerned with the fortune of the community but also with each member's obligation and good conduct. For, whoever wants to bring a complete political body properly in order must doubtlessly begin with the limbs" (130).[26] Mattheson was no stranger to John Locke's philosophy and at times referred to him in support of his own theories. Lockean epistemology, in which understanding arises from sensation, certainly informed Mattheson's metaphor of the political body. Music's intimate command over the body and the soul through sensations or the passions enables one to imagine using music to control the state's subjects and cure both social ills and physical ones.[27] Harmony and order are, as we have seen, the two essential aspects of this disciplinary control, for "God has sent us music so, besides other things, that after praising Him we are to moderate our spirit and its emotions and constrain the body or restrain it within fixed limitations" (VC, 130). In such a society of containment, dissonance is to be controlled or avoided at all costs.[28]

In the context of music's effect on the body and social body, Mattheson devoted a section of his *Der vollkommene Capellmeister* to the use of music to treat disease, both physiological and psychological disorders. Arguing from theories of sympathy and medical knowledge of nerve diseases as well as from what appears to be Rameau's theory of overtones generated in the *corps sonore*, Mattheson saw the wide application of music in curing disease through the reestablishment of physiological order brought about by harmonic vibration in which sound positively affects the muscles and nerves of the human body.[29] In a series of amusing anecdotal medical histories that range from the well-known rondeau cure for tarantula bites and the quotidian concert cure of the black melancholy of the king of Spain to more anthropological observations on the *savages* in his contemporaneous, eighteenth-century America, Mattheson showed how music can be applied scientifically and medically as an effective therapy and regulating practice to a number of physical ailments and social ills.[30] Implicit in all these diseases, many of which he merely copied from Plutarch's *De Musica*, was an imbalance or disorder that he equated with musical dissonance: "Health is so musical that all sicknesses consist of nothing other than discords and dissonances: as has been reported of *Arion* and *Terpander*, who happily cured many Ionians and Lesbians with strings. *Ismenias* cured sciatica with the flute, which *Theophrastus* confirmed in the ninth book, and attributes such force to Phrygian songs. *Asclepiades* found that music worked against madness, and *Democritus*, against many other illnesses" (VC, 103).[31]

Such language and examples were found similarly in the Vitalists of Montpellier, a group of medical doctors in eighteenth-century France surrounding the famed medical center of Montpellier (including such illustrious names as Barthez, Bordeu, Bichat, and Cabanis) who, following the animist theories of the Swiss Georg Ernst Stahl (1660–1734) and arguing against Cartesian and Iatromechanist theories, believed that all living organisms share a vital principal or life force that cannot be explained mechanically. Through the concepts of sensibility and organicism, the Vitalists also incorporated a more holistic approach to the treatment of disease and understanding of life.[32] Although not linked to Mattheson in any way that I know of and writing two decades after the *Der vollkommene Capellmeister*, the Vitalists had a similar interest in regulating vibrations and using music to calm the nervous system and to restore order. Like Mattheson, the Vitalists borrowed heavily from antiquity and used the theories of Locke, among others, to articulate their music therapies, which they believed would have an effect not only on the physical body but on the larger political and spiritual body as well. To take one example, Joseph-

Louis Roger (d. 1761), a medical doctor from Montpellier and author of the *Traité des effets de la musique sur le corps humain*, saw music as integral to all aspects of disease and its natural corrective: "Music is thus a corrective of this false sensibility that constitutes in society a real state of sickness."[33] Music prevents suicide. It cures not only moral sickness but nervous disorders, such as catalepsy, hysteria, hypochondria, malignant fever, nervous and humoral melancholy, epilepsy, rheumatism, migraines, nostalgia, and phthisis. As an active catalyst of the passions and humors, it is an essential mode of treatment. Roger writes, "Music tempers the excessive sensibility of the nerves."[34] By tempering the pathological nerves of suffering individuals, music and medicine enabled the larger healing and tempering of the social body and helped prevent its dissolution.

Understanding Dissonance: The Empirical Shift and the Listener

Mattheson's rejection of dissonance as pathological in the medical, political, and musical realms was not uncommon in eighteenth-century discussions, even if many of the opponents of dissonance acknowledged its necessity in musical practice.[35] Even if dissonance was an integral part of musical compositions, it remained metaphorically and morally reprehensible, and this aspect informed its scientific discussion as well. The Cartesian majority of the Academy of Sciences in Paris, which played a pivotal role in the scientific discussion across continental Europe, still overlooked its use and the potential for its appreciation: previous explanations of dissonance were unsatisfactory and seemed too arbitrary given new accounts of human physiology and psychology as well as the greater desire for accuracy in scientific analysis.

Rousseau may have appreciated the recent scientific explanations of musical principles such as harmony by Joseph Sauveur (1653–1716) and others and seen in them a way to counteract the arbitrary judgments of the past. However, in his definition of "Dissonnance" in the *Encyclopédie*, even he stated that he had learned of no satisfactory scientific explanation for the generation of dissonance in a *corps sonore:* "No one thus having found to this point the physical principle of dissonance, we will content ourselves with explaining its generation mechanically, and we will leave aside the calculations."[36] And although there was an effort by music theorists such as Rameau to systematize and rationalize dissonance, most music experts in the eighteenth century continued to believe that the recognition, acceptance, and pleasure associated with dissonance relied on the sophistication and constitution of the listener.[37] As Albert Cohen notes in his analysis of Pierre Estève's *Nouvelle découverte du principe de l'harmonie* in 1751, the differences between consonant and dissonant sounds "derive from the interrelationship of several factors: the complexity of the sound itself; the physical motion of air particles that convey the sound to the ear; and the degree of aural sensibility of the listener, as well as his inner feelings ('âme')."[38] The theorist of acoustics and music Sauveur also felt that while dissonances and consonances could be explained in part by harmonics, in the end, calling a sound dissonant or not was in large part a matter of the sensitivity, experience, and training of the listener.[39] The encyclopedist and *philosophe* Diderot also commented on the subjective nature of dissonance, on the ability of a note to affect listeners differently, and consequently, on the need for trained and educated listeners: "if excellent music has few composers, there are hardly any true listeners."[40] Speaking about the relationship between sounds and images and noting the multiplicity of responses that even the same individual may have to a given note, chord, or interval, the Maître in his *Leçons de clavecin* observes,

> I am not saying that image which presented itself to my mind is the only one that could be connected to the same harmonic succession. It is with sounds as with abstract words in which the definition is resolved at the last moment by an infinite number of different examples that touch each other at common points. Such is the privilege and fecundity of the indeterminate and vague expression of our art that each one makes use of our songs according to the present state of his soul; and is it is thus that a same cause becomes the source of an infinite number of diverse pains and pleasures.
>
> What an astonishing variety of momentary and fugitive sensations would I not have excited if I had combined the dissonant harmonies to the consonant ones and put in place all the power of the art?[41]

In light of the limits of mathematical reason to explain the agreeability of dissonance and the growing contradictions between mathematical models and empirical findings, musicians and scientists from Rameau to Jean le Rond D'Alembert to Michel Puy Guy de Chabanon applied their scientific models and experiments to the listener instead.[42] As D'Alembert writes in defense of pursuing a musical science that is nonetheless cognizant of its affective qualities,

> One can consider music either as an art that has as its object the principal pleasures of the senses, or as a science by which this art is reduced to principles. This is the double point of view that we propose to consider in this work.

It was with music as it has been with all the other arts invented by man; chance first taught some facts; soon observation and reflection enabled the discovery of others; and from these different facts brought close together and reunited, philosophers did not hesitate to create a body of science, which in turn was gradually increased.[43]

But it is precisely dissonance's resistance to scientific explanation by music theorists such as Rameau and scientists such as Sauveur that placed it at the center of debates on music theory and aural judgment.[44] Dissonance presented an impasse. And although many theorists, Rameau and Diderot in particular, demonstrated its necessity and encouraged its use, it clearly defied the scientific theories that outlined agreeable or suitable intervals, and its discussion was inextricably linked to its metaphorical, metaphysical, and moral overtones.[45] As such, dissonance and its scientific study by music theorists was an essential catalyst in the move to more empirical explanations in aesthetics and music theory. As Cynthia Verba argues, dissonance plays an important role in the move from Cartesian or rational arguments to Newtonian or empirical arguments on aesthetic judgments.[46]

The new spirit of empiricism that was beginning to dominate French eighteenth-century science from the 1740s on informed the study of the effects of harmony and dissonance on the individual listener and groups of listeners, and many scientists and amateur scientists set about to create experiments of their own. Michel Paul Guy de Chabanon (1730–92), for instance, perhaps inspired by the common anecdotes of dolphins surfacing when they heard music played on ships, observed attentively as he played his violin for his fish, who would swim to the surface to listen, almost transfixed to the music, to conclude that all animals have a musical instinct, an aural sensibility, and not just humans. This was a refutation of Cartesian understandings of the animal soul that, as we see in van Maas's chapter in this volume, is still being contested in the twenty-first century.[47] The greater expertise in the study of physiology brought about by the works of Albrecht von Haller, Théophile de Bordeu, and others enabled a more accurate scientific study of the physiology of the listener and the affective qualities of music on his or her physiology. Anthropological studies and travelogues from the New World, Africa, and Asia, in addition to developments in natural science, also contributed to a new understanding of the listener and the different physical and moral effects of different types of music. As the Parisian doctor Louis Joseph-Marie Robert wrote, "Voyagers have found the use of music among all inhabitants of the globe, even the anthropophagi."[48] Scientists, medical doctors, and anthropologists gathering evidence on the effects of music on the listener readily assumed a close connection between the physical and the moral and did not fail to propose musical cures when encountering dissonances that would reinstate somatic or social normativity. Robert's book, for instance, provides a whole litany of ways in which music can reinstate regularity and normativity, whether it be performed in and for the benefit of military service, religious devotion, procreation, or education. Implicit in the move to diagnose and understand the effects of music on the listener was a regime to prescribe music as a cure (music as *pharmakon*). As noted earlier with Mattheson, an understanding of music combined with an understanding of the physiology of the listener could be used to prescribe different types of medical therapies and even social reforms. What Mattheson shared with his French counterparts such as Buffon, Rameau, Roger, and Robert was the belief in musical instinct, a universal ineffable quality that manifests itself in the individual listener, whether that listener be human or animal. This was what made music essential to the state, to the study of man, to an understanding of the body. Musical instinct, or music more generally, with its simultaneous ineffability and potential to be observed, was that which can speak for that which is silent, for that which Odello has said has "no voice." We suddenly can hear and understand the body when we speak of its fibers as strings. We suddenly hear and understand the *other* when we are told that *it* responds to our music and enjoys its own music. We suddenly know animals are no longer machines when they come to the surface to hear the violin. But as such, music is made to speak, it is harnessed to achieve normative physical and social ends, and its instinctual or ineffable qualities make these normative ends all the more invisible and effective. As Lawrence Kramer notes in his chapter in this volume, music is not "uniquely ineffable,"[49] and sensibility was perhaps equally ineffable; but music's supposed ineffability in this context is exploited to hide and/or communicate specific meanings of the body. Music's ineffability and its ability to speak are thus intimately intertwined. By making speak that which cannot speak, there is invariably a power and force in the translation, in knowing what music is saying.

Not every eighteenth-century thinker suggested, however, that we use music and its varied potential to affect a listener's sensibility for only these normative ends. Diderot, to take one, was equally interested in the therapeutic properties of music and in the role of music in helping the common good. (He had a number of scientific music projects/machines including a standardized tuning device and a mechanized organ that made organists, often poorly trained, superfluous.) Nonetheless, he situated his *musica moralis* around the figure of dissonance, and in doing so, he presented an alternative to the more typical applications of music therapy that persist to this day.[50] Diderot speaks about music much more than he plays it, and he seems more interested in the types of metaphors music invokes than in establishing a rigorous music theory. He was not an accomplished musician like Mattheson; but he shared Mattheson's belief that music was an elemental part of the public sphere, and like Mattheson, he played an active role in helping shape and transform that public sphere.

Diderot described the term *dissonance* with respect to the common good in *Le Neveu de Rameau*, when Lui comments on the productivity of dissonance in the social economy: "These are the dissonances in the social harmony that need skill in placing, leading in to and resolving. Nothing is so dull as a succession of common chords. There must be something arresting, to break up the beam of light and separate it into rays."[51] Precisely because of dissonance's ability to elicit competing sensations and interpretations in the individual listener and in the social body more generally, and because of its lack of Cartesian predictability, it became an essential figure for Diderot in rethinking communicative practices, acts of association, the body, the political body, and the relation between parts and wholes.[52] A good example can be found in the *Leçons de clavecin*, an inspired staging of Anton Bemetzrieder's theories of harmony. During a lesson on musical dissonance that Bemetzrieder was giving to Diderot's daughter Angélique, one that engenders the most vibrant and engaging discussions and scenes of the entire work, Diderot clearly reflects on the idea that without dissonance and complicated music, total conformity would ensue. For Diderot, the *practice* of dissonance was necessary. It prevented social conformity and the systematic control of the whole over the part, such as that advocated by Rousseau, to whom Diderot refers explicitly and maliciously in the *Leçons*. Whereas both Rousseau and Mattheson, albeit in very different contexts, saw this dissonance and disorder as dangerous and imagined music being used as a means of social containment, conformity, and consent, Diderot sensed its productivity and saw dissonance as a radical epistemological figure that increases relative autonomy. As such, he was even willing to celebrate dissonance and its therapeutic effects, for example, in the sapphic relationship between Suzanne Simonin and the Superior at Arpajon, the two principal characters in his novel *La Religieuse*. The "bizarre" music of the Superior, who has a reputation as both a musician and a seducer of young female novitiates, is only appreciated by the talented Suzanne, a musician herself. Their dissonant musical sessions, which usually intermingle music and intimate physical acts, have tremendous therapeutic effects for Suzanne. It is only at Arpajon—the last of three convents in which she had been locked up against her will, forced to take vows, and tortured—that Suzanne expresses a limited happiness and a desire to stay put for at least a short period of time. But the musical exchanges outlined in the novel are also integral to her defiant acts against the conformity and homogeneity of the institution of the convent.[53] Suzanne cannot be awakened and affected to join the unison or *concordia* of her sister nuns, who all sing and pray together in order to subsume her dissonance into God's unity: she uses singing to pass to an ally secretive messages and her legal testimony against the church; she makes alliances for her dissent through the singing lessons she gives; and she willingly partakes in banned erotic musical exchanges with her final mother superior. Whereas Mattheson gave examples of harmonic music that might cure lesbians of their passions, Diderot celebrated this passion through the figure of dissonance. Perhaps following Bemetzrieder's theory of dissonance in the *Leçons*, Diderot tried to imagine a way in which dissonance could become an essential mover or producer of shock, not only in musical composition but, more important for him, in the production and communication of knowledge and as the basis for political association and vitality. Diderot, however, never implemented such a system; he understood that dissonances could be encouraged but never fully delineated.[54]

The move in the eighteenth century from Cartesian approaches to music theory to experimental ones has been thoroughly noted by scholars.[55] As we have seen, this shift, which emphasized the aural sensibility of the listener, musical practice, and the communication of sounds from an instrument to a body, enabled a new set of therapeutic theories and ideas about the social benefits of music and its effects to arise, theories and ideas that sought to influence and even control the bodies of the listening public. Even now, scientists, militaries, and marketing teams, as well as DJs and performers, practice and research how to control bodies through music and sound. In the eighteenth century, dissonance, in particular, questioned the reigning systematic theories of aesthetic judgment and scientific predictability and thus played an important role in catalyzing the shift to empiricism and the sensibilities of the listener. But although dissonance was essential in engendering the success of new experimental approaches to music in the eighteenth century, music theorists, who used it only when necessary, seemed less inclined to imagine dissonance as a common good; it was rather a necessary evil, a danger to be controlled. Dissonance was not shared together in the same way as consonance; it did not form the same bounds. While the different actors discussed in this chapter were happy to make music speak for their various interests and positions, they preferred that dissonance remain silent. For Diderot, on the other hand, the figure of dissonance and the multiplicity it engenders was inserted not as way to "prostitute" music in order to reinforce the *logos*, as Odello would say, by making music subservient to its goals. Rather, dissonance, a musical figure, was placed precisely at this point in the *Neveu de Rameau* and was used in Diderot's work more generally to underline the very limit of the *logos* and its ability to speak, but also paradoxically to mark the very conditions that would make speech, and perhaps even true civic unity, possible.

Rousseau: Music, Language, and Politics

Tracy B. Strong

> Some people think music a primitive art because it has only a
> few notes and rhythms. But it is simple only on the surface; its
> substance on the other hand, which makes it possible to interpret
> this manifest content, has all the infinite complexity that's suggested
> in the external forms of other arts and that music conceals.
> There is a sense in which it is the most sophisticated art of all.
>
> —L. WITTGENSTEIN[1]

> Each of us contains music and truth but most
> of us have a hard time getting it out.
>
> —MARK TWAIN[2]

While Rousseau's cultivation of music is well known, as is the importance
he gave the relationship between music and language, there is still much
that can be learned about what it is to communicate with others and what it
is to be in a community. Rousseau took as his point of departure a debate in
which music criticism and music theory often stood for moral and political
criticism. In this chapter, I examine how Rousseau sharpened the terms of
this debate through a radical insistence that music represents what is at the
core of being human, that is, what is required of us as humans. Through
music, one may discover one's commonality with others and the source of
a truly human politics.

Rousseau first found a voice of his own in music, which he knew naturally and learned semiformally after running away from Geneva at the age
of sixteen.[3] It shaped the account he gave of himself. The *Confessions* are
from its first pages filled with music—the songs of his aunt Suzon, Swiss
folk songs that drive him to tears, a grandiose and disastrous concert he
organized in Lausanne for a piece he composed at a time when he was almost completely ignorant of music, his pretense to be an itinerant Parisian
composer. Indeed, in a somewhat Schopenhauerian mode, one might say

that the whole style of the *Confessions* answers to music. As Bernard Ga-gnebin and Marcel Raymond note, "His language will be meaningful, no matter what he means. The analogy to music is enlightening, if music can be thought to be essentially the art in which the manner of expression is completely coincident to that which is meant."[4] In the *Dialogues: Rousseau juge de Jean-Jacques*, that strange work of an ecstatic author, he is literally beside himself as he has various parts of his persona interrogate the other parts—he has the character "Rousseau" say to the "Frenchman" of "Jean-Jacques" (who is the subject of the dialogue), "He was born for music. He discovered approaches that are clearer, easier, simpler and facilitate composition and performance. . . . I have seen no man so passionate about music as he."[5]

In 1762, having been banned from France and Geneva upon the con-demnation of *Émile* and *Du contrat social*, Rousseau was living in the coun-tryside of Neuchâtel. He again took up the musical articles he had contrib-uted to the *Encyclopédie* some fifteen years earlier. Having had but three months to write them the first time, he apologized for the lack of scholar-ship. And he composed an eight-hundred-page *Dictionnaire de musique* as well as some important commentary on Gluck's operas (including a very interesting analysis of the effects of the disappearance of enharmonics[6] in contemporary music notation and thus also of the privileged position of the human voice in relation to the tempered scale).[7]

Despite Rousseau's dubious beginnings as a musician, such self-promotion was not without a certain justification. The concern with music sounds throughout his life. His first published work—*Projet concernant de nouveaux signes pour la musique*[8]—was a proposal in 1742 to the Academy of Sciences for a new system of musical notation, all on one line, using num-bers rather than symbols, a system of sounds; it would, he averred, permit a "more simple, more precise," and more natural relation of the performer to the musical vocabulary.[9]

Rousseau had not, at this stage, thought through what he thought about French music as a national form. Two events occurred. First, he lived in Venice as secretary to the French ambassador from June 1743 to July 1744. He wrote later, "I had for [the street music I heard there] the passion that it inspires for those who are made to appreciate it."[10] Second, in 1745 he had a nasty exchange with Jean Philippe Rameau when the latter was present at the first performance of Rousseau's *Les Muses galantes* and found the book thin and the Italianate music plagiarized (Rousseau denied it vehemently). Rousseau's first real musical success was the *Devin du village*, presented with great success before the king in 1752.[11]

Like everything in Rousseau's life, music was a subject of controversy. In the early 1750s, he became involved in two quarrels, which, while related to each other, need to be kept separate. The first was a celebrated dispute with Rameau about the relations of language and music.[12] The subject, if not always the substance, of the quarrel is important here.

Rameau had introduced a revolution into the understanding of music when, in 1722, he published the *Traité de l'harmonie réduit à ses principes naturels*. French writers on music at the end of the seventeenth and the beginning of the eighteenth centuries had generally favored mimetic theories.[13] Thus, in the operas of Lully, the most important composer of the period, the vocal music is as much declaimed as it is sung, and the difference between song and recitative is often hard to determine.[14] The melodic line imitates the rhythms of speech, but the cadence is given by the composer to the singer: to the modern ear, it contributes to an impoverishment of both. In Lully, music is linked to a text, and that text is unproblematically in French.[15] As is well known, Rameau insisted on thinking about music as a physical, rather than human, phenomenon, and this in turn governed his preference for harmony over melody. Harmonic modulation led the ear: nature governed the human. Melody was thus secondary to harmony; in fact, it was derived from natural harmonic privileges.[16] As he wrote in the *Treatise on Harmony*, "It is harmony that guides us and not melody."[17] In this view, rationality is the base of emotion. Our self answers to a Newtonian universe—in fact, Thomas Christenson refers to Rameau as the "Isaac Newton of music."[18] It is thus rather an ever-present reminder of the fact that, for Rameau (as Rousseau was to note), our experience of music is grounded in physical rules and not in human experience itself.[19] Rameau not only thought that music was mathematical but verged on the Pythagorean position that it transcribes and structures the order of the universe.[20]

In such a picture of music, although music was, as Rameau continually argued, an imitation of nature, it was only that: an imitation, laboriously arrived at, the product of work rather than of revelation. Nature for Rameau was not that which spoke to Rousseau's heart; it was rather the nature of geometry and physics.[21] Additionally, music must in this view be understood as a form of *representation*, that is, as a construct of that which makes an image of natural laws apparent to us. And since music is the least plastic of the arts, it can contribute best to such representation, by *sounding like* a storm or *adding* dramatic effect to a dance. Here Rameau's operas (e.g., *Dardanus*, 1739; *Les Indes galantes*, 1735) were especially innovative.[22] One might say that Rameau represented a development of the stance which had been advanced by Descartes in *Les passions de l'âme*; Rameau himself spoke of being "struck" and "enlightened" by Descartes's *Discours de la méthode*.[23] Catherine Kintzler remarks on two elements in this parallel. First, for both Rameau and Descartes, truth is abstract and rests on formal relations. Second, since we cannot perceive formal relations directly; their truth is revealed only in representation, that is, through illusion and artifice.[24] Rameau's work was thus an attempt to place music into a broader natural context.

Rousseau, on the other hand, would try to explain the aesthetic importance of music itself, as itself and without reference to an external natural world which might underlie it or to a universe of which it would be a part.[25] He understood music in relation to that which it *requires of us as human beings*. He thus placed it in a context which will inevitably be moral and political, one in which the aesthetic cannot be understood except in terms of the moral and political.[26]

The second quarrel in which Rousseau was involved, the well-known *Querelle des bouffons*, is different in kind but related in that it exemplified the moral and political questions at stake. The 1752 success of Pergolesi's opera *La serva padrona* set loose a conflict that had been brewing since the beginning of the century. The basis of the conflict was as much musical as political—or rather the two were not separate. All Paris took sides. Indeed, Baron Friedrich Melchior Grimm noted that other political questions were no longer discussed.[27] Rousseau says in his *Confessions* that the life of the *Ancien Régime* was extended as people had their attention turned away from the sins of the government.[28] The philosophers of the Enlightenment—d'Alembert, Holbach, Grimm, Diderot, Rousseau—grouped themselves in the pro-Italian camp, that of the queen, and against the older music, that of the other camp, the camp of the king (and Mme. de Pompadour) in a theater across the square. These were the partisans of French operas, including those of Rameau.

What came to be at stake was, on the one side, the human and the natural and, on the other, spectacle, imitation, representation, illusion for the sake of illusion. It was the popular against central power (and the respective themes of the operas merely reinforced that).[29] For Rousseau, in particular, in his *Lettre sur la musique française*, the debate between the primacy of melody or harmony became the debate between human expression and conventional artifice. Despite the large number of pamphlets and tracts (seventy in six months), Rousseau dominated the discussion. The reaction to his writings was so fierce that he was hung in effigy by the musicians of the Paris opera. "I was the declared enemy of the nation: it would not have taken much for me to have been declared a conspirator; one would have said that the fate of the monarchy was tied to the glory of Opera."[30]

In the end, this quarrel is not about the difference between *opera buffa* and *opera seria*. It is rather about the understanding of the nature of human association, as exemplified in language. The French language, declared Rousseau, is too heavy with consonants, without music, and crude. The French must thus pile up harmonies alongside devices that "the ear cannot endure and reason not justify; these are evidently remnants of barbarisms and bad taste, which survive, as do the porticos of our Gothic churches, only to manifest the shame of those who had the patience to make them."[31] For Rousseau, it was the degree of musicality that rendered one language more natural than another.

Rousseau's critique derived from Plato but had another target than that of the Greek. For Plato, the different modes produced different educations. Rousseau wished rather to establish the principles by which one might understand music in its relation to human life and experience—thus to discover what a natural "human" life might be. Let me recall that to be "human" was for Rousseau one of the most difficult achievements: neither kings nor slaves nor bourgeois are "human."[32] One is not automatically human.[33] If for Rousseau, as for Rameau, music reveals the secret of existence, for Rousseau this secret is in what music requires from us as "human" and not in the physical structure of the universe. Thus, it can *require* of us that we be "human."[34]

How might this happen? Rousseau tells us what music should do:

> For music to become interesting, for her to bring to the soul the feel-
> ings that she is able to call up, all parts of it must come together to
> reinforce the expression of the subject in question. Harmony must
> only intensify this; the accompaniment must make the subject matter
> more attractive without submerging or disfiguring it; the bass line must
> march, must, so to speak, guide the person who sings and the person
> who listens, without being perceived as doing such. In a word, the
> whole must transmit at the same time a melody to the ear and an idea
> to the soul.[35]

This does not correspond, as Robert Wokler has argued, to a preference by Rousseau for simple melody.[36] Rousseau called on the idea of melody to give us an idea of what a unified piece might be.[37] In the article on "imitation" in the *Dictionnaire*, he called for orchestral and vocal sequences to be experienced by the listener as a single experience. For Rousseau, "melody" brings about "moral effects that surpass the empirical realm of the senses" and thus cannot be thought of merely as a tune.[38] When, he argued in the *Dictionnaire*, one brings together music, oratory, rhythm, accompaniment, and voice, the result will be "one melody."[39] What was important to Rousseau was that a musical experience be a whole. In the article "Unité de mélodie," he reflected on the relation between the melodic line and harmony. He concluded that when music is what it should be, "harmony—which might have suffocated melody—animates it, reinforces it, determines it: the various parts, without becoming confused the one with the other, converge on the same effect; and though each seems to have his or her own song, when all these parts are brought together, one hears only one song. This is what I call the 'unity of melody.'"[40]

Rousseau was speaking of something much more complex than a song with strummed accompaniment. On a larger scale, one might attain such a unity, Rousseau tells us, in "opera," which he defines in his *Dictionnaire* as a "dramatic and lyric spectacle in which one tries to bring together all the charms of the fine arts, in a representation of a passionate action, in order to arouse, by means of agreeable sensations, interest and illusion."[41] That which was taken for "opera" in France, however, was not opera. In the French works, the illusion depended only on "flashy magical effects, on the childish din of apparatus, and on the fanciful image of things that no one has ever seen."[42] People began to think, he noted, "that the masterwork of music was to make itself forgotten."[43] Against this, Rousseau, as would Nietzsche one hundred years later, recalls for us Greek tragedy: "Their theater was a form of opera." "We know this," says Rousseau, as their "language was so accented that the inflections of speech during declamation constituted meaningful musical intervals."[44]

Greek "opera," however, was only recitative, with no airs. We moderns, because our languages are notably less musical, have had to invent particular forms, in particular, sung verse. The aim for modern opera should be to recover what Greek tragedy accomplished naturally in profiting from the musical nature of the Greek language.[45] The advantage of Italian opera over the French comes not so much from its themes but from the fact that Italian is more musical, that is, more "Greek." (One should note, however, that this is not, as is often thought, a blanket preference for the Italian: Rousseau is clear that even Italian opera has "enormous faults" and that "only instinct" has made possible what achievements they have managed.)[46] He asserted, "The Greeks could sing in talking."[47] In the article "Musique," he wrote that "the origin of art is . . . close to the human, and if speech [*la parole*] did not begin in song, it is at least sure that one sings wherever one speaks."[48] Such assertions—amply confirmed by contemporary philology[49]—had already been advanced by the Abbés Dubos and Batteux.[50] In ancient Greek, syllables and words in a phrase had a precise tone and length rather than a tonic stress.[51] These tones were different in different *poleis*. Speaking was thus a form of song; expression thus actualized the fact of participation in a particular musico-linguistic community.

But modern European languages, for Rousseau, give rise only to very diminished community, if any at all. Indeed, in modern times, "the resolution of a great and wonderful problem would be to determine to what extent one can make speech sing and music speak."[52] Rousseau's interest in Greek lyric drama is to find modern equivalents: he is quite aware of the changes wrought by developments in music. He seeks to discover or uncover what one might call the "spirit" of their musical theater.

Rousseau thus returned to a question that occupied the Italian humanists whose discussions led to the first opera around 1600. They sought to reinvent Greek tragedy. While the debates were not new, Rousseau channeled the question in a new direction, toward one of language in general. He thereby reframed the question from one of art to one of politics. What might be the equivalent of Greek for modern times, for times in which languages are less musical? We may seek his answer in another article of the *Dictionnaire* in which he tell us that nothing is more affecting, more ravishing, more energetic in all modern music than "*récitatif obligé*"—what I might translate as "entailed recitative." By "entailed," I mean simply that in this form of recitative the "speaker [*récitant*] and the orchestra" are required "to be attentive and expected to pay attention to each other." At that point, the "actor, agitated, carried away by a passion that does not permit him to say everything, interrupts himself, stops, hesitates, during which times the *orchestra speaks for him*, and the silences thus filled affect the listener infinitely more than if the actor had himself said all that the music gave to understand."[53] In the *Fragments d'observations sur l'Alceste italien de M. Gluck*, he says that "the spoken phrase is in some way announced and prepared by the musical phrase."[54] It is when words fail the actor that music expresses itself.[55] It is when that which wants to be expressed in words but cannot be that music (as it were) speaks. For the French composer in particular,[56] music should be not exactly a supplement but a manner of "speaking," of expressing, when one lacks words. More precisely, music can/should establish a space between that for which one has words and that for which one would wish to find one's own words, words to which one would have right, even if, in the end, they are words that will always be insufficient.

Rousseau notes that he is the only French composer who has used *récitatif obligé* to confront this question (in the sixth scene of the *Devin du village* and a part of *Pygmalion*; see example 5.1).[57] Rousseau's concept of

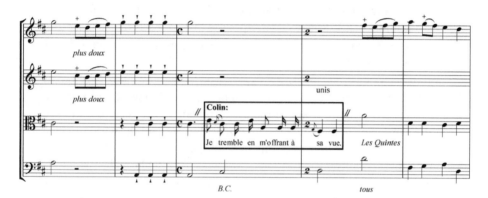

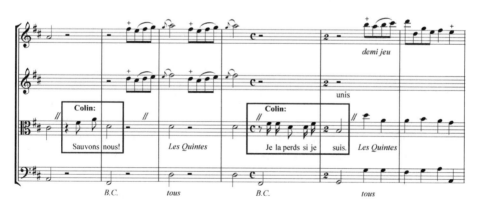

Ex. 5.1. Rousseau, *Le Devin du village*, scene 11

the *récitatif obligé* was not usual and not part of the usual categories of recitative (*secco*, *accompagnato*, even *obbligato*). Colin's part is not precisely *secco*,
although it is accompanied only by the basso continuo; nor is it precisely
obbligato, as it is not accompanied by the orchestra. What is of importance
to Rousseau is the *dialogue* between Colin and the orchestra, a mutual response of words and music.[58] In *Pygmalion* (1762), Rousseau and Horace
Coignet tried to link words and music even more.[59] There all the words
are spoken; the music makes sense in itself only in interaction or dialogue
with the words. The continuity of the piece changed by this interaction.
In *Pygmalion*, the actor speaks, as does the statue when it comes to life.
Instrumental music alternates with the spoken word and has the effect
of enhancing the emotional impact of the scene. It replaces vocal music
and especially sung recitative. One might thus think of the music as song
(but without words). Rousseau gave precise directions as to the place and
length of each musical number and to the emotion that each musical seg-
ment should convey.[60]

Rousseau's musical and critical exploration of the relation between what
can be expressed in music and what can be expressed in words leads to the
following conclusions. First, in the development of the relation of music
to the word, we find here that the interplay of music and the word can give
the listener access to the emotions of the character without those having
to be directly represented. Second, this can only be achieved by the development of an integrated and continuous art form. There is no difference
between declamation and song; music and word unite, and music suffers no
subordination to the word. Rousseau transforms this theoretical position
into musical reality through his thoroughly innovative use of the *récitatif
obligé*.[61]

All of this is important for an understanding of what it would mean
to use language naturally or in an appropriate fashion. In Rousseau's *Essai sur l'origine des langues*, we read that the first expressions that humans
used were "tropes," a term of seventeenth-century rhetoric that signified
the displacement of a word onto some object that was not appropriate or
natural to it; the meaning of the trope depended on this displacement.[62]
Thus, language was figurative before becoming natural. Rousseau gives us
an example:

> In meeting others a savage man will first be afraid. His fear will lead
> him to see these men as taller and stronger than he; he will give them
> the name of "giant." After much experience he will have recognized
> that these supposed giants are neither taller nor stronger than he, that

their stature did not correspond to the idea that he had first attached to the word "giant." He will thus invent another name common to them and himself, for example, the name of "human" and will leave that of giant to the false objet that had struck him during his illusion.[63]

A number of things can be said about this passage. First, it is our fear of others that leads to the misuse of language, or, more precisely, misuse corresponds to our desire to rid ourselves or protect ourselves from the other. Second, a correct or appropriate use of language is acquired in society and through experience. One learns it (much in the manner that a child learns language). Third, an appropriate usage consists in accepting that which we have in common with others, something that we had previously refused. There is, one might say, five years of psychoanalysis between "giant" and "human." To attain to humanity thus implies and requires that we share the world with others. The more language will be musical—that is, the more our emotions and our thought will be in tune—the more this will happen "naturally." Language may be conventional, but because it is conventional, we can work with it and make the words we speak "natural." That is, we can responsibly *mean* them.[64] *The natural, like the human, is learned.*

Finally, one only arrives at the appropriate usage by having gone through the figurative usage.[65] Illusion is necessary to attain the natural, and its possibility is always retained with the natural. Our capacity for the natural depends on our capacity for the figurative. A "correct" or natural usage is thus only possible by retaining the possibility of a bad or incorrect usage or, more accurately, by not trying to eliminate the possibility of incorrect usage.

For Rousseau, the central quality of the state of nature is negativity: humans, as themselves, so to speak, have no qualities aside from the faculties of pity (the ability to recognize that which is sentient like us) and self-love (the desire to remain in existence). As he tells us in the *Discours sur l'origine de l'inégalité parmi les hommes,*

Let us conclude that man in a state of nature, wandering in the forests without industry, without speech, without settled abode, without war, and without ties, without any need of others of his kind and without any desire to harm them, perhaps even without ever recognizing any one of them individually, subject to few passions and self-sufficient, had only the feelings and intelligence [*lumières*] appropriate to this state, that he felt only his true needs, saw only that which he had interest in seeing, and that his intelligence had made no more progress than had his vanity. If by chance he made a discovery, he was unable to communicate it as he did not even recognize his children. Art perished with the inventor; there was neither education nor progress; generations repeated themselves uselessly; and as each always started from the same point, centuries went by in all the crudeness of the first ages; the species had already grown old, and man remained ever a child.[66]

Almost twenty negations in this little summary! In this state, nature comes, one might say, "naturally": as there is no differentiation between human beings (and between the sexes), when I meet another, I meet one who is exactly like myself.

Once we have left the state of nature, the idea of the natural remains the same: it will be the recognition of that which in an other is exactly as it is in our self. Given, however, the distinctions between individuals that have accrued with society (the subject of the *Second discours*), attaining or acknowledging the natural will be much more complex. In *Du contrat social*, Rousseau explores the significance of this hard-won "nature," in particular, in his analysis of the general will.[67] The model for this is music.[68]

If, as Starobinski remarks, the remedy is in the illness,[69] we (social humans) will only be able to live "naturally" if we retain our concinnity, a simultaneous affirmation of motifs that lack a perfect consonance.[70] With this it is interesting to note that Rousseau, who had been a tuner of harpsichords, offers up an important metaphor at the occasion of the first meeting of Emile and Sophie: "There was an old harpsichord in bad repair. Emile fixes it and tunes it. He is a *facteur*, he is a *luttier* as well as a carpenter; he always had as maxim to proceed without the help of others in all that he could do himself."[71] The metaphor of "tuning" tells us that each element must play a role appropriate to what it is and that the whole must be a unity. The fact that Emile does it is a sign that community is something that humans make for themselves. In a passage I have quoted in part before, Rousseau tells us,

> How, in our system of chords and harmony, can music come to sing? If each part has its own song, all the songs, heard at the same time, will destroy each other, and there will be no more song: if all the parts have the same song, the context will be that of unison.
>
> It is remarkable how a musical instinct, a certain deaf feeling of genius, has dealt with this difficulty without seeing it and even turned it to its advantage. Harmony—which might have suffocated melody— animates it, reinforces it, determines it: the various parts, without becoming confused the one with the other, converge on the same ef-

fect; and though each seems to have his or her own song, when all these parts are brought together, *one hears only one song*. This is what I call the "unity of melody."[72]

It is precisely this concinnity of retained individuality that coincides and makes the whole actual, that actualizes the whole that makes music possible and constitutes the parallels between music and a democratic polity. In our collectivity, we retain each our own singularity.[73]

From this study of the *Essai* and these considerations on music, we can learn the following. It is in what we say to others that we recover and discover the possibility of our humanity. Second, it is the human voice that constructs and makes human association possible; thus, human association depends on the fact that our words carry or contain the quality of a human relation. A word or a phrase—*human* for example—is a feeling, a feeling that is not added on to the reference but is an integral part of the meaning and signifies and constructs a relation between persons, all the while allowing them to defend themselves against this relation, from fear, as Rousseau notes in his discussion of the origin of "giant." When we are able to acknowledge that which we share with an other rather than resisting this sharing in and from the fear that we have of him or her, we will need another name for this relation. It is this that allows Rousseau to assert that the origin of song and speech were identical. Finally, Rousseau sees in all of this a political opposition between different languages (vowel-rich in the South and heavy with consonants in the North) that corresponds to different attitudes toward public space.

How do we come to use language as *human* beings use it, as the source of our commonalty and thus our difference? What is or can be the role of music in this process? Three ideas are to be avoided, if we are to understand this.[74] Let us look at a passage that Rousseau repeats three times in his writings of this period. In a discussion of storms and other natural phenomena commonly represented on the stage, he writes,

> Music acts more intimately [than simple noise] on us, arousing in us, by means of a sense, feelings similar to those which might be aroused by another being. . . . May all nature be asleep, he who contemplates it does not sleep, and the art of the musician consists in substituting for the insensible image of the object that of the movements which its presence arouses in the heart of he who contemplates. . . . He [the musician] will not represent objects [*des choses*] directly but will arouse in the soul the same movements that one might have in seeing them.[75]

Note that Rousseau is quite clear that "imitation" in music is different from imitation in the other arts. Music imitates *itself without being in any sense a representation.* Thus, he continues,

> Imitation, in its technical sense, is the use of the same sequence of sounds [*chant*], or a similar sequence, in several partitions such that they are heard one after the other, in unison, at a fifth, a fourth, a third, or whatever interval there may be. *Imitation* is always well accomplished [*prise*], even if one changes several notes, as long as this same song is recognizable [*se reconnoisse*] and that one does not depart from the laws of a good modulation.[76]

Several things follow. First, whatever music does, it cannot claim to reproduce nature but only to arouse the sentiments which nature elicits. Rousseau views music thus much as one might view abstract painting today.[77] Second, music functions here as language in its own right, a language that does not persuade but convinces, does not tell but calls. In "melody," writes Rousseau, we seek to express the concinnity of language, emotion, and action.[78] Third, melody will also have to grasp what a *particular* culture can hear—that is, what a particular language experiences in the face of "nature." Thus, Rousseau insists, for instance, that "our most touching melodies are vain noise to the ear of a Caribbean Indian" and that "Italians must have Italian airs."[79] However, it is important to realize that language does not do this just by imitating the cadences of a particular language. It is not, as Rousseau makes clear in the *Essai*, an imitation of language. Rather, it is a voice calling to us, an interplay between an emotion transmitted and an emotion aroused.[80] Not everyone is called by the same song and voice; we are only called to that which can be known as our own. Music grounds and thus makes possible the enacting of (a) common experience. Lastly, the reliance has to be on the melodic voice, which may, once established, be supported harmonically. Most importantly, however, this passage gives us a sense as to what the art of the musician is: to make this happen.

These last considerations are central to Rousseau's thought. In antiquity, in ancient Greece, the harmony between words, music, and public space were the most in evidence. There "eloquence preceded reasoning [*le raisonnement*], and humans were orators and poets well before they were philosophers. . . . In the ancient festivals all was heroic and grand. The laws and the songs carried the same designation in this happy time."[81] Unfortunately, even in Greece, with the development of rationality, the forms became fixed, language became "more artificial and bolder." "In cultivating the art of convincing, one lost that of moving [*émouvoir*]. Plato himself, in the bosom of wisdom, jealous of Homer and Euripides, was harsh to the first and could not imitate the other. With the Roman conquest and the arrival of servitude, all was lost. In chains, Greece lost this celestial fire that warms only free souls and could find the sublime voice by which she had earlier praised her heroes only to praise tyrants." Latin is a "deaf and less musical" language than is Greek.[82]

In the entry "Musique" in the *Encyclopédie*, Rousseau tells us, "The great vice of our beat [*mesure*], which is perhaps a little that of the language, is not to have sufficient relation to speech." He continues,

> What do I wish to conclude from all that? That ancient music was more perfect than is ours? Not at all. On the contrary I believe that ours is without comparison more knowledgeable [*savant*] and more agreeable, but I also believe that that of the Greeks is more expressive and more energetic. Ours conforms more to the nature of song; theirs more to that of declamation; they sought only to stir the soul, and we wish only to please the ear. In a word, the very abuse that we make of our music comes just from its richness, and perhaps without the limits to which the imperfections of Greek music tended she would not have produced the marvelous effects that we hear about.[83]

In the *Dictionnaire*, however, under "Musique," he more boldly suggests that those who think Greek music inferior are wrong.[84]

A society that speaks in a language appropriate to life in common, to political life—a musical language—would rather value eloquence and rhetoric. As Rousseau remarks in the *Essai sur l'origine des langues*, the only form of speech appropriate to a people to whom it could be said "this is my pleasure" is that of the sermon, and such a people will be subject to paying taxes rather than gathering in assembly. In a society with a language for life in common, no one need listen. The language may degenerate even to the point that no one could be heard. "Herodotus read his history to the peoples of Greece as they were assembled out of doors, and the assembly rang with applause. Today the academician who reads a speech on the day of political assembly is hardly heard at the back of the room."[85]

This extraordinary analysis of Greece, with its practically Nietzschean condemnation of Plato, examines a central quality that a truly human society must have for Rousseau. There is to be no disjunction between expression and emotion, between words and tears, between meaning and saying. If there is such a unity, one can only take him or her who speaks for who he or she is. Speech must be heard as one hears music.[86]

What does this mean? I suggest that if it is the nature of music to place at the disposition of human beings the possibility to be in common with others, it is then the task of music to give us a world that would be abandoned neither to skepticism nor to religion and metaphysics. How might music accomplish this? For Rousseau, music does not call us back to our origins: it is not the voice of the primitive or even the call to that which would lie before words—even supposing that there were such a place. For Rousseau, music gives understanding, even if it does not give knowledge. For human beings, music is the experience of being called to that which they do not (yet?) have the words for. And it is in the call to express that, and in the pursuit of the capacity to express it—to wish to mean what one says—that one rediscovers that which one has in common with others, thus, that which one shares with them, thus, that which is natural or common or ordinary.

A last word: the hostility that Rousseau expresses for representation—be it in the theater or in politics—is well known. Let us remember, however, that Rousseau was not opposed to governmental representation but only to the representation of sovereignty, that is, of the general will, a will that was general because it was common. Because of this, for ontological reasons, sovereignty cannot be represented. As music offers us a world without representing one, it is music that offers us the vision of the possibility of a human world. Everyone—as Mark Twain says—"contains music and truth but most of us have trouble getting it out." For the political realm, the question is, From whence our difficulty, and what might we or might we not do about it? A human politics starts from the acknowledgment of our difficulty in articulating our commonality, from, one might say, being unmusical one with another.[87]

Listening to Music

Lawrence M. Zbikowski

Listening to Philosophy

Amid the clatter and din of contemporary philosophy—a cacophony that winds in and around and through language—Jean-Luc Nancy pauses to ask if philosophy is capable of listening. Listening, of course, takes as its object sound, and sound, as the material vehicle for arbitrary symbolic tokens, is basic to the process of signification on which language and philosophy are based. Nancy, however, is interested in sound not as object but as sense, and in listening not as the first step in a process of signification but as an activity *prior* to signification. For philosophy to be capable of listening, then, it must seize sound as sense, not as sign. This thought brings Nancy to music, for although sounds permeate our existence (as their resonance permeates Nancy's *Listening*), it is in music that sound—sound that shapes time and space without referring to either—becomes a substantive worthy of a more comprehensive contemplation. Listening, then, leads philosophy past sound and past resonance to music as the place where sound and resonance become complete.

In the course of following this path along its various twists and turns Nancy comes face to face with one of the originary moments of phenomenology: Husserl's analysis of time, in which the philosopher uses as his model the act of listening to a melody.[1] Here Nancy follows and adapts Gérard Granel's critique of Husserl, and together they note that, in his analysis, Husserl has perpetuated a "forgetting of being," which occurs "to the very extent that he does not concentrate his ear on musical resonance but rather converts it ahead of time into the object of an intention that configures it. Sound (and/or sense) is what is not at first intended. It is not first 'intentioned': on the contrary, sound is what places its subject, which has not preceded it with an aim, in tension, or under tension."[2] The consequences of this missed opportunity have deep resonance for Nancy, for they suggest that music, and indeed sound in general, is not exactly a phenomenon:

> That is to say, it [music] does not stem from a logic of manifestation. It stems from a different logic, which would have to be called evocation, but in this precise sense: while manifestation brings presence to light, evocation summons (evokes, invokes) presence to itself. It does not establish it any more than it supposes it already established. It anticipates its arrival and remembers its departure, itself remaining suspended between the two: time and sonority, sonority as time and as meaning.[3]

And this suspension between becoming and being is, finally, what music offers to the philosopher, a form of seeing beyond sight:

> Prophecy in the instant and of the instant: announcement in that instant of its destination outside of time, in an eternity. At every instant music promises its development only in order to better hold and open the instant—the note, the sustaining, the beat—outside of development, in a singular coincidence of movement and suspense.[4]

To listen to philosophy, at least as the opportunity is structured by Nancy, is to listen to it listening to music listen to itself.

But can music truly listen to itself? And, if it did, what would it have to say to language and philosophy?

Listening to Fernando Sor's Fantaisie élégiaque

Fernando Sor (1778–1839) was a composer and guitarist who spent almost all of his career outside his native Spain, principally in Paris and London.

His *Fantaisie élégiaque* for guitar, one of his last published compositions, was written in memory of Charlotte Beslay, who was his student and who died in childbirth 20 April 1835. Beslay was herself a pianist who had come to the attention of Rossini; perhaps because of this, the fantasy is written in a compositional register that is by turns operatic and pianistic. When all is said and done, the genre to which this fantasy belongs (and in Sor's hands the fantasy took many forms, including that of theme and variations) is the operatic potpourri. A work stretching out over some fifteen minutes, the *Fantaisie élégiaque* begins with a rather dramatic introduction (measures 1–34), dramatic both in its evocation of the varied instrumental resources of the opera orchestra and in the rapid shifts between markedly varied musical materials comprised in these measures. This introduction is followed by an extended soprano aria (measures 34–67), which gives way to a quasi-orchestral interlude (measures 67–82), which in turn yields to a snippet of a duet (measures 82–86), followed by a short bass aria (measures 86–100) which dissolves into a series of cadential gestures (measures 100–107). These are answered by a striking transition (measures 108–111) that initiates a return to the high drama of the introduction (measures 112–126) and an eventual arrival on an extended dominant chord (measures 127–140), which in turn leads to the funeral march that is the principal topic of the second section of the fantasy. I say the principal topic because the initial presentation of the funeral march (measures 1–16 of the new section) is followed by another soprano aria (measures 17–32) and another quasi-orchestral interlude (measures 33–57), which includes another extension of the dominant. Subsequent to the build-up of intensity associated with this focus on the dominant, the march returns (measures 58–73)—it is in fact the only thematic material within the fantasy that is recalled in this way—and is followed by a coda that brings the elegy to a conclusion (measures 73–101). As an opening into how music might listen to itself, I would like to focus on these last measures (which are given in example 6.1), for they present not only an instance of music reflecting on music but also an instance in which music supplants speech.

There are two things striking about this ending. First, there is the juxtaposition of the somewhat pompous funeral march with the rather more subdued music that commences in measure 73. The funeral march, both in its first statement and in its recollection in measure 58, is a perfect evocation of a tragic theatrical procession and as such is in keeping with the broadly operatic cast of the rest of the fantasy. There is a sense, indeed, that the funeral march of the *Fantaisie élégiaque* is meant to be *seen* rather than

Ex. 6.1. Fernando Sor, *Fantaisie élégiaque à la mort de Madame Beslay*, op. 59 (c. 1836), measures 58–101

simply listened to, even if what is seen is but the image of a confabulation inspired by fragments of scenes from operas long past. The music after measure 73, by contrast, is quieter, more contemplative, and its thoughtful character is all the more apparent when, with the *forte* of measure 81, it briefly returns to the major mode. There is a poignancy here that expands with the chromatic slide consequent to the *dolce* of measure 85, a slide that culminates in the cadential gesture of measures 88 and 89.

Equally striking is what happens next. Above a return to the pulsing quarter-note topic first heard in measure 73 there appear bare fragments of melody, little more than skips between E and G. The first of these, in measures 90 and 91, is complete and returns to E; the second, in measures 92 and 93, does not. The G that is left hanging is subsequently harmonized with a major chord—the same C major that provided temporary relief in measure 82—and the minor third E–G answered with the major third G–B. And then the music collapses back into minor, where it concludes with bell-like harmonics answered by a subdued and somber tonic chord.

Although the musical excerpt of example 6.1 provides only the briefest glimpse, the contrast provided by the coda of Sor's *Fantaisie élégiaque* speaks volumes. As suggested by the summary I offered earlier, the bulk of the work is occupied with operatic topics, presented as such: a succession of orchestral bombasts, heart-on-the-sleeve arias, and moments of light diversion, all of which conclude in a funeral march whose grandeur borders on preening self-importance. It is only with the coda that the work turns away from the projection of operatic topoi, turning its back on the musical journey just undertaken and searching for something not found therein. What this odd juxtaposition of musical materials enacts is a moment of commemoration befitting its elegiac topic. The ersatz operatic potpourri created by Sor (for there are in the *Fantaisie élégiaque* no traceable references to extant operatic works) is an evocation of countless hours spent enraptured by and later reenacting the music of the opera, hours that Sor and Charlotte Beslay shared as habitués of Parisian musical culture in the 1830s. The sudden change of compositional register in the coda is a recognition that, with Charlotte's death, these hours could be shared no more. The shift, then, is from music that is about something else—about operatic scenes or witnessing operatic scenes or re-creating the experience of operatic speculation—to music that is only about itself. Beginning in measure 73 we can hear music listening to itself and finally listening to itself mourning. Nowhere is this clearer than in the fragments of melody that resonate through the stillness that begins in measure 89, which summon a wordless cry of lament. And yet these fragments are not precisely

Ex. 6.2. Fernando Sor, *Fantaisie élégiaque à la mort de Madame Beslay*, measures 89–93

wordless, for, as shown in example 6.2, in the published score there appear over these fragments the words "Charlotte! Adieu!" These are not words meant to be spoken, and even less are they an instantiation of a hypertrophied form of signification melding phonemes and tonal structures; these are instead words whose sense resides only in sound as it is shaped through the resonance of music.

With this close reading of the conclusion of Fernando Sor's *Fantaisie élégiaque* I have, out of necessity, shifted the focus away from philosophy and onto music: I have wanted to explore not simply the *idea* of music listening to itself but the *actuality*. In making this shift I am motivated in part by the belief that Nancy has important things to say to musicologists, not the least of which is that music leads the listener to sound-as-sense and in doing so presents an alternative to sound-as-signification. But I am also motivated by a belief that a closer consideration of musical practice shows how Nancy's argument falls short of what it might achieve. For instance, although the body appears throughout Nancy's *Listening*, its role is invariably that of a symbol rather than that of a full participant in coming to know sense: the body resounds with sound, but it seems to have lost its capacity to listen, to *engage with* rather than simply *accept* (or serve as a receptacle for) sound. Symptomatic of this loss is Nancy's characterization of musical rhythm: "rhythm separates the succession of the linearity of the sequence or length of time: it bends time to give it to time itself, and it is in this way that it folds and unfolds a 'self.'"[5] Viewed in the abstract, this account captures perfectly the function of rhythm (and more specifically meter) within musical syntax (a function I have described, in similar terms, in work on musical gesture).[6] But on further consideration one finds nothing in rhythm for the body, no sense of the periodic movement of the body that *incorporates* the distinctions between one moment and the next. As has much of contemporary musicology, Nancy has left the body out of his conception of musical behavior, turning it into an empty shell into which can be poured the passions inspired by sonic phantasmagoria.[7]

A further limitation is imposed by Nancy's regard of what counts as worthy music. In expanding on the issue of whether musical knowledge is necessary to *know* music he writes,

> Musical science or technique does not by itself imply the most profound, original, or convincing musicality. To be sure, there are no examples—or almost none—of a naïve musician in the sense of Douanier [Henri] Rousseau (although his naïveté is far from being devoid of technical sophistication and savoir-faire), but there are many examples of talented technicians whose musical facility doesn't get beyond tepid academic compositions.[8]

The example of Rousseau is illuminating in its infelicity: Rousseau produced his art without the assistance or the imprimatur of the academy, but this is precisely the story of countless musicians working in the domain of "popular" or "commercial" or "folk" music. If Nancy means that Rousseau aspired to produce works worthy of the academy (an aspiration which seems probable and which has as its counterpart efforts made by certain nonacademic musicians to gain academic recognition), "naïveté" takes on the meaning of "innocent or unaware of the compositional strategies around which the academy has defined itself." As Nancy himself acknowledges, however, such naïveté does not preclude the development of an alternative set of strategies every bit as complex as those of the academy. More subtle, but no less telling, is Nancy's deprecation of "academic" composition. Without specific examples the observation is difficult to evaluate, but just this sort of critique has been leveled against innumerable composers who failed simply by not being Beethoven or Wagner. Indeed, my central musical example—an instrumental composition of uncertain genre by a Spanish expatriate musician, written for a "minor" instrument and influenced by Italian opera—is just the sort of work that has often been dismissed by analysts and critics as having nothing profound, original, or convincing to offer to the musical world.

In the end what is obscure in Nancy's vision/version of music is the cultural work that music is meant to do. Music can certainly be profound, original, and convincing; it can also be superficial, derivative, and dissembling. And in both cases it can do real cultural work, but of different sorts: Franz Schubert's "Der Leiermann" is unlikely to win a Eurovision song contest; Alexander Rybak's "Fairytale" is not a conclusion, or even the beginning, of a song cycle.[9] And who is to say that music does not listen to itself in both cases? Who is to say that resonance does not permeate the quotidian as well as the exceptional? Who is to say how music should evoke, support, or enact mourning?

Listening to Akpafu Dirges

During the 1980s Kofi Agawu undertook a study of music in the funeral traditions of the Akpafu, an ethnic group in southeastern Ghana who numbered around four thousand in the late 1980s. The models for death and burial among the Akpafu draw on traditional and (depending on the religious affiliation of the deceased) Christian practices and proceed in a number of stages across a day or more. Typical of these practices are the dirges that are sung during the section of the funeral rites in which the body is washed, which occurs after the death has been announced to the village but prior to the period when wake-keeping commences; notated versions of two such dirges are given in example 6.3. Agawu notes that, within this tradition, dirges pose challenges to simplistic conceptions of what counts as music. With respect to the delivery of the words, for instance, this can vary from singing, to a kind of *Sprechstimme*, to speaking. Performance of the dirge also involves various patterned bodily movements, in particular an agitated pacing that may or may not coordinate rhythmically with the delivery of the words. Of the two dirges given in example 6.3, "Itupiee" (example 6.3a) conforms for the most part to the rhythms of speech and has no set meter. Each of the rests between the different phrases indicates a considerable pause, a span which may be filled in with either silence or with nonverbal punctuations (such as wails, cries, or shouts).[10] (In thinking about sound before signification perhaps one should also include the cries wrested from our throats at times like this.) "Okwaisa" (example 6.3b), by contrast, has a set meter which correlates with the ritual pacing typical of Akpafu funeral rites.

The differences between "Itupiee" and "Okwaisa" are quite evident to even the casual listener: the dirges have different words, project markedly different senses of rhythm in performance, and are organized around different tonal centers: "Itupiee" has D as its final, above which appears a raised fourth degree (G$\sharp$); "Okwaisa" has C as its final and makes use of harmonizations in fourths. It is all the more striking that the Akpafu regard "Itupiee" and "Okwaisa" as equivalent. Agawu observes, "Asked about the relationship between the two dirges, the Akpafu often respond, 'Ne amē iɖe ne' ('It is the same thing')."[11] Agawu then goes on to reflect on Akpafu ideas about musical structure: "There seems to be little doubt that in the case of this pair of dirges, the response is primarily to the text

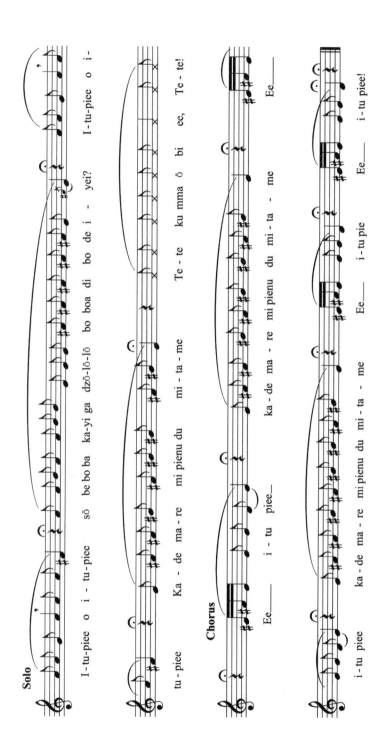

Ex. 6.3. Two dirges from Akpafu funeral traditions to accompany bathing of the corpse; transcriptions and translations by Kofi Agawu

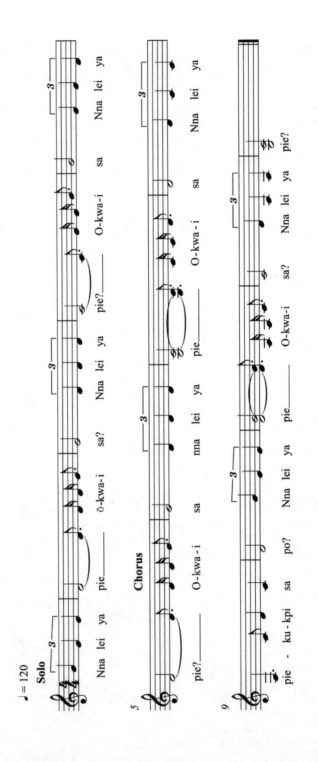

and its meaning, the elements that define their social function. Singing about bathing the corpse is what matters, not whether the singing is in free or strict rhythm, or is with or without harmony."[12] And yet the meaning of the text does not exhaust the meaning of the dirge: the resonance of the dirge as it sounds is far deeper than the words to which it gives voice.

So what is one to make of a situation in which music is so manifestly important to the realization of a ritual and in which the specific sounds organized by music matter so little? Or if they do matter (in the sense that incorrect renderings of either "Itupiee" or "Okwaisa" would inhibit the performance of the ritual), how can we account for the role of sound—still in its nonsignifying role—in the cultural practice of which these dirges are a part? It seems clear that music, as instantiated by these dirges, is just as much a part of the process of mourning enacted by the Akpafu as it is a part of the process of mourning enacted by Fernando Sor's *Fantaisie élégiaque*. But, going further now, how can two such different practices—one communal, traditional, and focused on ritual rather than music; the other private, stylized, and constituting through a succession of musical sounds a ritual wholly personal—be put in the same category?

Listening through Categories

To begin to answer the questions just posed—as well as ones asked earlier—I should like, for the moment, to become much more prosaic and to suggest how recent research in cognitive science can provide a novel perspective from which to view musical practice. I must emphasize that I do not mean to replace the rich tapestry of ideas woven by Nancy with a durable and plain cloth of "data" and "facts" but simply to sketch how that tapestry might be completed. As a beginning, let me take up the topic of categories and show how it can be used to clarify how we think about music, sound, and listening.

For the most part the categories through which we structure our understanding of the world are not cause for a great deal of reflection. To all appearances, these categories are simply givens. A book is a book, a tree is a tree, and any equivocal cases are just a matter of insufficient knowledge. During the 1970s this commonsense view of categorization began to be questioned by psychologists and cognitive scientists, who found that the notion that category membership was determined by necessary and sufficient conditions simply did not fit with how humans actually used categories. Research since that time has shown that the categories that humans use to structure their understanding of the world—what I call cognitive categories—is graded through a dynamic process in which the attributes of potential category members are compared with the attributes most typically found within the category.[13]

As an example of such a graded structure, consider the category *bird*. Experimental rankings show that subjects in the United States view robins and sparrows as the best examples of birds, with owls and eagles lower down in the rankings, and ostriches, emus, and penguins among the worst examples. All are considered members of the category *bird*, but some better represent the category than others. The structure of cognitive categories is thus graded according to typicality: category members range from the most typical to the least typical, with the former securely inside the bounds of the category (robins and sparrows) and the latter in danger of being excluded from the category (emus and penguins).[14]

Based on the evidence provided by empirical research, it appears that typicality effects reflect in part statistical correlations of functional attributes among members or potential members of a category. It should be clear, however, that cultural knowledge also informs judgments of typicality: while robins and sparrows are typical birds in the United States, they are somewhat less typical of birds found in the rain forests of the southern hemisphere, and much depends on why the birds are being categorized in the first place. As one way to understand how cultural knowledge informs processes of categorization, Lawrence Barsalou and others have proposed that judgments of typicality rely on conceptual models. In brief, conceptual models, which are central to reasoning and inference, consist of concepts in specified relationships, pertaining to a specific domain of knowledge.[15] (I should note that conceptual models, as I conceive them, can be formulated independent of language, such as those that might be used to structure our understanding of emotions or musical sounds.) With regard to categorization the primary function of the conceptual model is to supply a guide for reasoning about accepted and potential members of the category. This is accomplished through a simplified representation of category structure that incorporates knowledge about what values are most typical for a select group of attributes for the given category: the category *bird* is organized around a conceptual model which provides a means for deciding what sorts of things should go into the category. The attributes of a conceptual model are selected according to the goals of categorization, which are themselves informed by more global conceptual models applicable to a broad range of categorization tasks.[16] The conceptual model for a given category thus reflects statistical correlations of functional attributes, but conditioned by knowledge about the overall goals of categorization.

But what of music and of sound? To answer this question, let us return to "Itupiee" and "Okwaisa." Again, while there are manifest differences in the constituent musical materials of the two dirges, the Akpafu regard them as "the same." I would like to suggest that their inclusion in the same category is guided by a conceptual model organized around the function of dirges within funeral rites. Put another way, decisions about which category the dirges belong in—and here I am concerned with any possible instantiation of either of the dirges, whether sung or imagined or preserved on a recording—is made in accordance with the conceptual model that organizes the category. For a Western musicologist the function of a work is typically subsidiary to its rhythmic and melodic features, and as a consequence the two dirges would be put into different categories, organized around conceptual models rather different from those used by the Akpafu.

Although this notion of the function of a musical work may seem a rather coarse tool with which to make discriminations between musical works, it provides important insights into the role of music in human cultures.[17] In the case of the dirges one could simply equate this function with a particular section of the funeral rites—the bathing of the corpse—but such an equation would obscure the thoroughly embodied way this function is realized. The embodiment of the dirges is manifested in the way the singers bring their words into conformance with the pitch structures of the song, in the way these words resound with or against the ritual pacing that accompanies their delivery, and in other actions, seen or performed, that provide a context for the singing. The dirges might thus be seen as part of a process of *inscribing* the funeral rites on the bodies of the participants, preserving not so much the memory of the deceased as the act of remembering a member of their community. In this connection note the tempo that Agawu indicates for "Okwaisa": two quarter notes per second. The pacing that would be correlated with this tempo is not the leaden-footed step used in many Western funeral rites but a rapid movement that suggests both a need for action and anxiety about whether the action will be effective. Many of us use a similar kind of pacing when we have misplaced something important, whether a favorite book or the keys to our car, and one way to interpret its use in Akpafu funeral rites is as an enactment of a similar search for something crucial to the community that may be—and that in fact is—lost forever.

The process of embodiment I have just described is what Paul Connerton, in his work on memory, calls incorporation. Connerton, a social anthropologist, was interested in the means through which societies, rather

than simply individuals, remember. Key here were commemorative cer-
emonies and the bodily practices associated with these, which together
help to stabilize knowledge crucial to a society. Connerton writes,

> Both commemorative ceremonies and bodily practices . . . contain a
> measure of insurance against the process of cumulative questioning en-
> tailed in all discursive practices. This is the source of their importance
> and persistence as mnemonic systems. Every group, then, will entrust
> to bodily automatisms the values and categories which they are most
> anxious to conserve. They will know how well the past can be kept in
> mind by a habitual memory sedimented in the body.[18]

One of the roles of music in human cultures, then, is to organize and support the bodily automatisms that are crucial to commemoration. Music is,
in this context, more than sound: it is sound as a correlate for bodily movements. Here, then, is the correspondence between rhythm and movements
of the body missing from Nancy's characterization of musical rhythm: it
is not that the body *itself* must "separate the succession of the linearity of
the sequence or length of time," only that such separations are informed
by the experience of their bodily enactment; the "self" that is "folded and
unfolded" through the bending of time is an *incorporated* self.[19]

Returning now to one of the questions that I left hanging earlier: under what circumstances could the mourning practices of the Akpafu be
put into the same category as the mourning practices of Fernando Sor?
The first answer is, under only the most violent of circumstances. The
mourning practices of late twentieth-century western Africa are not those
of early nineteenth-century France, and to group the two together is to
misunderstand both. But a second answer is, under circumstances in which
we want to understand how music embodies—*incorporates*—experiences
and events that are beyond language.

The notion that music incorporates the supralinguistic points toward
a way to address the old question of whether music signifies. As treated
by semioticians, music is an example of a semiotic system that is purely
syntactical;[20] this perspective is similar to that toward which Nancy is
drawn by Pierre Schaeffer's reflections on musical structure.[21] I would like
to propose, however, that this view of signification is one that is too beholden to the mechanisms of representation that language exploits. The
mourning practices enacted by the dirges of the Akpafu and by Sor's *Fantaisie élégiaque* show that music does signify, but through a means markedly
different from that on which language relies.

Listening to Signification

It would not be advisable to attempt here a comprehensive review of semiotic theory, but it may be possible to set out a few points that are among the less contentious. The first is that human language relies on a system of reference in which arbitrary symbolic tokens—phonemes, written characters or ideograms, or (in the case of sign languages) coded physical gestures—stand for concepts. Perhaps one of the most important features of human language, and one that apparently makes it inaccessible to other species, is the organization of these symbolic tokens into a dense network in which symbols are linked both to concepts and to other symbols.[22] This network of interconnected symbols makes it possible to refer to objects and relations both proximate and distant, giving access to a system of reference with unparalleled resources for social interaction.[23]

The second relatively uncontroversial point is that music, with but few exceptions, does not make use of symbolic reference. And it is here that most applications of semiotic theory to music stop, for, focused as they are on language, the only mode of reference they countenance is symbol reference. There is, however, another possible mode of reference, one associated with the type of signs Charles Saunders Peirce called icons. Although Peirce's characterization of the icon was more than a little complicated (not least because Peirce wanted the notion to include reference to objects from the imagination as well as the real world), in the main the icon, as a representamen, needed to capture the essential features of the object to which it made reference. In some formulations Peirce characterized this function in terms of a similarity between the representamen and the object,[24] but it is more productive to conceive of the relationship as analogical.[25] In the case of similarity both attributes and relations are shared: a pencil and a pen are similar to each other both in appearance and in function, although the kind of marks each makes on a writing surface (permanent or impermanent; of relatively consistent coloration or subject to gradation) are different. In the case of analogy only relations need be shared: a finger is analogous to a pen in that it is an approximately cylindrical structure that can be used to trace characters on a writing surface; unlike a pen or pencil, however, the finger leaves no discernible marks on the writing surface, and its "cylinder" is firmly attached to the larger structure of the hand. The icon ☝ thus makes reference to the human hand not because it is *similar* to a hand (for what similarities are there between this diminutive, highly simplified line drawing, rendered on the printed page, and an actual human hand?) but because the lines proper to the icon mark off a group of proportional curvilinear relationships that correlate with the outline of a human hand as it might appear against a contrasting surface.[26] In his critique of iconism, Umberto Eco noted that the icon relies on both culture and convention for its interpretation,[27] but this reliance simply reflects the role of analogy in making iconism possible: analogies, whether in the service of reference or reasoning, are invariably constrained by contextual goals that are distinct from analogical process proper (goals that reflect the conceptual models proper to the analogical mapping).[28]

The fundamental difference, then, between analogical reference and symbolic reference is that in the case of the former the token needs to share analogical relationships with the object to which it refers; in the case of the latter the relationship between the token and the object (or the concept) to which it refers is essentially arbitrary. Analogical reference on its own, however, cannot explain how music signifies: in traditional accounts of iconism the object of reference is always an *object*, the static nature of which musical practice captures but poorly. What music can capture are *dynamic processes*. In some cases the dynamic processes analogized by music are easy to grasp: the ritual pacing that is a part of Akpafu mourning is one such process, for which the regularly occurring sonic materials of the dirge "Okwaisa" serve as analogical correlates. In other cases dynamic processes may be more subtle: to regard the highly personal and deeply somber reflection evoked by the conclusion of Sor's *Fantaisie élégiaque* as a *dynamic* process may seem contrived, but note that the practice captured by this music plays out over time, is subject to twists and turns as the reflection expands and contracts, and may, in its course, lead to sudden movements of both the body and the soul.

On the analysis I offer here music is not beyond signification but instead signifies in a way fundamentally different from language. It does this through analogical reference, which makes it possible for sequences of sound to represent a wide range of visual, kinesthetic, and psychological phenomena. Common to all these phenomena is their dynamic character, which distinguishes them from the objects to which icons conventionally refer; also prominent is their embodiment, both in their actual manifestation through bodily movement (kinesthetics) and in the physiological processes that accompany psychological phenomena. It bears mention that music is not the only form of human expression that offers analogs for dynamic processes—the spontaneous gestures that accompany speech, as well as dance and cinema, offer similar analogs—but music is somewhat exceptional in its lack of an essential visual or proprioceptive component and in its organization of sonic analogs into grammatical structures.[29] Finally, it should be noted that language can also make use of analogical reference—both through onomatopoeia and prosody—although when it does so, it begins to become more like music.

Analogical reference—as a mode of representation that cuts across perceptual channels and that offers a way to explain the role of the body in the construction of meaning—points to a different kind of knowledge from that on which philosophy has concentrated. This kind of knowledge is more diffuse than that captured by language but also more immediate, and together these offer an opportunity to interrogate knowledge itself. I would argue that it is just this opportunity that Nancy gestures toward when he describes the conceptual refraction that makes manifest the plurality of possible senses of a text:

> It is not, and in any case not only, what one can call in a superficial way the musicality of a text: it is more profoundly the music in it, or the arch-music of that resonance where it *listens to itself* [s'écoute], by listening to itself *finds itself* [se trouve], and by finding itself *deviates* [s'écarte] from itself in order to resound further away, listening to itself before hearing/understanding itself, and thus actually becoming its "subject," which is neither the same as nor other than the individual subject who writes the text.[30]

Listening to Mourning

Cognitive science is a diverse field, and its approach to human knowledge can scarcely be called unified. But here are some things it might tell us about music. First, "music" is not a single thing but a variety of different practices which often but not invariably involve patterned sound. *Music* is a cognitive category, which includes any number of subcategories (*music for mourning*), the members of which are individual musical works (which themselves may be viewed as cognitive categories comprising performances, recordings, notations, and imaginings of "the work"). As is typical of cognitive categories, all will have variable membership, organized around a conceptual model that specifies not only "musical" features but also the function of the particular type of music within a given musical culture. The category *nineteenth-century lieder*, for instance, would include Schubert's "Der Leiermann" but not Rybak's "Fairytale"; the category *Eurovision song contest entry* would include Rybak's "Fairytale" but not Schubert's "Der Leiermann."[31]

One of the important functions of music in human cultures—a function which is evident, in a superficial way, in the categories *nineteenth-century lieder* and *Eurovision song contest entry*—is to contribute to the commemorations through which societies remember. These contributions may take shape as a specific tune deemed essential to the performance of a ritual or, in the case of the Akpafu funeral rites, as a representative of a class of musical works, all of which perform equivalent functions. In both cases music often provides sonic analogs for stylized physical movements that inscribe the ritual on the bodies of those performing it and by this means preserve the act of commemoration in sound.

The second thing that cognitive science might tell us about music is that it connects to that-which-is-not-music through analogy. Such connections are often highly imaginative and may stretch across the boundaries of perceptual modalities, but they are not unconstrained. The successful employment of analogy will establish a dense network of relationships between the domains that are brought into correlation, but "success" must be evaluated with respect to the goals of the individual employing the analogy, goals that are shaped in part by the cultural practices that inform each individual's habits of reasoning. The sonic analogs basic to a musical practice may *appear* to be immediate and natural to people familiar with that practice, but they are in fact heavily mediated by cultural knowledge. In Western funeral rites, for instance, the movement of mourning is a slow, deliberate, leaden tread; the sonic analogs that correlate with these movements are similarly slow and deliberate and emphasize timbres with a significant degree of low-frequency disturbance.[32] In Akpafu funeral rites, by contrast, mourning is often accompanied by ritual pacing; the sonic analogs that correlate with this movement emphasize the rapidity of the tempo and the complex rhythmic relationships typical of human locomotion.

These contributions suggest ways to extend Nancy's insights into the kind of knowledge offered by music, for they provide a way to approach the full range of musical behavior and place embodied experience near the center of musical practice. At first glance they may also suggest an approach that abandons much of the poetry of Nancy's prose, the enthralling allusiveness of his descriptions of the relationship between sound, resonance, music, and the self. To reason carefully, however, is not to abandon poetry but to find its source in other interstices of knowing. When we catch music listening to itself, we may find ourselves confronting not the echo of sound but the memory of movement or the curling wraith of an image.

Listening to mourning—at least as instantiated by Sor's *Fantaisie élé-giaque* or by the Akpafu dirges I have discussed—is an invitation to confront what it means to be human. To be human is, in part, to be defined by language; but it is also to be defined by what language is not, and it is in the resonance of this absence of language that the sonic analogs of music have their proper home.

Listening to Jean-Luc Nancy

In the end what music has to say to language and to philosophy is nothing definite, *and this is its greatest resource.* By "nothing definite" I mean that music is focused on the representation of dynamic processes rather than on representations of objects and relations. Where language is predicated on the illusion that concepts are firm, stable, and unchanging, music celebrates all that is changeable and transitory. And so when music listens to itself, it does not hear meaningless sounds arranged in artful patterns but sonic analogs for the psychological and physiological processes associated with the emotions, for the gestures that shape our thought, for the patterned movements of dance, and for the prosody that vivifies language. Music is not beyond signification, but it does not signify in the way that language does; its philosophy is concerned not with being but with becoming.

For Jean-Luc Nancy music offers the promise of being in itself and for itself, of sound as nothing more than sound:

> Music is the art of the hope for resonance: a sense that does not make
> sense except because of its resounding in itself. It calls to itself and
> recalls itself, reminding itself and by itself, each time, of the birth of
> music, that is to say, the opening of a world in resonance, a world taken
> away from the arrangements of objects and subjects, brought back to
> its own amplitude and making sense or else having its truth only in the
> affirmation that modulates this amplitude.[33]

The vision offered by Nancy is seductive but ultimately untenable, for it cuts music off from the body that listens and grants music significance only by placing it beyond signification. There is an alternative to this vision, one that simply asks us to listen more carefully to music and to reckon with the cognitive processes that shape the transformation of sound into music. When we do, we will not only hear music listening to itself but also hear the resonance of what it means to be human.

Mi manca la voce:
How Balzac Talks Music—or How Music Takes Place—in *Massimilla Doni*

John T. Hamilton

In a letter to Madame Hanska, dated 2 November 1833, Honoré de Balzac barely conceals envy with skepticism when he writes, "I have read all of Hoffmann, he is below his reputation; there is something there, but nothing great; *il parle bien musique*."[1] The tone of the professional writer comes across fairly clearly. One craftsman judges the workmanship of another; popular opinion needs to be checked; yet, all the same, credit must be given where credit is due: E. T. A. Hoffmann "parle bien musique." Balzac does not say that Hoffmann talks *about* music ("il parle *de* musique"); rather "il parle musique"—"he talks music," like others "talk politics" or "talk shop." However much Balzac tries to discount the accomplishments of this famous German author of *Fantasy* and *Night Pieces*—a weak dismissal that cannot hide what we know to be a deep admiration and fondness—Balzac must at least acknowledge Hoffmann's capacity to deal successfully with musical topics and themes without talking simply about them, to capture something that may be called the essence of music, to depict the life of composers, performers, and listeners with psychological acuity, even to arrange texts that are deeply orchestrated, that is, in a manner that does not treat music merely as a metaphor. In regard to these criteria, Hoffmann's resonant characterization of Johannes Kreisler and his seminal review of Beethoven's C-minor Symphony would be exemplary. There can be heard in Balzac's curtly reductive remarks a hint of desire, the desire to emulate Hoffmann, perhaps some day to equal his level of expertise. In brief, he wants to "talk music" like an insider, like someone who is in the know, distinct from the outsider who can merely talk about music. Years later, Balzac strived to bypass Hoffmann altogether and vie directly with the paradigmatic composer: again to Mme. Hanska, the master of French Realism confesses that Beethoven is "the only man who ever made [him] feel jealous."[2]

Within years of Balzac's intense engagement with the work of Hoffmann, in 1837, he produced a pair of musical novellas—*Gambara* and *Massimilla Doni*—which clearly reflect his indebtedness to the German writer. In general, these narratives demonstrate how Balzac himself "talks music" in a way that to a large extent mirrors Hoffmann's approach. However, without entering into an extended or detailed comparison of the two writers, it can be shown that Balzac's particular treatment of musical material broaches issues and themes that move some distance away from his predecessor and, moreover, raise concerns over the act of "talking music" in a sense that may have even broader ramifications. To put it most abstractly, in concentrating on but one of the two works, namely, on *Massimilla Doni*, my analysis strives to understand both how Balzac creates a literary place or location for music and what precisely this gesture of localization (or dislocation) implies for larger considerations of the relationship between verbal and musical language.

In this novella, set in Venice in 1820, Balzac formulates the problem of providing a space in literature for music by focusing on the problem of exchangeability. Venice is depicted as an emblem of dignity and poverty; the city itself is described as a beautiful work of art devoid of substantial value. In this regard, Balzac's protagonist, the handsome but penniless prince Emilio Memmi, is paradigmatic. The point is that the case of Venice demonstrates how the glory of artistic beauty can still flourish in financial destitution, how aesthetic value is altogether distinct from monetary value. (Emilio at one point laments that he is prohibited by Austrian decree from selling off the artworks held in his palazzo, so as to get money for food.) If monetary value is grounded in exchangeability, then aesthetic value—so Balzac seems to suggest—is strictly nonexchangeable. Art is not a commodity. It must stay in place. Like the marbles in Emilio's ancestral home, art cannot be deployed on the checkerboards, or *saccaria*, that the Venetian exchequers famously introduced to European banking.

However, that said, in working to find a place for music within literature, Balzac also seems to imply that the arts, however resistant to commodification, may in fact be exchangeable among themselves: for example, that music may be exchanged for literature or that visual art may be exchanged for music and so on. The urgent question, then, is, Can the principle of exchangeability within the system of the Sister Arts preserve art from the aesthetic devaluation of the marketplace; or does it not, rather, expose art to a process that ultimately corrupts a particular ideal of aesthetic freedom (that is, a freedom from values imposed from without)? In relocating music to literature, can the basis of art's autonomy be maintained; or does it come under threat? If artistic dislocation does in fact instigate the collapse of art's noncommodifiable purity—a charge frequently brought against artistic decadence, where effects of synaesthesia reign—would a demonstration of an artwork's resistance to relocation allow art to hold on to its dignity: a dignity indifferent to its marketable poverty?

Balzac's distinctly musical aspirations spanned his entire career as a writer. As early as 1820, when he was but twenty years old, struggling to prove to his family that he could financially support himself as a writer, toiling away, as legend has it, in the solitude and obscurity of the garret rented in the Rue de Lesdiguières, Balzac dove into his first attempt at literature, not in the genre of epic poetry or tragedy, and certainly not in the form of a novel, but rather, less expectedly, in the form of an opéra comique.[3] The title was to be *Le Corsaire*, based on Byron's poem about the swashbuckling rebel Conrad and his free-roaming band of pirates. The stage of the opéra comique would be the testing ground for this young genius. Fame and compensation were on the horizon. However, work on the libretto was abandoned soon after the aspiring Romantic came to inevitable frustration: as he exclaimed to his sister Laure, "Where the devil am I going to find a composer?"[4]

Still, the fascination that opera exerted on this musician manqué, and the literary desire it engendered, persisted. In May 1837, Balzac, who had since found and put to good use his novelistic voice, reported to his friend Maurice Schlesinger of a particularly inspiring evening spent at the home of George Sand:

> *Nous parlâmes musique*—we talked music; there were many of us: although I would be a musician like one used to be a shareholder of the

Royal Lottery of France, when one would, say, procure a ticket for the price of a seat in the loge, I timidly expressed my ideas about *Mosè*. Ah! It will resound in my ears for a long time, that word of initiation: "You should write what you have just said!"[5]

No longer restricted to the outside, Balzac has gained entrance into the temple precincts of music. His relationship to music has progressed past the level of a mere theatergoer or amateur. Even though he concedes his outsider status—a status easily remedied, however delusively, by an inexpensive monetary transaction—he nonetheless celebrates his *initiation*, that is, his achievement of *going into* (*in-ire*) a place reserved for the privileged few. Having demonstrated his ability, like Hoffmann, to "talk music," however timidly, he is no longer prohibited but instead permitted at last to enjoy the mysteries of this sacred art.[6] The theme is Rossini's 1818 oratorio *Mosè in Egitto*, which continued to be performed regularly at the Théâtre Italien since its Paris premiere in 1822, together with the French adaptation *Moïse et Pharaon*, prepared for the Théâtre de l'Opéra in 1827. Evidence that Balzac took full advantage of this encouragement is seen in the novella begun at the time, *Massimilla Doni*, which repeats, in the brief dedication to Jacques Strunz, the metaphor of initiation and which, more importantly, features an extended commentary on Rossini's *Moses*, presumably one that more or less replicates the ad hoc interpretation offered at Sand's party.[7]

Balzac's commentary, as well as the novella that frames it, centers on the so-called Naples version of the oratorio, with libretto by Andrea Leone Totolla, who adapted it from Francesco Ringhieri's 1760 tragedy titled *L'Osiride*. The plot complicates the account from Exodus, in which Moses pleads with the Pharaoh for the release of his people, by inserting a love story between the Pharaoh's son Osiride and a Hebrew princess named Elcia. The ensuing drama, coupled with Rossini's setting, provides the essential elements for Balzac's own novella and, moreover, serves as the occasion for the writer to talk music. Balzac's intention to do what Hoffmann did so well has settled on its object, has lighted on a suitable place for expression, a satisfying *location* of meaning. Rossini's rendition of the biblical story about oppression and liberation has freed the novelist's voice from its inadequacies. It has revealed a glimpse of the Promised Land.

In *Massimilla Doni*, it is the title figure who presents the extended interpretation of Rossini's opera. As one of Balzac's "études philosophiques," the novella also offers some reflections on the qualitative differences between language, music, and the other fine arts. Massimilla explains:

[The language of music], a thousand times richer than the language of
words, is to speech [*langage*] what thought is to its utterance [*parole*]; it
arouses sensations and ideas in their very form, in that part of us where
ideas and sensations are born, but leaves them as they are in each of
us. That power over our inmost being is one of the grandest facts of
music. All the other arts impose on the mind definite creations; those
of music are infinite. We are compelled to accept the ideas of the poet,
the painter's picture, the sculptor's statue; but each one of us interprets
music at will according to his sorrow or his joy, his hope or his despair.
While other arts encircle our thoughts by fixing them on something
determined, music lets them loose over all nature, which it alone has
the power to express.[8]

These statements rehearse in many ways conventional, nineteenth-century
views, views that were in fact seminally codified by E. T. A. Hoffmann.
The series of antitheses—between music's immediacy and verbal mediation, between vagueness and determination, infinitude and definition,
interiority and exteriority—can be found in most aesthetic assessments
beholden to German Romanticism.[9] The innovation of Balzac's contribution, therefore, lies not in this regurgitation of ideas from across the
Rhine but rather in the way the novella tests and qualifies their ramifications. In providing a narrative, verbal space for the opposition between
words and music, Balzac obliges the reader to consider what happens to
music when it occupies literature and, conversely, what occurs when literature gives shelter to music. What are the consequences for literature
and for music when an opera takes place in a novella? This question seems
to motivate Theodor Adorno's reflections on Balzac when he attests to a
fundamental musicality at work within the realist project: "If music is the
world dematerialized and reproduced in interior space, then the interior
space of Balzac's novels, projected outward as a world, is the retranslation
of music into the kaleidoscope."[10] To be sure, this kind of internalizing
reproduction and subsequent "retranslation" depends in large measure on
the writer's ability to "talk music" or, at the very least, his talent for letting
music take place. Yet what precisely does this capacity accomplish? What
does it contribute to the grand social enterprise of the *Comédie humaine*?
How might it enhance our understanding of, or possibly even our engagement with, society?

  If someone talks music, then music, strictly speaking, does not speak,
it does not sound out. Even in the case of *Massimilla Doni*, in which a
particular composition, Rossini's *Mosè*, is specifically conjured, the music's

presence within a literary text is purchased with muteness, regardless of the reader's acoustic memory. If a musical creation is infinite and indefinable, as Massimilla claims, then its inclusion within the defined space of a literary work would appear to seal it off from being heard. This silencing is based on what I call literature's *localizing* function. The desire to immure music within the confines of verbal description or interpretation manifests itself either as a sincere gesture to hold on to that which is elusive, keeping music in place, like a Proteus bound, so as to allow it to give forth a determinate meaning; or as a terribly cruel strategy that robs music both of its liberating force and its freedom, leaving it to wither away behind walls of text. Elsewhere, in *Le Chef-d'oeuvre inconnu*, in which Balzac explicitly employs the metaphor of a "wall of paint," there is a vanishing of visual art that is somewhat similar to the kind of silencing I am noting here. Still, a close reading of that text would show that *ekphrasis*—the verbal representation of a visual representation—does not simply entail a looking away but rather includes an invitation to look again, that is, with eyes now informed by the verbal detour. In this sense, Balzac follows the didactic impulse that has accompanied ekphratic discourse from Philostratus on, an impulse that rests entirely on a decidedly iconological understanding of visual art. With music, however, the silencing appears to be more definitive and therefore more fatal, insofar as the verbalization strives to finalize a meaning, in an analogously iconological fashion, for an art that is presented as fundamentally aniconological. Once the threshold into declared meaning has been crossed, the music thus located is forever transformed into something representational. Visual art certainly differs from literature on the level of the medium, yet the two forms conventionally share a logic of representation that renders them homogeneous. Music, on the other hand, at least from the perspective of the Romantic theory that Massimilla pronounces in the passage cited earlier, is understood as nonrepresentational. The consequence here is that any verbal reformulation should be taken as heterogeneous to the sound and movement of performed music.

Music, then, would seem to exist within literature only as that which has been lost to literature. Balzac, however, does not end with this ending. To talk music is not the same as to talk art in general. Sound, Balzac seems to emphasize, has the penetrating power to bleed through obstructions, to evade topologies, to emerge afresh even after it has been localized. Like the voice from a soprano's mouth, like the tone from a violin's body, the curiously immaterial material of sound can detach from its source and readily flee from one place to another. Even though desire strives to locate the acoustic phenomenon of musical experience, sound can always find a way to dislocate itself. In a very specific sense, recognized by Ernst Bloch, the music that is sheltered within literature is essentially *utopian*.[11]

A number of dislocations, ascribable perhaps to something fundamentally acoustic, may be discerned regarding *Massimilla Doni*. To begin, unlike the majority of Balzac's fiction, this tale does not take place in France but rather in the Italian city of Venice. As mentioned, Balzac began work on the novella in 1837, upon returning from a brief re- or dislocation of his own in northern Italy. (Apparently, he had been fleeing his Parisian creditors.)

This Italian resetting points to a more fundamental dislocation, one that does not concern the narrative's geographical but rather its temporal coordinates. Specifically, I am referring to the relation between what narratologists define as the *énoncé* and the *situation d'énonciation*. Here, it would be instructive to compare *Massimilla Doni* with *Gambara*, a second novella directly concerned with music, on which Balzac worked almost simultaneously.[12] Together with *Sarrasine* (1830) and *Le Cousin Pons* (1847, at one time provisionally entitled *Les Deux musiciens*), the *Massimilla Doni–Gambara* pair constitutes Balzac's most sustained reflections on music.[13] In many ways, *Gambara* constitutes a nearly perfect counterpart to *Massimilla Doni*, with each text presenting a different side to musical experience. A story about a mad and destitute opera composer—a close analogue to Frenhofer, the deranged painter of *Le Chef-d'œuvre inconnu*—*Gambara* deals with the creative invention of music, whereas *Massimilla Doni* deals with its performance. Balzac himself envisioned the two novellas as working together in a strictly complementary fashion: both to Maurice Schlesinger and to Mme. Hanska, the author emphasizes this "double form," whereby *Gambara* and *Massimilla Doni* treat the dual aspects of "composition" and "execution," respectively.[14] However, this marked parallel is disrupted by each story's relation to its enunciation. Unlike *Gambara*, which is set in 1831, close to the narrator's present, the action of *Massimilla Doni* unfolds at a further point in the past, specifically in the year 1820, nearly two decades before the time of narration. Why would Balzac formulate his account of musical "execution" in a more distant time? Why would he disturb an otherwise clear complementarity between these two texts? The difference, I would argue, is not arbitrary. *Massimilla Doni* may be about the staging of music, but the sounds produced therein are fatefully consigned to the silence of a now remote world—a world deemed distant, not simply because of the time that has elapsed between the event and its recounting but rather because of the *qualitative* differences between these two epochs. From the point of view of French history, the temporal stretch between the events of *Mas-*

simitla Doni in 1820 and their recollection in 1837 is above all punctuated by the July Revolution of 1830. Autobiographically, the distinction between these two eras is characterized by Balzac's own shifting political allegiances, from the earlier liberalism of his associates in the journalism trade to the later monarchism and Catholicism of his mature aristocratic circles. The nearly twenty-year span further traces Balzac's rise from a failed librettist in the Rue de Lesdiguières to a renowned novelist. The historical caesura of 1830—Balzac's own breakthrough year—articulates, therefore, an important tension in *Massimilla Doni* that is far less emphatic in *Gambara*, which falls on this side of the July Revolution. The literary treatment of musical production calls for a temporal division that reinforces the geographical separation between Italy and France—temporal and spatial locations that invite travel, either by coach or by memory.[15] The fact that Rossini himself resigned from writing operas upon the abdication of Charles X is not irrelevant. By locating the events of his "musical-execution" novella in 1820 Venice, Balzac significantly dislocates its action from a qualitatively different, French present. In this light, *Gambara* would amount to a relocation: decisively grounding the event of musical composition in the subjectivity of the composer *qua* origin. The music of *Massimilla Doni*, however sheltered, enjoys no such anchoring.

The historical, geographical, and autobiographical caesurae of *Massimilla Doni* erect a series of barriers. It should come as no surprise, therefore, that the narrative opens with a reflection on loss, specifically, on what has been left behind on the other side of the various divides. The tale focuses on two young lovers, Emilio Memmi and Massimilla Doni, both of whom belong to an Italian aristocracy that has lost its political autonomy, first to Napoleon and then to Austrian sovereignty. As in the case of Elcia, the Hebrew princess in Rossini's *Mosè*, Emilio and Massimilla observe how their royal status has been severely compromised by the enslavement of their nation. Indeed, the island republic of Venice, which flourished for a thousand years, whose navy was the envy of Europe and a bane to the East, has now turned into a menial outpost in service to Vienna, emasculated, demoralized, and decrepit. The lion of San Marco has retreated into humiliating hibernation.[16] The ancien régime of Venice has become stale, mere crumbs on the banquet tables of foreign rulers. The nobility has taken on a spectral existence, wandering through their city as pale presences of glory long absent, of greatness long dead. Balzac sets up his story with vivid references to this debased nobility, which is "entirely ruined" (MD 543/2). Here, in Venice, the aristocrats lack a political voice—*gli manca la voce*. Balzac reminds us how these descendants of illustrious dukes, these members of patrician families, have been subjugated and dispossessed, how these inheritors of a brilliant, unequaled past have been unspeakably degraded, some even to the level of gondolier or rag-picker (MD 543/2).

Although certainly suffering a degree of disenfranchisement, Emilio and Massimilla have not sunk as low as other Italians. Their situation is nowhere near as grave as the lot of rag-pickers. Nonetheless, they live, as Massimilla at one point complains, in a "land of slaves" (MD 574/33); they exist, despairingly, beneath the burden of heteronomy (MD 577–78/34–35). Emilio is even further incapacitated. His powerlessness is not limited to political, societal, or financial matters: in his exaggerated adoration of Massimilla, he has turned her into an ideal, placing her on a pedestal so high and so spiritual that he is unable to consummate their love. Emilio is not only politically powerless; he is also sexually impotent, in love with a creature who is divine and therefore inaccessible. He is yet another victim of that typically Balzacian disease of sexual frustration, an illness that is generally debilitating and often self-destructive.

This is not the first relationship in which Massimilla has had to deal with an incapable companion. Her parents, clearly concerned with their daughter's stability in an unstable world, married her to the older, wealthy Duke Cataneo, who may have secured ample property and revenue for the young lady but who proves to be an unfit husband. Cataneo's problem is not idealization but rather melomania. He is obsessed with opera, tirelessly lusting after those fleeting moments of emotional power which alone bring him ecstasy. Cataneo wanted a duchess but had not the energy for a wife. As is often the case, Balzac, the physiologist of marriage, has endowed his character with enlightened tolerance: perfectly aware of his incapability, old Cataneo ungrudgingly has suggested that his young bride find herself a "cavaliere servente" (MD 547/5), who might take his stead and, incidentally, help him ensure the survival of his family line. Massimilla's mother takes her forthwith to all of Italy's great opera houses, not in search of musical *jouissance* but rather in search of a *jouissance* far more mundane. At last, one evening at Venice's Fenice, Massimilla discovers Emilio as he passes by her box. "The Venetian [Emilio] felt struck by lightning; while a voice cried: *Here he is!* in the ears of the duchess."[17]

The voice that intrudes on Massimilla's consciousness is incorporeal and compelling, not dissimilar to Socrates's *daimonion* or Kant's "voice of reason"—a voice that arrests, a voice that overtakes one's subjective position. It is a voice, most importantly, that cannot be located. Emilio, too, is overmastered by a voice, the voice of his beloved, that is, a voice whose source may be identified but whose efficacy lies in its capacity to dislocate and confuse sources: "By what moral phenomenon did his soul so seize his body that he no longer felt in himself, but rather entirely in this woman at the least word she spoke in that voice, which disturbed [*troublait*] the very sources of life within him?"[18] These voices that lack assignation, that come from outside and lodge themselves deep within, cause a commotion that perpetuates a love that is as ideal as it is paralyzing. For the first three months, the pair limit their meetings to the public space of the opera house; and then, with the approach of summer, Emilio joins Massimilla in her country retreat, where for the next six months their love remains entirely "intense" (*violent*) but perfectly "timid" (MD 548/6). Nine months pass without their desire coming to term.

A letter from Emilio's closest friend, Marco Vendramini, arrives to make some announcements: first, that Facino Cane has passed away, leaving the title of Prince of Varese to Emilio; and second, that the famous soprano Carla Tinti is to perform in Venice at La Fenice. The first piece of the news is essentially worthless: the former Prince of Varese died alone and penniless in a Paris prison.[19] Emilio therefore simply relates the more important information to Massimilla. He explains how la Tinti had been a mere tavern servant, just twelve years old, when a Sicilian nobleman discovered her "miraculous voice" and decided to make her his protégée. Today, fully matured and meticulously trained, she has been captivating audiences across Italy. As Emilio speaks, Massimilla vainly resists recognizing la Tinti's noble protector as her own estranged husband, the hideous Duke Cataneo.

Massimilla, who lost her husband to Carla Tinti's voice, will soon lose her lover to Carla Tinti's body. Unbeknownst to Emilio, the soprano and her entourage are now renting the rooms of his family's palazzo in Venice. It had all been set up by Vendramini, another member of the fallen nobility, now addicted to opium, who thought the rent income would greatly ease the burden of Emilio's financial distress. Unaware of this arrangement (which was probably related in the unread, latter half of the friend's letter), Emilio enters his bedroom and undresses, believing that the apartments' renovations and the luxuriant supper set out on the table are simply a surprise gift from Massimilla. But Emilio is about to learn that his place is no longer his. La Tinti soon arrives with Cataneo, who discovers the young man in his protégée's bed and flees the scene in despair. La Tinti, who was compelled to waste her youth with an elderly and rather ugly duke, and Emilio, who is condemned to lead a monkish life at the feet of his ideal love, quickly succumb to the pleasures of the flesh. Henceforth, Emilio is trapped within the snares of Venus duplex, caught between a celestial love for Massimilla and a vulgar lust for la Tinti. His spiritual empowerment is purchased with sensual impotence, while his sexual prowess jeopardizes his soul.

It is in conjunction with this classic plot between the spirit and the senses, between pure love and debauchery, that Balzac introduces his reading of Rossini's *Moses* oratorio. Massimilla, in her box at the opera house, while Emilio sits in the shadows pale and sickly, offers a detailed interpretation of the piece to a physician visiting from Paris. As mentioned, her lengthy exegesis is presumably very similar to the ideas Balzac himself presented to George Sand and company. Massimilla has begged the French doctor to cure Vendramini of his opium addiction and, above all, to rescue her Emilio, whose health has, to her mind, inexplicably suffered a recent, melancholic downturn. Her lecture on the oratorio's meaning is given as a kind of advance payment for the physician's services. Indeed, Massimilla's offer of aesthetic interpretation in exchange for the doctor's assistance already reveals her tendency to deal with art in terms of gross marketability.

That said, it would be misleading to suggest that Massimilla proceeds in a thoroughly base fashion. Her general aesthetic statements, as noted earlier, attempt to maintain an aesthetic of purity or nonexchangeability. For example, she insists on the impossibility of arriving at concepts of musical meaning. Although she respects medical science for matters of health, she is doubtful whether the doctor's training would enable him to appreciate Rossini's genius. She gently derides France as "a nation occupied with philosophical theories, with analysis, with discussion, and always disturbed [*trouble*] by civil divisions."[20] For her, "modern music, which demands a profound peace, is the language of tender, loving souls, inclined to emotionally noble exaltation."[21] Ironically, in this, one of Balzac's *études philosophiques*, he *identifies the problem* of the French reception of Italian opera as the tendency *to identify problems*. The Parisian novelist diagnoses Parisian insensibility as an incapacitating desire to diagnose everything. The typically French preoccupation with theoretical matters—a preoccupation that Massimilla connects with that nation's ceaseless divisiveness—essentially assigns a meaningful place for every aspect of experience. It nourishes itself on classifications, on locating significance. Consequently, according to the duchess, in terms that clearly allude to the famous *Querelle des bouffons* a century before, the French are deaf to music because of their intellectual and political partisanship. The French listen with their minds, the Italians with their hearts. The French physician may be able to cure the lovesick Emilio and the strung-out Vendramini, he may be able to put them in their place, but is it possible for him to understand an art form that would appear to elude all placement?

Despite Massimilla's suspicions concerning conceptualization, she does execute her own methods of localization, not only in her rash and reductive generalization of French audiences but also in her interpretive commentary of the opera. Upon relating France's ruinous analytic spirit to its divisive politics, the Italian duchess nonetheless submits the musical piece to a political allegory. "Moses is the liberator of an enslaved race," she remarks. "Remember that thought, and you will see with what religious hope the whole house of La Fenice will listen to the prayer of the delivered Hebrews, with what thunder of applause it will respond!"[22] To be sure, Massimilla posits a unified Italian audience, which is contrasted with the French citizenry, presumably split between liberalism and conservatism, between monarchists and republicans. Moreover, her understanding of national liberation differs significantly from the ideas of the Parisian doctor, as an earlier conversation has revealed. For Massimilla's dream is the return of the aristocratic republics of Italy's glorious past, hardly the rise of the bourgeoisie, whose guillotines, in her opinion, not only severed the heads of the nobility but also killed the noble fostering of high art.[23] Still, all things considered, Massimilla's revelation of a determinate, political message in Rossini's work fixes what she herself has claimed to be utterly elusive and indefinable. By locating the power of the oratorio in a specific political, nationalist meaning, she offers us a way to understand the audience's response as unified and unequivocal. In this way, Massimilla talks music and talks music well—but at what cost? Can any music be heard above her continuous commentary throughout the performance? Does not her interpretation of the opera as a story of liberation hypocritically enslave music to word, voice to meaning? We listen as Massimilla explicitly contradicts herself: having described music in explicit contrast to poetry and the visual arts, she goes on to offer analogies derived from the tradition of the Sister Arts, referring to the opera in turn as a "poem," an "elegy," a "painting," and an "edifice"—transforming the music, that is, into a transitive signifier, whose signified could just as well be expressed in words, colors, or stone. In a typical revulsion for the synesthetic confusion of the arts, the Parisian *médecin* eventually deplores Massimilla's rates of exchange: "As an analyst, a materialist, I must confess that I have always rebelled against the affectation of certain enthusiasts, who try to make us believe that music paints with tones" (MD 608/64).

Although Massimilla's exegetical procedures strive to be definitive, it is still possible that there remains an unaccounted residue; that her hermeneutics cannot hermetically seal off the sound emanating from the stage. Her voiced opinion is but one kind of confinement, one that may not be, in the end, all that soundproof. Massimilla has a voice, but hers is, after all, just one voice among many in Balzac's text. As the first violinist raises his bow, we read how Emilio flings himself into the dark corner of a back seat, uttering not a word.

The performance had been anticipated by the Venetians for some time, since la Tinti, in the role of Elcia, was to be joined this evening by the equally popular and astounding tenor Genovese, in the role of Osiride, the Pharaoh's son. Osiride, in love with Elcia, attempts to overturn the Pharaoh's decision to release the Hebrews. In the second act, however, Osiride is struck down by lightning, and the enslaved race is free to cross the Red Sea. The performance proceeds beautifully, as Massimilla makes her compelling points that interpret the Hebrew people as the oppressed aristocracy, forced to abandon their religion by the Egyptian mob of unbelievers. Throughout, the duchess suggests an allusion to the French Reign of Terror. Between the opera house, La Fenice, a crucial locale for Venetian resistance against foreign rule, and Florian's, the café that warmly welcomed the nationalists and discouraged an Austrian clientele, Massimilla's reading would not fall on deaf ears. The theatergoers who cross the Campo S. Moise in order to go from one institution to the next would have much on which to reflect. All aspects of the opera, from the libretto's verses to the harmonic progressions, thus fall, thanks to Massimilla, *into place.*

Suddenly, however, back on stage, the easy allegorical explanations are rudely interrupted as Genovese and la Tinti begin the climactic duet of the first act: "*Non è ver che stringa il cielo*—It is not true that heaven ties / the bonds between two hearts / if our love always cost the soul grief and pain." The problem is that Genovese's voice is failing miserably. He squeals and shrieks in the most dreadful manner. His performance is utterly unbearable and therefore altogether disruptive. Massimilla halts her explication. The audience is flabbergasted, the orchestra uneasy. Emilio for the first time speaks up, shouting from the back of the loge in dismay, "Genovese brame comme un cerf"—"Genovese is bellowing like a stag!" (MD 596/53). Whatever is happening, Genovese effectively interrupts Massimilla's desire to validate the opera's meaning; his botched singing dislocates. As though responding to her politicized interpretation, Genovese seems to be shouting, "It is not true!"—"non è ver!"

Genovese, who just the night before sang impeccably in la Tinti's absence, is now embarrassing himself before all of Venice. The beastly sounds emitted from his throat block Massimilla's interpretation, which will continue only after the tenor leaves the stage. Genovese the singer is no longer a sign; he has become opaque, no longer a pure, unobtrusive vehicle for conveying significance. Yet Genovese's horrifying performance not only disturbs the political reading; it also angers those members of the audience who in fact care little for the libretto and instead sit in their seats enthralled by the sheer beauty of the melodies and harmonies. Balzac gives us Capraja, another Italian melomaniac who often engages in lofty, quasi-mystical discussions with Cataneo on the power of music. In an earlier episode, Capraja explains precisely what he seeks when he attends the opera, namely, the perfect execution of a *roulade*, the rolling melismatic display of the virtuoso that blurs rather than channels verbal significance. In this earlier scene, Capraja relates how eager he is to hear Genovese in the upcoming performance of Rossini's *Mosè*: "[Genovese is] the first singer who has satisfied me. I shall not die without hearing a *roulade* executed like the ones I have often heard in certain dreams, in which upon waking I seemed to see the sounds float in the air. The *roulade* is the highest expression of art."[24] Capraja's desire hardly focuses on what the voice signifies but rather concentrates on the voice itself in its pure, presignifying effulgence. How utterly shattering and disappointing, then, when Genovese commits vocal atrocities like a shameless imbecile.

Genovese's disruptive, dislocating fiasco—his vocal impotence, which is clearly analogous to Emilio's sexual disorder—is a double failure of the voice, both a failure to communicate the import of the libretto and a failure to generate the beauty of the melody. Genovese lacks a voice because he is unable either to produce meaning or to provide an object for affective enthrallment. His performance disturbs both the semantic and the aesthetic functions of the voice; it is neither an instrument nor a fetish. In the first case, his bellowing breaks the mimetic illusion: the Egyptian Osiride is obfuscated by the bumbling Italian. In the second case, his artistic catastrophe affords no pleasure; it frustrates the listeners' chances to experience any *jouissance*. We could say, his voice disarticulates; it cannot be incorporated into the matrix of Massimilla's political allegory, and it ruins Capraja's fondest dreams.

Nonetheless, Genovese's inarticulateness does articulate something. As the performance progresses, it becomes clear that the tenor has not entirely forgotten his training or his art. In the second act, in the duet with Carthagenova, who is playing the role of Pharaoh, Genovese sings admirably and more than satisfies everyone's expectations. Moreover, later that evening, walking across the Piazzetta, Genovese proves to his small audience that he is still quite capable of performing brilliantly. There, beneath the moonlight, unaccompanied, he sings Crescentini's famous aria, "Ombra adorata," and powerfully brings the nearby listeners to tears. "Never did music more truly merit the epithet divine."[25] Capraja, who is among those present, steps forward to give an explanation for Genovese's inconsistency—an explanation that roughly rehearses Diderot's well-known "paradox":

> When an artist is so unfortunate as to be full of the passion he wishes to express, he cannot depict it because he is the thing itself instead of its image. Art is the work of the brain, not the heart. When you are possessed by a subject you are a slave, not a master; you are like a king besieged by his people. Too keen a feeling, at the moment when you want to represent that feeling, causes an insurrection of the senses against the governing faculty.[26]

According to Capraja, the cause of Genovese's fiasco is obvious: he is madly in love with Carla Tinti, a love that can further connect the tenor's disability with Emilio's impotence, as well as link the soprano's effect with Massimilla's. Altogether, the two couples form a dynamic quartet of desire and frustration, of intention and failed consummation. Genovese therefore articulates his infatuation by disarticulating the voice's other functions in Balzac's text, the semantic and the fetishistic. Whenever Genovese has to sing directly to or before his beloved, his voice fails him. Considering Capraja's diagnosis, this failure could be specified in at least three ways, all of which have to do with exchanging the music's location. To begin, one could say that his performance suffers when he locates the music in his own subjective desire, when he wants to express his own personal intention. Alternatively, one could agree more closely with Capraja (along with Diderot) and affirm that the passion to be voiced in song comes to be collocated with that voice, eradicating the distance or gap necessary for effective expression, since expressive efficacy seems to require that the voice conveying passion is not confused with the passion itself. Finally, a third interpretation would reveal Balzac's debt to Hoffmann, to Hoffmann's manner of talking music, specifically in his story *Das Sanctus*, which links the singer Zulema's loss of voice to her desire to express the inexpressible, to seek the Absolute.[27] Like Frenhofer of *Le Chef-d'oeuvre inconnu* or the mad composer Gambara, Genovese demonstrates with his impassioned performance that the impossible wish to render in art the highest truth culminates in the destruction of art itself.

If Genovese the singer did not identify with the song, if he did not locate the melody and text in his own subjective desire or relocate it to some inaccessible, transcendent place, his singing would have continued to serve as viable locations for Massimilla's political interpretation and Capraja's affective engagement. On stage, in the role of Osiride, Genovese shouts, "non è ver!" in a screech that shatters the voice's relation to truth, be it Massimilla's allegorical truth or Capraja's emotional truth. In the Piazetta scene, Genovese seems to allow Capraja and the others to satisfy their desire to locate the music; however, even here, Balzac's text alludes to an absence that frustrates any certainty. Genovese, we recall, performs the "Ombra adorata," the aria composed and famously executed by the castrato Girolamo Crescentini for Niccolò Zingarelli's *Giulietta e Romeo* (1796). In the context of Zingarelli's opera, Crescentini's Romeo performs the song directly after imbibing the fatal poison that he believes will allow him to reunite with his beloved. The voice that addresses his "ombra adorata" is specifically a voice about to die, the *moritura vox* that captivated Napoleon during an 1805 performance in Vienna. As Roland Barthes memorably argues in his reading of Balzac's *Sarrasine*, the text evokes the idea of castration in order to cut language off from its reference.[28] Is Balzac's light allusion to the castrato in *Massimilla Doni* accomplishing the same semiotic effect? To be sure, Genovese's performance reveals that every utterance is severed from the subjective voice that would ground it. Like la Zambinella, he produces a voice that cannot be located, a voice whose loud and impossible beauty barely conceals a loss, an absence, a lack.

Balzac's discourse essentially plots different functions along the evanescent axis of time. On the one hand, it is a Realist gesture that undermines any transcendent topology, any vertical ascension to a fixed place of significance. On the other hand, it is an eminently musical method, which ultimately dissolves the very referential sites of meaning that presumably validate Realist prose. In other words, Balzac talks music by attending to a series of voices lost to other voices; he presents us with a sequence of voices, each one entering in turn, where the latter is heard at the expense of the former, where the presence of one marks the absence of another. Tellingly, the high point of the opera is judged to be the grand quartet of the second act, *Mi manca la voce*— "My voice fails me," "I lack a voice." Balzac's characters take turns in the loge to voice their individual reactions to this song: a quartet of audience responses to a quartet of staged melody.[29] Massimilla regards the piece as expressing the timeless value of aristocratic nobility and therefore introduces it as "one of those masterpieces that will withstand everything, even time."[30] Capraja, in turn, applauds la Tinti's performance by exclaiming, "She pours floods of purple into my soul!"[31] An anonymous gondolier enthusiastically blesses the young soprano.[32]

And as Genovese continues to debase himself, plummeting to the level of the worst of chorus singers,[33] Emilio, his counterpart in powerlessness, remains utterly silent.

Rossini's song has the old form of a canon in unison, four voices entering consecutively with the same melody and ultimately merging into a collective that, here, sings in the first-person singular:

Mi manca la voce!
Mi sento morire!
Si fiero martire
Che può tollerar?

My voice fails me!
I feel I shall die!
Such cruel torture
Who can bear it?

This piece, in Massimilla's judgment, equals the entirety of Beethoven's C-minor Symphony, the entirety of Mozart's *Don Giovanni*—two works that figure large in Hoffmann's *Kreiserliana* series. Massimilla further compares it to masterpieces by Marcello, Cimarosa, and Pergolesi: "Mi manca la voce" will serve as the guarantor of Rossini's immortality. Over unobtrusive, graceful arpeggios, the melody passes through the simplest of harmonic progressions, gently floating from tonic to dominant and back. It is a curious conflation of infancy and maturity—a lullaby of pain, an innocent's lament. Elcia enters first, bewailing her decision to renounce her love. Osiride follows, regretting his resolve to abandon his nation. Amaltea and Aronne take up the melody in turn. In the end, the quartet communicates nothing other than the destruction of communication, a manifestation of ongoing disarticulation. Each singer expresses the incapacity to express. Balzac successfully talks music by allowing his voice, presented as Massimilla's political allegory, to be undermined by—to yield its place to—other voices. He allows his voice to fail. (Georg Lukács, following the judgment of Friedrich Engels, well recognized this feature of Balzac's project, which is said to describe with accuracy real social conditions, despite the author's own voiced sympathies and allegiances.)[34] To hear the voice is to hear it go missing, to listen as the voice becomes a revenant that haunts and thereby disorients every locale, as in the spectral glory of Venice or the dreamlike evanescence of the *roulade* or the hope of requited love.

In *Gambara*, Balzac suggests that music, which combines conceptual and aesthetic approaches, is an ideal means for the "search for the Absolute"—

"Music is simultaneously [*tout à la fois*] a science and an art."[35] Along these lines, Balzac reveals to Madame Hanska his high aspirations:

> In five years, *Massimilla Doni* will be understood as a fine explanation of the most intimate procedures of art. In the eyes of its first readers, it will be what it appears to be, a lover who is unable to possess the woman whom he adores because he desires her too much and who possesses a wretched girl. Make them therefore conclude from this that we are dealing with the birth [*l'enfantement*] of works of art![36]

The *enfantement* of fresh beginnings also marks an event of voicelessness, of lacking a voice (*infans*). At the novella's end, the *enfantement* occurs. It occurs, however, in terms of represented life and not represented art. Emilio Memmi consummates his love with Massimilla: she learns that she is pregnant. The Absolute—the simultaneous conjunction of the transcendent and immanent realms, the identification of celestial and corporeal Venus—has been reached, not in music but rather in its absorption into literature. The desired goal has been attained; impotence has been cured, but only after the music is over, only after sound has been definitively exchanged for written prose, only after the opera has *taken place*. The exchange of music for words, the way Balzac talks music in this text, preserves the aesthetic value of art, by revealing art not as something that can last but rather as something that must be lost: enjoying a dignity, like Venice's, grounded in its substantial poverty.

Speaking of Music in the Romantic Era: Dynamic and Resistant Aspects of Musical Genre

Matthew Gelbart

> Not content with success in the field in which he was free to
> design, with such perfect grace, the contours chosen by himself,
> Chopin also wished to fetter his ideal thoughts with classic
> chains. His Concertos and Sonatas are beautiful indeed, but many
> discern in them more effort than inspiration. His creative genius
> was imperious, fantastic and impulsive. His beauties were only
> manifested fully in entire freedom. We believe that he offered
> violence to the character of his genius whenever he sought to
> subject it to rules, to classifications, to relegations not his own,
> and which he could not force into harmony with the exactions of
> his own mind. He was one of those original beings, whose graces
> are only fully displayed when they have cut themselves adrift
> from all bondage, and float on at their own wild will, swayed only
> by the ever undulating impulses of their own mobile natures.
>
> —FRANZ LISZT, *F. Chopin* (1852)[1]

I start from the position that it is impossible to "speak of music" in more than the most vague and abstract terms without broaching the issue of genre. I mean genre broadly conceived as the place where music as text meets music as social act or communication: the place where expectations are met or defied, where individual performative utterances fit into cultural contexts and habitus—in short, the place where music makes its meaning.[2] Of course, genre in this broad sense is a huge and messy conglomeration of ideas and rules of engagement. It operates not only on several levels simultaneously but sometimes even on several levels that are contradictory or apparently mutually irrelevant. Nevertheless, we should muddle ahead rather than retreat from this challenge. The essays in this volume remind us that speaking of music in general is demanding, but such language is also revealing—and a necessary part of the very systems that create music's effects. The same is true of genre considerations. In this chapter, I propose that attempts, driven by Romantic ideology, to shift the language in which we discuss musical genre encountered some specific resistance that set music apart from other arts, due to the social nature of music-making itself.

There is a well-established narrative asserting that the concept of genre shifted fundamentally around 1800—in music alongside literature and other arts. Until then, literate Europeans took genre almost for granted as deriving from a set of natural rules. There were of course debates (such as the *Querelle des anciens et des modernes*) about the extent to which *new* genres might be valid extensions of the natural rules set out in well-established forms. Yet the idea remained that, in art, rules were essentially natural laws that inherently facilitated communication or made it possible in the first place, rather than limiting or constricting expression. Studies or explanations of genre from before 1800 largely lay out typologies and give instructions for communication within each genre, down to the smallest details of appropriate content, style, and form. Reading the passages on how to write a concerto from Johann Joachim Quantz's 1752 flute treatise can be a shocking experience for modern students, for example, because Quantz prescribes—in several dense paragraphs of numbered rules—every aspect of thematic content, form, meter, key, character, in addition to the length of each section and movement, and more. For instance:

> The last Allegro must be just as humorous and sprightly as the first is serious. To this end, the following meters prove useful 2/4, 3/4, 3/8, 6/8, 9/8 and 12/8. In no case should all three movements of a concerto be written in the same meter. But if the first movement is in duple time and the second in triple, the last may be written either in triple or in two-four time. In no case, however, may it stand in common duple time, for this would be too serious and hence as little suited to the last movement as two-four or a rapid triple time to the first. . . . To insure a proportional length, even in a concerto, consult a timepiece. If the first movement takes five minutes, the Adagio five to six, and the last movement three to four, the whole is of the proper length.[3]

Indeed, in this earlier period, style (and "mode") appear as almost completely dependent on and subordinate to genre. Style was linked primarily to function rather than to creative *origin*—that is, rather than to any specific period, culture, or person. Hans Robert Jauss has outlined, for example, how from the Middle Ages onward, literary scholars used the example of Virgil to praise the poet's adoption of a "high" style for an epic poem and a "low" style for an eclogue.[4] Virgil's place of honor depended on the craft he could bring to a variety of apposite styles rather than his development of a single, "personal" style.

On the other hand, in the years around 1800, rules of art were called into contention en masse. Their very status as "natural" (rather than artificial) was questioned, as part of a new valorization of individual creation—that is, rule-breaking or rule-giving individual "genius." In this shift, the concept of genre itself became a locus of strife, its historical contingency increasingly asserted. An apt representative of the newer viewpoint is Friedrich Schlegel's famous declaration that "of the modern genres there exists only one or infinitely many. Every poem is a genre unto itself."[5] In other words, each poem was a subjective interaction with the world around. Each resulted from its creator's intuitions over and above any rules of expression or form. Granted, Schlegel was, as Samuel Taylor Coleridge was to be, anxious to find a new genre theory that *would* encompass the interaction of valorized individualism and social (if not natural) rules or restrictions—because it might unlock the secrets of art. Still, as several prominent literary critics have charted, this meant that genre was being approached not as fact but in a historicized, "philosophical," even "phenomenological" manner.[6] Regarding *music*, Carl Dahlhaus treated the issue of genre frequently. His own narrative is parallel to that outlined by the literary critics; in fact, it is taken further. In a nutshell, Dahlhaus suggested that as musical "function" gave way to a new idea of "autonomous" (and organic) art music at the start of the nineteenth century, genre became an increasingly irrelevant category in musical discourse. The process finally culminated in the music of avant-garde composers after World War II, who, Dahlhaus argued, completed the process of rejecting genre by going as far as finding *titles* for their pieces that did not link them to any generic precedent.[7]

I find the broad narrative of the changing conception of genre around 1800 convincing. There are, however, some major problems in Dahlhaus's musical formulation. When Dahlhaus often seems to embrace the idea that we have happily "grown out of" genre, the better to exalt Romantic and modern "postgeneric" "genius," he falls into the trap of failing to recognize his own inherited Romantic ideologies.[8] Indeed, the very domain of "autonomous" music in which Dahlhaus considers postgeneric musical achievement has itself been so thoroughly deconstructed and problematized ideologically that I need not rehash this here.[9] Dahlhaus has surely had many counterparts among critics of the other arts—Benedetto Croce prominent among them—but the problem runs deeper in music. Jeffery Kallberg has critiqued Dahlhaus's engagement with genre in depth, noting especially that Dahlhaus tends to ignore the communicative side of genre, the sense of dialogue between composer and listener, because he is too focused on the creative process of the composer.[10] Put another way, Dahlhaus is thinking only about how composers and their champions "speak of music" when they make claims to justify their own work, while ignoring the fact that the most common types of discourse about music come from performers and listeners.

I approach the issue from a different angle—one even Kallberg downplays: I want to note that music is more inherently functional and physical than "literature" is. Different genres of literature may be consumed in the same place—for example, in a comfortable chair by the fire—and there was even in fact a tradition of "reading" drama as a kind of literary output, to the extent that Goethe could assume that reading Shakespeare would bring "purer joy" (*reinere Freude*) to any literate, educated person than seeing it on the stage.[11] Indeed, the *dramatic* was considered as one of the natural forms of literature taken for granted by the Romantics.[12] On the other hand, in music, genre is almost inalienably linked to types of rooms, accompanying movement, times of day, membership in a particular kind of audience, and so forth. Or at least it was linked thus in the nineteenth century, before the age of widespread recording—despite the development of a score-based culture. Any educated layperson could read different sorts of literature at home, but only a very few people could read scores and "hear" them in their heads. Critics in the early nineteenth century could hardly publicly claim the musical parallel of what Goethe claimed for Shakespeare: that certain works were better perused in score because they did not lend themselves to the practicalities of performance. Though music lovers might play through, say, a version of a symphony at the piano to enjoy it or study it at home, not only did this activity itself already require a physical engagement with the body and with space, but it would also have been seen as a means toward understanding the symphony rather than a full reading of the work in context. Robert Schumann wrote that "music—so different from painting—is the art that we enjoy most in company with others (a symphony, presented in a room with one listener, would please him but little)."[13]

In other words, music was intrinsically a more social experience. Richard Leppert has suggested an important reason for this: "Precisely because musical sound is abstract, intangible, and ethereal—lost as soon as it is gained—the visual experience of its production is crucial to both musicians and audience alike for locating and communicating the place of music and musical sound within society and culture."[14] (Still today, in a world of iPods, when most types of music *can* be consumed in the same comfortable chair, such elements linger in the background.) Thus, even if we confine ourselves to the elite concert music that Dahlhaus considered "autono-mous," we encounter a wide variety of subfunctions (appropriate commu-nicative contents and methods for different types of concerts, instruments, and audiences). This innately social, functional aspect of music lies at the heart of my consideration here of Romantic "speaking of music."

The practical aspect of music-making, the physical presence of musi-cians and audience communicating and listening to music in a room or hall, often seemed to confound even the diverse German Romantic musicians who wished, frequently on nationalistic grounds, to sublimate music to an abstract essence, in order to praise its ability to speak to the soul directly. The ideas of philosophers who sought to sever music from its environment are well known. Schopenhauer's conceptions of music and the will seem to exist almost perversely in a world without musical performance and praxis. Because "clothing" music "in the imagination in flesh and bone" when we listen does not provide "understanding or enjoyment, but rather gives it a strange and arbitrary addition," he argued, "it is therefore better to interpret it purely and in its immediacy."[15] Even this (foresworn) visual-ization of music as "flesh and bone" itself ignores the performance setting and venue as part of a social system. Similarly, Hegel, in his *Aesthetics*, contrasts music as a Romantic art with architecture, sculpture, and even painting. Music, he believes, transcends the physical, incorporeal medium of those other arts. Thus, while he briefly considers performance as a path toward uncovering the meaning of music, he too ignores it from a social or physical angle.[16] But musicians and music critics who championed modern "Romantic" music could not ignore its social and physical aspect as easily as idealist philosophers or literary critics could. While they often imported the word "poetry" as a metonym for all great art, including the music they held highest, these musicians and critics were constantly reminded of the bodily, physical creation of music and the effects of this on the type of communication that might work in different settings. They too may have wished at times to move into the ideal world where music existed outside of its performance settings and social ramifications, but they could not. Their writings often seem to fluctuate uneasily between discounting this reality and embracing it. Nowhere is this more evident than in discussions, implicit or explicit, of genre—for the realm of genre was where music as idealized text and as incorporeal experience met.[17]

Thus, certain discursive shifts in theory and criticism that occurred in literature as "escapes" from formally defined genres could not be paralleled in music. Consider, for example, Friedrich Schlegel's push to see the novel as a world-encompassing modern, Romantic genre—or, rather, a meta-genre that needed to obey no specific rules as it organically combined all other genres.[18] Franz Liszt and Richard Wagner were certainly enticed by such ideas of a modern all-encompassing genre.[19] Wagner conceived the music drama in part in this spirit, as did Liszt his symphonic poem. It is true that they were driven more by the idea of combining the arts than by the idea of combining genres within one art. Yet even to the extent that the music drama and the symphonic poem might be seen as parallel attempts to combine genres novelistically within music, Wagner and Liszt had to abandon their high-flying rhetoric quickly when they faced the practical considerations of theater space and the like. Similarly, Romantic sketches of progressive ages of lyric, epic, and dramatic art—a discourse solidifying and expanding through the work of Schiller, Friedrich Schlegel, Schelling, Jean Paul, Goethe, Hegel, and Hugo—enticed avant-garde Romantic composers and music critics. Although such teleological narratives became extremely common in tracts on music aesthetics and on specific genres, theorists of music agreed even less than theorists of literature about how to parse their art and its genres into epic, lyric, and dramatic categories, let alone on the specifics of progressive ages tied to those domains. The Romantic three-way categorization conflated mode and genre in a way that forced some reconceptions even in literature, where modes, like styles, had also previously been dependent on their host genres.[20] In music, where the underlying mode of communication could not be divorced easily from specific genres that tied expression to types of room, audience behavior, and the like, such conflation was even more difficult.

The inescapable presence of human action in the process of music-making is the reason, I propose, for some striking *continuity* in musical writing and criticism across the volatile nineteenth century. Let us turn from the abstract to some specific examples, starting with one from the beginning of the period at hand. Here is the definition of "chamber music" from Heinrich Christoph Koch's famous *Musikalisches Lexikon* (1802). Chamber music, says Koch, "is in the narrowest sense of the word, a type of music heard only at courts, and to which one can gain access only with special permission, since it is set up as the private entertainment of regents."[21] *Because* of its function as private entertainment, rather than as religious sentiment (as in church music) or moral sentiment (as in opera), and because it works in a small space with a small ensemble, chamber music tends to focus stylistically on fine nuancing and mechanical finish. (Koch compares chamber music to a painting meant to be seen from up close, as opposed to a large fresco to be viewed from far away.) In other words, from the genre's functional stipulations emerged a specific style, which Koch notes is still today known as the "chamber style" (*Kammerstyl*). He concludes, however, that "many modern composers have not been satisfied to abide by these maxims of their predecessors, and instead they avail themselves in opera of just as intricately worked-out voicings and just as difficult instrumental writing as in their chamber works. Thus it is hard work these days to draw a real line between the theater and chamber styles, or to isolate a distinctive character for either."[22]

Koch's definition is predictable in some ways as a summary of late eighteenth-century thought, captured in a compendium at the end of that century. We see here the longstanding governing tripartition of music into three large, overarching genres: "church, chamber, and theater" music. Furthermore, each of these functional (and thus apparently "natural") categories has its naturally derived apposite "style." (It should be noted that Koch's article on "style" [*Styl/Schreibart*] begins by explaining that each genre of musical piece has a specific functional goal and thus an appropriate style—there is no link of style to personality or to national background, etc., only to function and genre here. Certainly, concerns with some of these elements can be found in eighteenth-century writings.[23] They remain, however, much less dominant than they became shortly thereafter.) Next, we should remark that Koch's chamber music entry historicizes the genre, noting that the origins of chamber music and its associated style are culturally determined (as court music). Since music did not have ancient Greek and Roman precedents to refer to as static models, there was no point in pretending that all current forms of music had always existed, as had been more possible in some other arts.

However, there is no sense of Romantic teleology here, no sense that a genre, at least a large-scale genre such as chamber music, once introduced, may become archaic. For Koch, the originating circumstances of chamber music, exclusive court entertainments, would define the genre even as it began to move slowly (it soon moved quickly) away from such princely origins and toward a realm of domestic amateur and semiprofessional music-making. Koch can dwell on the court origins as determining the style without worrying that the present may not be "the age of chamber music." On the contrary, he can tacitly presume that the connection between function and style that originated in private *court* music is "natural," and he can transfer the modes and styles of chamber music to appropriate modern settings. Koch assumes the lasting nature of his rules to the point that he is flummoxed by (or even censures) those "modern" composers who take the chamber style outside its natural domains (i.e., to the theater).

Fast-forward fifty years, to the middle of the century. By this time, established genres were under constant attack in music as in the other arts, and Richard Wagner was busy disparaging "academic" composers who followed rules and established styles. Not only do Wagner's writings historicize genres; they suggest that genres become archaic as they work toward a more modern synthesis—a narrative obviously based on Schiller, Friedrich and August Wilhelm Schlegel, Jean Paul, Goethe, Hugo, and Hegel. New times demanded new acts of individual synthesis, epitomized for Wagner by Beethoven's addition of voices to the Ninth Symphony, a stroke which, for Wagner, basically thrust music forward into a whole new era, in the process making the symphony itself obsolete. Such innovations, however, must not become further forms or sets of rules; they should not degenerate into "mere" genres themselves. Thus, Wagner complains that too many composers do not understand the priority of individuality and genius over genre and standardization:

> The forms in which the master [Beethoven] brought to light his artistic, world-historical struggle remained only *forms* as such for his composing contemporaries and followers. They passed from style into mode, and in spite of the fact that not a single instrumental composer was capable of extracting from these forms even the slightest bit of new invention, no one lost the courage to continue on and on composing symphonies and similar pieces without the least realization that the last symphony [i.e., Beethoven's Ninth] *had already been written.* So we now have to live with the fact that Beethoven's great voyage of world discovery—that unique, thoroughly unrepeatable feat whose consummation we see in the last and boldest endeavor of his genius, his *Freude*-symphony—is subsequently retraced with an utterly dimwitted lack of self-consciousness, and interpreted without any trouble. A new genre [*Genre*], a "symphony with choruses"; that is all they saw in it! And why shouldn't any Tom, Dick or Harry [*Der oder Jener*] also be able to write a symphony with choruses? . . . Thus Columbus has discovered America only for the mawkish haggling of our own times![24]

Wagner discussed those who attempted to follow Mozart's forms in opera in similar terms.[25] In his apparent contempt for the idea that a genre, once established, remains valid by virtue of having formed a set of naturally determined rules, and in his assertion that each great composer must forge new forms and combinations, Wagner sounds worlds away from Koch's generation.

Yet consider the entry on "chamber music" in another musical encyclopedia, from this same, later period. The entry, from a three-volume set edited by Eduard Bernsdorf, introduces some new elements but nevertheless rings with numerous striking echoes of Koch's definition. As with Koch's, the newer lexicon entry begins with historical circumstances. It explains how "chamber music" as a category split off from both theater and church music:

> Theater music gradually distinguished itself from church music [as the art broadened and people wished music to be] not merely religious, as that music aimed to achieve, but also to express moral sentiment, as [theater music] primarily intended to do. . . . Both genres of music, church music and theater music, however, were from the very start, as they still are, suitable primarily only for public use, and allowed in some respects for no other purpose. For the *private* practice of music, therefore, a third genre would need to be spawned: chamber music— which was in some ways a combination or a point of mediation between church and theater music, taking something from both, but on the other hand made up its own distinctive whole.[26]

We also see here similar wording to Koch's about the new category being neither religious like church music nor expressive of "moral sentiment" like theater music. Next, the entry parallels Koch by noting the etymology of the term as an integral part of its essence: "The name chamber music comes from the fact that previously only great lords at their courts and in their staterooms (chambers) entertained themselves privately with music such as this—and only those especially privy to them had access to this music." The entry continues by stressing that "Nowadays . . . when in educated lands music has come to be spread among all ranks," the term really has to be distinguished not only in a wider sense from church and theater music but also in a narrower sense from a later developing category, *concert music*, which (though it grew from the chamber category) is also now a *public* genre, performed in large rooms. This narrower type of chamber music is also sometimes called *Hausmusik*. Thus, today "chamber music" means music for small rooms or private circles, using not a full orchestra but rather a few instruments or voices, for example, quartets, trios, duos, sonatas, nocturnes, lieder, and so on. The entry ends, "Finally, one can distinguish it from folk music (which encompasses folk dances and songs)."[27]

What has really changed since Koch's definition? There are differences, of course. One is the fact that the older "chamber" domain (which did not originally distinguish between small orchestral music and one-to-a-part music) has now clearly split into "chamber music" in the modern sense and what we have come to call "orchestral" music. While the treatment here shows an awareness that major divisions might emerge later from a single category, all these descendant genres are still traced back to historical origins that are functional in their demands. In this case, we are dealing with music for concerts that were neither theatrical nor liturgical. The historical origins of this broader genre are, as in Koch, rooted in the specific demands of music for small, exclusive court entertainments. The suggestion persists that this originating function will shadow the resultant styles.

Another, briefer, German handbook, an 1871 edition, actually classifies chamber music in a way even closer to Koch's earlier entry: Its definition runs simply, "a.) music intended for the private entertainment of a regent, which no one without invitation may gain entrance to hear, and b.) composition in classical genres for a small number of instruments, such as trios, quartets, quintets, etc.—to be heard in private circles."[28] In such a concise characterization, there is no time to draw connections, but it seems clearly implied that definition B derives historically from definition A and, furthermore, that the editor here (Julius Schuberth) believes that large concert music no longer fits in as a part of the chamber music genre but has become a separate genre with its own historical genesis, splitting off from chamber music just as chamber music originally split from church and theater music. This is even clearer when we see the still more laconic definition of "chamber style" in the same handbook: "composition in the strict sense [Compositionen im strengen *Satz*], that corresponds to chamber music."[29]

Of course, descriptive encyclopedia entries about music themselves constitute a genre, and one that, by building on earlier typologies and codes in the same form, may be expected to remain relatively consistent. Such typologies are one fixed way of speaking of music. Are these later definitions of chamber music just conservative encyclopedia entries then? Examples that do not yet take on board (even as a subject of critique) the radical intellectual breaks outlined in the more prescriptive writings of Wagner, Liszt, and their acolytes, inspired by philosophical and literary discourse? I do not think so at all. For a start, Liszt is listed as a consultant on the title page of the Bernsdorf encyclopedia. More telling, however, is that Wagner himself in his own prose never moved away from such ideas about "chamber music"—as a governing genre with appropriate corresponding style. In a famous passage of 1879, Wagner takes Brahms (who remains unnamed) to task for exporting a "chamber style" to the symphony—where such a style was inappropriate. Wagner writes,

> The . . . symphony compositions of our newest school—let us term it the "Romantic-classical" school—distinguish themselves from the natural growths of so-called program music, besides the fact that they strike us as lacking a program itself, also especially by a certain type of over-chewy melodic content. This has been imported into them from the so-called "chamber music" that their creators thus far cultivated quietly. That is to say, they have withdrawn to the "chamber." Unfortunately, however, this is not the intimate little salon in which Beethoven shared with a few breathlessly attentive friends all the unsayable things he knew could only be understood in that context—rather than in the expansive concert hall where he believed he must speak in broad plastic terms to the folk, to all humanity. . . . [Instead of taking care to speak differently in intimate and public music, as Beethoven did, the recent "Romantic-classical" composers] have already displaced *their* chamber to the concert hall. They now serve up as symphonies what was previously arranged as quintets and the like: fussy little melodic chaff, comparable to used tea leaves mixed with hay. No one knows what he is sipping, but it is ultimately concocted under the banner "authentic"— for the supposed enjoyment of world-weariness.[30]

Walter Frisch and others have traced the influence of this passage well into the twentieth century among critics (especially Wagnerian critics) of Brahms's symphonies, who continued to berate Brahms for this apparent generic impropriety.[31] But what concerns me foremost here is the familiarity of these *ideas*—if not the wording—from the encyclopedia articles we have examined. Wagner, though he might have hated the fact, sounds like Koch when he chides certain "modern composers" for taking the chamber style—with its private, refined, personal, intellectual connotations and meanings and its work on a small scale—out of the chamber! (Though here it is to the symphonic hall rather than the theater.)

So Wagner, the radical who longed more than any of his contemporaries to translate to music the most "Romantic" narratives of evolving "world-spirit," of individual subjectivity and genius trumping formal constraints, ultimately cannot go as far as his literary counterparts. He cannot—and often does not even *want* to—transcend functional categories and replace them entirely with modal forms or ideal approaches. Even in theory, let

Table 8.1. Diagram of Genre Systems: Seventeenth–Eighteenth Centuries

GENRE GENERATES MODE/STYLE

Metagenres	⇩	Inconsistent	◇	
Governing genres with commonly resulting or associated *styles*	**CHURCH** *"bound/strict style"*	**CHAMBER** *"free style"* *"chamber style"*	**THEATER**	**LABOR/ WORK SONGS**
Midlevel genres (On this level and below, function generally determined not only *style* but also [direct or stylized] *form*)	church sonata sacred cantata organ genres church symphony	sonata (da camera) trio sonata lied/song settings quartet concerto (solo versus grosso, etc.) (chamber/ concert) symphony	opera (including its parts, such as aria, duet, etc.) ballet overture (theater symphony)	for plowing field, for sewing, etc.
Microgenres	types of organ prelude, etc.	gigue-type finales, etc.	rage aria, etc.	e.g., Highland cloth-waulking song

alone in practice, when he speaks of music, his categories remain grounded in the functions of music within society.[32]

Let us pause and take stock here. In order to understand how musicians in the "New German" avant-garde could attack composers they saw as academically following generic norms, while often berating the same composers for *failing* to follow other generic norms, it will be helpful to separate more clearly the different levels on which musical genre has operated. Tables 8.1 and 8.2 are rudimentary sketches of the discursive levels at which genre can operate. I have called these levels, from broadest to narrowest, metagenres, governing genres, genres and subgenres, and micro-

Table 8.2. Diagram of Genre Systems: Nineteenth–Twentieth Centuries

MODE/STYLE CAN SEPARATE AND CUT ACROSS
SOME LEVELS, BUT NOT CONSISTENTLY

	"ART MUSIC"	"FOLK MUSIC"	"POPULAR MUSIC"
Metagenres The categories at this level at least claim to be determined *not* primarily by function but by origin (composer type or composer, nationality, etc.)			
Governing genres	**CHAMBER – ORCHESTRAL – OPERATIC – CHURCH** SMALL *"public"* GROUPS OR PIANO *"private"*	songs, dances, ballads	music hall, popular dances, etc. arrangements of hit tunes, etc. ◇ later many other domains
Midlevel genres and subgenres	quartet, symphony, grand opera, trio, symphonic poem, "music drama," etc. lied, vocal duet, character piece, etc.	reel, jig, etc.	
Microgenres	nocturne, prelude, intermezzo, etc.		"swell songs," etc.

genres.[33] Discussion of levels is prevalent in much of the existing literature on musical genre. For example, several German studies have considered whether the term "genre" (*Gattung*) applies to one level or more, though each conceives the levels differently. At the same time, it is easy for such discussions to become almost useless theoretical abstractions. As I outlined at the start of this chapter, I think it makes sense to consider genre in the most inclusive sense. There has never been consistency in the application of "genre" to only one or certain limited levels.[34] This very inconsistency is what makes generic contracts between composers, performers, and audiences range across and interconnect all the possible levels.

Beyond the question of levels as such, there are further concepts held separate by some people that I want to bundle together as part of the same interconnected umbrella category called "genre." There are not now, nor were there in the nineteenth century, clear lines between genre as an idea and related groupings such as medium, form, and apposite style. In the eighteenth century, genre discussions were generally linked to styles, as we have seen, and styles were closely linked to "characters." However, the boundaries between these categories were blurry. Johann Nikolaus Forkel, for example, considers "genre" (*Gattung*) as a subset of style (*Schreibart* or *Styl*) but suggests that genres are sometimes determined by form, sometimes by instrumentation, sometimes by their "inner essence."[35] A few decades later, the idea that the medium chosen for a piece might be independent of or even contradict the true underlying generic contract could become more explicit. For example, Schumann argued that the character of Schubert's Sonata in C for Piano Four Hands, D. 812 (the "Grand Duo") betrayed it as an imagined symphony despite its scoring. "One who wrote as much as Schubert does not trouble too much about titles and thus he probably hastily entitled his work 'sonata,' while a 'symphony' was what he had finished in his mind."[36] (Schumann speculated that Schubert disguised the work as a sonata because it was harder to find a publisher for a symphony.) Romantic conceptions of organic art seem almost by definition to infer a blurring, or a growing, fluctuating generic identity.

This same fluidity raises another important point, one that I wish to emphasize with regard to tables 8.1 and 8.2. Genres are by nature in a constant state of flux. Their very meaning often stems from the inflections they undergo.[37] As Wulf Arlt has observed, attempting to pin down a definition of genre too rigidly actually undermines the concept's usefulness and productivity for thinking about music.[38] Thus, these tables should in no way be regarded as attempts to reify definitions or to create an immovable typology. They are, rather, an attempt to lay a foundation for the discussion of some important relationships. Genres are never formed in a vacuum but rather in affiliation and opposition to each other.

It is this set of relationships that makes a schematic diagram useful even if the relationships are in a constantly changing state. I offer the tables as launching pads to make specific points about the interaction of levels. The groupings these discursive levels circumscribe are always inherently parts of complex systems of communication. (There will always be some categories that seem to stand outside the system shown here or that create their own concurrent networks. For the sake of clarity, such aspects are left off of these tables.) Table 8.1 sketches musical categorization in the seventeenth and eighteenth centuries, table 8.2 in the nineteenth and twentieth centuries.

My argument is basically that the most distinctive, and persistent, level in musical genre is the second level down on these tables—what I have called the "governing" genres. These are broad categories that are most closely linked to musical setting, audience, performing forces, and apposite content. (Should the ideas be public or private? Intellectual or spiritual and anthemic? And so forth.) There *can* be historical changes at this level—such as the separation of orchestral concert music out of the earlier broad "chamber" category, noted on the tables. On the other hand, this is the level at which the common ground between a Koch and a Wagner—and, for that matter, a Varèse—becomes evident. Meanwhile, at the lower, or narrower, levels, issues such as formal layout may take center stage, and it is thus on these lower levels where the avant-garde and the so-called conservative composers and critics of the Romantic period clashed. Wagner's and Liszt's disdain for "pouring content" into preexisting forms and Hanslick's contention that thematic and figural gestures created their own larger forms naturally were really phenomena that addressed these lower levels primarily.

Nevertheless, when a structure of musical categorization and reception depends on deep epistemic systems and evolving social interactions, one generic level cannot be rearranged without affecting another. And in fact, my final point here concerns the relationship between the levels. I want to suggest that the ideology that led the Romantic avant-garde to disparage the formal constraints on subgenres and microgenres did indeed have repercussions on the whole cognitive schema, but in a more complicated way than in other arts.

The Romantic desire to place the subjective individual and the creative *origin* of an artwork at the heart of its meaning made musical Romantics of a radical cast wish to see—in their art as in literature—every composition as a genre unto itself, a free combination. They hoped to place creative origin (personal, national, etc.) at the highest, regulative, level. It was easy to place this poietic level above the *formal* implications of the subgeneric and microgeneric levels. But Wagner, in his polemics against would-be followers of Beethoven or Mozart who could only see new forms (or formulas) in their innovations, attempted to move the stamp of the personal even higher—to affect style as well as form. Could not personal (or, often, national) style, once it was no longer subordinate to function and once it transcended many genres, become a basis of criticism and meaning in music?

Once again, though, there remained the practicalities of music-making: that middle level of the governing genres whose inherent stylistic prescriptions ("chamber music style," etc.) stood "in the way" of complete personal stylistic "freedom"—or at least needed to be taken into account. Since the level of the governing genres was relatively fixed and perhaps inescapable in conceiving and speaking of music, the solution turned out to be the creation of a new generic level that had not existed before and that, rather than replacing the "governing" level, was pushed discursively *above* it— generating new metageneric labels. These new categories amounted basically to a separation of art music (that is, "autonomous" music) from folk music and (soon) popular music as well (see table 8.2).

In the eighteenth century, I argue, no such metalevel existed. Or rather, there were several partially formulated concepts that sometimes sat atop the other levels. These included certain protective "professional" categorizations (the legacy of guilds from the Middle Ages), not to mention class distinctions, which were in flux throughout this period, and a growing sense of national identities. None of these forces, however, coalesced into a set of driving metageneric forces as the later folk, art, and popular categories did.[39] (I have thus marked the top line, the metageneric layer, as "inconsistent" in table 8.1.) The church-theater-chamber partition operated at the highest relatively consistent discursive level. Where music is discussed that falls outside of this tripartition, it seems to have had its own specific functional category (for example, work songs) operating on the same practical, "governing" level. In an era when genre—and style—were considered derivatives of natural functional rules, this should not be surprising: the governing level would *obviously* be a practical one, reifying these natural rules in action. The functional origin of chamber music, for example, would determine a large, shaping style *and* many subgenres.

Conversely, in the nineteenth-to-twentieth-century paradigm, the new metalevel becomes the most idealized and sacred. Here the concerns of genius (and that means either national or personal *creative shaping* forces) were presumed to regulate and sit above even the inescapable practical demands of music. In order to make Romantic musical discourse consistent with practice, this highest level became increasingly necessary but increasingly abstract. More and more was at stake at the top level. Hence, Wagner's writings lean heavily on the organic fertilization of the individual creative mind by the "folk" and elsewhere on a disdain for commercial "selling out" at the expense of individual synthetic, self-fulfilling creation. It could only be on this upper plane—where "art music" built on folk music and shunned the popular—that the spirit of Germany, of Beethoven, of Mozart, could prevail over all genres, even while, one step lower down, an idea of "chamber music" remained firmly in place, sometimes working independently and sometimes in tandem with the upper level to build musical identities for audiences.

The growing ideological significance of the new upper level is evident everywhere. Such was its import that it was even liable to permeate other discussions and analyses incongruously and sometimes illogically. Consider once again the 1856 Bernsdorf encyclopedia entry on chamber music. I focused earlier on the elements in this definition that were consistent with Koch's older entry for the same headword. The last part of the Bernsdorf encyclopedia entry, however, which I did not comment on before, in fact attempts a rather bizarre logical move, which betrays the newer paradigm at work. It sets chamber music apart first from public theater and church music and then from the later development of public orchestral music. So far, so consistent. But the paragraph ends by saying that chamber music is also distinguished from "folk music." This jarring conflation of levels amounts to an assertion that chamber music is a branch of "autonomous" art music. Yet, given this fact, it would have made more sense to say outright that chamber music was a *subset* of "art music" than to contrast it here to another category, folk music, that itself contained public and private, small and large forms. One senses that the rhetorical effect of the strange conclusion—appearing almost as an afterthought—was to remind the reader that the functional history and derivative styles of chamber music *were* indeed subject to a higher presiding force, the personal stamp of individual genius. The new metalevel operates almost in a parallel universe to the still-governing functional level but must discursively trump it in the end.

Certainly, an analogous new metalevel—the very idea of "literature"—was built for poetry and prose as well at this time, as Susan Stewart and Alastair Fowler have considered from different perspectives.[40] What seems unique to music is the constant mediation of that level through a more persistent middle ground—a middle ground that was the bread and butter of musical practice. No musician would have wanted to part with it really, but it strained the philosophical underpinnings of Romantic music at the same time. It seems to me that the very existence of this governing level, with its potential to contradict the values of the metalevel, was what *made* the metalevel in music so much more dominant, sometimes stridently so and sometimes insidiously so, in discourse ranging from the broad public sphere to the shoptalk of performers and musicologists, than it was in the other arts.

Furthermore, even though metalevel labels are treated by all audiences, marketers, and social arbiters as generic categories in the classic mold, it has been ideologically important in many cases to deny that this metalevel is a part of a generic system—since the very creation of the metalevel was part and parcel of claims to be abandoning genre(s). For example, consider Dahlhaus's language in his article on modern music and genre, once again reflecting and expanding Romantic tropes. Writing of the gradual "disappearance" of genre from the nineteenth to the later twentieth century, Dahlhaus asserts, "That it might be possible to discover additional functions for music, even in industrial society, which would enable one to develop new musical genres [i.e., versus "autonomous" music] without falling behind state-of-the-art compositional techniques is the hope of composers who feel unhappy about the present isolation of the avant-garde." Here "state-of-the-art" compositional techniques are directly opposed to the very idea of genre, since that is tied to "utility value."[41] (And it should be noted that here Dahlhaus is cleaving closely to the Horkheimer-Adorno model of modernist art defined only as resistance to a resurgence of genre brought about by the culture industry.)[42] Dahlhaus continues, "But attempts to close the gap between utility value and art character in the name of New Objectivity forced even composers of the caliber of Hindemith and Krenek to turn away from New Music."[43] Of course, "new music" as used here (a cover term for the most esoteric "art music") *is* a genre, in many senses. It is a label that determines (or at least conditions expectations about) concert settings, audience sizes, behavior, and expectations. Even as older genres were treated more ironically and fragmentarily, almost as *topoi*, new conventions emerged.[44]

Strikingly too, "new music" is a label of about the same breadth and limitation as earlier examples of groupings from the highest operative level, back when that highest level was the "governing" level. In some ways, "new music" is even a genre with arresting parallels to "chamber music." We could imagine a Koch-like definition: it starts with the first origins of "new music" around 1830 as exclusive music for small, initiated audiences to reflect on—in a concert setting in which it is inappropriate for them to make noise. The definition of "new music" when Dahlhaus was writing might have ended too as Koch's chamber music entry ended: with a perplexed musing on the newest composers who do not always maintain the established boundaries of the genre, mixing it with apparently incongruous alternative genres, in this case, popular music and the like, which not only courted different audiences and audience behavior but also used different venues (or used venues differently). It thus required a different social system. (Indeed, this is precisely the thrust of Dahlhaus's commentary on Hindemith and Krenek.) Here it becomes clear that even positioned above the more constant level of governing genres, the new level of metagenres, supposedly determined entirely by creative origins, was itself quickly permeated by considerations of practicality and function. Once again the governing level turns out to be extraordinarily tenacious and influential—essential in fact—in music.

I end with a demonstrative example drawn from the Romantic era itself. It is Liszt's famous 1852 biography of Chopin. The epigraph to this chapter shows Liszt rehearsing the familiar argument that using established genres simply limited and "fettered" genius. Predictably, Liszt follows through with the new Romantic gesture *par excellence*. Having made a show of downplaying established genres and their associated formal structures, he argues at length for a new, higher level at which style and other generic concerns are linked to personal and national creative origins:

> Like all truly national poets, [Chopin] sang spontaneously without premeditated design or preconceived choice all that inspiration dictated to him, as we hear it gushing forth in his songs without labor, almost without effort. . . . Chopin must be ranked among the first musicians thus individualizing in themselves the poetic sense of an entire nation, not because he adopted the rhythm of *Polonaises*, *Mazourkas*, and *Cracoviennes*, and called many of his works by such names, for in so doing he would have limited himself to the multiplication of such works alone, . . . compositions of similar form. . . . It is because he filled these forms with the feelings peculiar to his country, because the expression of the national heart may be found under all the modes in which he has written, that he is entitled to be considered a poet essentially Polish. His *Préludes*, his *Nocturnes*, his *Scherzos*, his *Concertos*, his shortest as well as his longest compositions, are all filled with the national sensibility. . . . All his writings are thus linked by a marked unity.[45]

The attempt here to make "Polish music" into a genre, and to make "Chopin" into a style (which Schumann had done musically in *Carnaval*), shows the ideological importance to the Romantic vision of music of subordinating familiar functional generic concerns to the new metalevel.

Yet, in the end, it still proves impossible to "speak of music" in the real world without genre conceptions at the governing level working persistently, in the background or the foreground. It soon becomes clear once again that Liszt's attack on established "genres," quoted in the epigraph, is primarily an attack on *form*, working at the lower generic levels.[46] As Liszt says in the next paragraph, Chopin "could not retain, within the square of an angular and rigid mould, that floating and indeterminate contour which so fascinates us in his graceful conceptions," for that inspiration required "disguising the skeleton, the whole framework of form" in a "mist of floating vapors" (6–7). Yet we need look only a couple of paragraphs earlier to find Liszt *praising* the same idea of limits and restraints that he scorns when discussing the classical midlevel genres, subgenres, and their attendant forms. This is because he is now dealing with what amounts to the governing genre level—in this case, with what is apposite for a piano piece:

> In confining [*se renfermant*] himself exclusively to the Piano, Chopin has, in our opinion, given proof of one of the most essential qualities of a composer—just appreciation of the form [i.e., here as instrumentation] in which he possessed the power to excel. . . . What strong conviction, based upon reflection, must have been requisite to have induced him to restrict himself to a circle apparently so much more barren [than the orchestra], what warmth of creative genius must have been necessary to have forced from its apparent aridity a fresh growth of luxurious bloom, unhoped for in such a soil! (2–3)[47]

Liszt goes on to praise Chopin for thus developing figuration that is idiomatic to the piano rather than being "modeled only on the *Fioritures* of . . . Italian song" (5). The thrust of Liszt's discussion about how Chopin's music was always delicate and refined and his description of how Chopin wrote and played only for a small circle and for special audiences who understood him (45–50) further confirms that, in fact, Liszt is speaking once again of that very persistent level of the practical governing genre. In other words, confinement to "forms" (here as implied structural layouts corresponding to established [sub]generic labels) is a fettered dead end; whereas, at the governing level in which pianism and "intimate" idiom are ideals, similar confinement (of timbre, mood, and intended audience) spurs creativity rather than killing it. Liszt is here, in essence, arguing that Chopin's music is *chamber music*—a particular kind of chamber music—and his use of the metaphor of the miniature painting versus the large canvas or fresco (3–4) is a now-familiar metaphor from the chamber music definitions we have encountered.

Liszt also discusses what is signified by much narrower labels than "piano music." Indeed, he does so in detail. For instance, he praises Chopin's modesty in expressing himself through newer microgenres such as the *étude* and the *prélude* (labels with less historical baggage than *sonata* and *concerto*) (5), and he devotes long chapters to discussing the *polonaise* and the *mazurka*. Here, however, Liszt consciously eschews any discussion of form (or indeed other musical specifics) in favor of a long (and very indulgent) discussion of the appropriate *character* of each type. Though framed here in modern, that is to say Romantic, garb, the discussion of character is actually a much older part of generic discourse than the minute prescriptions of formal guidelines published in the seventeenth and eighteenth centuries.[48] Character is linked to what René Wellek and Austin Warren called the "inner" attributes of genre (as opposed to the "outer" conventions of form or syntax used to articulate those attributes).[49] And character is what is largely at stake at the level of the governing genres, adding another reason for their particular persistence across other changes in attitude to musical genre. Liszt's discussion at this level is thus both new and old.

The model in which avant-garde composers and their champions, from the Romantic era onward, attack "genres" at what amounts to the lower levels, deal in a consistent way with governing-level generic concerns (of performance forces, setting, and character), and finally insist loudly on a new metalevel in order to obscure the persistence of the middle level or to subordinate it to new concerns about genius is a recurring pattern from the Romantic era onward. When we speak about music, we are frequently brought back to its paradoxical mix of the technical (acoustic) and practical (production technique and social place) with the unfathomable or ineffable. Perhaps much of the anxiety we still feel in "speaking of music" today—the very questioning that has spawned this volume—is due to the fact that, since the nineteenth century, the apparently ineffable aspect has been pushed to the top level discursively. We are expected to focus on this level, yet it is shot through with its relationship to the governing level of musical practice, and vice versa. If we start by noticing the structure in which the relationship occurs, we may be able to confront more productively and simultaneously the different layers of meaning in Romantic music and beyond.

Weather Reports:
Discourse and Musical Cognition

Per Aage Brandt

Through it all, Welser-Möst and the [Cleveland] orchestra
are dashing partners, surrounding their guest [Radu Lupu]
in *vibrant colors without washing out any of his.* On Thursday,
they also helped steady him during the Adagio [of Béla
Bartók's Piano Concerto No. 3], when a ringing cell phone
twice *poked holes in the silken musical fabric he was weaving.*

To listeners, the noise was simply rude. But to Lupu,
it must have been painful, *like lightning striking.*

—ZACHARY LEWIS, "Ensemble Offers Up an Appealing *Climate,*"
Cleveland Plain Dealer, 17 January 2009, italics mine

Clouds occasionally gather in the E-flat trio, though
Schubert is resilient enough to emerge from minor-key
territory and *let the sun shine* in his inimitable way.

—DONALD ROSENBERG, "Trio Conveys Wonder of Schubert's Work,"
Cleveland Plain Dealer, 27 March 2010, italics mine

Music in Space

The concert referred to in the first epigraph comprised meteorological
works such as Richard Strauss's *Alpine Symphony,* György Ligeti's *Atmosphères,* and Claude Debussy's *Nuages,* before the Bartók concerto. In
the history of written music, Baroque, Classical, Romantic, and Modern
manners of composition, exemplified paradigmatically by Beethoven's
"Pastoral" Sixth Symphony, has allowed rather explicit references to aspects of meteorology as constitutive elements of the meaning of music, of
musical semantics.[1] Composers, critics, lay listeners, and remarkably also
musicians find it meaningful to describe what music is "about" in terms
of such visionary experiences of nature and its elements and thus find it
relevant to account for properly musical events in terms of more or less
lyrical "weather reports."

This phenomenon is what I reflect on in this chapter. The question is extremely simple: Why does music solicit such atmospheric or cosmic visions—and inspire corresponding commentary in terms of "poetically" spatial discourse?

Semantics

Remarkably, this "aboutness" is of course semantic, in the sense that some sort of iconic sign relation must hold between the tonal signifier and this spatial signified; but it is *not referentially semantic*. It does not report that a meteorological event was really taking place at a certain time and a certain location. It just evokes an imaginable event of this kind, happening in some imaginary space at some imaginary time, paradoxically coinciding with the real time of the musical performance. It happens in an imaginary time-space of qualia: of light, colors, shapes, flows, movements, in which listeners are not bodily involved but are nevertheless present as observers, experiencers, travelers, insofar as they are listeners. Cognitive semanticists might call this signified a fictive space; but it is of course not a fiction in the literary sense. What it is may be intriguingly difficult to determine.

If we compare language and music with regard to their meaning and sense-making, we will find that the main semantic difference is, in fact, the general *referentiality* of meaning in language. We will sometimes say, "It is raining again," and this impersonal statement of a meteorological situation will necessarily refer to the state of affairs somewhere specifically at some specific time; impersonal constructions in language have implicit locative complements.[2] Not so in music; here, for example, in Chopin's "Raindrop" Prelude, if it rains somewhere, it would be "in the music," that is, in the semantics of the piece as performed, intended, and perceived. What do we mean by talking about "rain in the music"?

Allow me a linguistic digression on this point. In language, there are morphemes and lexemes such as the determiners (*a, the*), the pronominal forms (*I, you, it; this, that*), the deictic, anaphoric, and coreferential adverbials (*here, there; likewise, therefore, so*) that allow us to narrate, describe, and argue while referring to a stable space-time or conceptual referent, either in *the* world or in some other, imaginary "world." If we eliminate these linguistic devices, or reduce their efficient presence significantly in a text, we will get a poetic, lyrically floating effect, which listeners or readers will often qualify as "musical." This effect will imply a dominance of content experienced as imagery. Poetry is reputedly relying on images for this very reason: not because poetic texts contain more images than pragmatic texts but simply because the poetic, nonreferential mode makes content into imagery. Poetry works with what is left when the referential operators are blocked; it does not have to *add* iconicity to the arsenal of metaphors, comparisons, and the like already available and current.[3] "Images" are simply what semantic items become when their reference is eliminated. By contrast, there are no referentializing elements like *it* in music; a musical phrase cannot mean "the aforementioned idea" without replaying or quoting the idea in question; and it cannot just say *now* or *then*, as language, including sign language, easily can. In particular, tonal art has no pronouns; and experimentally, if we remove all pronouns from a verbal text, it will acquire a "musical" sound or character.[4]

Spaces, Intrinsic or Extrinsic?

Music critics extensively exploit as imagery what in a first approach appears to be a spatial or meteorological stand-in for the lacking reference.

In the article quoted in the epigraph, Zachary Lewis does so, and he adds a metalinguistic remark on the rhetorical status of his own phrasing: "Ligeti wasn't necessarily thinking about weather when he wrote 'Atmosphères.' But *shifting heavenly vapors* is certainly an apt metaphor for this dense, slow-moving work" (my italics).

So why would such a metaphor certainly be apt? Is there something in Ligeti's "dense, slow-moving work" that contains "shifting heavenly vapors"? Is there a cloudy sky, or something behind this image, *in this music*? Even if the metaphor is "only" a metaphor, as we often say, its target has to somehow match what the image offers. What is it? This is a truly embarrassing problem; no wonder that many musicians and musicologists prefer not to go there or to beg the question by declaring that spatial imagery is extrinsic to music. How does the intrinsic then evoke the extrinsic? If arbitrarily so, then the extrinsic weather reports simply cannot make sense, which is highly counterintuitive.

So, understandably, some composers of the modern era tend to reject "aboutness" altogether and to declare, as Igor Stravinsky famously did, tautologically, that music is about *music itself*.[5] Here is a significant fragment of a dialogue between Stravinsky and his friend Robert Craft:

R.C.: Have you ever thought that music is, as Auden says, "a virtual image of our experience of living as temporal, with its double aspect of recurrence and becoming?"

I.S.: If music is to me an "image of our experience of living as temporal" (and however unverifiable I suppose it is), my saying so is the result of a reflection and as such is independent of music itself. But this kind of thinking about music is a different vocation altogether for me: I cannot do anything with it as a truth, and my mind is a *doing* one. Auden means "Western" music or, as he would say, "music as history"; jazz improvisation is the dissipation of the time image and, if I understand "recurrence" and "becoming," their aspect is greatly diminished in serial music. Auden's "image of our experience of living as temporal" (which is also an image) is above music, perhaps, but it does not obstruct or contradict the purely musical experience. What shocks me however, is the discovery that many people think below music. Music is merely something that reminds them of something else, of landscapes, for example; my *Apollo* is always reminding someone of Greece. But in even the most specific attempts at evocation, what is meant by being "like" and what are "correspondences"? Who, listening to Liszt's precise and perfect little *Nuages* gem, could pretend that "gray clouds" are a musical cause and effect?[6]

Stravinsky needs to stress and repeat his rejection of the idea that music may be "about" or "mean" places, feelings, event-related emotions; such things are "below music," but they are persistently uttered. By contrast, however, Nicholas Cook explains in detail how a contemporary British composer, Roger Reynolds, derives the structure of an entire symphony from a peculiar rock formation on the shore of Honshu, in Japan.[7] Intimate relations as these between visual and sound images are easy to find in professional musical literature. Do we think they are external, indirect, secondary, inferior, metaphorical, whereas musical meaning as such is *unrelated to imagination*, and all its visual, in particular mentally visual, properties reported by listeners and musicians as core elements of musical phenomenology?

When we *speak*, and especially when we *write*, about music as experienced, there is evidently an important amount of cross-sensorial—visual, tactile, gustatory, olfactory, and even auditory—associations that are brought to the fore, some of which may be pertinently seen as mere conveniences of discourse rather than as constituents of the musical experience. Emotional experiences are often rendered by conventional comparisons and metaphors.[8] Other figurative components of our reports may, however, be intrinsically and indissolubly bound to the experience: the elementary feeling that *something is happening* cannot be done away with. In this sense, musical meaning definitely comes with an event-oriented "aboutness," an intrinsic narrativity justifying our extrinsic reports of induced spatiotemporal representations, even if this aspect can be felt as inessential by some subjects.[9]

On Quality and Space

So, basically, we may admit that there is, in our tonal imaginary, a multimodal or amodal spatial setup, which language-about-music can refer to, because *music itself* really has it. We may admit it, because we often have to report that it is there, and we wish to explore *what* is there—*what there is*—in the phenomenological reality of music, as a significant part of our shared human reality.

Consider the following utterance in a concert review by the Cleveland critic Donald Rosenberg: "The program's other extended work, Schubert's Fantasy in C major, D. 934, was an opportunity for the performers to *delve into profound and wandering terrain*."[10] The musicians "delve," and the listeners supposedly follow them in this locomotor activity. The "terrain," which is "profound and wandering," is a spatial setup surrounding or globally framing the local events that will happen during the trajectory of these imaginary delvers or travelers. If the performers are in fact to delve into the wandering depths of the alleged terrain, while simultaneously staying on the framing *extramusical* material stage as artists with their material instruments, we will have to suppose that they will delegate their imaginary, immaterial avatars to this *intramusical* space. Beyond the mental space of the present performance, another mental space is built, and subjects can miraculously be in both spaces simultaneously.[11] Not only is this semiotically possible, since Rosenberg's and an infinite amount of other reports every day say so, but it seems to be important to say so to evaluate the quality of the performance. It is aesthetically important that this space delegation be possible and take place; *good music* does this, whereas music is bad if it does not. We may ask, why is quality reportedly dependent on space delegation? There is a general problem for cognitive aesthetics in this normative phenomenon.[12]

Often, however, space delegation goes to uninhabited spaces: the tonally induced experience of imaginary space seems to be void of human beings, as in the following account, again by Lewis, from a review of a concert presenting compositions by Olivier Messiaen:

Most transfixing was "The Resurrected and the Song of the Star Aldebaran," from Part III, in which the strings and glockenspiel player Sindre Saetre evoked *a serene, otherworldly realm*. Active throughout "Canyons" were the percussionists, especially xylophonist Jennifer Torrence, whose vibrancy readily depicted *everything from warbling birds to rushing winds*. At several points, another player shook a sand-filled drum to *mimic the sound of rain* and ran a bow against a tiny cymbal in spine-tingling *evocations of vast space*.[13]

Otherworldly realms, vast spaces, with birds, winds, rain—we are enthusiastically sending unembodied observers to these imaginary spaces. Their properties are "evoked," "depicted," "mimicked," and like pictorial landscapes, potentially void of human presence. But they are still part of the excellence of the piece of music responsible for the delegation.

My generalization: it is part of the experience on both sides, the artists' and the listeners', to *mentally see spaces*, when music is produced and perceived, at least if enjoyed. The more important and meaningful the music is felt to be, the more clearly this spatial imagination is present. Space-building in the listener's mind is apparently precisely what this music is expected to achieve. The value of mentally spatial imagination must be somehow stably related to the value of beauty or truth or the morally good.[14] But why would spatial imagination at all be linked to the feeling of value in this Platonic sense? Why this connection, if it exists, between space and importance? How general may the connection be? Could it be something all art does or can do, to some extent?

Art in Semiosis

A general semiotic consideration may be useful here. It is extremely common to *perceive in two spaces*, as we do when we share intuitions of spatial meaning in music. This is what we constantly do in social life, which is built on symbolic signs: in one space we process signifiers, and in the other space we process the concepts signified by these signifiers. Signifiers and signifieds have to be connected by codes, and these can be of variable strength: *strong codes*—explicit lists of conventional concepts to be learned by their users—convey strong meanings, namely, orders, instructions to follow, deontic signals of many kinds; strong codes express the impersonal will of society itself (example: traffic sign systems). By contrast, weak codes are implicit, rooted in inherent structures of human cognition; express personal, individual thinking; and characterize the signs we call iconic: pictures, images of all kinds, diagrams, maps, and gestures.[15] We communicate interpersonally by using both types, symbolic and iconic signs; language combines them, since words are strongly coded, whereas the codes of syntax are weak.

Human semiosis is complex but can be approached through the study of dynamic sign processes. These will show how symbolization can develop out of iconic communication, as through a strengthening of codes, which leads to conventionalization, ritualization, and sedimentation of "history" in our social world. On the contrary, and interestingly, codes can be weakened; when used out of context or combined freely or recombined in new contexts, sign meanings change and are negotiated in what we call playful behavior. *Code weakening produces playfulness*, theatricality, simulation, mimetic activity, reflecting imaginative thinking of all sorts. In this way, symbols may again become iconic—the best example being what I think happens in art, literature, music.[16] The artist, the author, the musician, are agents of code weakening, in the sense that they inherit semiotic material that tends toward gaining symbolic strength, and they repersonalize this material by playfully recombining its components, until the result calls on principles "deeper" than knowledge, principles of human cognition as such, in order to make sense.

Weak coding or, dynamically put, *the weakening of codes* is, I believe, characteristic of all art (literature, painting, sculpture, architecture, etc.); so how does it work in music? The "strong code" of a musical expression would be the inventory of tonal (rhythmic, melodic) signals used in highly organized social situations: military trumpet signals, maritime horn signals, ceremonial bell signals, traffic honking and pedestrian-strip beeping, announcement jingles, telephone rings. The weakening of such signal codes is operated when signals become songs and extend into longer sequences that can inspire and coordinate interpersonal body movements (especially dancing, walking, running).[17] This operation of productive code weakening through extending and elaborating paradoxically entails increased formal complexity: technically it involves the cultural development of metric rhythms and tonal modes, melodic phrasing through tonal and modal variation over rhythms, and ultimately, polyphonic harmony and timbre. The weakening of tonal signals may have evolved into music; and music therefore may have to be just as symbolico-iconic as all other arts. They all *return*—reinstall—imagination in the space of meaning that social semiosis had filled with injunctions. When art itself becomes an educational injunction (code strengthening), it has to start all over again (code weakening), and of course this semiotic "dialectic" is its constant condition of instability.

The Other

> Schoenberg's music introduces us into a new realm, where musical experiences are not acoustical, but *purely spiritual.* This is where "Music of the Future" begins.
>
> WASSILY KANDINSKY, *On the Spiritual in Art*

The origin of semiosis in human evolution is hard to determine. Still, perceiving meaning that is only connected to the present by intentional signifiers is an ability we must have evolved as a species-characteristic sensitivity to *the mind of others*: there are other minds "out there," and they "intend" to address myself as a mind, just as I intend to show them what I "have in mind." This is, I think, what meaning means: other minds, other spaces. When minds meet, they "mean" to each other, and they are able to perceive what is "meant" by signifiers issued by others, in terms of contents of meaning spaces. To perceive an intending Other is to open a mental space behind the space of this perception—a space for the Other's mind, so to speak.

This peculiar, basic, semiotic double perception, perception in two spaces, one of which signifies the other, makes exchange of information possible and constitutes communication in the ordinary functional sense, when codes are strong and referential. But it generates what we sometimes like to call *emotional* communication, whenever codes becomes weaker and more iconic, and meaning therefore becomes partly or entirely generic, nonreferential, "imaginary."[18] This form of communication may be "emotional" or "affective" to the extent that it simply turns our attention to the content of the singular mind of the Other. We are rarely emotional without other persons involved. Here I am not only referring to basic emotions such as joy, fear, surprise, disgust, anger, shame, and so on but also to the feelings of *intensity*, elation, instant happiness and awe, shivering spines, piloerection, and the like, induced by experiences of beauty. I would suggest to subsume this affect under the anthropological concept of the sacred: *an instant state of presently felt sacredness.* The arts, and first of all music, have been associated with sacred rituals and religious practices since the dawn of humanity. In contemporary music, the religious reference in the framing is still predominant; the list of modern composers who were fervent religious believers is very long. Still, we are essentially talking about a form of semiosis, one that may generate "spirituality" as an experiential force inherent in the sharing of generic and emotional meaning. The "spirit" would cognitively be the unembodied "mind" of the shared meaning of this kind. When such meaning is shared by you and me, it is neither "mine" nor "yours," so it gets its own signature as the spirit "in" which we communicate.

There is in music, if I am right, a necessary connection between *spatial imagination and affective communication.* Attention focused on nonreferential, weakly coded expressions generates affective, interpersonal meaning effects; affect, in turn, can be related to world states, but in many different ways. We know that *desires* (volitive states of mind) contain an orientation to specific objects, acts or events; while *moods* refer to background qualities of experience such as lightness/darkness, color,[19] sound/silence, and vast/narrow scopes of time and space, and *emotions* are motivated by episodic narratives (offense → anger, loss → sorrow, danger→ fear, luck→ joy, etc.); and we know that *passions* (love/hatred) entail intense mental interest, concentration, obsessive awareness, linking the subjects to their targets, potentially for a lifetime. All these semantic aspects of affect presuppose spatial intuitions, whether the domain be natural, societal, or directly interpersonal. These intuitions, for a music listener, are *signed by the Other Mind, the "Spirit"*—not the composer or musician, but the state the composer or musician (the person by whom the music comes into being) was "in."[20]

What constitutes music (as distinct from space-inducing sounds in general) could in fact be this intentional reinforcement of an inherent semantic spatiality of auditive perception.[21] Beyond, or in front of or permeating, the material space of the musical performance, a second, immaterial, "spiritual" space emerges in the experience, giving rise to a "sacred" phenomenology, sometimes composed of shared experiences of supernatural presences and trancelike feelings of spatial alienation allowing our minds to encounter and address (at least sense the proximity of) divinities, ghosts, phantoms, dead people, magical forces, demons.

The effect of this spatial, transcendental alienation in social life is forceful, and its function is overwhelmingly important to all symbolic endeavors. Music "bathes" the celebrating community in fantasmatic nocturnal sunshine and so on,[22] and here is where social laws and principles, authority of all kinds, are constituted. Language—the great structural builder of immaterial (hypothetical, conditional, counterfactual, fictive) spaces of meaning—would not have had a chance without music (to constitute the spaces it fills).[23] When discourse now reports on spatial experiences of music, and typically on the basic, meteorological binding of our feelings to the weather—the elementary idea of time: (French) *le temps qu'il fait,* which has determined our lives and deaths over the millennia—it just gives back, so to speak, what it inherited from it in the first place: the culturally decisive human mental capacity to immediately transcend the immediate.

Postscriptum: Inverse Metaphor

Reconsider Rosenberg's "Schubert . . . let[s] the sun shine." As a simple conceptual metaphor in the critic's discourse, this expression does not work at all, since there is no intelligible mapping between notes and astrophysical objects. And yet it makes as much sense as the canonical reference to moonshine: chords, timbres, and melodic phrases somehow easily evoke beams of light. Here is a new way of analyzing this phenomenon: whereas in metaphor, the *signifying* imagery is presented as a *generic* content, mapped onto a *signified deictic* referent—as in "Achilles is a lion," where "lion" is generic and "Achilles" is deictically referred to—in the semantic structure of musical double-space experience, the *signifying* tonal event series is inversely given as the *deictic* percept, present here and now, and the inherently *signified* spatial content is given as its *generic* referent— namely, the light and darkness, meteorological visions of all kinds that the music evokes. To my knowledge, there is no name for this cognitive configuration, but it is known from rituals in magic and religion (which often call for musical accompaniment). Maybe we could dub it *inverse metaphor.* The weather reports would thus be the source and the tonal events their target; however, here we paradoxically access the source imagery through the target, not the target through the source. This configuration yields the "spiritual" character of music, since the acoustic act hereby opens the doors to the imaginary space of the spirits—which is what music invariably does.

Messiaen, Deleuze, and the Birds of Proclamation

Sander van Maas

The resurrection of mankind will be accompanied by the renewal
of the whole earth, including the birds, trees and flowers.

—OLIVIER MESSIAEN[1]

La structure d'origine du christianisme, c'est l'annonce de la fin.

—JEAN-LUC NANCY[2]

Messiaen and Ecomusicology

Olivier Messiaen is one composer of the twentieth century who has explored the connection between music and nature. The majority of his
works include references to the songs of birds, and many refer to inorganic
natural phenomena such as galaxies, high mountains, American canyons,
precious stones, and so on. Messiaen belongs to a generation of musicians
whose awareness of nature as a musical resource anticipated the rise of
the ecological composition practices in the 1970s.[3] In his long career as
a teacher at the Paris Conservatory Messiaen had witnessed the development of ecological approaches to composition. His own music, however,
was little affected by this emergent scene. Throughout his career Messiaen's musical inspiration remained religious. Even though he turned almost exclusively to birdsong in his works of the 1950s, his perspective on
nature remained markedly different from that of the ecological composers.
In Messiaen's music we are dealing with a remarkable mixture of scientific-
ornithological, naturalist-mimetic, and Christian-eschatological elements

which, as I intend to show, challenges the ways in which we address the natural references in this repertoire.

Messiaen's work on birdsong only received full scholarly attention from the mid-1990s onward. The recent publication of a monograph on Messiaen's *Oiseaux exotiques* by Peter Hill and Nigel Simeone is the apotheosis of this new development, which probably started with the pioneering work of Robert Fallon.[4] It is only now that Messiaen's bird works have received critical attention that we are able to engage in an informed debate about the religious aesthetics of this challenging music. To say it is challenging is to take a different tack from Messiaen's own students, some of whom, according to François-Bernard Mâche, found their teacher's interest in the songs of birds "a token of pious conformism rather than a bold exploration like those he was making in more technical fields like rhythm or modality."[5] I argue for the extraordinary religious-aesthetic position occupied by these works. Instead of being mere depictions of nature, Messiaen's bird works embody something unheard-of. Though originating from an act of mimetic transcription, they offer themselves as sonorous events reaching into a domain that few other composers have attempted to enter.

From the grand-scale birdsong-only piano cycle *Catalogue d'oiseaux* to the eighteen-part birdsong sequence featured by the orchestral *Chronochromie* Messiaen seems to have created, as he himself liked to say, music "for the angels" rather than for humans.[6] With Messiaen to speak of music means to engage with modes of time that open a certain futurity from within the nature he finds immanently present in the woods and canyons. In his work references to nature can only be fruitfully analyzed when ecomusicological approaches—which so far have focused precisely on natural immanence— are supplemented with an eschatological analysis.[7] This temporality will be complex in the sense that it stages a dramatic confrontation between, on one hand, nature as we know it and, on the other hand, the Christian logic of proclamation and the events "to come."[8] Speaking of the birdsong works requires not just an account of their relation to their natural models but also, and more importantly, an account of how these songs transfigure their natural embedding by changing its temporal modality. In Messiaen nature is read from the perspective of a radical future event which, as I suggest, should open our ears to the allegorical scene it creates. As I argue in my conclusion, this should also affect our account of the birdsong music and, by extension, Messiaen's work in general.

This ecomusicological debate takes as its starting point Gilles Deleuze's philosophical commentary of Messiaen. Deleuze is a philosopher whose work has been an important source of inspiration for ecocriticism in the arts.[9] He was acutely aware of Messiaen's musical and theoretical work and gave him a prominent place in his courses and texts on music. In turn, Ronald Bogue has elaborated on Deleuze's work, construing Messiaen's "rhizomusicosmological" innovations as instantiations of the Deleuzian concept of "the virtual" in the realm of music.[10] Arguably this line of interpretation of Messiaen has opened important new possibilities for the articulation of his aesthetic position. But it also underplays some of the key aspects of the temporal mode which make his "birds" enter their extraordinary domain. I focus this discussion on the philosophical and religious aspects of Messiaen's involvement with birdsong, leaving aside the ecomusicology of the birdsongs as songs which, as we shall see, has been taken on by others. First, however, I offer a few words on Messiaen's work on the birds.

Messiaen and the Style Oiseau

As Messiaen himself reported, he first developed an ear for birdsong as a child while staying with his aunt in the countryside of northeastern France. Later, his composition teacher Paul Dukas stimulated him to listen to the birds, the first traces of birdsong appearing in 1932 in the second movement of *L'Ascension* and even more prominently in *Quatuor pour la fin du temps* from 1940 ("Abîme des oiseaux").[11] Although birdsong remained in Messiaen's works and became ever more articulate (see the song cycle *Harawi*, organ cycles *Livre d'orgue* and *Messe de la Pentecôte*), it took another twelve years before Messiaen decided to temporarily shift his attention fully to birdsong. The first piece that evidences this new focus is *Le Merle noir*, a piece for flute and piano composed in late 1952. The flute part represents what remains the most naturalistic, realistic type of birdsong rendering in all of Messiaen's music. In the year after was composed *Réveil des oiseaux*, a piece for ensemble and solo piano populated by birds and based on the sequence of events from midnight until noon in the forest. Messiaen comments, "there's really nothing but bird songs . . . , without any added rhythm or counterpoint, and the birds singing are really found together in nature; it's a completely truthful work."[12] As Hill and Simeone show, however, on the basis of Messiaen's birdsong *cahiers*, these birds had not been found in a single forest; the work combines songs notated in the woods of Saint-Germain-en-Lay just west of Paris, in the garden of Messiaen's house in Paris, and in Gardépée in the Cognac, where lived Messiaen's great mentor, the ornithologist Jacques Delamain. The "truthfulness," then, largely pertains to there being relatively few interventions by the composer in the songs as he notated them *in situ* and few interventions in the chronology of their natural occurrence over the course of a day.

The next step in Messiaen's birdsong music was *Oiseaux exotiques*, a work in which the composer left behind the pretense of naturalism. Messiaen here brought together birds from all over the world which had never sung together before. The sources of these songs are revealing: Messiaen possessed a set of six recordings called *American Bird Songs* issued by Cornell University in 1942. Messiaen may have bought these when he visited Tanglewood in 1949 and used them as a source for half of the birds that appear in *Oiseaux exotiques*. Of the other birdsongs, the tropical ones were collected from—or inspired by—the birds in the *volière* of a certain Madame Billot, who lived near Paris and, secondly, by the birds heard at the Sixième Salon des Oiseaux in the same city in November 1955. As Hill and Simeone report,

> Messiaen's cahier is a spontaneous record of the birds as they were singing around him at the exhibition, with the long solos for the shama interspersed with interruptions from other birds. At one point Messiaen notes that the shama is imitating the Himalayan laughing thrush, identifiable in the score by the rocking ostinato figure, two bars after. Later, the shama imitates a nightingale: the result can be heard in the tremolos towards the end of this solo. These shama observations must have sparked Messiaen's interest in developing the motivic connection between different birds that is such a feature of *Oiseaux exotiques*.[13]

Because of the disparate sources of the birdsong, Messiaen seemed to feel less obliged to stick to mimetic "truthfulness" and allowed himself to use his free imagination and to *compose* "birdsong material."[14] The latter has in fact been a constant factor in his bird-style music since its early beginnings.

The birds in *Oiseaux exotiques* are very different from the "leisurely, even lethargic" and timid ones that appeared in the preceding *Réveil*. They have become dramatic, loud, agile, high profile, and above all colored. Messiaen brought harmony and (synaesthetic) color to prominence after a period of more abstract work and experimentation, not only to augment the aural profile of the birdsong but also to benefit from the colors of their plumage for additional highlighting.[15] Furthermore, the songs are here developed much more selectively, taking certain elements of the song phrases and leaving out others, thus creating more specialized material. Messiaen managed to bring a sense of "purpose and direction," whereas in *Réveil* long cadenzas and pauses occasionally make the music somewhat languid. The *style oiseau* of *Oiseaux exotiques* remained a signature element in Messiaen's later music, beginning with the two-hour piano work *Catalogue d'oiseaux* (1956–58) and continuing in the complex birdsong fields found in *Chronochromie*, *La Transfiguration*, and the "Sermon to the Birds" from *Saint François d'Assise*. Birdsong proved to be a versatile element for Messiaen. It could serve to highlight structural aspects of a composition, to provide free counterpoint in ways incomparable with other material, but it could also carry symbolic meanings, both through its recognizable structure and through its "character."[16] Messiaen used birdsongs as "attributes" of the characters in his opera *Saint François*.[17] In sum, then, Messiaen's bird style varies from the mimetic to the fantastic, from the realistic to the idealistic (and not merely the idealized), from the formalistic to the symbolic, and from the naturalistic to the artificial. In addition, the birds had affective and even emotional qualities for Messiaen.[18]

An Archeological Approach: François-Bernard Mâche

The work of François-Bernard Mâche, one of Messiaen's students, puts that of his mentor in context. Although Mâche was skeptical about Messiaen's obsession with birdsong early on, he soon followed in his teacher's footsteps. He relates, "Messiaen encouraged me to work at the Groupe de Recherches Musicales, which Schaeffer, after breaking up with Pierre Henry, had just founded with three or four young composers like Ferrari and me. When I manipulated rhythmic choirs of amphibians, for example in 1958 in my piece *Prélude*, which Messiaen highly appreciated, it was both a way of following his advice and staving off his example."[19] Although Mâche was influenced by Messiaen, a remarkable difference exists in the way each used the material they had gathered. While Messiaen sat in front of his loudspeakers to transcribe the songs he had collected, Mâche treated the actual recordings as sound material for his *musique concrète*.[20]

Mâche's approach is considerably different from both Messiaen's and James Fassett's in that it engages in a sustained conversation with biological and bioacoustical approaches of birdsong and animal sounds in general. He is widely known as the author who introduced, in the final chapter of his 1983 *Musique, mythe, nature, ou les dauphins d'Arion*, the notion of zoomusicology for the study of music in nonhuman species.[21] His more recent writings pursue the notion of "music in the singular," that is, music seen under the aegis of cross-cultural and cross-species constants, such as refrains, variations, repetitions, strophes, and polyphonies.[22] Mâche is not alone in this pursuit. Primatologist Frans de Waal, for instance, has long argued that many species demonstrate behavior that suggests that we should apply the concept of culture, and even the notion of art, to certain aspects of animal life.[23] Mâche points out in a statement typical for the ecological approach to composing, "The poetic I would like to outline is based on a monistic postulate affirming, in a double way, the unity of the universe: as an external *sonosphere* where noises and musics are crossing, getting interchanged and hybridized without stopping at cultural customs barriers—and, sometimes, not even on the limit of species, and as a unique internal and flexible legislation governing obliquely all sonorous signals, at least those of living beings."[24]

The biological concept of species is evoked here but not further elaborated. Yet it is clear that Mâche's approach welcomes the idea of "convergent evolution" between, for instance, humans and birds as regards their common use of certain sound forms.[25] This is markedly different from Messiaen's approach because it implies a common bionatural history, an evolutionary scheme that holds the species together in their use of sound.[26] Whereas Messiaen merely introduced himself as a "composer and ornithologist," Mâche draws the cultural consequences from the current developments in the natural sciences. This is not to say that he merely applies science to music. On the contrary, his "sonorous naturalism" ultimately relies on a fabulation of origins much in the way his friend and colleague Iannis Xenakis fabulated archaic scenes. Mâche practices an *archeology* in sound, integrating ancient cultures, distant languages, swarms of flies, miraculous glissandi, as they have been, or *could* have been, found on the face of the earth.[27] In this archeology the Darwinian notion of a community of living beings resonates with the ancient myths in which humans and animals share the same language, the same music, and sometimes even the same body.

In the following I develop the motif of time that resounds in Mâche's archeology. In Messiaen, too, the presence of birdsong is related to temporal modes. This fact is most evident in his use of birdsong as a resource for rhythmic innovation, both in terms of individual rhythms and, for instance, through the creation of textures with temporal implications. However, above and beyond this use of birdsong as compositional material there is the grander movement of time implicated in the symbolism of the birds. As Messiaen made abundantly clear in his multivolume *Traité de rythme*, his interest in things temporal extended well into the eternal. This extension not only plays on the level of symbolism—the birds being tokens of the Resurrection; they also play an active role in the structuring of the music on a conceptual and affective level. In order to access, and to account for, the temporal dimension of the birdsong on this level it will be necessary first to discuss the Deleuzian appraisal of Messiaen's work.

Deleuzian Messiaen: Birds without Organs

There has been a trend—a "minoritarian" one, to be sure—in the literature on Messiaen to use references by Gilles Deleuze to this composer as a starting point for an ecocritical appraisal of his music. This trend harks back to Deleuze and Guattari's remarks in *A Thousand Plateaus* and even earlier to Deleuze's comments during gatherings such as those at Vincennes in May 1977 and at Ircam in 1978.[28] At Vincennes and Ircam, Deleuze referred to Messiaen chiefly because the composer had dealt with time and with birds. Deleuze had clearly read key texts on and by the composer and, there as well as in *A Thousand Plateaus*,[29] often refers to these without mentioning Messiaen's name. I discuss two zones of contact between the two oeuvres.

Regarding birdsong in Messiaen, Deleuze is remarkably more reserved than later interpretations of the philosopher's work on music suggest. At first sight Deleuze's comments on music would not even allow Messiaen's bird works to be called music in the first place. If, according to Deleuze, music can be defined as "a creative, active operation that consists in deterritorializing the refrain," these works have two features that situate them outside the realm of music as Deleuze sees it.[30] First, in his 1977 Vincennes course Deleuze calls Messiaen's use of birdsong a form of collage: Messiaen has "pasted" (*plaqué*) the birdsongs into his works. The collage, Deleuze explains, does not yet entail deterritorialization, which only comes into play when elements become part of a "block of becoming."[31] Such a block of becoming—"transversals that continually escape from the coordinates or punctual systems functioning as musical codes at a given moment"[32]— are exemplified, for example, by Luciano Berio's loose citations of folk material in *Folk Songs* (1964).

The second point is no less surprising. According to Deleuze, the most condensed form of striated time, the refrain (*ritournelle*), is in fact *counter-musical*. He defines the refrain as "sonorous territorialization as opposed to music as such, which is process, the process of deterritorialization."[33] As he later writes in *A Thousand Plateaus*, "The refrain is . . . a means of preventing music, warding it off, or forgoing it. But music exists because the refrain exists also, because music takes up the refrain, . . . it forms a block with it in order to take it somewhere else."[34] Hence, insofar as birdsong quotations might be considered to function as a type of refrain, one is initially led to conclude that Deleuze could not and did not regard Messiaen's bird works as music. However, he also suggests that "all music is pervaded by bird songs, in a thousand different ways, from Janequin to Messiaen."[35] This "bird song," it seems, inhabits music in a way distinctly different from the mere quotation of birds' pitches and rhythms. One should not, in other words, generalize the idea that, as Messiaen often had it, birds were the first musicians on the planet and still offer the best example for human composers. By being, in a complex sense, nonmusical or countermusical Messiaen's bird works position themselves at the outer edges of music rather than at its center, a suggestion that I discuss at greater length later.

The ultimate figure for the infinite movement of re- and deterritorialization is Deleuze's notion of the "Cosmos refrain," that is, the cosmos regarded as "a little ditty."[36] This cosmic motif constitutes the second zone of contact between Deleuze and Messiaen.[37] In Deleuze's classification of refrains he speaks of "molecularized refrains (the sea and the wind) tied to cosmic forces, the Cosmos refrain. For the Cosmos itself is a refrain."[38] The movement of the first type of refrain, the "territorial or assemblage refrain," to this second, "Cosmos" type is effectuated by the machine (of sound), which opens the assemblage onto the interassemblage, for example, "in the case of birds that adopt alien songs."[39] The superb lyrebird, used years later by Messiaen in the orchestral work *Éclairs sur l'Au-delà . . .*, would have been fine example of this.

Next, according to Deleuze, these interassemblages may be opened up by the molecular, which decomposes whatever is left of sonorous *forms* (e.g., the little ditties in Proust and Nietzsche) into material and into planes of consistency, whose task it is to harness forces. Here we enter the realm of the Smooth, of "the continuous variation, the continuous development."[40] The metaphysical relation between matter and form is to give way to the relation between material and force. As Deleuze and Guattari suggest, "There is no longer a matter that finds its corresponding principle of intelligibility in form. It is now a question of elaborating a material charged with harnessing forces of a different order," that is, the forces of the Cosmos.[41] Deleuze warns that "all this may sound extremely general, and somewhat Hegelian, testifying to an absolute Spirit. Yet it is, should be, a question of technique, exclusively a question of technique."[42] This emphasis on technique, which reveals Pierre Boulez's influence on Deleuze, is a key to understanding Messiaen's dealing with nature as a musical-eschatological resource.

Returning to Messiaen, the question remains to what extent his music partakes of the Cosmic refrain. Deleuze mentions Messiaen as an example to illustrate his thesis on smooth time-space, which runs as follows: "The molecular has the capacity to make the *elementary* communicate with the *cosmic:* precisely it effects a dissolution of form that connects the most diverse longitudes and latitudes, the most varied speeds and slownesses, which guarantees a continuum by stretching variation far beyond its formal limits."[43] Messiaen is then referred to because of what later became the leading ideas of the first volume of his *Traité de rythme*: time is multiple; the macroscopic time of the stars coexists with the microscopic time of the insects; these and all the intermediary times are an expression of "Rhythm."[44] Deleuze translates this into his own language, saying that the elementary and the cosmic "combine to form a block, a universe fiber, a diagonal or complex space. Music dispatches molecular flows."[45] He then continues, "of course, as Messiaen says, music is not the privilege of human beings: the universe, the cosmos, is made of refrains; the question in music is that of a power of deterritorialization permeating nature, animals, the elements, and deserts as much as human beings."[46]

These remarks have inspired a Deleuzian line of interpretation of Messiaen in which Deleuze's vision of the musically Smooth is used to understand how extremely disparate phenomena might still be related through a plane that knows no discontinuities, gaps, or aporias. Ronald Bogue, who has written extensively on Deleuze and the arts, may be quoted as an example of this tendency to view Messiaen from the perspective of the continuous. In his interpretation, Bogue introduces Deleuze's conceptual distinction between "the virtual" and "the actual" in order to claim that the birdsong music not only involves deterritorialization but also partakes in the capturing of forces typical of the virtual. "The virtual," Bogue explains, "may be conceived of loosely as a field of vectors or potential development and metamorphosis, each vector a line of continuous variation along which an actual process of development and metamorphosis might unfold."[47] Regarding this distinction in Messiaen, he writes,

> In one sense . . . Messiaen's compositions are directly connected to the actual material world, in that he generates thematic material through a deterritorialisation of actual birdsong refrains. But in another sense, his compositions partake of a different realm—the virtual—rendering sonorous the non-sonorous forces immanent within the real. In this regard, his compositions may be seen as sonic bodies without organs, palpable planes of consistency that render perceptible what usually escapes perception—the speeds, affects, and floating time of the virtual.[48]

Before discussing the construal of the Smooth and the virtual in Messiaen it is necessary to shed some light on the way in which Messiaen transformed the birdsong material supplied by nature and to consider in what sense his work can be perceived as continuous with these natural sources.

Beyond Mimesis: Recording, Notation, Technics

As has often been noted in Messiaen studies, the birdsongs found in his music are never simply mimetic.[49] Although Messiaen took pride in being the first composer to have taken the transcription of birdsong to an almost scientific level of accuracy, it is clear that he never intended to subsume his creative powers to the stringencies of representation in a mimetic sense. As noted earlier, the birdsongs he presented in his works are not entirely birdsongs; they are, as will become apparent, both less than birdsongs and more. If, on a more philosophical level, it must be maintained that every act of mimesis is productive rather than simply reproductive, it should be asked what kind of nature Messiaen's birdsong renderings create before any assessment is made of its mimetic qualities.[50] The element of surplus appears under two guises, each of which I briefly comment on.

The first aspect of the manner in which Messiaen moves beyond mimesis, I refer to as the *alter-natural*. It involves a transfiguration of the natural through a process of negation. In Messiaen the power of the negative is apparent in his predilection for unmediated transitions, as in the montages of *Couleurs de la Cité Céleste* and the collages of the *Catalogue d'oiseaux*.[51] Such stark juxtapositions are not only present in the forms Messiaen uses but also in his bird-style poetics. As we have seen, Messiaen's fully developed bird style involves selection, ellipsis, and condensation. For instance, it deletes the long silences usually found in birdsongs heard in their natural environment; it brings together types of birds from distant regions and sourced from a variety of media (recordings, notations, viewings, other bird musics). Hill and Simeone highlight some aspects of this process in their discussion of Messiaen's wood thrush rendering.[52] Messiaen found this song on the *American Bird Songs* recordings and started out transcribing what he heard. In subsequent revisions of his transcription he can be seen to vary his approach dramatically, singling out some melodic features and downplaying others, sharpening the register contrasts, adding dynamic markings, changing the phrasing and rhythmic flow. In the final version used for *Oiseaux exotiques* the song of the wood thrush is carved out in granite gestures, interspersed with fermatas and *laisser vibrer*, with performance indications that prescribe an "*éclatant, ensoleillé*" (bright, sunlit) overall character.

Messiaen used such condensations, stylizations, dramatizations, and colorings not to re-create nature as he may have encountered it in the woods but to create a surplus: an "denatured" nature, as Rousseau would have it.[53] This "nature" is now a *hyper*nature (in its exaggeration and dramatization of "found" properties), now a *sub*nature (for instance in its disregard for other such properties, including microtones, sliding tones, extraordinary speed, extreme changes of register, particular patterns of variation, and so on).[54] As Richard Steinitz writes, in "Cedar Breaks" from *Des canyons aux étoiles* . . . "birdsong is metamorphosed into an abstract power, primeval, hallucinatory and cataclysmic: witness the monumental treatment accorded the red-shifted flicker and the blue grouse in the opening *tutti*. In such passages Messiaen's music becomes less harmonic than sculpted, hewn from elemental sonic matter like the music of Varèse."[55] Hence, the result is a sonorous texture that is musically appealing, full of beautiful gestures and gripping tensions, which arguably refer to natural phenomena but which ultimately point in a very different direction. This sonorous world is, one might say, too denatured to be natural and not enough musicalized to count as music.

Incidentally, the alter-natural is not an element that is exclusive for Messiaen's dealing with things natural. It belongs to a wider culture of animal keeping, breeding, and hence representation which involves similar processes of denaturing and has led to a great variety of practices in which animals appear under the aegis of a certain artificiality and technicity. The birds heard by Messiaen at the Paris exhibition belong to this practice of transposing animals to the realm of technics: they tell the story of the breeding, keeping, improvement, medicalization, trade, exhibition, and exploitation of animals.[56] Messiaen's ornithology (i.e., his musical keeping, molding, exhibiting of birds) is ultimately an example of a form of technicity that is less concerned with the coordinates of the real in the natural sense than with the Real in the *alter*-natural sense. It pushes nature beyond itself, unwittingly regressing to mythological animal figures (such as harpies), invoking the Surreal experience of the animal or extreme forms of breeding and transgenetics. To paraphrase Deleuze's Boulezian statement quoted earlier, Messiaen's nature is a question of technique, if technique is understood in the Greek sense of *technè*. The art and technics of music enable him to move beyond mimesis and to open a realm in which the aural imagination is free to project natures beyond nature as we know it.[57]

Announcement: Opening the Open

If Messiaen engages in the play of mimesis only by moving beyond it, the question remains what is won by means of this strategy. What kind of economy is involved in this sacrificing of nature? The answer to this question leads back to the issue of temporality. In the work of Mâche the extension of the concept of music toward the kingdom of animals is construed in terms of the past. His archeology in sound seeks to situate human music-making within a historical perspective that operates under naturalistic and scientific concepts of nature. Human music is thus treated as an aspect of a broader category of music that includes the sonic and aural activities of other species. In Messiaen's mind there is no such continuity. Although humankind shares the totality of Creation with the birds, trees and flowers, there remains the fact of the divine hierarchy of created beings. Messiaen generously places the birds above humankind as supreme musical artists and as images of the Resurrected, but they are not allowed to leave their assigned ontological place. No doubt this is a consequence of his theological view of Creation: Messiaen never engaged in ecological debates in theology. As regards the ontological place of animals in Creation he subscribed to the anthropocentric theological tradition.[58]

In the musical works themselves, however, this hierarchy is less stable and permanent than it appears. The lack of historical depth in Messiaen's dealing with nature is balanced by an extreme sense of futurity that permeates all of his work. From his earliest compositions Messiaen addressed the events to come at the End of Time, both on the scale of the universe and on the individual scale, after each individual death. Work titles such as *Les Corps glorieux* (The Glorious Bodies, for organ), *Quatuor pour la fin du temps* (Quartet for the End of Time), and *Des canyons aux étoiles . . .* (From the Canyons to the Stars . . . , the points referring to the beyond of the stars) underscore the idea that, for Messiaen, the present world (both the human world and the natural world) have always already been directed at and oriented by their ultimate renewal in and through Christ. What this renewal will comprise is something none of the faithful knows with any certainty. However, Messiaen was greatly inspired by glimpses of the beyond offered by the Revelation of John and by theological expositions about life after death. These and other sources helped him to create a personal view of things to come, occasionally assisted by his religious imagination. For instance, he imagined himself as a glorious body flying effortlessly from galaxy to galaxy after his death.[59] Yet, as I intend to show, in his music such concrete anticipations are less important than the tendency to suspend all determinations. Rather than pinning down in his music a vision of life after death, or after the End of Time, Messiaen loosens the nuts and bolts of the perceptual world, beginning with its temporal structure.

In earlier birdsong works the temporal unfolding of the sonorous landscape is more or less respected. Messiaen attempted to describe musically the integral experience of birds singing in their natural habitat in an apparently undirected temporal flow. In *Réveil* Messiaen tries to accommodate this lack of direction within his musical language. The solution he experimented with, and which he reused in *Catalogue d'oiseaux*, was to put the songs in a narrative framework. They would tell the story of how nature awakes in the early morning and progresses through various times of the night and day.[60] While this articulated the ebb and flow of the piece, it did not yet provide a sense of direction. The temporality still remained close, too close for Messiaen's purposes, to the world of animals and plants. His preferred poet, Rilke, described this world in terms of "the Open." As Rilke wrote in one of his letters, explaining this notion to a Russian reader of his *Elegies*, "You must grasp the concept of the 'open' that I attempted to put forward in this elegy in such a way that the animal's degree of consciousness place it into the world but without the animal placing itself each moment athwart [*gegenüber*] the world (as we are)."[61] "The Open" refers to the ontological openness of nature. However, it does not engage with the awareness of the things to come, the eschatological perspective. This is why Francis of Assisi, in Messiaen's opera, needed to sermon to the birds.[62] Their "poverty in spirit" puts these creatures of the Open in an advantageous position, but they need to be enlightened by the knowledge of the promises made God, by the message of the good news, that is, by the announcement of a new world.

Rather than communicating the contents of this message, Messiaen's birdsongs present the gesture of its announcement as such. In *Dis-Enclosure: The Deconstruction of Christianity* Jean-Luc Nancy offers a description of Christian temporality that can be used to understand the power of Messiaen's music to inspire beyond the doctrinal core of his faith. "Christianity," Nancy writes, "is not proclamation [*annonce*] as a predisposition in one way or another of [*sic*] the end; in it, the end itself is operative in the proclamation and as proclamation, because the end that is proclaimed is always an *infinite end*. This is what truly makes up Christianity, what constitutes, as the theologians say, the 'kerygma' of Christianity, that is, the essence, the schema of what is proclaimed, the schema of the proclamation."[63] The schema of the proclamation, that is, the very temporality of the announcement, is what Messiaen adds to his birdsong transcriptions. The Open of the birds is, as it were, opened by this schema.

The example of the wood thrush illustrates how this is accomplished. By emphasizing the singular, Gestalt-like character of each musical gesture in the song phrases, Messiaen manages to evoke a sense of limitation, of finitude.[64] This finitude is then allowed to produce its own afterlife by means of the piano's sustained pedal and the long resonance that fills the fermatas. Messiaen's complex color chords and the consistent use of terraced dynamics in the loud range add aural luminosity to this process. Through this process Messiaen introduces a tone of grandeur, a feeling of the sublime, of infinity extending beyond the finite signals. Messiaen's birds, indeed his oeuvre as a whole, is constituted by this reiterated gesture toward, and production of, a "to-come." It is an openness that is introduced to answer, to open up, as it were, "the Open" of natural life.

Animating Allegories

The temporal aspects of Messiaen's work cannot easily be incorporated into Ronald Bogue's Deleuzian interpretation of Messiaen in terms of the virtual. In Bogue's comments on Messiaen's innovative rhythmic procedures he is right to refer to the *valeur ajoutée*, or added value, as one of the techniques used by Messiaen to unlock a temporal mode which differs from that of metrical time. The *valeur ajoutée*, which consists in the minimal extension of the shortest value of a rhythm, gives regular rhythmic patterns a surprising plasticity and sense of flux while retaining the reference to metricality. For Bogue, this fluid, ametrical time, if taken in its pure manifestation, can be understood as the elusive fluctuating time of Becoming that Deleuze and Guattari describe. It is the time of the event which, according to them, has "neither beginning nor end, neither origin nor destination—it is always in the middle."[65]

Combining this reading of time with an appreciation of Messiaen's work on birdsong, Bogue then contends that in *Catalogue d'oiseaux* "each piece ultimately creates a specific atmospheric configuration of interpenetrating elements [landscape motifs, birdsongs] in flux." As multiplicities these configurations are expressed in the temporality of the event, in the "this-ness" (*haecceity*) of pure duration, which, in turn, gives the bird works their wondrous sense of eternity. The logic of the virtual, mentioned earlier, is thus intimately connected with a notion of time based on a continuous relation between, and interpenetration of, the past, the present, and the future, which Deleuze refers to as duration.

Furthermore, duration, however continuous its structure may be, is never completely given and remains fundamentally open. As Constantin Boundas argues, Deleuze's ontology of the virtual can only be understood as an inversion of Platonism.[66] Whereas recollection in Plato enabled the authentication of the Idea in the world of (its) shadows, in Deleuze the eternal return, that is, the memory of the future, "dispels the illusion of the One and severs the relation between the will to power and its self-identical preservation for the sake of all possible worlds."[67] The eternal return expresses the ultimate triumph of difference over the Platonic logic of the same.

But what would these "possible worlds" be in Messiaen? How unconditional is this openness once it is oriented toward the coming of worlds? Messiaen defined religion as "the relationship with the extraordinary Spirit which is outside everything, which is wholly other."[68] The motif of the wholly other determines the balance between the "futures" found in, or opened by, the various readings of his work. It is clear from his writings that he argued for a breakthrough (*percée*) toward the beyond of time rather than for a Deleuzian, immanent breakaway (*échappée*, lines of flight).[69] The play with lines of flight, which must be acknowledged as being an important element in the aesthetics of many of Messiaen's works (in particular from his wartime works onward), must be placed against the radical transformation "to-come" of the present world of nature, culture, and human life. The works are structured in order to speak from this present world while articulating this world's finitude and evoking an otherness from it beyond its current horizon. This articulation is informed by a poetics of discontinuity, by absences that will probably remain forever beyond the mending powers of an immanent reading of these works.[70] In Messiaen, the announcement of the end is infinite and allows for infinite reiteration.

An example of this infinitization of the End is produced by the so-called bird *tuttis*. These are sonorous textures—fields—which are (almost) entirely composed of birdsongs, played simultaneously by multiple players. The most striking example is the sixth movement of the orchestral *Chronochromie*, entitled "Épôde."[71] This movement features an uninterrupted tangle of eighteen solo strings that abstractly resembles its model, the bird *tuttis* that can be heard in the forest at dawn. More than mimetic, the texture of such movements produces a great sense of vitality—a confused vitality. The confusion is not only due to the tangle of individual voices; it is also due to the instable meaning of the vitality itself. As Lawrence Kramer notes, vitality, understood as the feeling of animation that music may produce in its listeners, is one of the most common yet mysterious aspects of music.[72] The sense of animation is usually interpreted in anthro-pocentric terms as the proximity of music to, and power over, the human soul. Although Messiaen's bird textures exert the same power, they inter-rupt this music-human intimacy by displacing it to the realm of animals. They transfer the feeling of animation to the birds as though it were their vitality. Listening to the birds as they engage in their cacophony, one is invited to recognize oneself in the songs and vital energy of birds. It is the birds that now possesses, and to a certain extent control, the soul's sonic mirror. Furthermore, the textures—by directing the human soul to its ultimate destination, uplifting it as they do from its current life toward an experience of life in its pure state, the Life of the living—doubly dispossess the listener of the felt animation.

Whereas the presence of birdsongs invokes a concept of nonhuman life in a musical context that mostly lacks human presence, the implication of their raw vitality for the (human) listener remains enigmatic. For Mes-siaen, the birds carried a number of symbolic meanings, ranging from the naturalistic representation of nature to the divine act of creation and, on the level of the human individual, a promise of ultimate freedom. They embodied, for him, the four aspects of the glorious human bodies of the Resurrected: power, agility, joy, and luminosity.[73] By contrast, on the musi-cal level we find series and textures, finite melodic gestures and resonance spaces that open up infinite announcement. On the level of animation we find a movement of multiple dispossessions in which the intensification of life is carried beyond the one who listens and feels. Rather than coming to rest, as Messiaen intends, in religious symbols or metaphors, or indeed in a set of purely musical gestures, these movements create deflected, al-legorical meanings.[74] For what does this raised vitality, this surplus of life in the face of the infinite End ultimately mean? Does it ever come to rest in a vision of life after death? It arguably does not. The force of Messiaen's sonorous allegories, speaking as they do *differently* (literally *allegorein*), will leave the listener with a mixed sense of joy and impossibility. For listening to the birds in Messiaen's works is like being asked to perform an impos-sible task: to decide whether this is life actually—or something wholly other, to-come.

Here, finally, we encounter a challenge that may not be an exclusive feature of Messiaen's work or of his explicitly religious aesthetics. I have argued that in speaking of Messiaen's music we cannot dispense with the specific temporality which it presupposes, at least not without losing a sense of the radical nature of its proclaiming. Its mode of proclaiming ties in with the more general problematic of apocalyptic utterances. Having been written in the tradition of the Apocalypse of John, the music of Messiaen addresses its listener in a mode that is both ineluctable and puzzling. *There shall be (no) . . .*[75] Derrida comments on the structure of apocalyptic phrases, saying that if the tense of such phrases is clearly future, "nothing in what comes before or after the sentence allows one to decide whether the grammar of this future is that of a description or of a prescription."[76] In our response to such utterances, then, the evaluation of their religious content is less important than to philosophically analyze their modalities and to document their performative effects. In musicology the latter would take the form of an account of the rhythm of their occurrences and the textures created by their echoes and precursive doubles. This account would ultimately need to allow itself to be affected by the temporal mode of the music it attempts to respond to.

Put differently, it should be proclaimed that, in musicology, of (the) music shall be spoken.

Parole, parole:
Tautegory and the Musicology
of the (Pop) Song

Peter Szendy

Chanson,
Toi qui ne veux rien dire,
Toi qui me parles d'elle
Et toi qui me dis tout.
Ô, toi . . . ,
Toi qui me parles d'elle,
D'elle qui te chantait

—"india song"

You might know this song. You might know it in its instrumental version, without words, as it haunts Marguerite Duras's film *India Song*, released in 1975. The film was adapted by Duras herself, from her stage play of the same name written in 1972. In her stage directions at the beginning of the play, Duras wrote,

> A tune from between the two wars, *India Song*, is played slowly on the piano. It is played right through, to cover the time—always long—that it takes the audience, or the reader, to emerge from the ordinary world they are in when the performance, or the book, begins. *India Song* still. Still. And now it ends. Now it is repeated.[1]

This song from between the two wars is really a song from between two worlds: the ordinary world and the world of dreams, fictions, or plays. It is repeated throughout the film, and it accompanies the images of the strange and uncanny love story that *India Song* is.

You might know this song. You might know it even if you have never heard it. For in its *betweenworldliness*, if I may, it seems to have always already haunted all the songs that we know or do not know.

The music was composed by Carlos d'Alessio, a little-known French musician born in Buenos Aires in 1935. But indeed, as Duras herself wrote in the liner notes of the soundtrack, the origins of the composer are of as little importance as the origins of the song itself: "To tell the truth, I do not really know where he comes from, Carlos d'Alessio, they say from the country of Argentina, but when I heard his music for the first time, I saw that it came from the country of everywhere."[2] After the release of the film that made the song famous, it was sung and recorded by Jeanne Moreau, with words especially written for her by Duras. Many other artists have given their own renditions of this haunting bluesy melody, now adorned with lyrics—among them Carla Bley (on *Coup de tête*, the album produced by Kip Hanrahan in 1981) and Murray Head (on his *Rien n'est écrit*, in 2008).

What do these words say? In their ambiguous simplicity, they are quite difficult to translate accurately. But let us try, word by word, inelegantly, lending an attentive ear to the pronouns as they shift between the personifying apostrophe to the song itself and the imaginary character being evoked by it:

> Song (*Chanson*),
> You who do not mean anything (*Toi qui ne veux rien dire*, you who do not
>   want to say anything),
> You who tell me about her (*Toi qui me parles d'elle*)
> And you who tell me everything (*Et toi qui me dis tout*).
> O you, . . .
> You who tell me about her,
> About her who was singing you (*D'elle qui te chantait*)

I cannot render in English the unfathomable play between the two feminine pronouns in French: "you" stands for "toi," the song as it is being apostrophized; and "her" or "she" stands for "elle," the ghostly character from the past that the song seems to evoke. But in French, "elle" could also designate the song itself, for "chanson" is a feminine noun. To account for this internal ambiguity, I could propose the following nontranslation, an ugly and unpolished gloss, indeed, but accurately polysemous: "O chanson—the words would now say—you who tell me about her, she who stands for you, for you under the guise of another, the other that you, the song, have to evoke in order to be able to sing yourself."

Not intending to mean anything but telling everything, the song: this song, from nowhere and from everywhere that *India Song* is, utters itself. It sings itself, it says and tells itself, it means itself.

The figure of speech that my unrefined gloss excavated from the apparent banality of these words closely resembles what Coleridge, Schelling, and Jean-Luc Nancy after them have called the *tautegory* of the myth.[3] Whereas "allegory" (from Greek *allos*, "other," and *agoreuein*, "to speak publicly") refers to some hidden meaning, to another sense, tautegory (from Greek *tautos*, "same") is self-meaning or self-utterance, as Nancy recalls in *The Inoperative Community*:

> As Schelling put it, myth is *"tautegorical"* (borrowing the word from
> Coleridge) and not "allegorical": that is, it says nothing other than
> itself. . . . Myth becomes (wants to become, through the will to its own
> power) its own enunciation, its own *tautegory*, equivalent to its truth
> and its own realization. . . . This is what Schelling demands with his
> "tautegory." Myth signifies itself, and thereby converts its own fiction
> into foundation or into the inauguration of *meaning* itself.[4]

Nancy also briefly enlists Nietzsche in his deconstructive genealogy of mythical or mythological thought.[5] But we should go somewhat further than he does into Nietzsche's view of the myth, namely, into the text of *The Birth of Tragedy*. For it is there that we find the mythical articulation between *melos* and *logos*, between music and words, that accounts for the tautegory of song, of popular song in particular:

> But above all else we regard folk song [*Volkslied*] as a musical mir-
> ror of the world [*als musikalischer Weltspiegel*], as original melody
> [*als ursprüngliche Melodie*] which then *seeks for itself* a parallel dream-
> appearance, and expresses this in poetry [*die sich jetzt eine parallele
> Traumerscheinung sucht und diese in der Dichtung ausspricht*].[6]

Music, then, or the popular melody—I am even tempted to say the pop song—searches for its own dreamlike phenomenon in words. In other words, it seeks words, other words again and again in order to appear to itself, tautegorically. For Nietzsche continues:

> Thus *melody is the primary and general element* which can therefore
> undergo several objectifications in several texts. . . . Melody gives birth
> to poetry [*die Melodie gebiert die Dichtung aus sich*], and does so over and
> over again, in ever new ways [*und zwar immer wieder von Neuem*]; this
> is what the *strophic form of the folk song* is trying to tell us [*nichts An-
> deres will uns* die Strophenform des Volksliedes *sagen*], a phenomenon
> which always astonished me until I eventually found this explanation.
> Anyone . . . with this theory in mind will find countless examples of
> how the melody, as it gives birth again and again, emanates sparks of

imagery [*wie die fortwährend gebärende Melodie Bilderfunken um sich aussprüht*].[7]

So what do the verses of the pop song try or want to tell us? Apostrophizing their strophic structure, we could say, letting Duras translate Nietzsche into lyrics: *toi qui ne veux rien dire*, you who do not want to say anything except yourself, *toi qui me dis tout*, you who tell me every word that you can give birth to, you speak of the music you are.

But we could also rename the tautegory through which the pop song speaks about itself and sparklingly interprets itself (with its "sparks of imagery," *Bilderfunken*). We could designate it, quite simply, as *the musicology of the song*. Yes, *of* the song, in the double sense of an objective and subjective genitive. For the song, as Nietzsche and Duras suggest, is both the object and the subject of its own musicology.

Musicology—which we could define in a very economical way as the practice of *speaking of music*—then, does not come after the fact, in the more or less scholarly belatedness of a *logos* (discourse, speech, or reason) that would tell and establish what the music was or what it meant. If there is something like musicology, it will have begun from within the music: in the gap that opens between the music and its quest for itself *as* music.

We should recall, at this point, Carl Dahlhaus's position, while radicalizing it. In his admirable work on the genealogy of absolute music (that is to say, pure music without words, music severed from language or *logos*), he wrote,

> Literature about music is no mere reflection of what happens in the musical practice of composition, interpretation, and reception, but rather belongs, in a certain sense, to the constituent forces of music itself. For insofar as music does not exhaust itself in the acoustical substrate that underlies it, but only takes shape through categorical ordering of what has been perceived, a change in the system of categories of reception immediately affects the substance of the thing itself.[8]

Literature about music—musicology, musicography, or musical ekphrasis in the widest sense—is constitutive not only of its reception but also, if we agree to trust provisionally such a distinction, of its production. For there is no music that produces itself as such, that appears as such without diverging from itself, without letting a gap open at its heart. An *in-between* in which music, so to speak, speaks about itself, in which words, more and more words, resonate.

I have analyzed elsewhere many examples, many hits and successes that exemplify the tautegorical or (self-)musicological structure of songs:

Prince's "Musicology" (with its portable or pocketable history of music, from James Brown to Public Enemy); Serge Gainsbourg's "Je suis venu te dire que je m'en vais" ("I came to tell you that I am leaving," says the song, describing its own mnemonic comings and goings); Irene Cara's "Fame" (a big hit that tells of its own quest for survival in eternity). Since we have no time to evoke them all, I would like to recall just one of them: "Parole, parole, parole" (Words, words, words), sung by the wonderful Italian singer Mina, in 1972.⁹

"Words, words, words": this banal little phrase, which has become one of the most often sung refrains in the world, this triple and trivial repetition of the word "word" (*parola*) could become a motto or a slogan as important as the one musicians and musicologists have borrowed from Salieri's opera *Prima la musica e poi le parole*.¹⁰

Salieri's *divertimento teatrale* stages a composer (*maestro di cappella*) and a poet as they argue during the preparation of an opera. I cannot resist the temptation to quote their dialogue at the beginning of the show:

> POET.—You think, then, that we can have words and music in four days? MAESTRO.—As for the music, don't worry, it's ready; and you only need to adapt the words to it. POET.—But that would be like making the garment first, and then the man who fits it. MAESTRO.—You poets are mad. My friend, believe me, who do you think is going to pay attention to your words? Music, music is what we need today. POET.—But the music still has to express feelings, aptly or badly. MAESTRO.—My music has the excellent quality of being adaptable to anything.¹¹

In the end, the distance between "Parole, parole, parole" and *Prima la musica e poi le parole* is not so great: both statements insist that words have no importance at all, that only the song, only the music matters.

But, in order to be complete, the generative grammar of the possible relations between music and language should also include the reverse proposition. Historically, it can be attributed to Monteverdi, with the birth of the operatic genre. When the canon of Bologna, Giovanni Maria Artusi, defended the established values of polyphony, criticizing the confusion of voices in Monteverdi's works, the latter published a reply, written by his brother, in his *Fifth Book* of madrigals (1605), explaining his intentions as follows: "to render the discourse master of the harmony and not slave" (*far che l'oratione sia padrona del armonia e non serva*).

So here we are confronting three statements: 1. *Parole, parole, parole;* 2. *Prima la musica e poi le parole;* 3. *Che l'oratione sia padrona del armonia e non serva.*

The first one apparently agrees with the second, and both seem to contradict the third.

Apparently.

But let us take a closer look, since Mina's motto might well change the issue radically.

Let us listen. Listen *to the letter*, if I may say so. Let us listen word by word, word for word, to what is being said and sung. For while Mina sings her words ("words, only words"), the actor Alberto Lupo plays the opposite role with his spoken lines. Of course, she is the girl and he is the guy, the eternal protagonists of so many hit songs. But she is also the Song or the Singing, while he is the Word or the Discourse, in what appears then as an allegorical—or tautegorical—play, like Salieri's: a little drama between Speech and Melody in person, personified.

Alberto Lupo impersonates Language itself, with its perpetual complaints: *Non vorrei parlare*, he says, "I would rather not talk." He would like to be able to stop the stream of signifiers, to stay silent or to reach the fullness of the song and the cry.

Mina, on the other hand, who impersonates Melody or even Music, seeks to get rid of the words in order to soar up toward the sky of the absolute refrain. *Caramelle, non ne voglio più*, sings the Song itself: "I don't want any more sweets," meaning no sweet words anymore, no words at all.

The scene—a sort of domestic dispute between Language and Music—then takes a more dramatic turn. *Una parole ancora*, "one more word," one last word, says Language, begging, while Melody answers by a multiplied echo that empties the words of their power: *parole, parole, parole*—words, only words, nothing but words.

Words are worth nothing. This is what Song would like to sing. Or maybe, more accurately, words *should be* worth nothing *in order for the song to take off and soar* as the song that it wants to be. Up to this point, the domestic drama between Mina and Alberto Lupo seems to do nothing but develop or amplify Salieri's tautegory. But Mina soon introduces, at the end of the refrain, something unheard-of, something that urges us to completely rethink the apparently worn-out question of the relations between music and language.

For Mina sings, *Parole, parole, soltanto parole, parole tra noi*. That is to say, "Words, words, only words, words between us." Can we hear what she sings? Can we hear it *to the letter*?

She ("elle" in French, that is to say, the Song itself, the "chanson") asserts that between them, between Language and Music, there is nothing but words. Which is to say, in other words, that between Melody and

Words, there are other words. Words, again. The *in-between* is made of words, words, words.

And consequently, if Music *needs* this gap in order to constitute itself as the Music it seeks to be (rather than mere sound, mere "acoustical substrate," as Dahlhaus puts it), we should even claim that the *difference* that allows Music to appear as such is *wordy* again. Or maybe, to play once more with the neologism that *India Song* suggested to us, we could say that, in its *betweenworldliness*, the difference that constitutes Music as such is *other-wordy*.

Let us put it more simply and straightforwardly, to conclude: Music becomes the Music that it is by giving birth to other words.

Is this not a paraphrastic translation of Nietzsche's statement about the "original melody which then *seeks for itself* a parallel dream-appearance" and "gives birth to poetry . . . over and over again, *in ever new ways*"?

But it could also be an unashamed adaptation (rather than a translation) of Duras's lyrics: *Chanson, toi qui me parle d'elle, d'elle qui te chantait.* In tautegorical and (self-)musicological English, this would mean, "Song, you who speak of song, of the song that sings you."

Speaking of Microsound:
The Bodies of Henri Chopin

Kiene Brillenburg Wurth

> The lines separating music and poetry, writing and
> painting, are purely arbitrary, and sound poetry is
> precisely designed to break down these categories.
>
> —WILLIAM BURROUGHS, introduction to Henri Chopin's
> *Poésie Sonore Internationale* (1979)

Introduction

Between 1983 and 1992, at the San Francisco Exploratorium, Charles Amirkhanian and KPFA radio copresented the celebrated *Speaking of Music* series.[1] Amirkhanian, the well-known composer, sound artist, and percussionist, produced the show, which featured John Cage, Astor Piazolla, Pamela Z, Laurie Anderson, Steve Reich, Sarah Hopkins, Meredith Monk, and many other leading music makers. Typically, the series would involve a conversation, a performance, and audience questions. Appearing on *Speaking* in 1987, Cage answered a final question enigmatically: "there's no reason," he said, "to listen to music rather than to sounds around us." He did not object to people making records, but he did not have a playing machine in the house.[2] Why would he play music, the implication was, when there are sounds hanging in the air offered to us as event that we do or do not want to hear?

We know all this, and yet the core business of musicology—the legitimate "speaker" on music—in America and Europe continues to be music in a classical and strict sense: music that lends itself to music theory.[3] Why would one discuss a performance artist for this volume and not, say, Pierre Boulez's *Pli selon pli*, which is identifiably "music"? To use Edgar Varèse's terminology, is this "organized sound"? What would it mean not to be music? Since the twentieth century, music makers, composers, poets, and sound artists have precisely sought to diversify music, as well as our conception of it, and to test the artificial boundaries between "music" and "nonmusic," "music" and "sound," "music" and "poetry." And yet many scholars still ask for something that is identifiably music. Who knows, maybe Cage still inadvertently implied something that is identifiably music, as a contrastive figure against which sounds can appear "as such"—or even "music" as a mental frame in which accidental sounds can emerge as melodious, harmonious, striking. Perhaps we cannot stop thinking and speaking of music.

Cage was a great listener. Yet while being open to sounds around him, he never mined an entire soundscape *within* the body. It is this inner soundscape, the recorded and manipulated sounds of body organs and body cavities that I am concerned with in this chapter. I focus on a sound explorer—perhaps we should call him a speleologist—who, half a decade after Cage visited the anechoic chamber and discovered the sounds of silence, was swallowing microphones to disclose a factory of sound beneath the skin: Henri Chopin (1922–2008). The reason that I am interested in Chopin is not simply because his sound works cannot be compared with anything else, unsettling, appalling, and amazing as they are. It is because, as such, they test our very register to speak of and interpret sound worlds. Interpretation, Lawrence Kramer has recently affirmed, is the activity of subjectivity as it has been defined since the Enlightenment in terms of knowing, feeling, and creating meaning freely—an activity preeminently taking shape in relation to musical listening.[4] Chopin's *L'Énergie du sommeil* (1965, released in Chopin's *revue OU* 23/24), I argue, probes the limits of interpretation as such a humanist practice. A study in sleep, it teases out the decomposition of subjectivity, making audible an impersonal life that leaves little room for affective engagement: the biophysical vibrations prior to the I. How can we speak of sounds that are precisely meant to foreclose the symbolic order?

French Sound Poetry in the 1940s and 1950s

Henri Chopin stands as a singular figure in the history of sound or audio poetry, a form of acoustic art that aims to tear down the walls between poetry and music, speaking, crying, screaming, and singing. Rooted in the technology of the microphone and the tape recorder, sound poetry is a mode that is almost uniquely tied to the practice of one poet—Chopin himself.[5] Nevertheless, in retrospect, Chopin has repeatedly identified the breath-poet Gil Wolman, as well as Antonin Artaud and François Dufrêne, as important precursors. We will have occasion to return to Wolman, Artaud, and Dufrêne later.

If sound poetry questions the disciplinary boundaries between the arts, it also questions the conditions of possibility of these arts: what these arts would "be." Thus, poetry, in Chopin's practice, has nothing to do with text anymore. It is born as sound, even though the recording and subsequent manipulation of body sounds counts as writing, as audiography, all the same. It also has nothing to do with words. Sound poetry, as Steve McCaffery has put it, is the "high-energy expulsion of inarticulate sounds, cries, and grunts."[6] Indeed, the history of Chopin's work is the history of the progressive disappearance and disintegration of words and, as a result, the ever greater prominence of phonemic sounds and bare, vocal as well as buccal, vibrations. Sound poetry is the technological and creative organization of these sounds and vibrations. What it does (in Michael Lenz's comprehensive description of sound poetry after World War II) is mobilizes "all speech organs, auxiliary parts, and the breathing mechanism that contribute to the articulatory process and makes the entire range of human sounds perceptible."[7]

Chopin has been associated repeatedly with Lettrism (Isidore Isou) and Ultralettrism (Dufrêne, Jean-Louis Brau), but his work can be reduced to neither. Like Wolman, Chopin is—was—above all separationist. Unlike the Lettrists, Chopin's main interests were not with the articulation of letters separated from words and devoid of content.[8] After he discovered the tape recorder in the mid-1950s, Chopin went further than they did. He started to investigate the sounds of phonemic particles and the vibrations of bodily spaces and cavities that preceded articulation. What he set out to do with electromagnetics was in fact to liberate the voice from "itself" (though the voice has never had a place) and to stretch it all over the body, in numerous cavities whose possibilities for artistic expression had never been considered before. Swallowing microphones, which were increasingly small and sensitive, Chopin explored a territory beyond the voice as we know it, extending it to all the places where breath is formed and making it heard anew from within the stomach, lungs, gullet, and glottis. Thus, "voice" became plural—as it had become with Artaud, who had made the voice speak through different bodily locations.[9]

Chopin shared his interest in audio technology with the Ultralettrists of the 1950s. Ultralettrism was a faction of Lettrism for those who were dissatisfied with Isou's universal visual alphabet of preliterate sounds. Dufrêne initiated Ultralettrism in 1953 at age twenty-three with Jean-Louis Brau and others. He aimed to go beyond letters by amplifying microparticles of his own voice with microphones and a tape recorder. At first Dufrêne used the tape recorder to store his sound poems, but increasingly he came to deploy it as a compositional tool. What he produced were *crirythmes*, or improvised screams, which recalled in some ways the cries and grunts of Artaud's *Pour en finir avec le jugement de Dieu* (1948). Produced live or audiographically, the *crirythmes* made the noises of the mouth audible. The point was not just to create new noises but somehow to reach and capture the nonsignifying dynamic of things.

Lenz has aptly characterized Dufrêne's *crirythmes* as "an extensive play of nonverbal-paralinguistic signals, emotional in origin (e.g., tongue clicking, throat clearing, coughing, sobbing, whimpering, moaning, laughing, babbling, panting, gargling, screeching), of 'unarticulated' screams and breath sequences all the way to snoring and spittle noises."[10] It is the foregrounding of sounds that come before or are kept out of the symbolic order—physical, intrusive, "beastly," abject. Interestingly, Dufrêne would juxtapose his *crirythmes* with such icons of classical music as Richard Strauss and Mozart, much as ad-busters might contrast their socially conscious transformational productions with the unthinkingly accepted products of traditional culture today.[11] The result was a creative and hilarious commentary on classical music from the viewpoint of the body and its respiratory sounds, manipulated electronically and at times so painful to the ear as to become tortuous. This, perhaps, is how bodies come to tamper and interfere with regulated, instrumental music: they make listening—linear, focused listening—nearby impossible. They make noise.

Dufrêne's *crirythmes* are also known as *musique concrète vocale*, and it is no secret that they were a major influence on Pierre Henry and his *musique concrète* (music composed on magnetic tape by the electronic manipulation of natural sounds and noises). "Concrete vocal music" wonderfully captures a dynamic between sound, music, and poetry. The term is an appropriate starting point for a consideration of Chopin's more expansive mode of electronic body sound—from sounds of digestion to sounds of nasal hairs. How does the body sound, and how is this sound animated? By way of breath, through respiration. This is where Wolman comes in. Chronologically, he already comes in before Dufrêne, in 1951. As Chopin notes,

He—historically—is our turning point because he passes beyond the phonetic poem made of letters. He invents his *Mégapneumes* (breath poems, superinhalations) in 1951, that is, spitting poems, without words, or semantics, from the viewpoint of the word given to negation, from that of the breath to the concrete quality of *air*, to expression.[12]

Wolman was the young poet who, during a series of Lettrist performances in October 1950 (entitled *L'Univers des Bruites*), rose and recited not abstracted letter-sounds but organic noises that ranged from burping and humming to loud exhalations. Greil Marcus evokes this performance marvelously in *Lipstick Traces*, when he describes it as "a pre-phonetic explosion that denies any lexical description. Unknown tongues flow from his mouth—not languages, but the linguistic organs as such, searching the air and slamming his cheeks and teeth."[13] With this performance, Wolman did not concern himself with the mere decomposition of language. He turned instead to the very regions where speaking begins: to the body, to breath, to air, to exhalation. There is a connection between this physical movement of exhalation in Wolman's sound work and a phase in poetry that Isou called *ciselant* in his *Introduction à une nouvelle poésie et à une nouvelle musique* (1947).[14] *Ciseler* means "to chisel, cut, or consume" (and in English to chisel is also to cheat). For Isou, poetry had run its course in the nineteenth century as an evocative art—evocative of personae, images, figurations, and giving rise to interpretations. Up until Victor Hugo, poetry had been in its lively or amplified stage (*amplique*): inventive, expansive. What then followed was the *ciselant* phase of creative decomposition— that is, a destructive working-through—that started with Baudelaire and culminated in Tristan Tzara's letter poems of the early twentieth century. Cut-ups, collage, reduction, and the expenditure of words and language "as such" now set the poetic scene. Knowingly or unknowingly, Wolman rendered this phase of consumption audible—or epitomized it—in pure breath works. Wolman's sound art was, to that extent, a sign of the times: a sign of expiration. Chopin would follow suit.

Expiration, in an archaic sense, means death. There is a whole network of meanings connecting death, breath, and consumption (expending, devouring, wasting), and this is a conceptual network that can be used as a grid to analyze Chopin's electronic sound work: death and exhaustion are palpably present as aural traces in that work. The sounds of breath and bodily noise in works such as *L'Énergie* echo the devastating soundscapes that Chopin, imprisoned at the forced labor camp of Olomouc, witnessed during the last cruel phases of World War II, those of the death marches between eastern Prussia and the Lithuanian border. Frédéric Acquaviv notes in his obituary of Chopin, "Thousands died on those journeys and it was then that [Chopin] listened to the voices of his fellow marchers, sounds which would infuse his work for the rest of his life."[15] The "signal" of expiration is thus also an intensely personal one with Chopin, one that gives a particular, historical twist to the idea of a concrete vocal music: the idea of the concrete, the "given" that will be given to manipulate, here recalls the index as a semiotic type. These sounds become traces of past presences—they act as aural fossils that continue to be heard concretely, that is, distinctly, physically in the present.

Orality, Buccality, and Interpretation

So far, I have briefly discussed a limited number of sound poets whose practices have been immediately relevant to Chopin's sound poetry in post–World War II France. As the Belgian musicologist Herman Sabbe has suggested, these practices occupy a "specific territory [of noise], born out of the certain death of two preceding territories: poetry and music."[16] As, precisely, a deterritorialization of these territories, sound poetry of course extends far beyond the 1950s, from the nineteenth and even the late eighteenth century onward into the twentieth century and the avant-garde practices of Dadaists, Futurists, Lettrists, Ultralettrists, Fluxus, Beat poets, and so on.[17] Indeed, it is owing to Chopin, as well as to the magazine *Cinquième Saison* that he started in 1958 (later *OU*), that we have become aware of a history of sound poems in the first place—and of landmarks such as Kurt Schwitters's *Ursonate*. What connects Chopin to this history (Surrealism, Lettrism, and Ultralettrism) is a common concern with and even consecration of orality, orality as the work of the mouth (the physicality of the mouth and the sounds and noises that emanate from it) but also as a "lost culture"—a vast expanse of time preceding poetry as a printed tradition. In Chopin's writings and interviews, he never tired of pointing this out: we have had seven thousand years of oral poetry and only a couple of hundred years of print culture. Why should we abide by the laws and conventions of print poetry? How do we process poetry? By reading silently? Or do we listen to sounds as aural events communally? What is poetry in the first place? Attaching this question to the question, What is a body? Chopin sought to create a sound mode that circumvented the symbolic order and the repressive systems of writing.[18]

Anticipating Althusser's notion of interpellation, as well as Deleuze and Guattari's notes on the imperative law of the language of the father in *L'Anti-Oedipe* (1972), Chopin regarded language as an instrument of obedience.[19] As Martin Heidegger and Jacques Lacan have also suggested, language is a system of rules we have to enter and abide with. It then can speak through us and situate us. (Hence, "what comes first is . . . a collective assemblage resulting in the determination of relative subjectification proceedings, or assignations of individuality and their shifting distribution in discourse.")[20] For Chopin, linear writing is the organizing structure of this system of obedience. His sound poetry gestures toward a different organization—a materiality "before" subjectification uttered by means of the recorded and amplified work of body organs "below" or "before" the dimension of organized speech.[21] This materiality is epitomized in the idea of buccality, a more primitive opening than orality that Jean-Luc Nancy has evoked as follows:

> *Bucca* . . . is puffed up cheeks; it is the movement, the contraction and/ or distension of breathing, of eating, of spitting, or of speaking. Buccality is more primitive than orality. Nothing has taken place yet; nothing has been spoken there yet. But an opening—unstable and mobile— forms at the instant of speaking. For the instant, one discerns nothing: *ego* does not mean anything, *ego* only opens this cavity. Every mouth is a shadow mouth, and the true mouth also opens onto this darkness, and as this darkness, so as to form its heart of hearts.[22]

What Nancy intimates here is an opening prior to self-presence, prior to the articulation or figuration of self ("I," "I am"). *Ego*, in Nancy's text, embodies this prior instance, this impossibility of self-positing and self-grounding. Orality cannot cover this instance. It comes from *os/oris*, the mouth for voice and speaking, also meaning "face" and "entrance," and it is, as such, the mouth of figuration. Bucca is the inarticulate opening where "nothing has been spoken"; yet it is also the mouth of breathing, swallowing, growling. It is the mouth that disfigures the face. I think of Chopin performing fellatio with a microphone in his mouth (or rather, castration, since we are speaking of buccality here), a mouth, swollen and retracted, an old man's mouth, a mouth disposed toward its dedisciplinarization— toward its deformation as an echoing receptacle of "the Word." In 1967, Chopin wrote, "The buccal sound, the human sound, in fact, will come to meet us only around 1953, with Wolman, Brau, Dufrêne, and sometime later with my audiopoems."[23] It meets us as the materialization of "mouth," the opening or *béance*, as Nancy calls it, around which the mouth as figuration sculpts itself.[24]

How can we speak of this materialization? How can we speak meaningfully of an amplified breath—a fart? Could we even interpret such sounds? Would they be "worth" the effort, to the extent that these sounds foreclose any "exchange value," any meaning, any attempt at being understood? I address this issue of worth also because sound poetry is not only one of the most intriguing but also one of the most difficult, unappealing, and marginal of musical-poetic modes. There is little in Chopin's work to ingratiate itself with a listener, to induce pleasure or to trigger deep and weighty thoughts and feelings. There is also little in the practice of sound poetry—typically performed in the unspaces of modern culture—to include it in the kind of heritage making that hermeneutics familiarly enables and sustains. Sound poetry, Gerald Bruns has noted, "has nothing of the solemnity and monumentality of the *Grande œuvre*. The world of high art is deaf to it. It rarely or never makes its way into museums, performance halls."[25] It is an *other* art. Otherness, however, should be no impediment to interpretation. Indeed, the whole project of musical hermeneutics in the new musicology has been triggered by the persistence of the Romantic idea that music goes beyond (or before) language, an art that is, as such, "other" and can therefore not be spoken about in the way we speak about, say, literature. And yet, as Kramer points out in this volume, we do it all the time. Let me pause to reflect on this speaking a bit so as to position my speaking of Chopin more accurately.

As "meaningless," "empty" sound, instrumental music has been endlessly spoken about since it turned into a venue for creative self-expression and inwardness in the later eighteenth century. Thomas Twining, speaking of music in 1789, epitomizes this creative activity when he writes about the merits and pleasures of a sonorous and suggestive art:

> But, whatever we may call it, this I will venture to say,—that in the *best* instrumental Music, expressively *performed*, the very indecision itself of the expression, leaving the hearer to the free operation of his *emotion* upon his *fancy*, and, as it were, to the free *choice* of such ideas as are, *to him*, most adapted to react upon and heighten the emotion which occasioned them, produces a pleasure, which nobody, I believe, who is able to feel it, will deny to be one of the most delicious that Music is capable of affording.[26]

This famous passage from Twining's *Treatise on Poetry* illustrates well the link between instrumental music and subjectivity that Kramer posits in his project of musical hermeneutics: music enables a listener to create meaning precisely by allowing him or her to associate freely and to project freely these associations onto the music heard. Music becomes meaningful as a screen or mirror of subjectivity *because* it "has" or "carries" no specific meanings. Indeed, as Sander van Maas has observed, by the nineteenth century, music, as an open sign, had become "a medium in which the listening self does not only see itself reflected, but in which a window opens to other possibilities of individual existence. A window that is undeniably obscure, but evocative precisely because of it."[27]

For Kramer, when it comes to speaking of music, this listening self becomes the very medium of music. The latter requires a "free, rich subjectivity" to be heard at all, a subjectivity that was invented with the rise of instrumental music as an art triggering infinite, indeterminate interpretations. Indeed, Kramer claims, classical music was *devised* for such subjectivity.[28] Not surprisingly, perhaps, when we now speak of music, we often do so as if we were approaching and interpreting a meaningful presence: a self—or, more precisely, a reflection of self—that moves. To put this differently, interpreting music inevitably takes on the form of interpreting a subjectivity of some sort. Thus, in the volume *Musical Meaning and Human Values*, Kramer speaks of Beethoven's String Quartet in C major, op. 59, no. 3, as sustaining "a mood of mysterious brooding" and possessing a "dark, contemplative state," while the contemplative movement of the Molto Adagio of the Quartet in F major, op. 59, no. 1, is said to "continuously [heighten] its intensity of feeling and concentration until it passes the point where such heightening seems tolerable. Its hiccoughing reminders of care have been a portent."[29] Likewise, Marshall Brown, writing on music and fantasy, turns Beethoven's Symphony No. 5 in C minor into a presence with subject-like qualities (it is "attuned . . . to questioning rather than responding") that is only "ever on the verge of a grand statement . . . because it never finds the proper way to open its mouth."[30]

Such writing is, of course, metaphorical; it happens again and again when we speak of and try to make sense of musical movements—we make them human—but it also indicates the extent to which musical interpretation (or at least the interpretation of classical music) rests on the assumption that music, as an object of interpretation, is an art form addressing itself *as* a (feeling, acting) subject *to* a (feeling, responding) subject. What happens when one of the two subjects disappears—or changes beyond recognition?

The question is an urgent one. It propels us to think about the challenges to a mode of interpretation modeled on a music that takes a distinctly humanist subjectivity as its very medium. More specifically, it is Chopin's sound art that propels us to think about these challenges because it leaves us nothing but the sounds of a human animality—even though that animality does not exclude the hermeneutic enterprise per se. There is nothing else—no movements, no tensions and resolutions, no deep structure, no semblance of communicative action allowing us to participate imaginatively and meaningfully—there is just the human, without the ordering and mirroring subjectivity. (Or perhaps, there is an excessive presencing of the human as animality in Chopin, more human than a humanist subjectivity could be made to bear). Does Chopin's work thus test the limits of interpretation as a creative activity, or does it displace the subjectivity from which the work of interpretation in its hermeneutic tradition starts—and thus intervene in this tradition? In the next section, I try to answer this question by approaching *L'Énergie du sommeil* as a theoretical object:[31] an object raising theoretical questions, obliging us to think through theoretical issues, and indeed itself producing theory, rather than a mere object or case study to be "spoken about." It speaks back. *L'Énergie* speaks back about the body asleep, prompting us to reconsider its relation to listening and subjectivity. In what follows, I propose to frame this reconsideration within Jean-Luc Nancy's philosophical work on the body, discourse, and the soul in works such as *Corpus* and *The Fall of Sleep*. How do Chopin's sounds allow us to reconsider the body and the soul, that which was once that intensely "Romantic" seat of expression, emotion, and indeed, subjectivity?

L'Énergie du sommeil

The energy of sleep, the force, the work, the being at work, the activity (*energeia*) of sleep. *Energeia*, the term that Aristotle used to refer to a realized potential or the process of its realization—the "actual" or, one could also say, the activity of realization. I would hazard the guess that "energy" with Chopin is a poetic term, probably even a specification of poetry *as* free activity that recalls Wilhelm von Humboldt's use of *energeia* in relation to language. Humboldt advocated a view of language as being always open and in process rather than fixed and completed. It is a creative activity that is real only in the moment of speaking and can change anytime.[32] Humboldt's focus on language as living discourse touches on Chopin's emphasis on orality and, as we have seen, buccality in his dealings with poetry as living body sounds. Energy is the force that works, the activity of working, the *work* (of art) itself.

Sleep is an absence of self, retrievable and recurrent, an "effacement of my own distinction," as Nancy puts it, when "'I' no longer distinguish 'myself'": "I can no longer hold anything as an object, as a perception, or a thought." A self that is working, digesting "itself" and yet that is absent to "itself"—absent and present all at once, a "simultaneity of what is one's own and what is not one's own."[33] This simultaneity is heard in the sounds of respiration, the process by which I am "traversed."[34]

Absence, self-digestion, respiration: why is it so significant that Chopin would record the body, his body, himself, in sleep? There is the element of experimentation: how far can we go in letting the body speak "for itself"? By swallowing small microphones so as to record the bronchial cavities, putting them in his ears, nose, hair to amplify the imperceptible sounds they make during sleep, he cuts out the speaking voice and instead hears it breathing, sighing, heaving: this is how Chopin aims to write and touch the body. And "touch" here has the sense of a transformative intervention.

The discourse of invention and experimentation—actions whose outcomes are unknown and unforeseen—is everywhere in Chopin's reflections on his work. In an interview with John Hudak, he explains how he came to sound his body:

> Being curious, I put the microphone in my mouth, and when you put the microphone into your mouth, you have immediately four or five different sounds. . . . Inside you have an echo with the liquid way in the mouth, with breathing, with a strong sound from the tongue, you have respiration with the body. . . . Altogether, it's like a factory for sound. It was a great surprise for me. The body is like a factory that never stops. The body ignores silence.[35]

The body speaks. When the body sleeps, this unheard noise is most poignant. The body goes on making sound when "nobody" is "there." It is like an automaton, given over to the rhythm of its organs. And yet Chopin is "there" like a phantom, a soul in the form of all-hearing audio technology that is never asleep, recorded from the inside out (organs) and the outside in (skin, hair, reverberation). This is why *L'Énergie*, lasting but five minutes, is an exemplary "case" in Chopin's small corpus. With it, Chopin shows how we might be able to speak *out of* the body in sound, rather than only *of* it. This would not be Artaud's miming of ex-corporation—*ex corpore*, speaking out of the body—that Nancy refers to in *Corpus*.[36] It may seem so, but it is not. *L'Énergie* belongs to the order of writing rather than miming, a writing in sound or audiography that affects and disrupts the body, rather than merely voicing it. A technological evocation of the body asleep,

L'Énergie offers a "discourse coming out of the body," an "ex-corporate" discourse (the "incorporeal" in our tradition) that touches on—mediates, interrupts, alters—the body (the "corporeal"). Indeed, it may be that this discourse here produces "body" *as* an interruption of sense: the body becomes present through the bounds of mediation.[37]

In short, the question that *L'Énergie* raises is not simply how the body can be made to speak out of itself but also how this body can be accessed and invoked through writing (audiography). The issue has thus shifted. The speaking of sound has slipped into the speaking and concept of the body. I would not be the first to slip in this way. Roland Barthes's evocation of Robert Schumann's *Kreisleriana* readily comes to mind:

> In Schumann's *Kreisleriana* (Opus 16; 1838), I actually hear no note, no theme, no contour, no grammar, no meaning, nothing which would permit me to reconstruct an intelligible structure of the work. No, what I hear are blows: I hear what beats in the body, what beats the body, or better: I hear this body that beats.[38]

This body, this body of music and of Barthes, the former pricking and ravishing the latter, cannot be touched by "professional [i.e., musicological] analysis"—what Charles Rosen has called the "railway timetable" that identifies themes and phrases and motifs and turns and that moves along quite thoroughly, indicating where and how the music is proceeding.[39] For Barthes, it is precisely speaking of music, of *Tonkunst*, that should be affected and interrupted by the body of music, just as our speech necessarily interrupts the music.

Chopin's *L'Énergie* takes place in this reflexivity between "corporeality" and "incorporeality"—it shows that our access to the body *is* this reflexivity. Chopin himself, Chopin the author, at times liked to suggest otherwise. He liked to suggest that his access to the body was unmediated, that *his* evocation of his body—his bodies, to be more precise, as every work of Chopin invokes a different body—offered its sonorous realities or, at least, that the "raw material" of his work was the pure, unaffected body sound spontaneously produced during acts of improvisation recorded on a Revox tape machine. Chopin would then memorize these recordings as a mental score and tamper with them during editing to create the final sound collages as a second creative intervention: "It is just by heart and using only my memory that I conceive the expressions of my body, basically through my mouth with its breathing etc., which become my only solid score."[40] Such references to spontaneous body expressions create the impression of a being in touch with the body, having immediate access to it, and allowing it to express "itself."

I would suggest, however, that the breath work we hear in *L'Énergie* renders the body *inaudible* while offering its sounds: Chopin's body sounds offer us the body *as they remove it from us*. Again, this positions Chopin with writing—with what Nancy has called ex-scription: what is present in writing only through its absence.[41] We cannot hear what is left out of inscription, or perhaps we can hear it tentatively here. What we do hear in *L'Énergie* is an "outside" of the body—a body listening to itself. The inability to move through or around this "outside" (and of course this is no obstacle at all but rather a condition of possibility for the body in the first place) is here in fact rendered audible through a superimposition of inhalation and exhalation that makes it impossible to hear any body sound "as such."[42] Echoes, speed changes, and audio feedback have created a sound sculpture in which intake and waste are layered on top of each other. This layering allows the sounds of breathing in and out to be replayed as occurring simultaneously: they create a sonic wall that sounds the body's very impenetrability to itself.

Such an impenetrability calls forth the figure of *espacement* in Derrida's work to refer to the invisible space dividing the self from itself while looking at itself in the mirror. This space blinds us: when we look at ourselves in the mirror, we always see an other. Spacing or *espacement* precedes the self (the body) and its other. My fascination with *L'Énergie* stems from the fact that it renders *audible* the impossibility of self-presence: of a self, a body, being present and identical to itself. It literally allows us to hear this body—which we share, to a certain extent—emerge as its outside. For, as body sound, *L'Énergie* yields the sounds of rustling leaves, the whistling of the wind high on a mountain, a raging storm, or an undefined machine sound.[43] Serge Brindeau once remarked that superimposition enabled Chopin to trigger a world of sounds: "the work of a sawmill, the chirping and singing of birds, the arrival of trains, the roaring of airplane motors, sirens and liners, diverse metallic vibrations with accelerations in movement, and successive entries of different parties, a bit as with the orchestra."[44] Because we know that such "external" sounds are the special effect of edited sounds of body organs and amplified microsounds of skin and hair, *L'Énergie* triggers a curious sensation: the sounding body appears to be nothing but an interface between two ubiquitous soundscapes, "within" and "without," a fold in a continuity of sonorities. Are we nothing but a fold, a zone in an omnipresent surround-sound that feeds on us, that wastes us? Are we effects of spacing?

Michel Serres has suggested that it is not just our ears but our skin and entire body that hear and listen to sound and that produce it at the same time. Our ears and skin (ears *are* skin, as Steven Connor rightfully underlines)[45] listen by "receiving," by producing sound in turn and rendering it intelligible. This reciprocity parallels conceptually the idea of a bodily zone marking the convergence, the folding and unfolding, of "within" and "without," that emerges out of Chopin's work. As Serres evokes the sounding body,

> We hear through our skin and feet. We hear through our skull, abdomen and thorax. We hear through our muscles, nerves and tendons. Our body-box, strung tight, is covered head to toe with a tympanum. We live in noises and shouts, in sound waves just as much as in spaces, the organism is erected, anchors itself in space, a broad fold, a long braid, a half-full, half-empty box which echoes them. Plunged, drowned, submerged, tossed about, lost in infinite repercussions and reverberations and making sense of them through the body.[46]

Bodies are resonances, touching "self" (Serres's "organism") and space (the echoing "broad fold") at the very same time, which makes them, as we will see in the next section, souls.[47]

Sound Body in Performance: Soul or Substance?

In "On the Soul," written for a symposium on bodies, Nancy speaks and writes about souls in terms of the weight of the body in our time and our culture. Since bodies are, for him, (about) a rupture of sense, he writes of souls. He writes about souls in order to provoke such a rupture in discourse, when he puts the word "soul" in place of the body. Yet it was also Aristotle who wrote on the body as he wrote on the soul in *De Anima*. It seems that Nancy thinks along comparable lines. He thinks the soul as the body, as the body's relation with itself, as the body outside of itself: "The soul is the body's difference from itself, the relation to the outside that the body is for itself." And again: "the soul is the difference from itself that makes the body."[48] This is a reflexivity that indicates that the body cannot properly be called inaccessible as it is only ever accessible *to itself* from the outside, *as* outside. That is to say, "I am an outside of myself"—or to speak with Serres, "I am beside myself"—as "I have to be in exteriority to touch myself."[49] Clearly, Nancy is not trying to recall the soul in its Platonic and Christian mode, as a self-enclosed interiority, a little something, a little light or breath of air residing in our midst. What he is trying to do is to use the word "soul" to help us understand the production of such an inside from the outside: the soul is the "rest" or "interval" of the body to itself.[50]

Chopin listens to his body as a sound mass: one day he put a microphone in his mouth and discovered that his "body is like a factory that never stops." Factories concentrate, and in concentrating they mix substances. With Nancy, when bodies are masses—here, a mass of breath, snoring—there are no more bodies. A mass is a for-itself, a given: it is an absolute, without individuation. Most of the time we tend to think of the body as such a closed-off substance: "A mass is what is massed, gathered up in itself, penetrated with self and penetrated within itself such that, precisely, it's impenetrable." What this means is that "there is nothing that articulates a mass to itself"—it has/is no extension or soul, no relation. It's an absolute ground.[51] Over against this "substantial" body would be the "insubstantial": the spirit. A body without extension is a "concentration within itself," and concentration "for us today is effectively the annihilation of the body as extension, of the body *of which there are always several.*" A mass of bodies, a body as mass, is a body of (mass) destruction.[52]

Chopin acts in his work in part on this idea of the body as a closed-off substance: he *opens up* the body with his microphones. He mines this substance, as it were; he ventures within and allows us to hear what we cannot hear through the seal of our skin. Willingly or unwillingly, he thus also elaborates on the familiar idea of the body as self-contained. The sheer effort and pain of swallowing microphones—or more accurately, microphones attached to a thread so that they may be pulled out again—to record the sounds of one's inner cavities in a way pays tribute to the body as a sealed entity. To be opened up, and to be opened up from the inside out, presupposes being closed off.

During performances, Chopin exposed this body to a public. He played the tape and "performed" it, as a score. At first sight, such scoring may confirm the impression of a body as substance, rather than Nancy's alternative of a body as *espacement*. In metaphysics, Nancy points out, substance is "that which is *under* something." It is solid.[53] What is solid or substantial in music practice is a score: performances are fleeting; scores are concrete. A score is the matter we can study and to which we can return. A score could even reveal a composer's "intentions." It is the foundation "underneath" a performance. Even though Chopin reconceived of the idea of a score as an audiographic rather than a printed notation, his scored body continued to function in this foundational manner. During performances, he interacted with this body. One could say that he "exhibited" this body, amplifying and revealing its sound sources during live action. Once more, Chopin put the microphone in his mouth and voiced himself over against his recorded body, as he gesticulated like a director, some say a magician, to the public and the sound technicians at the back:[54]

> The poet uses complex vocal and non-figurative sounds, edited at several levels—electronically manipulating and broadcasting them at top volume—and adding to them in live performance with voice and microphone. . . . Despite his diminutive height, Henri Chopin radiates such an intensity that he seems to grow to a gigantic scale, the gravity of his expression suggesting some kind of vampire or evil spirit. The process by which this spirit emerges on stage can be really terrifying . . . because the real process of the work is non-mimetic, deriving from what the artist—in this case Chopin—is actually doing. In other words, the emergence of this spirit is inherent in the live performance of the work.[55]

Chopin performed a score: he performed a body-score written in sound. He seemed to transcend the score that was his body: he emerged over it as a "spirit" and controlled it. We are a long way from Nancy's body and soul here. A comment on Chopin's presence in his live performances shows us just how far. McCaffery writes, "Into this recontextualized technology (as performance) Chopin enters as conductor to demonstrate the mind's control over processed human sounds, through [their] expert orchestration." What we hear and see is an "audio-graphic imprint capable of controlled appearance and sequencing."[56] What we hear and see is the mastery of mind over matter: virtuosity.

While I recognize this dimension of Romantic genius in Chopin's work, I also think it does not do full justice to the kind of bodies this work evokes. In works such as *L'Énergie*, there is an ambiguity that also leaves room for the body, and the "spirit," to be heard differently, and so does Chopin's performance practice. Could we not (also) see this practice as the encounter of a body with a body, of a body in its relationship to itself? That is to say, while Chopin clearly projects the body in "old" metaphysical terms of substance, this body is nevertheless at the same time deconstructed as its own outside.

We have seen how *L'Énergie* stages and renders audible the silent and invisible spacing that separates the self, the body, from itself (according to deconstructive logic, the body instates itself *as it* separates itself from itself; it only appears *to itself* on the condition of this separation). What Nancy refers to as soul, the outside of the body to itself, is this spacing or blind spot, this movement of reflexivity. I believe that Chopin's performances revolve around this blind spot, this inability of the body to coincide with itself, insofar as they are staged as dramatizations of propriocentric hearing or, at least, propriocentric hearing of some kind: hearing oneself speak, the inability to pull one's ears away from one's body sounds. Steven Connor captures this state or condition. It is "the gurgling of the viscera, the cracking of the bones, the thudding and pulsing of the blood, even the firing of the neurons, to which all of us are continuously exposed and that for most of the time, unless we are subjected to the rending tortures of tinnitus, we integrate unconsciously without effort."[57] Nancy has related this kind of hearing to silence, as Cage and Chopin have done. Silence is when "you hear your own body resonance, your own breath, your heart, and all its resounding cave." Silence unveils the body, the self, as an "arrangement of resonance."[58]

Silence is the rest referred to earlier, the interval of the body to itself. In this interval, we may realize the sonic presence of our breath, our organs, and so on. When I say that Chopin dramatizes this interval in his performances, I mean that he stages a situation in which his "internal" body sounds become the focus of listening, as if they cannot *but* be listened to, of his live body—listening, not hearing, as this is a willed, directed activity, rather than the helpless exposure to body, sounds typical of propriocentric hearing proper. What Chopin shows us in these performances, body to body, is that the body as relation can never escape its constitutive movement of reflexivity: there is always noise in between itself. While Connor follows Serres in regarding propriocentric hearing in terms of a closed circuit of consciousness, Chopin's performances suggest a vibration, a relation, a self being projected back on itself as other—a self hearing itself, its body, as outside, as surround sound. The circuit is broken, not closed, when one cannot overcome one's awareness of oneself as a body, of one's body at work.

As I have proposed in the previous section, *L'Énergie*, a work on tape, makes us aware of an "outside" of the body, a body listening to itself, which is like a hypochondriac listening, capturing all the minimal sounds that the body is making. Chopin's performances render this impression of a body listening to itself visible. These are rare performances. I mean to say that we rarely get the chance to look at and listen to some body listening to itself.[59] We have no access to such experiences. What does it hear?

Peter Szendy has given us one exception in his fine book *Listen*: arrangements. Arrangers, such as Franz Liszt, Szendy observes, "sign their listenings. We hear them hearing; and that is why . . . we sometimes *believe we observe ourselves listening.*"[60] While the circularity implied in the phrase "listening to ourselves listening" is deceptive—listening to ourselves listening, Szendy observes, is a matter of reflexivity instead of circularity alone—there is the possibility of the circuit becoming closed. We no longer hear anything. Listening becomes deafness.[61] If there is anything terrifying about Chopin's performances, it is that we as listeners are closed in by this deafness: implied in this deafness, we have become deaf listeners. This is not only a physical deafness to "what is available to be heard."[62] It is also a deafness that interrupts the possibility of communication: communication of feelings or impressions. We cannot "identify" with the body sounds in *L'Énergie*; we do not easily have any "feelings" on account of them—as we may frequently have in classical music—or attribute any human trait, mood, or movement to them. They refuse us. They *are* refuse, fragmented body noise, the body as fragment instead of a semblance of subjectivity. These sounds communicate nothing to us, and want nothing from us—except, perhaps, for the kind of amazement that we feel on hearing any sound from any unexpected sound source (let us say, the singing of whales). Is that a body? Is that how a body can sound? Or even, is that my body that I hear? Do I hear myself never coming past my body?

I have interpreted *L'Énergie*. There may be no limits to interpretation, even while there are limits to a humanist subjectivity in sound. We may interpret a stone, as the Japanese do with the philosopher's stone, inkblots, white, "empty" paintings, or "empty" sounds. I have even honored part of a "humanist" hermeneutic practice by using Nancy's discourse on the body and the soul to frame my reflections on Chopin's sound work and performance practice. How can we speak of such work? As I have tried to show, we speak of Chopin's sound poems by speaking of the body. They raise the question of how we can speak out of the body and how the body listens to itself. Thus, they redirect us to the haptic modes of musical "analysis" offered by writers such as Barthes.

Chopin's body of work stands in a technological tradition that has troubled "old" philosophical notions regarding self-presence and auto-affection. It is a body of work that displaces voice as the locus of auto-affection. David Toop has traced these troubles thus:

> Throughout the 20th century, the voice was a prime site for the redefinition of the body in relation to the machine age, particularly during a rapidly developing era of disembodying technologies such as wireless telegraphy, radio, telephone, cinema, television, the tape

recorder, electronic amplification and the microphone. Temporal shift, spatial displacement and the physical absence of the vocalizing agent, both implicit and explicit in such communicative extensions of the body, suggest a disintegration of the image of the body as a symbol of unity.[63]

The body is redefined as a corpus, to use Nancy's term, and the voice is all over it. The voice comes to signal an absence of a self within itself, instead of a self coinciding with itself. I have tried to analyze this disintegration of the image of the body as a symbol of unity in Chopin's work by teasing out a productive inaccessibility of the body to itself: the body is always an outside to itself. It is a soul. If we cannot speak of sound without speaking of the body in Chopin, we cannot speak about the body without bringing up this soul.

Because *L'Énergie* is a breath poem, we cannot evade the soul here. For Aristotle, breath (*pneuma*) contained the heat that allows the soul, located near the heart, to circulate and regulate movement and sense perception. Listening to breath might thus be listening to the transmission of soul or self-movement or, at least, to its condition of possibility. We no longer hear it in this literal way, but neither can a poetic evocation of breath entirely escape this old connotation of breath, heat, and soul. Even when Nancy transforms self-movement into self-reflexivity, breath retains this connotation.

Yet when self-movement veers toward an autonomous movement, reflexivity is about relation and differentiation. Just like Nancy, Jean-François Lyotard has redirected the soul and the self from such self-enclosure to openness and relation. In "Anima Minima," for instance, Lyotard shows the dependence of the soul or anima on an outside. It is not itself, as an already available force or energy, but an other that propels its animation and apparition. "Soul" is to be affected by an other. It is a productive openness.[64] Despite the ambiguities of Chopin's *L'Énergie*, hesitating between the body as substance and *espacement*, it stages this openness, the vulnerability and precariousness of a body, a soul, that may be awoken into "presence" and that cannot defend itself against it.

And then I have not even started on the name "Chopin."

On the Ethics of the Unspeakable

Jairo Moreno

Preamble

Among the many things language addresses, one elicits singular qualifica-
tion: music. Examples abound in the history of language and music relations. Prompted to speak *of* the meaning of a particular composition, Robert Schumann, an otherwise loquacious writer *about* music, would respond
by playing the piece once again: music, like the sovereign, accounts for
itself and does so in deed, not word. Martin Heidegger, whose philosophical thought is rich in linguistic allusions to listening and hearing, is said
to have exclaimed after a performance of Schubert, "That we cannot do
with philosophy": music is a being-in-the-world that differs from philosophical language.[1] The famous "case of Nietzsche" (*der Fall Nietzsche*)
might best exemplify how language's reticence before music becomes a
full-blown incapacity, pushing all the way to what could be fairly called the
limits of language. As John Hamilton reckons, "After the word has been
exhausted—be it the *logos* of philosophical inquiry or the verse of lyric
poetry—there is only madness and music": music overflows the limits of
language and of reason.[2]

A small but powerful lexicon quickly gathers expressing the qualified relationship of language to music. Music limits language; it excludes it; it exhausts it; it is inhospitable to it; it is immune or indifferent to its conceptual advances; it resists or subverts its rational force. This is a lexicon heavily accented by a certain interdictory force.

A common denominator to qualified and/or failed attempts to address music linguistically is of course the notion of ineffability, forcefully expressed, for example, by Vladimir Jankélévitch, who renders it as constitutive of music's singularity.[3] The ineffable and its corollary the unspeakable, however, index more than the mere ban on language. Giorgio Agamben observes how "the ineffable, the un-said, are in fact categories which belong exclusively to human language; far from indicating a limit of language, they express its invincible power of presupposition, the unsayable being precisely what language must presuppose in order to signify."[4] On the one hand, we find here the intuition that language and speech, in naming their own negation (i.e., the unspeakable), affirm their sovereignty. On the other hand, this sovereignty has as its condition of possibility a category (i.e., ineffability) that another sovereign, music, claims for itself, so to speak, as fundamental to its constitution. From this perspective, an unresolved tension exists between these two sovereigns: there might be a limit, yes, but also an enigmatic hinge in the category of the unspeakable, which as an element common to both compromises their sovereign status.

There may be something about this unresolved tension in attempts by several commentators to explore the possible relationship between language and music. They represent widely circulated perspectives of this relation developed in the latter part of the twentieth century. Roland Barthes exemplifies a classic reorientation of language about music, famously denouncing the poverty of the adjective. For him, the adjective is the default mode of language's failed address of music's rich expressivity, specifically of the singing voice, and the luxuriant pleasures and powers of musical materiality, or at least of what he theorizes as sonic materiality, namely, "the body in the singing voice."[5] Others have sought to calibrate the appropriate grammatical devices that might best address music. Christopher Small tried to deobjectify music, betting all on the substitution of a noun (*music*) by a verb form (*musicking*) in order to engage music as an emergent, irreducibly active, and always embodied process.[6] Emmanuel Levinas offered another grammatical option, cryptically proposing that "music . . . bends the qualities of the notes into adverbs."[7] Music here is the rendering-sonic of an essence—more precisely, the whatness—of whatever produces it. This rendering-sonic opens up that essence into a living present; that is, it temporizes that essence. Music's singularity resides in the *how* of sound, less so in the act of its production (Small's "musicking") or its embodied materiality (Barthes's "grain"). By this adverbial logic, music is meant as the sonority of sound as it becomes a modality of being—in short, music as a sonorous *modifier* of being.

Even when delimiting or refusing language's power, these more recent critical considerations work with its logic, exploring grammar as a means to experiment with how language and music might relate and how we might best speak of music—or not at all. As a set, they might invite the adoption of the Wittgensteinian position according to which "grammar tells us what kind of object anything is."[8] Accordingly, Barthes's repudiation of the adjective tells us that music is pure bodily materiality; Small's embrace of the verb tells us that music is untrammeled action; Levinas's advocacy of the adverb tells us that music is a sonorous modifier of something more essential.

But what about the unresolved tension suggested earlier, between two sovereigns—music and language? Why should music be the object of such grammatical approaches? Could it be that music tests the limits of grammar, telling us in fact what these grammatical devices can and cannot do—the adjective merely accentuates, the verb does, and the adverb modifies, and so on? If so, one could well rewrite Wittgenstein and say that "music tells us what kind of object grammar is," inscribing in music's hospitality (Small, Levinas) and relative hostility (Barthes) toward language the very difference and limit between host (music) and guest (grammar). Yes, "music tells us what kind of object grammar is," but in the process, we are also told, it seems, what kind of object it—music—is not.

Where there is a limit, an impassable barrier may yet arise. Another option exists: to guard silence and heed the call of a certain other Wittgenstein who said that "whereof one cannot speak, thereof one must be silent."[9] He might well have had music in mind, for as he told Maurice Drury, "it is impossible for me to say one word about all that music has meant to me in my life; how, then, can I hope to be understood?"[10] When it comes to music, there might be no available guidelines for playing language games, no social regulation of what can be said about it and thus an invitation to retreat into the private realm of the modern self.

Speaking of music, then, is speaking of limits, speaking through limits, or not speaking at all. These limits mark "speaking of music" as a particular kind of linguistic trespassing. Questions remain. Is trespassing here something that *ought not* to be done, *should not* be done, or *cannot* be done? Is it a question of "representation" or of "prohibition"?[11] Is it a "decision," or is it a "norm"?[12] At what point, to whom, and in whose interest can the limit between music and speech become a norm, a decision, a prohibition, and so on? Here we confront the inevitably public dimension of such limits, at a register larger than the minimal social unit of the individual that predominates in discussions of the unspeakable, anywhere from Schumann's autoexpressive musicking, Heidegger's muted resignation, and Barthes's embodied pieties, along with the others.[13] I am interested in this chapter in exploring this public dimension, examining the social life of these limits—their logic, their constitution, their effective power. I do this by considering an episode in U.S. political life, the spring 2006 marches by hundreds of thousands in support of undocumented immigrants' rights. As in so many massive public demonstrations, music was in abundance throughout these marches, as was speech. The relation of music and speech was the stuff of actual political struggle, although its implications were mostly lost in the critical and media reception that followed, only to be taken in the polemical reaction to a Spanish-language version of the U.S. national anthem that was not directly related to the marches. In what follows, I theorize the nature of the limit in general, but with an ear to the challenges and contradictions that emerge philosophically and politically when drawing boundaries around music, language, and speech. For in these marches, the relation of music to language and to public speech became emblematic of the wagers made on each of these—music, language, speech—as discrete but always potentially interrelated domains of social life. These wagers mobilize, in my argument, the possibility of ethical decisions, and those decisions have as a condition of possibility aesthetic exposure, where aesthetics is broadly understood as general sensuous experience and its consequence cognition. I use the term *interdiction* to refer to the time and place in which ethical decisions become speech in all its various modalities, a transformation that always threatens to end in a troubling and politically devastating silence. Interdiction, understood this way, informs my proposal to understand the *unspeakable* as a limiting force driven by *aesthetic* exposure and as the *ethical* outcome of decisions made on the basis of that exposure. My itinerary follows a broad arc from the abstract to the concrete. Beginning with philosophical and critical accounts of the limit (what I call a general liminology), I proceed in the second section to an examination of a foundational relation of *logos* to political life and, in the final section, to an analysis of the marches.

Liminologies

In Barthes, Heidegger, Levinas, Nietzsche, Schumann, Small, and Wittgenstein, limits between music and speech are first assumed a priori and then variously delineated, either in an attempt to find a way to cross them or in a gesture of resignation—an acceptance that these barriers cannot or should not be crossed. Agamben's claims about the unspeakable obey a different logic to determine the impossible limits between language and the unspeakable. Either way, the question of the limit appears to be central to a critical examination of these delineations. As way of introduction, here are some schematic and general considerations about the main ways this question has been addressed in the West:[14]

(i)   A limit helps constitute an entity as bound, delimiting what lies inside and outside.

(ii) This entity is formed according to some criteria, be it shared properties, functions, or relations among its elements, parts, or minimal units, even and especially when these relations are heterogeneous.

(iii) The passage across boundaries or the relations among bounded entities can be multiply characterized: it can take place by an expansion of whatever criteria determine a limit; there may be some overlap between bounded entities; it can take place at the point where binding criteria are interrupted and some other criteria put into effect; in an extreme case, there may be no passage outside a bounded area, with that which lies beyond a given boundary constituting a terrain of radical unknowability.

At this level of generality, many things remain unaccounted for: Is it possible for a bounded entity to be construed as a self-contained whole? If so, what are the mechanisms by which this might be accomplished? To what degree does the installation of a limit indicate that the entity it bounds is limited according to some set of capacities that cannot or may not be exceeded? In short, the force of potential negation at play in the limit opens onto issues of identity and difference, positivity and negativity, and inclusion and exclusion, suggesting that the logic of limit plays a key role in political life. To map out some of these questions, I outline responses by two key thinkers of the limit—Kant and Hegel—as well as the intervention of Saussurean and post-Saussurean criticism and theory. Although I present these responses as a formal taxonomy of the logic of limits, their implications carry on to the aesthetic, ethical, and political discussion in the sections that follow.

(i) Radical alterity. Here, two bounded entities have no overlapping terms. There is an unbridgeable chasm between them. A number of dichotomies exemplify this. Take the principle of noncontradiction. By asserting that nothing "can be *and* not be" at the same time, this principle maintains the absolute nonidentity between these mutually exclusive poles. As a key consequence, this principle allows for the identity of each pole to itself. But it also disallows any grouping of the two poles together under a single category of being. There is no common ground outside these poles to mediate their dichotomous relationship, no bridging of the chasm between them, and the real possibility of a radical antagonism. We have here the basis for what Ernesto Laclau might call a "real contradiction."

There is a long history of thinking opposition in this way, from Parmenides ("The one—that [it] is, and that [it] cannot not be; . . . the other—that [it] is not and that [it] needs [and] must not be")[15] to Aristotle and the most hardened versions of Cartesian dualism. In modern thought, Kant influentially deployed this dichotomic logic of constitutive exclusion, giving it a central role to the notion of limit in his critical philosophy in order to frame the conditions of possibility for experience, on the one hand, and understanding, on which experience relies, on the other. Indeed, limitation ("reality combined with negation") was one of the categories.[16] (Combined with the a priori forms of intuition of time and space, the categories of the understanding were what made experience possible at all.) And Kant was clear about the constitution of limits: "that which *limits* must be distinct from that which *is* thereby *limited*."[17] Kant theorized limitation via the distinction given in the German terms *Schranke* and *Grenze*, both translatable as "limit" and/or "boundary," albeit with subtle distinctions. He regarded limits (*Schranken*) as "mere negations, which affect a quantity so far as it is not absolutely complete."[18] Boundaries (*Grenzen*) had a more restrictive and regulatory sense; they "always presuppose a space existing outside a certain definite place and enclosing it."[19] Through this distinction, he qualified the nature and possibility of knowledge of, on the one hand, mathematics and scientific knowledge—limited (*sensu Schranken*) in that it is confined to experience and never complete—and, on the other hand, of reason and metaphysics, which address the boundary (*sensu Grenzen*) between the knowable and the unknowable. This latter sense is what, following Laclau, I have in mind for thinking the logic of radical alterity, as though music and language replicate the difference between noumena and phenomena.

One of Kant's most salient ideas about human cognition is the boundary-concept (*Grenzbegriff*), which, says Michael Inwood, "marks the boundary beyond which real concepts cease to be applicable" and serves "as a 'Keep Out' notice."[20] It is in this Kantian critical realm that the dichotomy between two poles of the noumenal and the phenomenal constitute a prototype for a relationship in which two terms, although inconceivable without each other, are nonetheless to be understood in fundamental opposition. To drive the point home, Kant posits this in terms of the law of noncontradiction.[21] As is well known, the noumenal marks the finitude of the phenomenal, limited as the latter is to the sphere of appearances. The noumenal itself lies in absolute unknowabilty: "we are unable to comprehend how such noumena [things-in-themselves] can be possible, and the domain that lies out beyond the sphere of appearances is for us empty."[22] Of this beyond, we have no intuition or even the concept of a possible intuition, but we have what Kant calls "an understanding which problematically extends further [beyond the phenomenal]."[23] Nonetheless, according to the logic of the limit, there is no doubt that something other than an object of intuition lies beyond the boundary, "otherwise," as Herbert James Paton puts it, "there would be no sense in talking about limits at all."[24] Laclau is emphatic on this point: the Kantian limit is "an object which shows itself through the impossibility of an adequate representation [by the phenomenal]."[25]

The limit obeys a logic of self-identity given in the law of noncontradiction. But we have seen that it performs a negative function as a mark of finitude, writ large, an expression of absolute opposition, a determining but not determinate negation. Whatever it is, the limit in Kant is not neutral; that is, it always signals a hierarchy and therefore a relation of dependence, the force of which increases as things become more metaphysical. Thus, for instance, the overall structure of the phenomenal-noumenal dichotomy is such that the pole of the noumenal has clearly delineated limits according to a very specific reason: to uphold the sovereignty of the regulative Idea (God, the soul, the totality of the world) that alone guarantees reason.[26] The limit, then, is also a function of this sovereignty, and the ban imposed by this limit constitutes the condition of possibility for the very existence of the other, subordinate, and ultimately nonsovereign pole.

Calling attention to the subordination of the phenomenal pole glosses over a subtle distinction at work in the Kantian dichotomy. Žižek points out a difference between claiming that the phenomenal pole is "*non-noumenal*" (indeterminate judgment) and that the phenomenal pole is "*not noumenal*" (negative judgment).[27] The limit simultaneously mobilizes and is constituted in a negativity ("A is not B," or "the noumenal negates the phenomenal") and a positivity ("A is non-B," or "the noumenal delimits the phenomenal"). Moreover, while "A is not B" follows the logic of identity and the principle of noncontradiction in asserting a positive content both to that which is (i.e., the noumenal) and that which, in relation to this content, is not (i.e., the phenomenal), "A is non-B" operates according to a relational logic with no positive content outside of that relation and the interdiction it animates (i.e., the "Keep Out" sign that Inwood suggestively proposes). The limit, it follows, has a constitutive and a regulative dimension in the dichotomy.

This overview of the Kantian dichotomy paves the path toward a more comprehensive view of the interplay of negativity and positivity in an opposition. This is Hegel's thought, which indeed places negation at the heart of thinking the limit.

(ii) Dialectical model. Here we also find an opposition between two distinct elements, labeled schematically as A and B. These elements are constituted, however, by a relation between them that actually drives their opposition. A is understood as containing, internally to its constitution, an element—B—that contradicts A such that this element may be expressed as a "negation-of-A," using the Hegelian terms that characterize this opposition. Unlike the more static Kantian model, this opposition unfolds along a temporal axis implying an incipient movement from the first to the second element, for whatever happens in and as B must be present in A. This movement is one propelled by the force of determination. What does this mean? A is determined in large part by what inside of it negates it, and that determination produces two sequential moves. First, the negation is presented in opposition to the first element. Although internal to the first element, that negation is temporarily exteriorized. Second, that opposition is shown to be overcome and incorporated (i.e., *aufgehoben*) by the first element, which now "negates its negation." The resulting element constitutes the goal of the sequence. At this final stage, the totality is shown to be the identity of identity (A) and nonidentity (negation-of-A).

This basic gloss of the Hegelian dialectic shows the complexity of the limit in the dialectic. For one, if the first element already contains its negation, there is no limit at this stage, strictly speaking. Instead, the two terms of the opposition coexist within the space of that element. At most, we might think of the limit here as an internal frontier. An external limit emerges through the movement that expresses this negation of A. The limit is a symptom of this movement and as such is determined by its temporality. In its momentary exteriorization, it too is temporary, for it will have always returned to its proper location as an internal limit within the totality to which the dialectic progresses. It makes more sense to refer to the *moment* of the limit than its place or spatial location. Temporality emerges as the dimension on which the limit gains a new form but also as the dimension on which any clear opposition of one term to the other becomes blurry. This is why there is no void or ban at play in the movement from one moment of the dialectic to the next and why there is no real opposition here, at least not in the way outlined in the Kantian model. We might say that A and its negation are not so much opposed as varyingly distinguished from each other relative to the temporal unfolding of the dialectic process itself. This logic makes it possible to think of the limit as something that might simultaneously separate and unite the elements.

It is small wonder, then, that Hegel critiqued Kant's limit as an indeterminate negation that fails to conceive of a "mediation through which something and other each as well *is*, as *is not*," in clear contravention of the law of noncontradiction.[28] Furthermore, every time a limit is overcome, that limit corresponds to a *Schranke*, which Hegel links to an imperative "ought to" (*Sollen*).[29] In short, there is a prescriptive, albeit incipient, ethical dimension to the Hegelian limit.

(iii) Differential model. The identity of each element in this model—labeled A, B, and so on—is constituted as a pure differential relation between them. We might express this in the formula "A is constituted as A insofar as it differs from B." The formula is not only reversible ("B is constituted as B insofar as it differs from A"); it is extensible to all elements as well ("B is constituted as B insofar as it differs from C," etc.). Because all elements are subject to the same differential identity, they are equivalent, though not for that reason equal. All elements are equal, however, to the degree that each element has no positive content other than the differential relations it maintains with every other element.

This model, which is archetypally given in Saussure's linguistics, posits the existence of a contiguous space of representation within which A, B, and so on all operate. Within this space, difference functions as a nonantagonistic force, and so this model differs from Kantian "real contradiction." In contrast to the dialectical model, an underdetermined notion of content emerges here that does not saddle each element with the weight of its negation or with the imperative to overcome that negation. The limit such as it operates here consists basically of the movement of equivalent differences linking all elements.[30] As it dissolves into a relation of pure difference, this limit neither separates (as in the first model) nor negates in the movement across differences (as in the second model). Importantly, the limit does not fold inside a final totality where all differences might be *aufgehoben* (subsumed).

Widely rehearsed, this model drives what Jacques Derrida calls a "play of differences." Indeed, it was Derrida who called attention to the question of boundaries within this logic.[31] Let's remember that Saussurean linguistics is premised on structural relations that constitute what I have been calling "elements," with one relation—that between signified and signifier—being particularly salient in the formation of the element "sign." For Derrida, the structural relations organizing this linguistics enable one powerful system (i.e., language) and a set of *dispositifs* (i.e., speech, writing, communication, and meaning) that combined threaten to become, in a word, unlimited. But here we must note that the differential model has as its ideal basis an unlimited flux of differences prior to any actual representation or systematization. It follows that the demarcation of a system, which is how this model works in Saussure, presumes a privileged partition a posteriori of an originary play of differences to form a system, and such a system contains an incipient (Kantian) antagonism or else a homological relation to another system.[32]

Here at the encounter of language-as-system with the logic of differential identity, we find no objective ground to determine where the limit of that system might be. Or rather, we are confronted with the possibility that the same logic of differential identity extends as well to the relations among and between systems. Music is, of course, one such system, in potential relation to the system "language."[33] In other words, there is no force internal to the logic of differential identity that might close off the open-ended equivalences set in motion here. The structural impossibility of closure, however, occurs only at a logical, one might say ideal, plane, for in effect something else takes place: systems function with the presumption of a possible limit, a demarcation that becomes at the same time a threshold to another system. An example of this would be how grammar could be at once part of one system and yet function as a passage for the comprehension of another system (e.g., music), in the case of Small and Levinas. In this sense, each of these systems potentially constitutes an effective but porously bounded entity. Here, three questions arise:

(i) How is a bounded entity configured out of a set of equivalent differential identities; that is, how can one difference in effect break the series of equivalences in order to determine that from some point on some element is no longer part of the same system?

(ii)   What is the relation of this bounded entity to the elements which constitute it?

(iii) Does the existence of a potential equivalence across systems imply a common space—or imagine a totality of systems—in which they might coexist as differential identities?

The structure of differential identity is such that in order for there to be a limit at all, one difference along the set of equivalent differences must break the series. This single, decisive difference becomes the threshold after which other equivalent differences belong in some other series of equivalent differences. Laclau terms these series a "chain of equivalences." For him, this process for delimiting difference that might signify how a bounded entity is formed from within a system that logically allows for no closure means that the limit is internal to the system—internal to the system but not its negation, as we find in the dialectic model. The system of differential identity makes the limit impossible: to break the chain of equivalences is to interrupt the structure of differential identity. But because of this, the limit becomes in fact necessary.[34] Otherwise, there will be nothing but an endless dispersion disallowing not just systems of signification (in a way what concerns us when thinking about the music-and-language and/or music-and-speech divide) but also the construction of actual social formations where differential relations are all there might be.

The second question introduces a peculiar condition to the relation of elements in a differential identity to the bounded entity. It is not the case that elements stand in simply as parts in a part-to-whole relation in which the whole is the bounded entity. Rather, it is the case that, on the one hand, each element is always accompanied by all other elements but, on the other, all these other elements withdraw when one single element is deployed. For instance, in the case of a linguistic utterance, that utterance is possible and intelligible only on the condition that language, functioning here like a bounded entity, "withdraws itself from every concrete instance of speech," as Agamben puts it.[35] At that point and moment, the "bounded entity" is absently present, or present in its absence: language can never be present as bounded. I like to conceive of this as a torsion of the idea of limit in such a way that we cannot think of the bounded entity as something that simply constrains its elements in the manner of a container.[36] Instead, given the equivalence of differential identity that structures each element's relation to all others and to the bounded entity, there is no positive ground on which a limit might be located exclusively inside (between elements) or outside (as a totality that binds all elements). As a corollary, we find that the break of the chain of equivalences at once asserts the power of differential identity (i.e., it can by its own logic determine a limit) and subverts it (i.e., that determination interrupts its own logic).[37]

The torsion of the limit is more complex at the level of differential relations among and across systems. Our third question is, why? Because however unstable and susceptible to relocation along a "chain of equivalences," limits imply that what lies beyond a threshold is not just another differential identity but something that might actually threaten what lies before that threshold. In other words, the formation of a limit reintroduces the kind of dichotomy that characterizes Kantian "real contradiction." Constitutive of any and all economies of inclusion and exclusion, the limit is never neutral.

Even at this abstract level of analysis, we begin to see how the limit might be transposed to the analysis of the dynamics underlying social inclusion and exclusion: drawing the line means adjudicating to one difference among many possible differences the power to mark off those social boundaries, effectively closing what is constitutively an open system of differential identities. The potential impossibility of any closure here, combined with the necessity to do so, accounts for the violent force with which closure is achieved and limits set. This general condition of a potentially impossible closure, according to Laclau, is the ground of *the political*, the constitutive order which *politics* (i.e., actual actions carried out by social actors) then mobilize in the contestation or affirmation of power. In the passage from the political to politics, the drawing of boundaries forms a central—if not the central—mechanism. Remarkably, one such mobilization takes place at a founding moment of Western political logic that imposes a limit around sound in the constitution of politics. I turn now to that moment.

Logos and Its Partitions

Logos is subject to two couplings. In the first, it is inscribed into the very core of Being. In the second, this inscription of *logos* into Being shifts into a terrain in which *logos* will become a trace for politics. In both, sound and signification play primary roles.

(i) *Logos*-Being. Parmenides famously inscribed Being into *logos*, declaring that "it is necessary [that] speaking and thinking [is what] a being is: for Being is, and nothing is not" (*khrê to legein to noein t'eon emmenai esti gar einai, mêden d'ouk estin*).[38] Foundational for a particular but influential conception of Being in the West, the declaration elicits a fundamental question concerning the conjunction of speech and thought in that conception.[39] Grammar—the proper conjunction of thinking and speaking that organizes language and seeks to regulate all possible utterances—is of the essence, as I detail later. But the actual poetic lines of Parmenides luxuriate in an exquisitely elliptical grammar that has perennially obscured, if not mystified, what it may be telling us. Derrida, for one, observes how "thought—that is, what goes by that name in the West [*logos*]—was never able to emerge or manifest itself except on the basis of a certain configuration of *noein* [infinitive of "to think"], *legein* [infinitive of "to say," "to speak of"], *einai* [infinitive of "to be"] and the strangeness of *noein* and *einai* mentioned in the poem of Parmenides."[40] What may this strangeness be? At the most obvious level, there is a profusion of impersonal infinitive verb forms which, as is the case in many languages, do not require a subject. To say "*einai*" is to say "(it) is." Coupled with the initial impersonal indicative (*khrê*—"it is necessary to") that governs *einai*, however, something much less obvious happens. First, speaking (*legein*) and thinking (*noein*) constitute the *necessary condition* for "a being" (*eon emmenai*) (or grammatical subject) to be. Second, *at the same time*, a being is or exists by virtue of the power of speaking and thinking. The decisive articulation of Being and thinking and speaking forms the *logical condition* under which a being (you, I, anyone) *is* (i.e., the logical condition of its Being at all) by virtue of speaking and thinking. This constitutes the foundational ontological predicate of Parmenides's claim: "Being is [*esti gar einai*], and nothing is not." This sentence guarantees that thinking, speaking, and a being, on the condition of their consubstantiality, all are. To say "guarantees" is of course to grant Parmenides and the power of speech and thought an immoderate modicum of sovereignty. Derrida is onto something by noticing the "certain configuration" in which verbs are arrayed, which I take to be the silent work grammar does to elicit and indeed produce signification and to do so, moreover, in the act of obscuring itself and seducing the listener and reader by means of the rhythm and resonance it too can produce—here the two forms of "to be" (*emmenai* and *einai*) plus the third-person singular of "to be" are decisive in shaping the initial dactylic hexameter. In other words, these poetic lines tarry with nonsense, but precisely by straddling the porous borders between the meaningful, the not-yet-meaningful, and the meaningless, they allow grammar (again, the effective conjunction of speaking and thinking), even and particularly at its breaking point, to articulate Being to the production of meaning in and through grammar, which is to say, in and through thinking and speaking.

It should be clear, I hope, that in order to operate, the simultaneously playful and deadly serious ambiguities of Parmenides's famous lines have, as conditions of possibility, the presupposition, at once logical and necessary, of *logos*. Far from revealing its limits, and like the "unsayable" that Agamben refers to in relation to language, *logos* enables these ambiguities as dimensions of its power to signify. They are inscribed in a sovereignty that sanctions the musicality of Parmenides's poem and allows it to resonate because in the end it is grammar (thinking and speaking) that accounts for the play of meaningfulness and meaninglessness. It is small wonder that Jean-Luc Nancy calls the formation of Being here a "silent being."[41] Nancy may be pointing out the fact that despite the consubstantiality of thinking and speaking, thinking can always subtract the sonorous from assertions of Being. In this case, Being simply thinks itself as it speaks silently, or, more simply, Being simply speaks itself as resonanceless thought. Taking this one step further and paraphrasing Derrida, we might say that there is no one or nothing to manifest *logos* other than what it already is: Being itself.

Taking Parmenides literally, there would be no proper limit between *logos* and Being. But from the comments by Derrida and Nancy just quoted, we glean something more vexing, namely, that there is a residual causal relation between *logos* and Being insofar as Being calls on *logos* in order to "let be seen," as Heidegger puts it.[42] We encounter a situation in which a limit both is and is not—at least one in which there is a mark of distinction between *logos* and Being. And because one (*logos*) is the exteriorization of the other (Being) at the same time that it (*logos*) is interior to that other, we find the paradoxical interior exteriority of the third model of limit outlined earlier.

Parmenides's portentous words straddle both description (i.e., this is the relation between *logos* and Being) and prescription (i.e., in order for anything to be at all, it must be thought and spoken). In its prescriptive quality, the inextricable link between *logos* and Being carries enormous consequences for definitions of the political. First, however, Aristotle remarks of Being that it is "spoken in multiple ways" (*pollakōs legetai*), in reference to his own categories of being.[43] In a way, speech, which binds itself to Being in Parmenides via *logos*, disperses Being as well. As a result, Being is an abundance in need of being gathered. (Nancy reminds us of the etymological links between two apparently dichotomous sets of expressions: abandon and abundance, on the one hand, and banding and banning, on the other.)[44] It will take a formidable force to install a regime in which Being has a monological character, a regime in which it can be spoken in a singular way (*monōs legetai*). This corresponds to what I call a second coupling of *logos*, which occurs in the articulation of a political terrain.

(ii) *Logos*-political being. In a celebrated passage from the *Politics*, Aristotle builds on a distinction between voice and speech to construct a model of proper political being. Shared by animals and humans, voice (*phonē*) merely indicates pleasure and pain. Speech (*logos*), on the other hand, expresses a uniquely human potential to be concerned with the just and the unjust, good and evil, and the harmful and the harmless.[45] This fundamental capacity constitutes the binding force that gathers the community into the political order of the Greek polis: "It is the sharing of a common view in these matters [perception of just and unjust, etc.] that makes a household and a state."[46] We witness the linking of political order to the capacity for a number of determinations (i.e., ethical, in the discernment of the just and the unjust; moral, in the recognition of good and evil; juridical, in the adjudication of the harmless and the harmful), all made possible by *logos*. This move returns to *logos* the univocality that Being's dispersive character could potentially disrupt. *Logos* becomes equal to proper political being, while the proper political being becomes the life-form constituted in its power and capacity for good life (*to eu zēn*).[47] In this sense, *logos* becomes the limit par excellence. It delimits the boundaries giving form to the political community: *limên* signifies "gathering place," and *legein*, the root of *logos*, signifies "to gather." The political life whose existence *logos* guarantees is thereby given a proper place in the social and economic hierarchy of the polis. *Logos* determines who can and who cannot participate in political life. Those who are banned from participation are those other humans who live lives that are, by the mere fact of living (*to zēn*), limited and in a way captive to voice alone.[48] Our Kantian model of contradiction hovers over this arrangement of inclusion and exclusion.

But the banned are not expelled; they remain in the political order as the excluded inclusion that ensures that some will always take their place as the labor force of the community. This is what Jacques Rancière calls the "part of those who have no part," made out of those whose speech the proper citizens of the polis consign to a space of radical unintelligibility.[49] But because they *are* a part, however, they have a unique position within the economy of expression and communication of the political order: they recognize *logos* but do not possess it.[50] Thus, the Kantian contradiction accommodates a more Hegelian model of incorporation of difference in the name of economic expediency.

Rancière draws radical conclusions from this partition of speech from voice, for there is a potential passage from recognizing *logos* to taking possession of it by those who do not yet possess it. Noting that the excluded would attempt to "constitute themselves . . . as speaking beings sharing the same properties as those who deny them these," politics takes place "because the *logos* is never simply speech, because it is indissolubly the *account* that is made of this speech."[51] *Logos* is of course split between speech as such and its (*logos*'s) power to give a reasoned account of the affairs of the world; the distance opened by that split constitutes the space for political struggle in the first place. That space is internal to the split constitution of *logos*, and there a mobile limit can be installed but also removed and moved, endlessly. Why is this split so important? Because at stake in this reasoned account is intelligibility. It is here where the vociferous requirement of *logos* enters into the picture: this account depends on its sonorous emission as much as on its perception as an actual resonant event.[52] Rancière's insight is to show how the link between intelligibility, perception, and what I am calling sonorous emission, in short, between the phonic and the logical, makes the political inseparable from sensuous perception, that is, makes the political *constitutionally aesthetic*.

The relationship between the phonic and the logical is imminently aesthetic, albeit irreducible to it. After all, as the common denominator in a system of relations linking Being to politics and politics to aesthetics, *logos* remains a constituent power. It remains problematically as the zero degree determining the political order and the order of Being while being inseparable from those orders, as seen in the ambiguities of Parmenides's poem. *Logos*: the power to declare what order is and is not, what is to be included and what must remain excluded. *Logos*: the order of order that apportions shares in political life, naming and constituting all limits, all law. Indeed, no stranger to considering the dynamics of limits, Hegel remarked how "the perfect element in which inwardness is just as external as externality is inward is once again speech."[53] Following this line of thought, Agamben makes an intriguing parallel, placing the argument at the level of language, not speech: "language is the sovereign who, in a permanent state of exception, declares that there is nothing outside language and that language is always beyond itself."[54] In full exercise of sovereignty, language simply declares what its others are; it ushers them into being and draws a limit that it alone can trespass. In a sense, whatever is excluded remains captive within the limits of language.

Here, we return to the models for thinking the limit. Adopting the analysis of *logos*'s sovereignty, we find at play the dialectical model of an outside that is contained inside of one entity or system. It remains to be seen if there is a linear movement toward a consolidation of these into something greater, or even a totality, in accordance to a more technical Hegelianism. We also find the paradoxical limit drawn out of differential identities. This happens in the case of the partition of life into proper political existence and lack of political existence. The "chain of equivalence" given in the common ground of human life, possession of voice, and recognition of *logos* is thus violently broken by the elevation of the possession of *logos* as the specific difference that organizes the social field and establishes tightly controlled hierarchies. This gives rise, of course, to an antagonism that is experienced as a Kantian real contradiction, in other words, as the partition of the political field into one sphere of radical unintelligibility, on the one hand, and one of radical intelligibility, on the other. But because the unintelligible may yet become intelligible—this is the stuff of political struggle—the strict antagonism posited in a Kantian contradiction will be subject to endless reconfigurations and possible shifts in the laws which inscribe and legitimize these reconfigurations. There is, in other words, no transcendental term that may once and for all secure and guarantee the political claims made in the name of *logos*.

We find, in short, that the three models of the limit operate and are variously in effect across different registers of political order, an order formed by the institution of these various liminologies according to decisions made by political actors. The complexity of this interrelation of the limit as it took place in recent U.S. politics is the subject of the following section. Here we bring music into the fold of the logic of the limit.

Music Making at the Limits of Speech

By any standards, the spring 2006 immigrant-rights demonstrations in the United States were an extraordinary display. The demonstrations were in response to H.R. 4437 (the Border Protection, Antiterrorism, and Illegal Immigration Control Act of 2005, commonly known as "Proposition 4437"), passed by the U.S. House of Representatives in December 2005. On 7 March, an estimated 20,000–40,000 people gathered in Washington, D.C.; three days later, 300,000 marched in Chicago, with organizers putting the number at 500,000. On 23 March, between 10,000 and 15,000 marched in Milwaukee, and as many as 20,000 demonstrated in Phoenix the next day. Downtown Los Angeles was the scene for the single largest demonstration, known as "La Gran Marcha," with at least 500,000 people participating, on 25 March. On 1 April, some 10,000 assembled in Foley Square in downtown New York City. Somewhere between 350,000 and 500,000 walked in Dallas on 9 April. The following day, over 170 events took place across the country, with rallies of 5,000–10,000 people in states such as Iowa, Kansas, Tennessee, and Wisconsin and larger demonstrations in New York City, Atlanta, and Boston, among others; smaller rallies took place in states such as Nebraska. Sporadic marches were reported as late as July 2006.[55]

There were multiple dimensions to the marches' political display. Cristina Beltrán notes that people whose share in late-modern U.S. life is given in their raw laboring force—raw in the sense of being produced by bodies/minds that are juridically and politically nonexistent and socially unfree—willingly displaced their energy in order to perform something other than labor, becoming Arendtian subjects of action.[56] One thing is certain: it seemed impossible to ignore, to be blind or deaf to, the sonorous materiality that these marches mobilized. For weeks, these demonstrations, rallies, and marches took over public spaces and places, filling them with people and the sound they make. Marchers and demonstrators shouted, spoke, chanted, and made music. The vociferous sonorization of public spaces suddenly occupied by thousands was not in itself unique. Unheard-of was that fact that it was carried out by those who, as illegal immigrants and migrants, had no right to do so.[57] My commentary on the marches tracks the dynamics of this sonorization through relations of intelligibility and the marking of limits that made of this a political-aesthetic event.

It would be easy and by no means misguided to side with Small and say of the marchers' music that it was neither objectified nor removed from the act of its making. Indeed, whether it was *corridos* blasting out of store fronts in Los Angeles, labor-union-led chants in Manhattan, or the improbably brilliant duet of amateur trumpeters in whose wake a small group marched through desolate streets in Chicago's scorching midday July heat, where there was music, there were bodies, and vice versa. Music making was integral to the repertoire of Arendtian action taken by demonstrators. Indeed, by emphasizing the material dimension to all these resonating bodies unfurling through streets, public malls, and plazas everywhere, we might equally conjure up the aesthetics of Hardt and Negri's multitude (so indebted to a Spinozist vision of ethics), in which the joining of one body to another increases the capacity of each body to think, act, affect, and be affected—taking care, with Spinoza, not to reduce the meaning of "body" to human bodies. Likewise, we might call on Barthes to celebrate the specifically human embodied dimension of this sonorous materiality, leaving all verbal accounts and their effusive adjectives for another day.[58] A Levinasian adverbial reading is also suitable, insofar as the marches rendered sonorous an otherwise inaudible body politic.

I write "body politic" intentionally, not because the assembled multitudes were part of the national body politic but because they were not: the marches represented their becoming political, to follow Rancière, and the marchers did so precisely by presenting themselves as subjects of aesthetic intelligibility, there to be counted as speaking and music-making beings. Indeed, I would propose that the sheer sonic materiality of speech and music in these multitudinous assemblages made it difficult, if not impossible, to section the sonic materiality of speech from music and make either one a privileged field of the sensate.[59] From this perspective and in this specific context, there was no limit between speech and music, a situation that complicates, though does not fully evade, the limit structures outlined earlier. In the last instance, it is impossible to understand the demonstrations without understanding music's share in their constitution.

But if the music making of illegal immigrants and their supporters was unheard-of at this scale, it was also largely unheard. Neither the media (including mainstream and cable TV news, bloggers, and video reporting on sites such as YouTube) nor activists or politicians attended to the sonic dimension of the demonstrations qua political force. Although in the great majority of videos posted online, voices, noises, and music could be heard, the sonic dimension was hardly the focus of any commentary, being simply what happens when people gather in demonstrations. The sonic was partly muted by verbal overlay using technology designed to let some things be heard clearly and to cancel out others or by sound-recording technology overwhelmed by the magnitude and quick dispersion of the sound in open spaces. Attention, particularly in mainstream media, turned toward the written word on banners and placards seen in almost every audiovisual media report. There was good reason; they were multilingual, although mainly written in a combination of Spanish and English. This placed the focus on the hot-button issue of bilingualism, long the "surrogate terrain" for political struggles between the "Hispanic" population and both the civil society and the State.[60] "Language," once again, emerged as the zone where the potential movement from voice to logo-political intelligibility was interdicted, becoming itself the limit.

Many questions arise. Is it the case that the situational specificity of the multitude's aesthetics fails or is insufficient on its own to resonate beyond the bodies and sounds that help constitute it? Does the sonorous materiality of music making, its acoustic decay, constitute its own internal limit, in this case? If so, music, like so many other forms, contains its limit within, as in our third model of the limit. Or is it the case that the specifically pitched sound—that ancient partition of the sonic under the name *phthongos*—is contained within the totality of the sonic dimension but is incapable of overcoming it, stopping at the second stage of the dialectical model?[61] Or else does music exists as a separate and autonomous domain of the sonic, as in our first model of the limit? If so, might that separation not render it politically ineffectual? Either way, we would be juggling various liminologies. And neither bodies nor sounds nor music nor speech on their own can control whatever limits emerge in their interaction. Music cannot be said to test boundaries that it transforms into dialectical limits or that it alone overcomes, as their absolute contradiction. In fact, could we not also imagine that the resonant Being of the demonstrations and the demonstrators is abandoned precisely because of the abandon (i.e., plenitude) with which sound constitutes this Being? This is a thought that Nancy has placed in a very different register but that I invoke here for the manner in which it weaves abandonment into the ban and the limit: "to *abandon* is to remit, entrust, or turn over to such a sovereign power, and to remit, entrust, or turn over to its *ban*, that is, to its proclaiming, to its convening, and to its sentencing."[62] Music would be heard to ban those who abandon themselves to it. If nothing else, the force of this dialectical impasse cannot be ignored in the name of music's intrinsic "power."

Whatever the answers, it might seem as if at the intersection of sonic materiality and its necessary spatialization and temporization, we fall back into Derridian *différance*. Try as we may to find the better grammatical fit to the music making of those months in 2006, those many instances of sonorization remain captive to a certain poverty of their trace, the poverty of their ineffability, or what is the same, captive to the excessive abundance of their trace.[63] We might of course respond by asking if it was not enough that hundreds of thousands of people declared their existence, however fleetingly, and leave it at that.

These are impossible questions to answer. Some authors, however, have addressed the intersection of music and politics in these demonstrations. In a rare and welcome venture into the musical, Judith Butler heard in the singing at the marches an immanent freedom of resonant bodies. In the singing, she heard a claim to equality that, she said, after Arendt, cannot be limited by "a priori features or properties of an individual." As a collective act, the singing was more "an articulation of plurality" than a demand for inclusion, a sung claim that there can only be a "we" if there are many and equal "wes" all of whom can make claims to possession to national symbols and to belong, differentially, to that nation. Noting that despite Arendt's attention to the politics of hearing, she cannot quite theorize this act of singing, Butler calls for a language for understanding song capable of rethinking "certain ideas of sensate democracy, of aesthetic articulation within the political sphere, and the relation between song and what is called 'the public.'"[64]

Butler here echoes Adriana Cavarero, who articulates vocality qua resonance—that is, the acoustical fact of speaking and singing—to an emancipation of voice from the restrictions of a *logos* that makes of speech the demand to signify. Cavarero aims "to free logos from its visual substance, and to finally mean it as sonorous speech—in order to listen, in speech itself, for the plurality of singular voices that convoke one another in a relation that is not simply sound, but above all resonance." As a short circuit, resonance undercuts semantic communication as such, allowing instead a fundamental—for Cavarero, *the* fundamental—modality of convocation that humans are capable of. "This resonance," she writes, "*is* the music of speech, . . . the way in which the speaker cannot help but communicate him- or herself by invoking and convoking the other."[65] What is communicated, in the end? The unique sonic signature of any individual voice, which is considered to be the a priori condition of possibility for communicating anything at all, including any political demand.

Like Butler, Cavarero outlines a relational model by which to understand the ways in which vocality and uniqueness open up to collectivization and the communal. After all, as Cavarero insists, the linking in *legein* operates across multiple registers, not only in its power to gather under a system of signification and reason. Community is forged through "the acoustic link between one voice and another."[66]

The force of Cavarero's argument on behalf of vocal sonority and its capacity to link speakers is undeniable, though, as I will argue later, vocalic resonance cannot be rendered as a political universal: some people can afford to rescind linguistic signification; others can do so only at great political cost.

At present, I wish to register a related event. In the context of the marches, and oddly enough, Butler's appeal to Cavarero grafts an analysis of one object onto another: in the marches, there was no actual performance of the singing that Butler refers to, namely, the performance of the U.S. national anthem in Spanish.[67] This version of the anthem, the brainchild of a British-born music entrepreneur with a long trajectory recording youth-oriented, urban, Latin music acts, was a carefully orchestrated act in which, on 26 April 2006, five hundred radio stations across the country premiered the Spanish language "Nuestro Himno."[68] The release—a glossy pop and hip-hop version of the "Star-Spangled Banner" recorded by a bevy of well-known performers led by Pitbull, a Cuban American hip-hop artist with a fatal weakness for melismatic histrionics, and including, among others, Haitian Wyclef Jean, Mexican starlet Gloria Trevi, Puerto Rican reggaeton star Ivy Queen, and Puerto Rican singers Olga Tañón and Carlos Ponce—was partially intended as a show of support for pro-immigrant movements. There may be some reason, from this perspective, to yoke the marches to the anthem as Butler did, but not as part of their acoustical reality. In the public sphere, it is true, the anthem served to frame ongoing debates about the issues of Hispanic migration that instigated the demonstrations in the first place. But as I suggest in the brief comparative analysis that follows, the debates around the anthem could be seen to inadvertently impose limits on the music making of the marches.

In the anthem debates, the relation of music to words and to speech took various turns. President George W. Bush responded to the anthem—but did not address the demonstrations, let alone their sonic dimension. On 28 April 2006, he spoke. He was unequivocal about his position on the English-only issue, reducing the music making (or elevating it, depending on where one draws a limit) to an issue of the proper language of the nation-state and its symbols: "I think people who want to be a citizen of this country ought to learn English. And they ought to learn to sing the anthem in English."[69]

Further controversy followed Bush's de facto ban, creating for the first time since the beginning of the demonstrations a public sphere discourse with music at its center, albeit taking a highly charged musical-linguistic symbol as its main axis, not the sonorization of the marches. During a live interview in the widely seen TV news show *Face the Nation*, on 30 April 2006, Secretary of State Condoleezza Rice, an accomplished musician herself, was asked about the Spanish version of the national anthem:

> Bob Schieffer: Let me ask you about an issue where domestic policy
>   and foreign policy converge, and that is the issue of immigration;
>   and now, all of the sudden, a lot of people on the right are saying
>   that this whole issue of "The Star-Spangled Banner" being sung in
>   Spanish is a bad thing. . . . Where do you come down on that?
> Condoleezza Rice: Well, I have heard "The Star-Spangled Banner"
>   in any number of ways and—in any number of ways. I think—I
>   think what's really being expressed here is that our immigration
>   policies really need both to be humane and to defend our laws and
>   defend our borders and to recognize that when people want to come

here, they want to come here because they're seeking a better way
of life. . . .

Schieffer: So—so what language the national anthem is sung in is not a
problem for you?

Rice: From my point of view, people expressing themselves as wanting
to be Americans is a good thing. But we have laws about how they
do that, how they become Americans. . . .

Schieffer: I think you kind of dodged that question.

Rice: Well, we hope—Bob . . .

Schieffer: I mean, does it make any difference or not?

Rice: What, what, what language the national anthem is sung in? I've
heard the national anthem done in rap versions, country versions,
classical versions: the individualization of the American national
anthem is quite under way. I think what we need to focus on is an
immigration policy that is comprehensive, and that recognizes our
laws and recognizes our humanity.

Schieffer: All right. Thank you very much, Madame Secretary.[70]

Rice did not condemn or condone singing the anthem in languages other
than English, subtly withholding support of Bush's position as she also
cleverly avoided public disagreement with the president. And it is in fact
not clear from the interview that Rice actually had heard the Spanish version. A politician's rhetoric aside, Rice's brief speech on music is of interest not only because she (taking Schieffer's bait) yoked the polemics of
"Nuestro Himno" to the question of illegal immigration but also for the
way in which she highlighted the process of individuation embodied in a
particular musical style.

Individualization, an outcrop of individualism, is a classic liberal value
and sine qua non of the American right's ideology, amplified here to encompass the collective expression of a particular sector of the overall body
politic: "From my point of view, people expressing themselves as wanting
to be Americans is a good thing." To be sure, rendering stylistic individuation as a process of collectivization is a well-known strategy for reconcil-
ing the contradictory claims of individualist liberalism and democracy in
the context of "liberal democracy." For Rice, musical style—as much an
abstract musicological typology as a possible cultural marker for concrete
social actors—serves as a hinge to connect a "people" and their political
aspiration. Engaging a potentially polemical debate in terms of musical
style allows Rice to focus on the form in which music is imagined to carry
meaning (i.e., a modern, pop style) while shifting attention away from the

materiality of its production. Moreover, Rice adroitly dislocates the limit between music making and speech away from the contested area of language and places it at an unreachable location. Let me explain. First, Rice inadvertently creates an ellipsis between generation (youth) and political class (the demonstrators at large) that viewers and commentators could simply fill in as they pleased. That is, was it that the aesthetic proclivities and affective constellations of younger generations steeped in the contemporary and fashionable stylistic details of "Nuestro Himno" represented the most feasible political horizon for other immigrants today? Or was is that the cosmopolitan musical style of "Nuestro Himno" demonstrated the immanent Westernization and Americanization of cultural expression for the new generations of immigrants—presumably not those actually in the marches—and, because of that, perhaps their immanent suitability for social and political participation in the United States? Broadly speaking, in "Nuestro Himno" coalesced three general conditions for music and political associations: (i) traditional nationalism linking musical symbol and the spirit of the nation, a nineteenth-century formation; (ii) the belief in mass-popular music's resisting powers, a more recent ideological formation dating from the 1960s; (iii) the inseparable nexus between consumption and citizenship within the logic of late capitalist democracies, a formation that begins in the 1970s and reaches a high point in the 1990s and the new millennium.

I offer a simpler but complementary explanation. Combined, collective expression as an act of individuation of musical style functioned, I think, as an avatar for the only model in which the political establishment, whether on the moderate right or the left, could accommodate social and political heterogeneity, namely, multiculturalism—"accommodate" but not fully address. For in the facile ethics of cultural diversity and expression, no decisive political shift takes place other than to reaffirm the boundaries of what already exists as the final frontier of social life, namely, the State and its institutions. That is, in the tolerance and recognition of multiple but bounded entities (i.e., expressive collective individualities), the State both helps define the limits between these entities (i.e., there might be people expressing their political aspirations through classical versions that are different from country versions, soul versions, and so on) and ensures that they all remain firmly ensconced within its own all-encompassing limit, what Rice calls "our laws, our humanity." The dynamics of recognition are such that they enable the counting of certain forms of audibility and their concomitant visibility, situating whatever is recognized within a predetermined grid of comprehensibility and indeed amplifying preexisting standards of the aesthetic, and the continued delimitation of those aesthetic forms that remain uncounted within the order of official circulation.[71] All along, an urgent and constitutive conflict of contemporary American society is silenced in the very act of letting it be heard—in a word, abandoned in its abandonment.

Musical form served as a catalyst for Rice's recognition of certain claims to expression, whereas for her boss, words alone or, more exactly, language was what counted—one might imagine that another highly symbolic performance could have replaced the anthem, for example, the Pledge of Allegiance. But as the occasion for the reaffirmation of existing limits, music too contributed to the neutralization of the more complex political claims of the demonstrations. In the terms of liminology, if Rice's acceptance of music-stylistic and linguistic heterogeneity correspond to the model of differential identities (the third model), the effective politics affirming the State as the final frontier of such acceptance corresponds to a dialectical model in which the State negates and overcomes that which might negate it: the potential cultural and linguistic erosion of a monolithic American society. The sovereignty of *logos* displayed by Rice—as speech and as reasoned account about music making—as well as the effective power mobilized by *logos* on behalf of the State seemed irrefutable.

In the end, the controversy, the version and the story, like the demonstrations and sound they made, receded into the past. In the months that followed, the U.S. government increased border security, continued to link illegal border crossing to terrorism, dealt with illegal immigrants as felons, and engaged in a series of massive raids, many of which led to the incarceration of migrants without recourse to the law—the law outside the law, the exception given by sovereignty.[72] In light of this aftermath, it is difficult to remain silent, pace Wittgenstein, and to draw a limit around the unspeakability of the marches' sonorous materiality and/or its music making on account of its ineffability or the punctual force with which it partook in the demonstrations. We are reminded of a social distinction between those who possess the right, or indeed the luxury, to remain silent and those for whom speaking of music might be part of a strategy for political participation.

To conclude, I note the multiplicity of forms through and positions from which limits between speech and music are enacted, enforced, lived, thought, avoided, embraced, and so on. The heterogeneity of the limit, even in the case of a more or less bound set of events such as the demonstrations, goes a long way toward mitigating claims about a priori rigid boundaries in speaking of music. For instance, in the theoretical frame I have elaborated, within the particular political scenario I have briefly analyzed, and for the specific actors I have presented, I delineate ways in which music and language are possible negations of each other. But they appear also as elements of a differential identity that makes them subject to partitions according to a specific chain of equivalences that are formed in the service of various and competing political interests. Where Bush adopted a Kantian opposition, Rice engaged a differential model only to carry out a politically effective dialectical move through it.

I wish, then, to think of the *unspeakable* not as a limit but as an *interdiction*, which in a fictional etymology (*inter*, between; and *dicere*, to speak) hosts a double movement. On the one hand, it commonly implies a prohibition or a forbidding by decree, a speech act that silences. On the other hand, an interdiction is a speaking-across, an act of translation. In both these movements, there is no positive content to the interdiction outside the political investment each makes and the force each mobilizes in the interest of that investment. By the same token, the interdiction—and the unspeakable—cannot be explained simply through the logic of something like a negative theology in which what is known of it is known insofar as it cannot be said. Interdiction connotes the tracing of a relation that is always possible, between inside and outside, inclusion and exclusion, expansion and contraction, presence and deferral. It is not simply the failure of rationality to account for the aesthetic or the insufficiency of the aesthetic to articulate a politics in words or the gap between the semantic content of an experience and the corporeal content of that or another experience. It is not simply a dormant threshold to be crossed. If it is a hollow or empty space at the heart of music and language—or music and speech—it is one that is always rendered temporal in the actualization of a particular politics. This is where spatial analogies to describe and indeed define limits open up to another dimension. Interdiction obeys no temporality other than that of its actualization, remaining exposed to the finitude of all punctual affairs. I do not wish to accentuate the aporetic dimension of this condition of exposure and finitude; rather, I wish to call attention to this condition as the possibility of futurity, without anticipation or prescription attached to it, of course, but open to ever new interventions and struggles. By the same token, this condition requires that those who wish to make their interdiction permanent—the State, for example, in the case of the marches—constantly renew their efforts to maintain a ban that they know from the start to be impossible. To act otherwise and under the assumption of a fixed limit between music and speech is simply to disavow the future. And that, too, would disavow the political.

By following Rancière's claim that there is no political order anterior to the partition of the field of the perceptible and that this makes of politics a contest over this partition, I see this interdiction as imminently *aesthetic*. Aesthetics, in this sense, entails perceptually attending to something or somebody, even in the event of ignoring or being indifferent to it—after all, Bush did address his perception of the anthem, even if it is highly unlikely that he actually heard it, and so did Rice, who, to judge from her observations about musical style, may very well have heard it but attended to it only to remain politically indifferent to its claims while perceiving it through the apparatus of multicultural individuation and diversification. In turn, I consider this attending-to to be *ethical*. Here I think of *the ethical* as the condition of possibility for *ethics*. This means that on the aesthetic ground of the ethical, there is no a priori or originary displacement toward the Other on the basis of which a prescriptive, positive, empathy-motivated, and nonviolent relation might be always already valued. Yes, there is an occasion for aesthetic and ethical attending-to in the sense of recognizing and acknowledging the Other, and it may be highly mediated—we might consider tele-ethics as a way to describe the spatially and temporally displaced aesthetic encounters of the media, for example. And there is the possibility of indifference. Thus, demonstrators might have partaken of one or several of these ethical options. It appears, for instance, that organizers themselves remained largely indifferent to the sonorous aesthetic of the demonstrations. No single statement is known to have articulated even that old trope of the "people's voice" to the music making of the multitudes. So these organizers could be said to engage in an ethics of indifference that is not one of willful ignorance, which is not to say that they were unethical. This indifference challenges the notion of limits, of course, although one could argue that practically it allows for enactments of limits or the opening of interdictory zones by those who have a vested interest in speaking of music. Interdiction, then, always contains effectively the double movement I propose it hosts. That is, it is an act in which a decision is always already made that suppresses some other option precisely in the name of an ethical imperative. Such an imperative is at work when Rice invokes "style" alongside "our laws" or in the appeal to a final frontier (e.g., body, mind, speech, or meaning) where music truly is what it is, as in the cases with which I began.

In the end, the model I have sketched suggests an alternative to traditional comparative analysis of music and speech or music and language, one that perhaps critically complements the priority given to the perennial questions of meaning in linguistic and semantic reference. Likewise, it refuses the awed silence enacted in the name of corporeality, embodiment, expressivity, performativity, and other late-modern avatars for music's power. While agreeing with Cavarero's idea of politics and speech as a different way of thinking their relation in which "saying" is not subordinate to the "said" and with the action-determined reason of sonorous invocation, I do not follow her to the ultimate conclusion positing that this rethinking holds "logos to be oriented toward resonance rather than toward understanding."[73] She is correct in saying that as the modern state's song, the national anthem calls on individuals to lose themselves in it. Her response, to take resonance "like a kind of song 'for more than one voice' whose melodic principle is the reciprocal distinction of the unmistakable timbre of each—or, better, as if a song of this kind were the ideal dimension, the transcendental principle of politics,"[74] strikes me as a wager possible for someone for whom language and intelligibility are not at stake. Being with others in resonance entails a relation, and so does being with others in speech, in the form of dialogue. Cavarero's "transcendental principle of politics" idealizes acoustic binds at the risk of ignoring the fundamental antagonistic nature of the political as well as its material ground. I hope to have made clear that interdiction, no matter what its lack of positive content, is no metaphysical affair and that it functions on a material ground. It is the terrain where sonic materiality and the intelligibility to which that materiality is subject are both contested.

The emphasis on materiality raises intriguing possibilities for thinking about music, first, that it is not only something that simply coexists with other dimensions of social life. Coexistence is the logic organizing the claim that music serves as an interface, medium, or mediation. Steven Feld and Aaron Fox, in an insightful mapping of various scholarly paradigms exploring the music-and-language nexus, identify a number of such mediations. Music functions "in a variety of social formations: as an emblem of social identity, . . . as a medium for socialization, . . . as a site of material and ideological production, . . . as a model for social understanding and evocations of place and history, . . . as a modality for the construction and critique of gender and class relations, . . . and as a medium for metaphysical experience."[75] This is absolutely correct but inscribes a limit between music and "life" that is then sutured by the preposition "as." My thinking of interdiction would show each of these interfaces and mediations to be already enactments of particular logics of the limit and consequently of struggles over aesthetic (and thus political) intelligibility. Further, each of these struggles would be a zone of interdiction and thus constitute an occasion for ethical decisions. Second, considering the Arendtian notion according to which singing occurs from a place of equality, as Butler reminds us and as Beltrán too affirms in a more general political sense, I suggest that the emphasis on sonic materiality in the politics of aesthetics makes it possible to think of music and its makers and perceivers in terms of cosubstantiality and not in terms of equality that could be easily co-opted under empty signifiers such as "our humanity." Cosubstantiality lies behind the notion of the resonant modification of Being of Levinas, for instance, and shows why it is so essential for political order that limits be drawn, bans imposed, and interdictions enacted. Bush secretly knows that this sonorous cosubstantiality might yet subvert the order of things and give lie to the ongoing, most often unremarked, imposition of a limit between voice and *logos*, music and speech, the proper language of a tune. The demonstrators know it too, operating from the obverse side of this cosubstantiality, enacting it and affirming it. From this perspective, I disagree with the following claim that Butler makes: "the discourse of equality or the discourse of labor—we are the labor you need, we are the labor you depend on . . .— that strikes me as very different from the national anthem moment and it may well be a different kind of we as well."[76] First, cosubstantiality is not the same as codependence (i.e., "you need us") or coexistence (i.e., "we all exist in light of our tolerance for our individualities," à la Rice), for, as Elizabeth A. Povinelli proposes, the well-being of the citizenry is "substantially within" the precarious existence of the noncitizens.[77] Here, the illegal immigrant is a producer of life, his or her own and everybody else's. Povinelli's proposition is barely concealed Spinozism, with which I wholeheartedly agree. That is, there is no movement in the lives of any people in this society that does not affect the lives of all. Furthermore, the substance monism that undergirds Povinelli's position should not be made apparent or experienced solely in the exceptionality of music making, the marches, or the moment of social demand: it is the very constitution of any social formation. Second, because the partition of citizenry and noncitizenry is given in the relation of voice (and song) to *logos*, as I have elaborated, to separate discourse from singing, as Butler does, is in fact to affirm that partition and to enact yet again the interdiction that places limits between music and everything else.

What then of *logos*, that pesky rationality that in its presumed sovereignty and political efficacy seems to tear apart my claims for cosubstantiality? Butler elsewhere glosses Cavarero, according to whom "it is not because we are reasoning beings that we are connected to one another, but, rather, because we are *exposed* to one another, requiring a recognition that does not substitute the recognizer for the recognized."[78] Agreeing with the basic principle of exposure—after all, Cavarero echoes Heidegger's *Mitsein* and Nancy's exposure, both of which help ground what I have said of the nexus between the aesthetic and the ethical—but rearranging its limits, I would say that it is time to recognize rationality as being itself cosubstantial, although most often in unsolvable tension with what I take to be the aesthetic exposure (*sensu* Rancière) that Cavarero invokes. This is my modest wager: to insist that the interdictions of *logos* and *aesthesis* be thought as particular traces of an ultimately inseparable relation, for then the possibility of a more comprehensive political intervention—always rationally mediated, affectively moved, and aesthetically experienced—might emerge. But we might also enable a criticism that grasps the strength of interdictory practices that so effectively render the abundance of the speakable as an unspeakable abandoned in the abyss of a politically ineffective silence.

Récit Recitation Recitative

Jean-Luc Nancy

the subject as subject of art,
myth and story [*récit*]
(is there any other?)

—PHILIPPE LACOUE-LABARTHE[1]

A story [*récit*] cannot end, having had no beginning—
Existing, it comes to the same thing, finished for a long time.

—PHILIPPE LACOUE-LABARTHE[2]

I

The narrative [*récit*][3] puts to work and brings into play its narrator [*récitant*]: there is no narrative without narration and no narration without narrator. The narrator always presents himself as distinct from the narrative, even when he is the subject of it, as he is supposed to be in an autobiography or in a novel whose narrator refers to himself in the first person, as in *In Search of Lost Time* or *Tristram Shandy*, which are not accidentally such special *exempla* in the history of the modern narrative. The "I," by itself and by its nature as well as by structure, distinguishes itself. Essentially, it exists in distinction and discretion: distinct, apart, separate, and discrete in the mathematical or semiological sense, discontinuous, isolated, and impossible to take apart to be inserted into a continuity. On account of this, the "I" of a first-person narrative is neither more nor less withdrawn than the absent, anonymous, and even aphonic narrator of narrative in its most classical form.

Distinction and discretion set the narrator apart from the narration. Him or it—for it is not clear if we must refrain from designating a "person," even though the word *person* might be considered as derived from *personare*, "to resound through," just as the voice of ancient actors reciting the drama had to speak through a mask. Not a person as interiority— unless we understand interiority as nothing but an infinite antecedence always more withdrawn into the very utterance of exteriority: the unsupposable, unbearable, impossible to submit supposition of a subject of speech.

The narrator is the necessary, improbable supposition of the narrative. He is the anteriority of the narrative to itself. The anteriority of the voice to itself.

II

Auto- or allographic, the narrative grows from a twofold necessity. On one hand, it must be narrated: it must be uttered, pronounced, and it must even be announced, it must be introduced as a narrative. There is always a "once upon a time" that hides or is hidden, that reveals or is revealed in a precise time, even if it is an imaginary one (thus Faulkner plays at beginning "Old Man"—in *If I Forget Thee Jerusalem*—with "Once upon a time (this was in the state of Mississippi, in May, during the flood of 1927)"). On this account, narrative requires its subject, its narrator, its voice. In "Once upon," there resounds—musically, we will have to come back to this—an utterance, a vocal articulation. If there is text, discourse, or whatever you like, that is not a narrative (which may be only a hypothesis-limit of an exclusively mathematical text, for instance, if that exists and if that is an instance and not a unique case . . .) or that is not a narrative in some respect—then it is also a text without a voice and without an enunciator, which comes down to saying that it is not a text.

On the other hand, as soon as the narrative is at least virtually present— and it can, even must, be so in the background of the poem, the philosophical, legal, or scientific text, and of anything in short that makes a *diegesis* and not a *mimesis*, anything that is not a declaration in the first person, that is, anything that does not suppose that the speaker is in effect speaking in our presence—then it implies its reciter, its subject, or its voice as being absent but indicated or suggested in this absence: it detaches it as *sub-jectum* or *sup-positum*, it positions it on the margin, in the background of the recitation itself.

What is more, the narrative can go looking for this subject to make it come into presence, unmasking it in a way, as when Henry James suddenly makes the narrator speak in the first person after having kept the narrative for three hundred pages in the absence of any traditional narrator (in

What Maisie Knew). A procedure of this kind, however, only shows how fragile the separation between *diegesis* and *mimesis* is when the presence in a person shows itself to be the equivalent of and substitute for an absence. "Literature" might mean uttered by no one—and "recital" could be the name for this utterance that is not "mine" in the sense it is so in the speech of ordinary life and not literary life. At least it is supposed to be so, for it is not evident that the simplest act of speech does not imply that "I" who speak (as "I," subject of my speech, and at the same time putting myself forward as speaker) should not withdraw into the interchangeability of all "I's," an interchangeability which is nothing but a general condition of language as speech.

From this perspective, the *narrative* defined—story, narration, novel, novella—is nothing but the specific treatment and intensification of a very general condition of speech—of language [*langage*] in action, of language freed from linguistics but not from language as *langue*, for this impregnates and colors the action—and is the condition of *orality*. The latter—enunciation, utterance, address—is far from being limited to the instrumentation of a phonatory apparatus. Orality is not merely phonation: it is the emitting body, the body open to the outside as emitter of its "inside" that gives itself only by this emission. Vocal production puts into play a resonance of the body by which inside and outside separate, then respond to each other—and about which there is no doubt that the initial opening is of the order of the shout and the song together, the signal and the invocation (we could refer here to all the religious, legal, and political values linked to the utterance of the voice and even to the vocabulary of the *vox* as well as to that of the *opa/epos* in Greek). As we see, we would find our literature at its birth, and we would find it adorned with the solemnity of an utterance that can put into play nothing else than the possibility of producing outside, in the world, the thing or person that is in search of the meaning or truth of the world or its absolute outside (reversibility: the inside of the body is the outside of the world, and vice versa). Nothing here takes place that does not imply a twofold dissociation: that of the given world and of an "incorporeal" meaning (as the Stoics said) and that of the narrator as he recites *himself*, or else—which comes down to the same thing—as he divides himself, producing himself as narrator, in between narrator and narrated.

What we call *writing*, with the modern value of the word, is nothing but the form wherein is exemplified by being amplified (by the material inscription where movement, the journey of pro-feration and pro-duction, is retained and exposed) the clearing the way [*frayage*] of meaning straining toward its escape. In writing, the dissociation between subject and speech is concretely inscribed, along with that infinite escape.

Narrative stems from this dissociation. It refers to it: not only does what it tells precede the report it makes of it, but even if it speaks in the present—the so-called narrative present or else the present of a "mimetic" declaration—it cannot help but open a gap through which it reveals itself preceding itself. A narrator will always have taken the initiative to recite, or else he will have received the order to do so. Actually, speech bears an absolute antecedence: in it, "I" withdraws to the other side of the "self" that speaks—but that it is how it comes to itself. No "I" comes to be "I" except by narrating itself as such or by being the narrator of some story.

III

Only narrative puts into play the tension—expectation and attention, beyond all intention—in which the undeniable and irreducible privilege of the path lets itself be felt the way, the *method* as philosophy recognizes it but, while recognizing it, cannot prevent itself from reducing and resorbing tendentially. If, as Hegel says, Truth is the result yielded by the path, it means that the path is integrated, engulfed in the result for which it will have been the means. It has been so since Platonic dialectics and the path climbing to the sky of Ideas and of *theos*. Truth is not inside the path as being interminable or even as deprived of termination or direction—a path that leads nowhere and gets lost in the woods that Descartes taught us to go through always straight ahead: for on such a path, it is the nullity of direction and destination that at every instant, at every step, is accomplished as truth and confers on movement, surreptitiously, the quality of a result.

In all the cases of philosophical and methodical path, the result is presupposed. This presupposition can remain relatively undetermined, like Cartesian intuition, Kantian freedom, or the Hegelian absolute; but it still remains a preliminary position, an already formed reservation and the provision for the journey. Despite the impressive travels philosophers can accomplish, despite the distances they cover, their paths harbor a secret immobility. This immobility stems from their gaze, fixed—even if it is through closed eyes—on the idea of the result: of the fulfillment of intention and the resorption of tension. Movement can and must be regulated according to this idea: it must be such that its trajectory and its speed can follow an outcome, a consequence that in return illumines the entire path and justifies its route. The route will be regulated according to its end, it will have its end as its rule, guide and model: mimetic path of the goal, movement imitating final stop.

All of Philippe Lacoue-Labarthe's thinking stems from a profound rejection, early on and radical, of this mimetic conformation. He very quickly recognized in it a subjection and immobility—*typological* fixation—against which an essential revolt animated him. I want to posit here that this revolt stemmed from a sense of the narrative that was no less profound and no less innate in him—even if he never really put it into practice, although he came close—and that this sense of the narrative flourished in his attention to music, by which he set himself apart from the more ordinary practice of narrative. I do not want to do this by clinging to a literal interpretation of his texts but by trying to join in their fundamental movement, working from a consideration of narrative that I will outline in my own way and at my own risk, in memory of him.

Or rather, I will outline it in order to follow in my own way the narrative of his life and his thinking, the narrative that was his thinking, the recitation of the interminable yet too-soon terminated novel of his existence . . .

IV

I say "novel" to express what for us subsumes or exemplarily represents the narrative, namely, not the narration of picturesque adventures and lively episodes (not novelistic) but the thinking that maintains itself under the major sign of happening/arrival, of appearance and disappearance, the thinking that obeys what Lacoue-Labarthe formulates thus: "What we must think is the *It happens that* . . ."[4]

The first condition in which to consider this "it happens" is to understand that the subject of this phrase, the "it" of "it happens," is inseparably both impersonal and personal. This or that "happens," a "that" happens, effectively and fully occurs—*arrives*—only when this "it" becomes someone. No longer "it happens *that*" but simply "it happens." "It happens that 'He' arrives." ["*Il arrive que 'Il' arrive.*"] All Lacoue-Labarthe's thinking will have turned toward—and turned back to, overwhelmed by—this obsession that "He" arrive, He, himself, specifically, so that he arrives at himself, so that he himself arrives.

For someone to arrive, for something to happen, is as infrequent and as difficult to determine as the event of birth (in the same passage, Lacoue-Labarthe speaks of "us to whom it has been 'given birth'"). This event, we know, is a forever-deferred advent. Being born seems punctual but begins before coming into the world and lasts—as Freud suggests—until we leave the world. Being born continues into dying.

That is why he—Lacoue-Labarthe—continues by writing, "But how is it thinkable without the threat that the *It happens* stops happening?" But this threat is inscribed in the nature and structure of *happening*. For that to happen, it must also leave. It must first of all have gone—absent, not given, estranged, even lost, nonexistent—for it to come or return. Coming and coming back are the same thing here, for coming always returning from one single void anteriority, coming returns from nowhere, and returns to it. (Coming, *jouir*, of course.)

That is precisely what philosophy ignores, rejects, or banishes. Hegel denies that philosophy has a beginning in the sense of the other sciences, that is to say, in the presupposition of a particular object.[5] Absolute knowledge is not a total, integral, terminal knowledge: it is knowledge for which nothing is presupposed as an object but which gathers into itself all objects and dissolves its objectivity—its exteriority. Knowledge as subject of self, return to self, to the "concept of its concept" as consequently resorption of any *arriving* and any *coming*. (Hegel speaks here of "satisfaction," that is to say, that which profoundly contradicts *jouissance*. Coming goes beyond the opposition of satisfaction and need. That too belongs to the narrative.)

If there can be a question in philosophy of a beginning, it will only be, writes Hegel, to consider it as a "relationship to the subject he intends to philosophize, but not to science as such."[6] Beginning is external to knowledge; it is empirical and contingent. It is inside a *Once upon a time there was a subject—for example, Georg Wilhelm Friedrich Hegel—who wanted to philosophize*. In the end, you will tell me this subject must be reabsorbed into the knowledge-of-self of knowledge. That is true, but this truth pushes itself infinitely outside any presentation that is not strictly the return to self of the concept of its own concept. Hegel himself knows this: that absolute return does not strictly speaking *happen*. On the contrary, it is what, not happening, opens the possibility for anything *to arrive*.[7]

This return to self is the nothing, the insignificant, the inconsistent of an anteriority and a posteriority to all *coming, coming-and-going*. In Hegel, that is called the "being" as "empty copula." The void of being—or else the void being, that is to say, philosophy itself—forms for Lacoue-Labarthe both what the narrative rejects and what it refutes.

It rejects it, for it declines to set itself up as pretending to grip itself, to join the void to its satisfaction—either because it deems this dialectic accomplishment impossible or because it dreads its too-unbearable truth. Both together, needless to say. Refusal is also a terror. But it refutes it, for by opening the narrative, by trying to say that *it happens*, by straining *to arrive at saying that it happens*, and to say *that it happens that* He *arrives*, it effectively, practically, and with an exemplary tenacity—the tenacity of the narrator himself—engages resistance to the mutual annihilation of the void and of satisfaction.

That is what he, Lacoue-Labarthe, calls *mimesis without precedent* or *original mimesis*. The "he" of the narrative, "he" or "I," it does not matter, we understand, or else "we" or no one, the anonymous voice, is one who, "making up his mind to narrate," sets out to imitate an absolute narrator who has never arrived, since the absolute is impossible to narrate.

V

In these conditions, not only does the circle closing onto itself of the concept (or the concept of the concept) by which the difference between void and plenitude is annulled turn out to be a strangling of self—and of *the* self, of any "he" or "someone" capable of arriving—but even the *path* dear to Hegel and to all philosophy is annulled. The path that matters to the result disappears in it, or even as it.

Narrative consists first of all in straying from the metaphor of the path and of any concept of means, whether it be ordered according to an end or itself mediatized as end. Narrative is not path. It is clearing the way [*frayage*], which is completely different. In clearing the way, the path is neither given nor even open.

Clearing the way opens up a possibility for the narrator to identify himself with the production and completion of the narrative itself. Without such an identification, the narrator will remain lost just short of or just beyond the limits of the narrative. That, of course, is what happens with every narrative. Never does a narrator end up merging with his narrative, no more than he manages to reabsorb it into himself. The past of the ordinary narrative is only a secondary effect of the being-already-past, that is to say, never yet come, of the narrator.

The narrative will have begun before its narrator, who however must have preceded it: such is the lesson of literature—a lesson that philosophy rejects in principle, itself resting on the decision to be contemporary with its beginning. Narrative, on the contrary, dissociates origin from beginning. When it begins, it already has its origin behind it. Any beginning of a narrative can tell us so. When we read, "For a long time, I used to go to bed early," we learn before any other information that this *long time* preceded, at length, with an irreducible length of time that is lost before this first word. And this length of time immediately affects the "I" that means to speak, that is written here. It stretches it out—here visibly, legibly, but every *incipit* stretches it out in the same way: "Once upon a time" dissociates the narrator of this unlocatable "time" that he however claims to be in a position to locate.

In Lacoue-Labarthe's terms, we can say that this distension—the very dissociation of the narrator in his narration—is the fact of the failure to identify himself, to become *himself*.[8]

The dissociation *itself* represents the impossibility of there being "sameness": here it represents the difference (or *la différance*) with which the subject establishes itself or rather initializes or initiates itself or, even better, clears a way for itself toward what can only conceal itself from him, being given only as something already withdrawn into a *long time* or into a *one time* that no narrative will ever come to reclaim.

Narrative sets into movement what is so withdrawn that nothing could connect with it to shake or animate it: the absolute antecedence of the subject of speech. But "the subject of speech" is not independent of it: it is speech "*itself*," and it forms this speech, it makes it speak, at the cost of coming to expire in it—literally and in every sense. I quote Lacoue-Labarthe, who writes and describes "a precise trajectory that I would readily identify, as best I can, with the passage, between neck and larynx, of thought to enunciation; at that elusive and probably nonexistent moment, withdrawn from time, in which, next to the back of the throat, *thought*, then (what other word can one use?), takes on a sort of intangible consistency—I'll say approximately: takes *breath*—and comes to be confused with expiration where it seems to me it is not lost but is simply changed and, changing itself, is articulated or modulated into a vague atonal song."[9]

This—that or the one—that expires not in speech but *into speech*—that or he or she who is here called "thought," for lack of a better word, that is to say, for lack of a word for what beyond words goes back to absolute antecedence, to original separation, always more withdrawn than any assignment to a "one," to a "some one" speaking subject, to some one speech-subject. Far from having to be thought of as separation *from* a larger unity, or else from a unitotality (represented as maternal, oceanic, cosmic, whichever you prefer), according to the well-known schema ("castration," "loss" . . .), this separation is to be understood as the separation of the "one" in himself and from himself. This "one" who has always-already been what he is but who becomes so only by ex-spiring—death and speech together, speech and breath losing themselves to find themselves, formed in the hyphen [*trait d'union*] between the immemorial and the nonarriving [*inadvenant*].

VI

Recitation is the regime of this hyphen [*trait d'union*], this little line drawn from before to after and from inside or in-self to outside or for-self that are the two poles of the infinite torsion by which "one" looks for oneself and without ever finding oneself still stretches out and draws itself out, outlines itself and withdraws, is inspired and expires.

Recitation recites this ins-ex-piration, the rise and fall, the beating, the beat of this breath. *Citare* is to set in motion, to make come to oneself (the Latin word is related to the Greek *kinein:* there is cinema in all narrative). *Ex-citare* is to awaken, *sus-citare*, to cause to rise (and *re-sus-citare* is not far), *in-citare*, to launch forward. All these motions and emotions are at play in recitation: it excites, arouses, and incites a "saying" that is not any old saying but the saying that says an arrival and a departure, that says the tension of the fact that something arrives and that this something, necessarily, is some "one" or becomes or calls someone. That this someone is labeled as "author" or as "hero," that he is caught up in a "personal" or imaginary story, matters little, or matters only in order to take into account the extraordinary wealth of reciting possibilities, the limitless multiplicity of twists of narration: this profusion corresponds to the absence of a single Narrative—and this absence is inscribed in the very fact of the narrative, in its universal presence among speakers. For the narrative makes this come to pass, that nothing comes without narrative.

Recitation in fact is not content with "saying" in the sense of uttering, expressing, telling events that took place. It makes them occur, it makes them *come forth* [*évenir*]. Nothing happened but the sequence of facts so long (but this time is never very long) as these facts are not grasped, carried, pushed toward their manifestation. This thrust is the work of speech. Speech is not a tool; it is itself—in its phonation as well as in its phrasing, its syntax, its prosody—the thrust or drive of "meaning." Meaning is not added to or supposed in facts; it is their *arriving*, it is their *coming*. In short, it is the fact of the fact, the thrust and pulsation that *bring it into the world* and thus that *make* a "world," that is to say, a space of circulation of meaning.

The world is a world of narratives, of recitations of narratives. Beginning with all those narratives of the world that all cultures have always recited and of which our "literature" is itself in turn the narrative: it tries to tell where we are, and how, not only with this fact of the world and our being-in-the-world but how we relate to our own narratives of the world, to their oldness and to their loss, to what seems to us their naïve illusions or lost promises. How we have interrupted the myths and what voices are anxious to speak through this interruption. Myth—a world reciting to itself, a *tautegory*, as Schelling said—interrupted itself at the command of *logos*: truth appeared to itself as object of an *allegory*, a way of saying another object, unpresentable, only representable.

But actually, all narrative remakes *mythos*: not because it fabricates more or less powerful, seductive, or believable figures but because it opens speech to itself, to its own impulse and pulsation. The speech, the voice, the perceptible narrative of meaning.

VII

That is why the narrative comes afterward. It comes after nothing and after everything: after no meaning that may have preceded it and after everything, for everything always settles outside-meaning, in erratic blocks. Narrative comes back. *Recitare* is to recommence calling out the names at the courthouse. The names that the one who is reciting summons to appear are his own names—his own names that are never wholly adapted, in their non-significance, to that remarkable, unnamable own-ness that forms the truth of what happens, the truth of its arriving, the truth of the story told, recited, truth summoned, invoked, evoked, unverifiable, itself erratic and spread everywhere throughout the narrative, weaving the narrative itself without ever showing itself there except through the art of the narrator. What we call "art," here as well as elsewhere, is a knowledge of unverifiable truths modeled, figured, disfigured, and transfigured to the rhythm and speed of a narration. ("The figure is never *one*. . . . There is no unity or stability of the figural; the imago has no fixity or proper being. There is no 'proper image' with which to identify totally, no essence of the imaginary.")[10]

For *narration* is knowledge (*gnarus, co-gnosco, i-gnoro*); it is knowledge that reports, that relates what has taken place, that it took place and how it took place, how the order and succession of things occurred and then modified, modulated, altered. It is not a knowledge of things learned (*mathemata*) but the knowledge of things as they take and mistake themselves according to their incalculable provenance and destination.

Narrative or narration supposes the course of things, and that it has always-already begun. Whereas philosophy wants to suppose—and impose on itself—the beginning itself, the point of origin and of the end, the narrative knows that these points are infinite and, according to infinity, join together and cancel each other out in an identical absence of dimension. With narrative we marry dimension itself: the distension of the always-already and the never-yet, the suspense of the event. "But how to establish the exact moment in which a story begins? Everything has already begun before," writes Italo Calvino.[11]

Taking up a Faulkner narrative that Lacoue-Labarthe liked, *As I Lay Dying*, I read its first sentence: "Jewel and I come up from the field." Everything is already given, everything has already been given, begun and continued until the instant I read it. Jewel and I are known, like the field and like this moment of return, at an undetermined time. Far from Valéry's irony on the excursions of the Countess or the Marquise, this phrase brings with it a rhythm, a pace, a proximity already marked by the sonorous stroke of a name—a jewel?—and the other characteristic, the first person of a speaker. He is there, he is speaking to us. We go off with him, at his pace. We have *already* left.

Around two hundred pages further on, the narrative ends with this sentence: "'I'd like you to meet Mrs. Bundren,' which he says just like that."[12] The somewhat comical or cynical conclusion—the replacement of the dead wife—which actually ends the story, is added to the resonance, itself ironic but also vague and indeterminate, of the "like that" of this speech that in fact opens up another possible story.

As implacable as the end of the narrative may be, it resounds beyond it. It opens up its unworking [*désoeuvrement*] in Blanchot's sense. The same is true for Malcolm Lowry's *Under the Volcano*, to which Lacoue-Labarthe was attached through literary connections as well as personal ones of identification.

The Consul falls into the volcano's ravine, and "it was as though this scream were being tossed from one tree to another, as its echoes returned, then, as though the trees themselves were crowding nearer, huddled together, closing over him, pitying."[13] This resonance of the last cry is followed, in the next paragraph, with this sentence: "Somebody threw a dead dog after him down the ravine." This coda, which could be described as expressly musical, takes up and amplifies the tonality of the cry with a precision foreign to the whole narrative. In French, the "*crevé*" [dead] revives the "*cri*" [scream] while at the same time stifling it. A sonority, as extinguished as it is interminable, keeps the voice, tone, and song of the narrative open.

What has already begun and what continues beyond any narrative "end" is what music brings to light. The characteristic shared by music and narrative stems from a precedence and subsequence that are always open. What I hear when music "begins" has already begun. What ceases being heard when the music stops still resounds. "In song," writes Lacoue-Labarthe, "we demand something of the voice other than what it does spontaneously, we demand, perhaps, that it find a little of the music of *before* (birth)."[14]

Music does not just mobilize the actual resonance of sounds that it amplifies, intensifies, works on, and modulates. It mobilizes their anterior and posterior resonance, the incompletion and nonbeginning that belong in essence to resonance. Repetition—reprise, return, theme and variation, haunting melody, *da capo*, and so on—that haunts music, that punctuates it and measures it, governs the *re-* of *récit*, the iteration that takes up and plays again what never took place and what will not take place—but what defines the *musical moment:* the passage of time outside time, the composition of presents past and to come in a present that is not that of presence given but of recollection and expectation, the present composed of a tension toward the infinite return of a presence never at hand, always essentially—eternally—escaped.

A singing master said to his student, "You shouldn't make us feel that you're beginning. It has already begun to sing."

This distension of the present, this dilation of presence beyond itself and even to an absence full of its own beating, replete with the repeated call of the absent seized with its "desire to reach itself,"[15] that is what forms the foundation and true issue of narrative.

Music is a narrative. Not a story. Not what we try to invent in order to transform a piece of music into narrative, as when someone says that the clarinet is conversing with the orchestra or that the fast movement picks up and carries forward in its passion what the slow movement had put down and so to say abandoned—or else the opposite, for almost anything can be said when this register is being used. But one can and one must use it, provided one does not imagine adventures or episodes between characters, landscapes, or images. Imagelessness is precisely the determinant here (imagelessness, or the intimate destabilization of the image as it has been evoked): it is there, if one may say so, to give way to the element that I call here "narrative": that is, the *coming-and-leaving* or else *reciting and citing oneself, calling and hearing oneself*, but losing oneself as well as finding oneself in this echo of self.

The echo of the subject, a title by Lacoue-Labarthe—title, one could say, of all his work and title of his life, of his narrative. In an echo, I find myself and lose myself. I resound in the space that must be open to permit resonance. Instead of reunion in the absolute knowledge of emptiness and satisfaction, it is the repercussion in a yawning gap of an arrival that is about to go away. The yawning gap is the one that opens the subject and that opens itself to him so that he can be called to it, so he can cite and recite himself there.

VIII

For Lacoue-Labarthe, musical recitation is not, or is not essentially or primitively, that of melody. The melodic line can close over a subjective figuration (a lyricism, an expressiveness, an effusion as they have been understood since the romantic era).[16] The rhythmic beat touches the structure of the Subject as such,[17] that is, the difference and *différance* of self from self, the *"A* différant *from/in himself"* of Heraclitus.

The beat of this differ/ance does not happen to a given Subject: it opens up its possibility, chance, and risk. It is born in the archaic pulsation around which—respiration, heartbeat, listening, inside/outside—originally crystallized the enigma of "someone."

Rhythm involves the tempo of a relationship to itself by opening it, in its midst, onto the suspense of the beat, onto the caesura or syncope that connects and disconnects tempos in this time. Music, par excellence, has already begun and will go on further into silence. No doubt there is no silence without rhythm.[18] There is no silence. There is no need to think of *pianissimo* introductions: when the first measure of Beethoven's "Great Fugue" (another of Lacoue-Labarthe's references) bursts into the silence, cutting or tearing, demanding, imperious, the sheer attack of sound and the thrust of its movement reveal an anteriority that one could call tonal and rhythmic (the melody does not come until later). Already we hear something of what had been inaudible. Already a thrust, an impulse and a pulsation behind the sound of the instruments, in an arch-sonority that is in a way sonority itself: the opening of the possibility of echo. (One could say the same thing, to add another of Lacoue-Labarthe's references, about Albert Ayler's saxophone attack in "Love Cry.")

Before music and before speech, like their obscure common thrust, there is what we will call the *recitative*. Not in the strictly musicological sense of the word (which, in any case, has varied and which today covers such large musical territories)[19] but in the sense in which it designates both what, in speech, precedes song, goes toward it without detaching itself in the form of an "air," and what, in music, enters into speech to space out time and lift it from a cadence foreign to its meaning. Neither declamation (which is regulated according to *pathos*) nor song (guided by *melos*), recitative forms an *ethos*: a position, a conducting of language. This conducting immediately recognizes in itself a "before" and an "after," knows that it comes from further away and that it goes further away than its linguistic constitution and its phonetic emission. Recitative awakens and maintains in language the *voice* that utters it, while it summons and retains in music the *meaning* that it is alone in causing to vibrate.

It recites to itself in such a way a story whose whole plot or adventure is not tied up without untying from moment to moment its progression in a cadence and without bearing its signification in a pulsation that puts back into play, incessantly, the birth of speech: the starting-up of this echo by which a subject knows himself and feels himself—and here it is the same thing—preceded and followed by himself in an infinite, eternal alterity. Lost, consequently, further than any narrative, but reciting from this loss that he calls that of

> his own
> voice, which belongs to us no more than our
> way of moving or our gaze.[20]

So

> Does not discover what one expected to see, but a shadowless expanse, with nothing to divide it (like the sea when no breeze ruffles it and when it rests not sparkling but motionless dazzling—so as not to be seen), in a rustle scarcely disturbing.[21]

Translated by Charlotte Mandell

SPEAKING OF MUSIC: A VIEW ACROSS DISCIPLINES
AND A LEXICON OF TOPOI
Keith Chapin and Andrew H. Clark

1. Christopher Small, *Musicking: The Meanings of Performing and Listening* (Hanover, NH: University Press of New England, 1998).

2. Downing A. Thomas, *Music and the Origins of Language: Theories from the French Enlightenment* (Cambridge: Cambridge University Press, 1995); Andrew Bowie, *From Romanticism to Critical Theory: The Philosophy of German Literary Theory* (New York: Routledge, 1997); idem, *Music, Philosophy, and Modernity* (Cambridge: Cambridge University Press, 2007).

3. Boethius, "From *Fundamentals of Music*," trans. William Strunk, Jr. and Oliver Strunk, rev. James McKinnon, in *Strunk's Source Readings in Music History*, ed. Leo Treitler, revised ed. (New York: Norton, 1998), 142.

4. "In the beginning was the Word, and the Word was with God, and the Word was God." The Gospel of John 1:1. See *The Interpreter's Bible*, 12 vols. (Nashville, TN: Abingdon, 1994–2004), 8:442ff. As Robert Grimes, S.J., has noted to us, John is taking the Logos as Jesus, the second person of the Trinity but also is linking it to the Creation account in Genesis 1—"Let there be light!" So all is created through the Word—through Christ.

5. The Derridian concept of the supplement is one that arises out of Derrida's close readings of Rousseau. Jacques Derrida, ". . . That Dangerous Supplement . . ." in *Of Grammatology* (Baltimore: John Hopkins University Press, 1994), 141–64. The chapter on supplementarity is followed by a chapter on Rousseau's *Essay on the Origins of Language*, in which Rousseau speaks of the fall from full presence and immediacy. Derrida, "Genesis and Structure of the Essay on the Origins of Languages," in *Of Grammatology*, 165–94.

6. W. J. T. Mitchell, *Picture Theory: Verbal and Visual Representation* (Chicago: University of Chicago Press, 1994), 151–81.

7. Other recent invocations of the term include those of Siglind Bruhn, who designates musical pictorialism as "musical ekphrasis," and Lawrence Kramer, who speaks of "paraphrase" or "ekphrastic paraphrase." By limiting

the translations between media to those into words (as Kramer does also), we wish to link the issues surrounding speaking of music to those surrounding speaking of visual artworks. By preserving the word *ekphrasis*, we wish to emphasize the possible, if partial, survival of music even when it is transferred into words. All is not (necessarily) lost, whereas a "paraphrase" emphasizes the transition. Siglind Bruhn, *Musical Ekphrasis: Composers Responding to Poetry and Painting* (Hillsdale, NY: Pendragon, 2000); Lawrence Kramer, *Musical Meaning: Toward a Critical History* (Berkeley: University of California Press, 2002).

SPEAKING OF MUSIC
Lawrence Kramer

1. See especially Carolyn Abbate, "Music—Drastic or Gnostic?," *Critical Inquiry* 30 (2004): 505–36. For a more considered defense of ineffability, see Nicholas Cook, "Theorizing Musical Meaning," *Music Theory Spectrum* 23 (2001): 170–95.

2. See, for example, Susan McClary, *Conventional Wisdom* (Berkeley: University of California Press, 2001).

3. The task is taken up in my *Interpreting Music* (Berkeley: University of California Press, 2010) and entails, among others things, a critique of hermeneutics, a reconsideration of meaning and interpretation, and a rethinking of the complex categories of work and performance. See also my earlier *Musical Meaning: Toward a Critical History* (Berkeley: University of California Press, 2001).

4. Jacques Derrida, *Without Alibi*, ed. and trans. Peggy Kamuf (Stanford, CA: Stanford University Press, 2002), 111–12.

5. The liar, says Derrida, "must know what he is doing; . . . otherwise he does not lie"; in other words, the liar, who aims to deceive, must know what he says to be false (*Without Alibi*, 34–35). J. L. Austin argues that speech acts, though themselves neither true nor false, carry an implicit claim of correspondence with fact, whereas statements, though only supposed to be true or false, also have performative effects. The result is the strange bifurcation of speech-act theory, which is rooted in a still-operative distinction between statements and speech acts that the theory itself renders moot. For the short version of this argument, see Austin, "Performative Acts," in *Philosophical Papers* (Oxford: Oxford University Press, 1979), 233–52.

6. Immanuel Kant, "On a Supposed Right to Lie Because of Philanthropic Concerns" (1797), in *Grounding for the Metaphysics of Morals*, trans. James Ellington (Indianapolis: Hackett, 1993), 63–68.

7. Derrida, "History of the Lie: Prolegomena," in *Without Alibi*, 28–70.

8. Derrida, *The Post-Card: From Socrates to Freud*, trans. Alan Bass (Chicago: University of Chicago Press, 1987).

9. On the imagetext, see W. J. T. Mitchell, *Picture Theory: Essays on Verbal and Visual Representation* (Chicago: University of Chicago Press, 1994), 83–107; and my *Musical Meaning*, 145–72.

10. Emily Dickinson, poem 1129, in *The Complete Poems*, ed. Thomas H. Johnson (Boston: Little, Brown, 1960), 506.

11. On being under a description, see Ian Hacking, *Rewriting the Soul* (Princeton, NJ: Princeton University Press, 1998), 234–35.

12. For more on the connections between the sonata and the symphony and further discussion of the meanings of the former, see my "Eroica-traces: Beethoven and Revolutionary Narrative," in *Musik/Revolution*, vol. 2, ed. Hanns-Werner Heister (Hamburg: von Bockel Verlag, 1997), 35–48.

13. For further discussion and context on this point, see my "The Mysteries of Animation: History, Analysis, and Musical Subjectivity," *Music Analysis* 20 (2001): 151–76.

14. Heidegger continually reiterates the theses that care is the being of Dasein and that it is grounded in the mode of temporality by which Dasein is always "ahead of itself." See Heidegger, "Care as the Being of Dasein," in *Being and Time* (1927), trans. Joan Stambaugh (Albany: SUNY Press, 1996), 169–212.

15. Paul Ricoeur, "Narrative Time," *Critical Inquiry* 7 (1980): 169–90.

16. For a recent defense of this credo, see Steven Rings, "*Mystéres limpides:* Time and Transformation in Debussy's *Des pas sur la neige*," *19th-Century Music* 32 (2008): 178–208. Rings is writing in part to rebut Abbate's polemic in favor of ineffability, cited earlier, and to that extent, his argument and mine share common ground. We part company, however, over whether analytical understanding either can or should ground musical understanding.

17. Friedrich Nietzsche's distinction between *Erfahrung* and *Erlebnis* (the latter designating "lived," that is, finished, delimited, experience) was of signal importance to Walter Benjamin, who associated modernity with the decline of *Erfahrung;* see Benjamin, "Some Motifs in Baudelaire" (1939), in *Illuminations*, trans. Harry Zohn (New York: Schocken, 1969), 155–200.

18. See Hugh Macdonald, "G♭ Major" [key signature], in *19th-Century Music* 11 (1988): 221–37.

19. Lawrence Kramer, "Chopin at the Funeral: Episodes in the History of Modern Death," *Journal of the American Musicological Society* 54 (2001): 118–19.

WAITING FOR THE DEATH KNELL: SPEAKING OF MUSIC (SO TO SPEAK)
Laura Odello

1. Vladimir Jankélévitch, *Music and the Ineffable*, trans. Carolyn Abbate (Princeton, NJ: Princeton University Press, 2003), 72. (Translation slightly modified.)

2. Editors' note: *Ipseity* (from the Latin *ipse:* "self"): "selfhood."

3. Jankélévitch, *Music and the Ineffable*, 75.

4. Ovid, *Metamorphoses*, Book V, 552–63, my translation. I am using the following edition of the Latin text: Ovide, *Métamorphoses*, vol. 1 (Paris: Les Belles Lettres, 1925).

5. "All objects have sound (*phone*) and shape (*skhema*), and many have color (*khroma*)." Plato, *Cratylus*, 423d. I am using the following edition of the Greek text: Platon, *Cratyle* (Paris: Les Belles Lettres, 2003). Unless otherwise noted, all translations of Plato are my own.

6. Plato, *Phaedrus*, 258e–59d (*Phèdre* [Paris: Les Belles Lettres, 2002]).

7. Ibid.

8. Maurice Blanchot, *The Book to Come*, trans. Charlotte Mandell (Stanford, CA: Stanford University Press, 2003), 9. "The narrative has that *other* time, that other voyage, which is the passage from the actual song to the imaginary song, the movement that causes the real song, little by little although right away . . . , to become imaginary, enigmatic song, which is always far away, and which designates this distance as a space to travel, and the place to which it leads as the point where singing can stop being a lure."

9. Ibid., 8.

10. Ibid.

11. Ibid.

12. Max Horkheimer and Theodor W. Adorno, *Dialectic of Enlightenment: Philosophical Fragments*, trans. Edmund Jephcott (Stanford, CA: Stanford University Press, 2002), 46.

13. Ibid., 26.

14. Ibid., 46.

15. Ibid., 47.

16. See, among other essays, Jacques Derrida, "Plato's Pharmacy," in *Dissemination*, trans. Barbara Johnson (Chicago: University of Chicago Press, 1981), 63–155.

17. "Plato appreciates the austere modes for their moral value, as much irenic as polemical: in war, they exalt courage, in peace, they serve well for prayers and hymns to the gods, and for the moral edification of youth. In effect, such 'music' is more a moral than musical phenomenon." Jankélévitch, *Music and the Ineffable*, 7.

18. Plato, *Republic*, III, 401d (*La République*, livres I–III [Paris: Les Belles Lettres, 2002]).

19. Ibid., 413e.

20. Plato, *Republic*, VIII, 549b (*La République*, livres VIII–X [Paris: Les Belles Lettres, 2003]).

21. Plato, *Republic*, IV, 424d (*La République*, livres IV–VII [Paris: Les Belles Lettres, 2002]).

22. Plato, *Phaedo*, 61a (*Phédon* [Paris: Les Belles Lettres, 2002]).

23. Ibid., 60e.

24. Ibid., 61a.

25. Ibid.

26. Franz Kafka, "The Silence of the Sirens," in *The Complete Stories*, ed. Nahum N. Glatzer (New York: Schocken Books, 1995), 430.

27. Friedrich Nietzsche, *The Birth of Tragedy*, trans. Douglas Smith (Oxford: Oxford University Press, 2000), 76–80, §14 (translation adapted).

BACH'S SILENCE, MATTHESON'S WORDS: PROFESSIONAL AND
HUMANIST WAYS OF SPEAKING OF MUSIC
Keith Chapin

1. Johann Mattheson, *Exemplarische Organisten-Probe im Artikel vom General-Bass* (Hamburg: Im Schiller- und Kissnerischen Buch-Laden, 1719), 120–21.

2. Johann Mattheson, *Das Beschützte Orchestre* (Hamburg: Schiller, 1717; reprint, Laaber: Laaber-Verlag, 2002), vi–x. In *Das Beschützte Orchestre*, Mattheson also asked Bach about a detail of his genealogy: whether he was related to Johann Michael Bach (who was in fact J. S. Bach's father-in-law).

3. Bach's name is the first on the alphabetically organized list and may owe its capitalization to this position. However, the first name on Mattheson's list of collected biographies is not singled out typographically. The capitalization might also be due to a typesetter's desire to keep his lower-case letters in reserve, but later pages in the manual contain far more words. Presumably, type shortage would not have motivated the capitalization.

4. Earlier musicians had occasionally entered the public sphere through their publication of semiautobiographical novels. See Stephen Rose, *The Musician in Literature in the Age of Bach* (Cambridge: Cambridge University Press, 2011).

5. Stauffer speculates that Bach felt intimidated by Mattheson's skill as a writer. George B. Stauffer, "Johann Mattheson and J. S. Bach: The Hamburg Connection," in *New Mattheson Studies*, ed. George J. Buelow and Hans Joachim Marx (Cambridge: Cambridge University Press, 1983), 362–63.

6. Two well-known signs of Bach's engagement are his extensive theological library and the music he set to the "Coffee" Cantata, BWV 211, a conservative commentary on the roles of women in Leipzig during the 1720s and 1730s. See Robin Leaver, *Bachs theologische Bibliothek* (Neuhausen-Stuttgart: Hänssler, 1983); Katherine R. Goodman, "From Salon to *Kaffeekranz:* Gender Wars and the *Coffee Cantata* in Bach's Leipzig," in *Bach's Changing World: Voices in the Community*, ed. Carol Baron (Rochester: University of Rochester Press, 2006), 190–218.

7. On the beginnings of the learned tradition of professional musicians as a distinct group, see above all Rob C. Wegman, "From Maker to Composer: Improvisation and Musical Authorship in the Low Countries, 1450–1500," *Journal of the American Musicological Society* 49, no. 3 (1996): 409–79; Wegman, *The Crisis of Music in Early Modern Europe, 1470–1530* (New York: Routledge, 2005).

8. The family relations between these different forms of lettered communities has been stressed in Dena Goodman, *The Republic of Letters: A Cultural History of the French Enlightenment* (Ithaca, NY: Cornell University Press, 1994), 12–52.

9. Carl Dahlhaus, "Der Dilettant und der Banause in der Musikgeschichte," *Archiv für Musikwissenschaft* 25, no. 3 (1968): 157–72.

10. "Ich weis nicht ob er [Kuhnau] dem Orden der Tonkünstler, oder den anderen Gelehrten mehr Ehre gebracht. Er war gelehrt in der Gottesgelahrtheit, in den Rechten, Beredsamkeit, Dichtkunst, Mathematik, fremden Sprachen, und Musik." Jacob Adlung, *Anleitung zu der musikalischen Gelahrtheit*, ed. Hans Joachim Moser, facsimile ed. (Erfurt: J. D. Jungnicol, Sen., 1758 [facs. ed., Kassel: Bärenreiter, 1953]), 195.

11. On the development of the galant habitus in German musical traditions, see Keith Chapin, "Counterpoint: From the Bees or For the Birds? Telemann and Early-Eighteenth-Century Quarrels with Tradition," *Music & Letters* 92, no. 3 (2011): 377–409; David Sheldon, "The Concept Galant in the 18th Century," *Journal of Musicological Research* 9, nos. 2–3 (1989): 89–108; David A. Sheldon, "The Galant Style Revisited and Re-evaluated," *Acta Musicologica* 47, no. 2 (1975): 240–69.

12. Ralf Georg Bogner, "Die Formationsphase der deutschsprachigen Literaturkritik," Universität Rostock, https://www.phf.uni-rostock.de/institut/iger man/forschung/litkritik/litkritik/Epochen/ea.htm (accessed 3 January 2013).

13. Anne Catherine Le Bar, "Musical Culture and the Origins of the Enlightenment in Hamburg" (Ph.D. diss., University of Washington, 1993).

14. Manfred Beetz, "Ein neuentdeckter Lehrer der Conduite: Thomasius in der Geschichte der Gesellschaftsethik," in *Christian Thomasius, 1655–1728*, ed. Werner Schneiders (Hamburg: Meiner, 1989), 199–222.

15. On Weise, see Carol Baron, "Transitions, Transformations, Reversals: Rethinking Bach's World," in Baron, *Bach's Changing World, 14–17*.

16. Le Bar, "Musical Culture," 155–68.

17. As the reorientation of public discourse progressed, burgher writers began to critique the genre and the aristocratic *galant* habitus on which it fed. The Leipzig professor, critic, and journalist Johann Christoph Gottsched, for example, critiqued its irrationality. On Gottsched's critique of opera, see Gloria Flaherty, *Opera in the Development of German Critical Thought* (Princeton, NJ: Princeton University Press, 1978), 93–101; Wilhelm Seidel, "Saint-Evremond und der Streit um die Oper in Deutschland," in *Aufklärungen: Studien zur deutsch-französischen Musikgeschichte im 18. Jahrhundert, Einflüsse und Wirkungen*, ed. Wolfgang Birtel and Christoph-Hellmut Mahling (Heidelberg: Winter, 1986), 46–54.

18. The following biographical information is drawn from Beekman C. Cannon, *Johann Mattheson: Spectator in Music*, ed. Leo Schrade (New Haven, CT: Yale University Press, 1947). Cannon's biography relies heavily on Mattheson's various autobiographies and corroborates and supplements them with information from other primary sources. Despite occasional errors of translation, it remains the most complete biography of Mattheson available.

19. "Ruhe Kammer für Herr Johann Mattheson weyland Grosfürstlicher Holsteinischer Legations Raht [*sic*] und dessen Ehe Genossin Zu ewigen Tagen." Quoted in ibid., 107.

20. For example, in 1717 Mattheson translated the *Letters Which Passed between Count G., the Barons Gortz, Sparre, and Others, Relating to the Design of Raising a Rebellion in His Majesty's Dominions, to Be Supported by a Force from Sweden* (London: Published by Authority, 1717). The British government had illicitly opened diplomatic dispatches from the Swedish ambassador, Count Gyllenborg, to Sweden. The act caused much outcry, and the British government published the contents of the letters to explain and excuse their actions.

21. Chapin, "From the Bees."

22. George Buelow, for example, writes, "For what occurs in the volumes by Mattheson and Buttstett is the last struggle of German conservative, traditional music theory, with its noble and decisive 17th-century heritage inevitably defeated on the battleground of the 18th century, where new music from Italy as well as France had compelled such writers as Mattheson to formulate an entirely new theoretical approach to the understanding of their art." George J. Buelow, "Buttstett, Johann Heinrich," in *Grove Music Online, Oxford Music Online*, http://www.oxfordmusiconline.com/subscriber/article/grove/music/04473 (accessed 21 October 2009).

23. A good summary of the debates can be found in Dietrich Bartel, introduction to *Die drei Orchestre-Schriften,* by Johann Mattheson (Laaber: Laaber-Verlag, 2002), v–xlix.

24. "Aus würklichem ernsten Eifer vor unsere heutige schöne *Music,* kan ich mannnichmahl nicht umhin, wenn hie und da in Büchern sich eine fantastische Klage erhebet, *daß wir der Alten* Music *nun unter die verlohrnen Dinge rechnen, dabey zu schreiben: GOtt Lob!* Denn es kommt mir fast für, als wenn ein *Theologus* unter uns betaueren wolte, daß das Brand-Opffer des alten Testaments nunmehro verloschen sey, oder daß in einer Catholischen Bauer-Kirchen von einem alten Marienbilde das Gold abgefallen. Leute die so reden und schreiben, sie mögen sonst so gelehrt seyn als sie wollen, machen der Lauß eine Steltze, und geben eine grosse Einfalt in diesem Stück ans Licht, welche alsdenn noch mehr hervorgucket, wenn etwan überhaupt von *Professionen* geurtheilet wird, und man so schreibet: Er sey *Theologus* oder *Philosophus, Juridicus* oder *Medicus, Historicus, Orator, Poeta, it.* alle *Grammati*sche, *Rhetori*sche, *Logi*sche, *Physicali*sche, *Metaphysi*sche, *Mathemati*sche Reguln *&c.* ohne daß dabey des *Musici* und der *Musicali*schen Reguln gedacht wird, gerade als wenn ein *Musicus* oder die *Music* so verachtete Dinge wären, daß sie gar keinen *Locum* verdienten, sondern als *Umbrae* under dem &c. begriffen werden müsten." Johann Mattheson, *Das Neu-Eröffnete Orchestre,* facsimile ed. (Hamburg: Author, 1713; reprint, Laaber: Laaber-Verlag, 2002), 245–46, emphasis in the original.

25. On the debates, see above all Georgia Cowart, *The Origins of Modern Musical Criticism: French and Italian Music, 1600–1750* (Ann Arbor, MI: UMI Research Press, 1981).

26. The collection passed from musician to musician until it eventually formed the core of the music library of the Berlin Staatsbibliothek. Its history could be a history of the discipline. Its story is told by Harald Kümmerling, *Katalog der Sammlung Bokemeyer,* Kieler Schriften zur Musikwissenschaft, vol. 18 (Kassel: Bärenreiter, 1970), 9–18.

27. Mizler reported on the foundation of the society and listed its bylaws in April 1738. The bylaws were subsequently revised. Lorenz Christoph Mizler, *Neu eröffnete musikalische Bibliothek,* 4 vols. (Leipzig: Author, 1739–45; reprint, Hilversum: Frits Knuf, 1966), 3:346–62.

28. This biographical information on Bokemeyer is taken from George J. Buelow, "Bokemeyer, Heinrich," in *Grove Music Online, Oxford Music Online,* http://www.oxfordmusiconline.com/subscriber/article/grove/music/03435 (accessed 30 November 2009).

29. Telemann's response to a questionnaire circulated by Mattheson appears in Johann Mattheson, *Critica Musica,* 2 vols. (Hamburg: Author, 1722–25; reprint, Laaber: Laaber-Verlag, 2003), 1:358–60.

30. Mattheson gleefully published the letter immediately following Telemann's response in ibid., 1:361–63.

31. Ibid., 1:257–58. On the ideal of intimate conversation as a pillar of traditional learned circles of European humanists, see Marc Fumaroli, "Les abeilles et les araignées," in *La Querelle des Anciens et des Modernes: XVIIe.–XVIIIe. siècles*, ed. Anne-Marie Lecoq (Paris: Gallimard, 2001).

32. "Denn er beweinte bitterlich die Ausschweiffungen der itzigen melodischen Setzer: wie ich die unmelodischen Künsteleien der Alten belachte." Georg Philipp Telemann, *Singen ist das Fundament zur Music in allen Dingen: Eine Dokumentensammlung*, ed. Werner Rackwitz, Taschenbücher zur Musikwissenschaft, no. 80 (Wilhelmshaven: Heinrichshofen, 1981), 202.

33. "Die Feder des vortreflichen Hn. Johann Kuhnau diente mir hier zur Nachfolge in Fugen und Contrapuncten; in melodischen Sätzen aber, und deren Untersuchung, hatten Händel und ich, bey öfftern Besuchen auf beiden seiten, wie auch schrifftlich, eine stete Beschäfftigung." Ibid., 201.

34. Mattheson, *Das Neu-Eröffnete Orchestre*, title page.

35. Mattheson, *Das Beschützte Orchestre*, title page.

36 Johann Mattheson, *Das Forschende Orchestre* (Hamburg: Benjamin Schillers Witwe und Joh. Christoph Kißner, 1721; reprint, Laaber: Laaber-Verlag, 2002), title page.

37. "Ich wünsche nicht nur, daß dieser mein Leser ein *habiler*, sondern auch, daß er dabey ein gelehrter, und mit scharfer Urtheils-Kraft versehener *Musicus* sey." "Ad Lectorem," in ibid., paragraphs 5 and 22.

38. Arno Forchert, "Polemik als Erkenntnisform: Bemerkungen zu den Schriften Matthesons," in *New Mattheson Studies*, ed. George Buelow and Hans Joachim Marx (Cambridge: Cambridge University Press, 1983), 199–212.

39. Johann Mattheson, preface to *Der vollkommene Capellmeister: Neusatz des Textes und der Noten*, ed. Friederike Ramm, Bärenreiter Studienausgabe (Kassel: Bärenreiter, 1999), 9.

40. Steffen Voss, "Did Bach Perform Sacred Music by Johann Mattheson in Leipzig?," *Bach Notes: The Newsletter of the American Bach Society*, no. 3 (2005): 1–5. I thank Daniel Melamed for pointing me in the direction of this article.

41. Such criticisms are summarized in Stauffer, "Johann Mattheson and J. S. Bach."

42. Fux had his own spats with Mattheson and may have harbored his own resentments. See Joel Lester, "The Fux-Mattheson Correspondence: An Annotated Translation," *Current Musicology* 24, no. 1 (1977): 37–62.

43. Johann Mattheson, *Grundlage einer Ehrenpforte*, ed. Max Schneider (Berlin: Leo Liepmannssohn, 1910), xi.

44. David Ledbetter, *Bach's Well-Tempered Clavier: The 48 Preludes and Fugues* (New Haven, CT: Yale University Press, 2002), 2, 118–25.

45. The various pieces from the debate are reprinted in Hans T. David and Arthur Mendel, eds., *The New Bach Reader: A Life of Johann Sebastian Bach in Letters and Documents*, revised and enlarged by Christoph Wolff (New York: Norton, 1998), 337–53.

46. On the debate, see George Buelow, "In Defense of J. A. Scheibe against J. S. Bach," *Proceedings of the Royal Musical Association* 51 (1974–75): 85–100; Keith Chapin, "Scheibe's Mistake: Sublime Simplicity and the Criteria of Classicism," *Eighteenth-Century Music* 5, no. 2 (2008): 165–77; Günther Wagner, "J. A. Scheibe–J. S. Bach: Versuch einer Bewertung," *Bach-Jahrbuch*, 1982, 33–49.

47. The report comes in the middle of Christoph Gottlieb Schröter, "Die Nothwendigkeit der Mathematik bey gründlicher Erlernung der musikalischen Composition," in *Neu eröffnete musikalische Bibliothek*, vol. 3, part 2, 204; translated in David and Mendel, *The New Bach Reader*, 353.

48. On the relationship between Mattheson's *Fingersprache* and Bach's *Kunst der Fuge*, see Gregory J. Butler, *"Der vollkommene Capellmeister* as a Stimulus to J. S. Bach's Late Fugal Writing," in *New Mattheson Studies*, ed. George J. Buelow and Hans Joachim Marx (Cambridge: Cambridge University Press, 1983); Stauffer, "Johann Mattheson and J. S. Bach," 364–68.

MAKING MUSIC SPEAK
Andrew H. Clark

1. See Odello, "Waiting for the Death Knell," in this volume, 39–48.

2. Johann Mattheson, *Der vollkommene Capellmeister: A Revised Translation with Critical Commentary*, ed. and trans. Ernest C. Harriss (Ann Arbor, MI: UMI Research Press, 1981), 127.

3. One reason for this might be that the arts were being forced to rethink their purpose and lines of support as traditional patronage and collecting from the church and royalty began to wane.

4. "Il n'y a plus, à proprement parler, de spectacles publics. Quel rapport entre nos assemblées au théâtre dans les jours les plus nombreux, et celles du peuple d'Athènes ou de Rome? Les théâtres anciens recevaient jusqu'à quatre-vingt mille citoyens. On employait, à la construction de ces édifices, tous les moyens de faire valoir les instruments et les voix. On avait l'idée d'un grand instrument." Denis Diderot, *Entretiens sur le fils naturel*, in *Œuvres complètes*, ed. Herbert Dieckmann, Jean Fabre, Jacques Proust, and Jean Varloot, 33 vols. (Paris: Hermann, 1975–), 10:118 (hereafter cited as DPV).

5. See Penelope Gouk, "Music, Melancholy, and Medical Spirits in Early Modern Thought," in *Music as Medicine: The History of Music Therapy since*

Antiquity (Aldershot, UK: Ashgate, 2000), 189. Gouk locates the first uses of this metaphor in terms of music therapy with Ficino in the 1490s. Bernard Mandeville, *Fable of the Bees* (1714); Adam Smith, *Theory of Moral Sentiments* (1759); Laurence Sterne, *Tristam Shandy* (1759–69); Pierre Jean Georges Cabanis, *Rapports du physique et du moral de l'homme* (1802).

6. Anthony Ashley Cooper, 3rd Earl of Shaftesbury, *Characteristics of Men, Manners, Opinions, Times*, 3 vols. (Indianapolis: Liberty Fund, 2001), 2:179.

7. One thinks naturally of Descartes, Kircher, Mersenne, Voltaire, Smith, Sterne, d'Alembert, Bernoulli, Shaftesbury, among many others in this context.

8. Eighteenth-century treatises that address music from at least DuBos on attempt to grapple with the effect of music on the "masses" and the consequences of their judgments. See for instance, Michel Chabanon's chapter, "Quels sont les Arts qui plaisent davantage à la multitude, quels sont les jugements qu'elle en porte," in *De la musique considéré en elle-même et dans ses rapports avec la parole, les langues, la poésie et le théâtre* (Geneva: Slatkine Reprints, 1969).

9. Many critics have noted Mattheson's contribution to a more empirical understanding of music theory. See John Neubauer, *The Emancipation of Music from Language: Departure from Mimesis in Eighteenth-Century Aesthetics* (New Haven, CT: Yale University Press, 1986), 76. We see a similar move from the metaphysical to the more empirical in Rameau's music theory texts. See Thomas Christensen, *Rameau and Musical Thought in the Enlightenment* (Cambridge: Cambridge University Press, 1993).

10. On Mattheson's eclectic sources and pragmatic approach, see Beekman C. Cannon's "The Legacy of Johann Mattheson: A Retrospective Evaluation," in *New Mattheson Studies*, ed. George J. Buelow and Hans Joachim Marx (Cambridge: Cambridge University Press, 1983), 1–14. Also see Keith Chapin's chapter in this volume for his discussion of specialist discourse in Germany in the eighteenth century and his analysis of Mattheson as a musical man of letters deeply rooted in the public sphere.

11. Mattheson, *Der vollkommene Capellmeister*, 51 (my emphasis). Nature produces sound and all its proportions (most of which are unknown and math cannot bring into order). There is an infinite possibility of tones. This infinite diversity precludes any privileged order or universal harmony.

12. Ibid., 54.

13. On German reception of Rameau's theory, see Joel Lester, *Compositional Theory in the Eighteenth Century* (Cambridge, MA: Harvard University Press, 1992), 150–57, 193–230. Rameau's name was certainly known in German, but real knowledge of his writings was scarce there. Most writers had

more preconceptions about Rameau than real understanding. However, he generally was considered a musical mathematician.

14. Jean-Philippe Rameau, preface to *Traité de l'harmonie* (1722), quoted in Cynthia Verba, *Music and the French Enlightenment: Reconstruction of a Dialogue, 1750–1764* (Oxford, UK: Clarendon, 1992), 54.

15. This move from mathematical models in music theory to experimental ones has been closely examined in the works of Thomas Christensen and Cynthia Verba. Both Christensen and Verba have argued that even Rameau, who is often labeled as the partisan for mathematical models in music theory, moved more and more to scientific models (experimental and physical) to justify his theories. "Music is a physico-mathematical science; sound is its physical object, and the ratios found between the different sounds are the mathematical component" (Rameau, *Génération harmonique*, 30, quoted in Verba, *Music and the French Enlightenment*, 59). For more on Mattheson's relationship to French music, see Herbert Schneider, *"Mattheson und die französische Musik,"* in Buelow and Marx, *New Mattheson Studies*, 425–42.

16. Cannon, "Legacy of Mattheson," 8.

17. Tracy B. Strong, "Rousseau: Music, Language, and Politics," in this volume, 86–100.

18. Louis Sébastien Mercier, *Tableau de Paris*, ed. Jean-Claude Bonnet, 2 vols. (Paris: Mercure de France, 1994), 1:1050. "Que j' emploierais cette musique ambulante et délicieuse, prolongée et diversifiée, comme un moyen pour changer en grande partie les moeurs du peuple et l'attacher encore plus à son gouvernement."

19. Mattheson, *Der vollkommene Capellmeister*, 103n23. Subsequent references to this source are cited parenthetically in the text, abbreviated as VC.

20. Cannon, "Legacy of Mattheson," 3.

21. Ibid., 10.

22. The fear of music as a potentially disruptive force was not uncommon in the eighteenth century. In France, for instance, Mercier laments the Archbishop of Paris's decision to end music at the evening *Te deum* and midnight Masses because of the increasingly unruly behavior of the masses at the overcrowded churches and cathedrals of Paris. Mercier adds that in hoping to preserve the sanctity of the church by banning music, the archbishop ended up chasing everyone away, as the people were only there to see the organist anyhow. Louis-Sébastien Mercier, *Tableaux de Paris*, 12 vols. (Amsterdam, 1782), 1:86. Also see ibid., 3:72. For more on the Archbishop's bans, see Loïc Métrope, *Les Grandes orgues historiques de Saint-Roch, œuvre de Clicquot (1755) et Cavaillé-Coll (1858): "L'Orgue témoin de l'histoire"; d'après une idée originale de Loïc Métrope; monographie* (Paris: Paroisse Saint Roch, 1994), 16.

23. Cannon, "Legacy of Mattheson," 4.

24. Ibid., 6.

25. Mattheson praises the English and French for having ministers who have knowledge of and support music.

26. See Leslie Bunt, "Music Therapy: Historical Perspective," in *The New Grove Dictionary of Opera, Music, and Musicians Online*, ed. Laura Macy, http://www.grovemusic.com (accessed 13 February 2009): "In Book 3 of the *Republic* Plato promoted the discovery of rhythms expressive of harmonious and courageous lives, and warned against the use of certain modes that could promote indolence or sorrow, recommending those with stronger qualities. The astro-musicology of the Renaissance master Marsilio Ficino gives insights into the care of the soul throughout 'a well-tempered life' that are as relevant today as 500 years ago. Karen D. Goodman traces the growth of a therapeutic approach to music in different cultures from its use in magical and religious healing to the evolution of rational and scientific ideas about medicine and music."

27. On the links for Mattheson between the senses or passions and the soul, see Cannon, "Legacy of Mattheson," 7. Although the subject was widely discussed since antiquity, there was an increasing presence of treatises on the salutary effects of music on the body and its ability to cure illness in the second half of the eighteenth century, particularly around the Vitalist school in Montpellier.

28. It should be noted that Mattheson was an early supporter of Italian music in Germany, and as such, he gave preferences to the less complicated, more "flowing" melodies of the Italian composer over elaborate contrapuntal scores of religious music. As Keith Chapin has astutely pointed out, the music-theoretical situation is a bit more complicated than I have purposely presented it. Because traditional counterpoint depended on the quick successions of dissonances and consonances, it could be perceived as more dissonant than Italian melodies. However, dissonance was more tightly controlled in conservative styles than it was in more modern ones, and theorists such as Mattheson and Heinichen were well aware that operatic styles relaxed dissonance control at the local level in order to achieve the *galant* negligence associated with the social ideal of the *galant homme*. At the same time, harmony was certainly the overall goal. "Part of Mattheson's insistence on consonance and harmony," notes Chapin in an email to me, "is a defensive strategy to combat criticisms of the relaxed dissonance practice of modern musical styles."

29. "In the Veritophili Deutliche *Beweis-Gründen,* published in 1717 with my foreword, the sixth chapter deals rather well with the use of music in bodily infirmities: and the recently deceased Doctor J. W. Albrecht, who was professor at Göttingen, also brought out several things which are pertinent

here, but especially a great deal of testimony which maintains that music has a wholesome effect on all sorts of pains in limbs. Wherein he illustrates very well, because sound works strongly on the muscles of the human body, that for example all sudorific measures and dances or movements do not nearly accomplish without music what they do with music. So much for the fourth point [of the natural theory of sound]" (Mattheson, *Der vollkommene Capellmeister*, 103).

30. Athanasius Kircher and others had already written extensively on tarantualism.

31. These names return frequently in treatises on musical effects. Almost a century later, Louis Joseph-Marie Robert lists musical cures as well by Pythagorus, Aesculapius, Theophrastus, Ismene of Thebes among many others.

32. See Elizabeth Williams, *A Cultural History of Medical Vitalism in Enlightenment Montpellier* (Burlington, VT: Ashgate, 2003).

33. "La musique est donc le correctif de cette fausse sensibilité qui constitue dans la société un état réel de maladie." Joseph-Louis Roger, *Traité des effets de la musique sur le corps humain, traduit du latin et augmenté des notes, par Etienne Sainte-Marie* (1758) (Paris: Chez Brunot, 1803), xxvi.

34. "Elle *tempère* la sensibilité excessive des nerfs." Ibid., xxx (my emphasis).

35. As Elizabeth Williams and Anne Vila (*Enlightenment and Pathology: Sensibility in the Literature and Medicine of Eighteenth-Century France* [Baltimore: John Hopkins University Press, 1988]), among others, have shown in their work on the Montpellier Vitalists, this pathological language of discord was not uncommon in medical theories of the nerves at the time, and many diseases were understood as an overstimulation or imbalance of sensibility.

36. "Personne donc n'ayant trouvé jusqu'ici le principe physique de la *dissonnance* employée dans l'harmonie, nous nous contenterons d'expliquer mécaniquement sa génération, & nous laisserons-là les calculs." Rousseau, "Dissonnance," in *Encyclopédie, ou Dictionnaire raisonné des sciences, des arts et des métiers*, ed. Diderot et d'Alembert, 17 vols. (Paris: Briasson, David, Le Breton, and Durand, 1751–72). "For a long period," writes Rousseau, "harmony had no principles, just rules which were almost arbitrary or based solely on the judgements of the ear, which in turn determined the quality of consonant progressions, which were also formulated in mathematical terms. But then, M. Mersenne and M. Sauveur made the discovery that every sound, no matter how simple in appearance, is always accompanied by other less audible sounds, which formed the perfect major chord. M. Rameau subsequently used this for his point of departure, and made it the basis of his harmonic system" (Rousseau, "Harmonie," quoted in Verba, *Music and the French Enlightenment*, 70).

37. Béatrice Didier, "La Réflexion sur la dissonance chez les écrivains du XVIIIè siècle," *Revue des Sciences humaines* 205 (1987): 13–14.

38. Albert Cohen, *Music in the French Royal Academy of Sciences: A Study in the Evolution of Musical Thought* (Princeton, NJ: Princeton University Press, 1981), 86.

39. See Cohen, *Music in the French Royal Academy of Sciences*, 24, 28–29, 79.

40. "[S]i l'excellente musique a peu de compositeurs, elle n'a guère de vrais auditeurs." Diderot, *Leçons de clavecin*, in DPV, 19:354.

41. "Je ne dis pas que l'image qui s'est offerte à mon esprit, soit la seule qu'on pût attacher à la même succession d'harmonie. Il en est des sons comme des mots abstraits dont la définition se résout en dernier lieu, en une infinité d'exemples différents qui se touchent tous par des points communs. Tel est le privilège et la fécondité de l'expression indéterminée et vague de notre art que chacun dispose de nos chants selon l'état actuel de son âme; et c'est ainsi qu'une même cause devient la source d'une infinité de plaisirs ou de peines divers.

"Quelle étonnante variété de sensations momentanées et fugitives n'aurais-je pas excité, si j'avais entrelacé les harmonies dissonantes aux harmonies consonantes et mis en œuvre toute la puissance de l'art?" Ibid., 354.

42. This follows a general trend in the medical sciences to focus on an individual's physiology and its reception of various sensations. On changes in medical treatment in the second half of the eighteenth century informed by the growing expertise and reach of Vitalism, see Alexandre Wenger, *La Fibre littéraire* (Geneva: Droz, 2007).

43. "On peut considérer la musique, ou comme un art qui a pour objet l'un des principaux plaisirs des sens, ou comme une science par laquelle cet art est réduit en principes. C'est le double point de vue sous lequel on se propose de la traiter dans cet ouvrage.

"Il en a été de la musique comme de tous les autres arts inventés par les hommes; le hazard a d'abord appris quelques faits; bientôt l'observation et la réflexion en ont découvert d'autres; et de ces différents faits, rapprochés et réunis, les philosophes n'ont pas tardé à former un corps de science, qui s'est ensuite accru par degrés." Jean le Rond d'Alembert, *Discours préliminaire aux éléments de musique théorique et pratique suivant les principes de M. Rameau éclaircis, développés et simplifiés par M. d'Alembert* (1762), reprinted in Catherine Kintzler, *Jean-Philippe Rameau: Splendeur et naufrage de l'esthétique du plaisir à l'âge classique*, 219–38 (Paris: Le Sycamour, 1983), 219.

44. Verba writes, "In the *Traité*, for example, [Rameau] allows an otherwise forbidden extended chain of dissonant seventh chords by saying that 'good taste obliges us sometimes to break the rules'" (*Music and the French Enlightenment*, 52–53).

45. Rameau writes, "The necessity of dissonance is found first in the three fundamental tones which constitute a key [the tonic, dominant, and subdominant]. Since each of them in turn can give the impression of being the key, . . . [the musician] with the help of dissonance attached to the harmony of a fundamental chord which is not the principal tone, has the means of making it clear which key he intends to present" (Rameau, *Nouveau système*, quoted in Verba, *Music and the French Enlightenment*, 56). Although Rameau emphasized the importance of dissonance, dissonance was used to reinforce the primacy of the tonic. In many ways, Rousseau and he agreed on this point. As we will see, Diderot gave much more autonomy to dissonance as a concept, although even he uses it primarily to create movement but to reinforce the tonic. For more on the function of dissonance in the eighteenth century and beyond, see Carl Dahlhaus's *Studies on the Origin of Harmonic Tonality* (Princeton, NJ: Princeton University Press, 1990).

46. On this point, see in particular, Verba, *Music and the French Enlightenment*, 56–57; Christensen, *Rameau and Musical Thought*, 98–102; and John Neubauer, *The Emancipation of Music from Language: Departure from Mimesis in Eighteenth-Century Aesthetics* (New Haven, CT: Yale University Press, 1986), 71–84.

47. Chabanon, *De la musique considéré en elle-même*, 43. See pages 41–43 for his discussion of musical instinct. In addition to sea creatures, Chabanon also observed the effects of slow harmonious music on spiders and quotes Buffon extensively on the various effects of music on elephants and dogs.

48. "Chez tous les habitans du globe, même parmi les anthropophages, les voyageurs ont trouvé l'usage de la musique." Louis Joseph-Marie Robert, *De la musique, considérée sous les rapports de son influence sur les mœurs, les passions et la santé* (Marseille: J. Mossy, 1807), 9.

49. Lawrence Kramer, "Speaking of Music," in this volume, 19–38.

50. See for instance the unsurprising effects of AC/DC on cancer growth in cells in Peregrine Horden's article in *Music as Medicine: The History of Music Therapy since Antiquity* (Aldershot, UK: Ashgate, 2000), 6.

51. "Ce sont les dissonances dans l'harmonie sociale qu'il faut savoir placer, préparer et sauver. Rien de si plat qu'une suite d'accords parfaits. Il faut quelque chose qui pique, qui sépare le faisceau, et qui en éparpille les rayons." DPV, 20:177; Diderot, *Rameau's Nephew and D'Alembert's Dream*, trans. Leonard Tancock (New York: Penguin, 1976), 111. As Chapin has pointed out to me, Gioseffo Zarlino also warned against the boredom produced by consonance alone.

52. For a more in-depth study of Diderot's use of the figure of dissonance, see Andrew H. Clark, *Diderot's Part* (Aldershot, UK: Ashgate, 2008).

53. See ibid., 173–88.

54. On Bemetzrieder's theory of the "choc" as the dynamic quality underlying all music, see Thomas Christensen, "Bemetzrieder's Dream: Diderot and the Pathology of Tonal Sensibility in the *Leçons de clavecin*," in *Music, Sensation, and Sensuality,* ed. Linda Phyllis Austern (New York: Routledge, 2002), 39–56.

55. Christensen and Verba are the best sources on this. Also see Béatrice Didier, *La Musique des lumières* (Paris: PUF, 1985).

ROUSSEAU: MUSIC, LANGUAGE, AND POLITICS
Tracy B. Strong

The present essay is extracted from a larger work in progress in which I attempt to identify and analyze themes common to the development of music and political thought during the period that goes more or less from Rousseau to Nietzsche, the period, that is, that initiates and to some degree accomplishes what we call modernity. These themes are summarized in the two quotations that serve as epigraphs to this chapter.

1. Ludwig Wittgenstein, *Culture and Value* (Chicago: University of Chicago Press, 1984), 8–9.

2. Mark Twain, quoted in Carl Dolmetsch, *"Our Famous Guest": Mark Twain in Vienna* (Athens: University of Georgia Press, 1992).

3. On Rousseau's musical education, see Michel Termolle, "L'Éducation négative dans l'apprentissage de la musique," in *Musique et langage chez Rousseau,* ed. Claude Dauphin (Oxford, UK: Voltaire Foundation, 2004), 131–43.

4. See their introduction to Rousseau's *Confessions,* in *Œuvres completes,* 5 vols. (Paris: Gallimard, 1959–), 1:xxxix. Subsequent references to Rousseau are from this edition (abbreviated as OC). Translations are mine. See Béatrice Didier, *La Musique des lumières* (Paris: PUF, 1985), chapter 5.

5. Rousseau, *Dialogues 2,* OC, 1:872–73.

6. Rousseau has a premodern approach to enharmonics. He understands enharmonics in the context of unequal temperament, as for him, enharmonic refers to the fact that in a nontempered system a C♭, for example, is slightly lower than a B♮. In a tempered system, by contrast, they are the same pitch. See Julian Rushton, "Enharmonic," in *Grove Music Online, Oxford Music Online,* http://www.oxfordmusiconline.com/subscriber/article/grove/music/08837 (accessed 29 August 2011).

7. See Alexander Rehding, "Rameau, Rousseau, and Enharmonic Furies in the French Enlightenment," *Journal of Music Theory* 49 (2008): 141–80. The most comprehensive general history of temperament is probably Owen H. Jorgensen, *Tuning* (East Lansing: Michigan State University Press, 1991); on Rousseau, see 134–54.

8. Rousseau, *Nouveaux signes pour la musique,* OC, 5:129–65.

9. Ibid., 5:130.

10. Rousseau, *Confessions* 1, OC, 1:313–14.

11. See the important discussion in Rita C. Manning, "Rousseau's Other Woman: Collette in *Le Devin du village*," *Hypatia* 16 (2001): 27–42.

12. See Melissa Butler, "The Quarrel between Rousseau and Rameau: Evidence from Contemporary Psychology," in Dauphin, *Musique et langage chez Rousseau*, 183–91.

13. See the discussion of imitation in Lydia Goehr, *The Imaginary Museum of Musical Works* (Oxford, UK: Clarendon, 1997), 141–46. There is a detailed discussion of mimesis in John Neubauer, *The Emancipation of Music from Language: Departure from Mimesis in Eighteenth-Century Aesthetics* (New Haven, CT: Yale University Press, 1986).

14. To be fair, Rameau argued that Lully's operas exemplified his understanding but that Lully did not perfectly realize it and that the faults of his work were the result. See, by way of comparison, Rameau, *Observation sur notre instinct pour la musique*, in *Jean Philippe Rameau: Musique raisonée, textes choisis et présenté*, ed. Catherine Kintzler and J. C. Malgoire (Paris: Stock, 1980), 172–73.

15. See Catherine Kintzler, *Poetique de l'opéra français de Corneille à Rousseau* (Paris: Minerve, 1991), 364–66. See Charles Dill, "Rameau Reading Lully: Meaning and System in Rameau's Recitative Tradition," *Cambridge Opera Journal* 6 (1994): 1–17, in particular, 1 and 14; Cynthia Verba, "The Development of Rameau's Thought on Modulation and Chromatics," *Journal of the American Musicological Society* 26 (1973): 69–91.

16. Rameau, *Observations*, in *Jean Philippe Rameau: Musique raisonée*, 146.

17. Rameau, *Traité de l'harmonie*, in *Jean Philippe Rameau: Musique raisonée*, 52.

18. Thomas Christensen, *The Cambridge History of Western Music Theory* (Cambridge: Cambridge University Press, 2002), 759. See Jairo Moreno, *Musical Representations, Subjects, and Objects: The Construction of Musical Thought in Zarlino, Descartes, Rameau and Weber* (Bloomington: Indiana University Press, 2004), 51–127, esp. 97.

19. Rousseau, *Dictionnaire de musique* (hereafter DM), s.v. "Basse fondamentale," OC, 5:657.

20. Rameau's calculations had numerous problems, as Jean d'Alembert and Leonhard Euler have shown. See, for example, Pierre Bailhache, *Une historie de l'acoustique musicale* (Paris: Editions CNRS, 2001). See Rameau, *Lettre à M. D'Alembert*, in *Jean Philippe Rameau: Musique raisonée*, 121.

21. Rameau, *Lettre à M. D'Alembert*, 125. See Kintzler's comments in ibid., 19, as well as those in Rousseau, *Essai sur l'origine des langues*, ed. Catherine Kintzler (Paris: Flammarion, 1993), 14–16. D'Alembert was to warn

Rameau about his efforts to "find the principle of *geométrie* in that which sounds [*le corps sonore*]." D'Alembert, *Elements de musique, Discours préliminaire*, quoted in *Jean Philippe Rameau: Musique raisonée*, 30.

22. Thus, Rameau develops a mechanical correspondence between certain musical motifs and particular passions: e.g., chromatics represent sadness; enharmonics "bring disorder to the passions." *Jean Philippe Rameau: Musique raisonnée*, 101. Compare Kintzler, *Poetique de l'opéra français*, 371. See also Rehding, "Rameau, Rousseau, and Enharmonic Furies."

23. Rameau, "Demonstration du principe de l'harmonie," in *Jean Philippe Rameau: Musique raisonée*, 66; René Descartes, "The Passions of the Soul," in *The Philosophical Writings of Descartes* (Cambridge: Cambridge University Press, 1989), 325–403, esp. 373.

24. Catherine Kintzler, *Jean Philippe Rameau* (Paris: Le Sycomore, 1983), 132. See Rémy G. Saisselin, *The Enlightenment against the Baroque: Economics and Aesthetics in the XVIIIth Century* (Berkeley: University of California Press, 1992), 41–48.

25. As Kinztler reminds us, one thinks here of Aristotle. See her notes to Rousseau, *Essai sur l'origine des langues*, 24.

26. This difference has been noted by Jacques Derrida, in *De la grammatologie* (Paris: Minuit, 1967), 280. Rameau was indifferent as to the cooriginality of music and language. See Rameau, "Nouvelles Réflexions sur le principe sonore," in *Jean Philippe Rameau: Musique raisonnée*, 117–18.

27. G. Snyder, *Le Goût musical en France aux XVIIième et XVIIIième siècles* (Paris: Vrin, 1968), 87. Rameau, *Lettre à M. D'Alembert*, 125.

28. Rousseau, *Confessions* 8, OC, 1:384.

29. Catherine Kintzler, *Jean Philippe Rameau: Splendeur et naufrage de l'esthétique du plaisir à l'âge classique* (Paris: Minerve, 1983), 132. See Rémy G. Saisselin, *The Enlightenment against the Baroque: Economics and Aesthetics in the XVIIIth Century* (Berkeley: University of California Press, 1992), 41–48. See also Daniel K. L. Chua, *Absolute Music and the Construction of Meaning* (Cambridge: Cambridge University Press, 1999), chapter 12, esp. 99ff. For a description of the relation between the architecture of opera halls and social hierarchies, see James H. Johnson, *Listening in Paris* (Berkeley: University of California Press, 1995).

30. Rousseau, *Lettre à de Beaumont*, OC, 4:928.

31. Rousseau, *Lettre sur la musique française*, OC, 5:308. A similar judgment can be found in Montesquieu, *Mes pensées*, in *Œuvres complètes*, vol. 1 (Paris: Gallimard, 1949), 1021.

32. Cf. Rousseau, *Émile* 1, OC, 4:250 : "He will be neither man nor citizen. . . . He will be a person of our times; a Frenchman, an Englishman, a bourgeois; he will be nothing."

33. The distinction between "human" and king, bourgeois, gentleman, and so on is made in detail in my *Jean Jacques Rousseau and the Politics of the Ordinary*, 2nd ed. (Lanham, MD: Rowman and Littlefield, 2002), esp. chapters 2 and 3.

34. Not that we will necessarily meet this requirement. The passage could be used to explicate the notorious passage about "force to be free" in *On the Social Contract*. See Steven Affeldt, "The Force of Freedom: Rousseau on Forcing to Be Free," *Political Theory* 27 (1999): 299–333.

35. Rousseau, *Lettre sur la musique française*, OC, 5:251–22; see the excellent article by Jacqueline Waeber, "Jean Jacques Rousseau's unité de mélodie," *Journal of the American Musicological Society* 61 (2009): 79–144.

36. Robert Wokler, *Rousseau on Society, Politics, Music and Language* (New York: Garland, 1987).

37. See the discussion in Jean Starobinski, introduction to Rousseau, *Essai sur l'origine des langues*, OC, 5: esp. clxxxviii.

38. See Rousseau, DM, s.vv. "Imitation," OC, 5:861, and "Mélodie," OC, 5:885.

39. Rousseau, DM, s.v. "Expression," OC, 5:823.

40. Rousseau, DM, s.v. "Unité de mélodie," OC, 5:1144.

41. Rousseau, DM, s.v. "Opéra," OC, 5:948. As Wagner does later, Rousseau questions the judgment that mixing poetry and music harms each component.

42. Ibid., 5:954. See Marian Hobson, *The Object of Art: The Theory of Illusion in the Eighteenth Century* (Cambridge: Cambridge University Press, 1982), 257.

43. Rousseau, DM, s.v. "Opéra," OC, 5:951.

44. Ibid., 5:949.

45. Ibid., 5:951.

46. Rousseau, *Fragments d'observations*, OC, 5:445.

47. Rousseau, DM, s.v. "Récitatif," OC, 5:1008. The theme recurs in, for example, *Fragments d'observations*, OC, 5:445. See also the editor's appendix: "Notes sur la musique grecque antique," OC, 5:1658–64.

48. Rousseau, DM, s.v. "Musique," OC, 5:916.

49. See, for example, the writings of Thrasybulos Georgiades, *Greek Music, Verse, and Dance* (New York: Da Capo, 1973); M. L. West, *Ancient Greek Music* (Oxford, UK: Clarendon, 1992); Paul Allen Miller, *Lyric Texts and Lyric Consciousness* (London: Routledge, 1994). See the important discussion of this issue and these and other texts in Babette Babich, "*Mousiké techné*: The Philosophical Praxis of Music in Plato, Nietzsche, Heidegger," in *Gesture and Word: Thinking between Philosophy and Poetry*, ed. Robert Burch and Massimo Verdicchio (London: Continuum, 2002), 171–90, as well as in my "The

Tragic Ethos and the Spirit of Music," *International Studies in Philosophy* 35 (2003): 79–100.

50. Dubos argued in his *Réflexions critiques sur la poésie et la peinture* (1719) that "les grands siècles" reformulate musical taste. He advanced a hedonistic appreciation of art, admired the ancients, and emphasized the importance of art for the audience. Batteux defended many of these claims in *Les Beaux-arts réduits au même principe* (1746). See Starobinski, introduction to *Essai sur l'origine des langues*, OC, 5:clxv–cciv.

51. See, for example, the contrast exemplified by Thrasybulos Georgiades, *Music and Language: The Rise of Western Music as Exemplified in Settings of the Mass*, trans. Marie Louise Göllner (Cambridge: Cambridge University Press, 1982), 4.

52. Rousseau, *Fragments d'observations*, OC, 5:445.

53. Rousseau, DM, s.v. "Récitatif obligé," OC, 5:1013. Much ink has been spilled on this topic over much time. An informal but convincing entry into the topic is Jacques Barzun, "Is Music Unspeakable?," *American Scholar* 65 (1996): 193–202.

54. Rousseau, *Fragments d'observations*, OC, 5:448.

55. See the similar remarks in Jean-Francois Perrin, "La Musique dans les lettres selon Rousseau," in Dauphin, *Musique et langage chez Rousseau*, 27–28.

56. One might maintain that Italian would offer more chances for true opera, whereas the poor composers who are condemned to French could only have recourse to the "melodrama" or the "monodrama." Cf. Catherine Kintzler, *Poétique de l'opéra de Corneille à Rousseau* (Paris: Minerve, 1991), 500.

57. Rousseau, DM, s.v. "Récitatif obligé," OC, 5:1012–13. There is no spoken dialogue in *Le Devin*, a departure from standard French practice. See Manning, "Rousseau's Other Woman."

58. See Rousseau, "Supplément à l'encyclopédie," 4:590–91, online at http://artflx.uchicago.edu/. However, Rousseau notes in the very late *Lettre à M. Burney* (possibly written as late as the beginning of 1778) that Gluck uses the "*récitatif obligé*" in his *Alceste* (1767; French revision, 1776) and elsewhere (*Lettre à M. Burney*, OC, 5:451). See Peter Branscombe, "Schubert and the Melodrama," in *Schubert Studies*, ed. Eva Badura-Skoda and Peter Branscombe (Cambridge: Cambridge University Press, 1982), 105–6. See also Cynthia Verba, "Music and the Enlightenment," in *The Enlightenment World*, ed. Martin Fitzpatrick, Peter Jones, and Christa Knellwolf (London: Routledge, 2004), 302–22, esp. 315. For an overview of eighteenth-century French understandings of the different forms of *recitative*, see Charles Dill, "Eighteenth Century Models of Recitative," *Journal of the Royal Musical Association* 120 (1995): 232–50, esp. 237.

59. See Julia Simon, "Rousseau and Aesthetic Modernity: Music's Power of Redemption," *Eighteenth-Century Music* 2 (2005): 41–56; and Shierry Weber, "The Aesthetics of Rousseau's *Pygmalion*," in *Jean-Jacques Rousseau*, ed. Harold Bloom (New York: Chelsea House, 1988), 65–81.

60. Edgar Istel, "La Partition originale de Pygmalion," in *Annales de la société Jean-Jacques Rousseau* (Geneva: Chez A. Julien, 1905), 1:149ff. The complete set of instructions is found in OC, 2:1929–30. See J. Van der Veen, *Le Mélodrame musical de Rousseau au romantisme* (Nijhoff: La Haye, 1955), 8–13.

61. Cf. Chua, *Absolute Music and the Construction of Meaning*, 101–2.

62. See Bernard Lamy, "Trope," in *La Rhétorique ou l'art de parler* (1675), http://openlibrary.org/details/larhetoriqueouloolamygoog, 119–35; and the commentary in Starobinski, introduction to *Essai sur l'origine des langues*.

63. Rousseau, *Essai sur l'origine des langues* 3, OC, 5:381. See my *Jean-Jacques Rousseau and the Politics of the Ordinary*, chapter 2. Stanley Cavell (*The Claim of Reason* [Oxford, UK: Clarendon, 1979]) has drawn attention to Freud's comment that our first experience of an other is one of fear.

64. On the notion of responsibility for, and meaning, what one says, see Stanley Cavell, *Must We Mean What We Say?* (New York: Scribner, 1969), chapters 1 and (on music) 5 and 6.

65. Starobinski (introduction to the *Discours sur l'origine et les fondements de l'inegalité*, OC, 3:iii) insightfully compares the narrative of that piece to that of the Fall. Accordingly, one might say here that Rousseau has secularized the "*felix culpa*," that "happy sin" of Adam (cf. the Good Friday Mass) that makes redemption in Christ possible.

66. Rousseau, *Discours sur l'origine de l'inegalité*, 1, OC, 3:160–61.

67. See the detailed analysis in my *Jean Jacques Rousseau and the Politics of the Ordinary*, chapter 2.

68. See here the excellent Julia Simon, "Singing Democracy: Music and Politics in Jean-Jacques Rousseau's Thought," *Journal of the History of Ideas* 65 (2004): 433–54, esp. the last three pages.

69. See Jean Starobinski, *Le Remède dans le mal: Critique et affirmation de l'artifice à l'âge des lumières* (Paris: Gallimard, 1989).

70. For a discussion of concinnity, see Babette Babich, "On Nietzsche's Concinnity: An Analysis of Style," *Nietzsche-Studien* 19 (1990): 59–80. The term has its origins, as she notes, in the work of Seneca and Cicero and was taken up by Alberti. See idem, *Words in Blood, like Flowers: Philosophy and Poetry, Music and Eros in Hölderlin, Nietzsche, and Heidegger* (Albany: State University of New York Press, 2006), 300–1, with additional reference to other works.

71. Rousseau, *Émile* 5, OC, 4:790. See Simon, "Singing Democracy," 448. The *facteur* built and repaired keyboard instruments and harps as well

as flutes, bagpipes, and so on; the *luttier* (now *luthier*) did the same for string instruments.

72. Rousseau, DM, s.v. "Unité de mélodie," OC, 5:1144 (my italics); also quoted in Simon, "Singing Democracy," 448. See Waeber, "Jean Jacques Rousseau's unité de mélodie." See also Rousseau, DM, s.v. "Accorder," OC, 5:634–35.

73. See, for example, the very interesting discussion by Arnold Steinhardt, violinist (he refuses the designation of "first") of the Guarneri Quartet, as to the necessary efforts to attain this complex unity: *Indivisible by Four: A String Quartet in Pursuit of Harmony* (New York: Farrar, Straus and Giroux, 2002).

74. See Kintzler, introduction to Rousseau, *Essai sur l'origine des langues*, 35–36.

75. Rousseau, DM, s.v. "Imitation," OC, 5:861; See Philip E. J. Robinson, *Jean-Jacques Rousseau's Doctrine of the Arts* (Bern: Peter Lang, 1984). The other references are in the article "Opera" (DM, OC, 5) and the first part of *Essai sur l'origine des langues*, OC, 5, chapter 15. Cf. Rousseau's letter to D'Alembert, 26 June 1751 (OC, 2:160), where the same point is made.

76. Rousseau, DM, s.v. "Imitation," OC, 5:861. See the discussion of the same passage in Simon, "Rousseau and Aesthetic Modernity," 52. The rendering of "chant" as "sequence of sounds" is authorized by Rousseau's discussion of "chant" in Rousseau, DM, s.v. "Chant," OC, 5:694.

77. Cf. Michael Fried, *Art and Objecthood* (Chicago: University of Chicago Press, 1998), 148–72. I shall not enter here into the controversies over Fried's views but only note that those views are somewhat like those I find in Rousseau. See also Tracy B. Strong and C. N. Dugan, "A Language More Vital than Speech: Music, Politics and Representation in Rousseau," in *Cambridge Companion to Rousseau*, ed. Patrick Riley (Cambridge: Cambridge University Press, 2001), 329–64.

78. Rousseau, DM, s.v. "Expression," OC, 5:823.

79. Rousseau, *Essai sur l'origine des langues* 15, OC, 5:418.

80. Rousseau, *Essai sur l'origine des langues* 14, OC, 5:416. On this, see Hobson, *The Object of Art*, chapter 11.

81. Rousseau, *L'Origine de la mélodie*, OC, 5:333 (also translated in Wokler, *Rousseau on Society, Politics, Music and Language*). In the *Laws*, Plato notes that the word *nomoi* (laws) was also used to designate song. See Plato, *Laws* 799c and 700b, for a study of inappropriate ideas in music. See also Dugan and Strong, "A Language More Vital than Speech."

82. Rousseau, *L'Origine de la mélodie*, OC, 5:338.

83. See *Encyclopédie, Musique*, at http://www.alembert.fr/index.php?option =com_content&view=category&id=714335161:musique&Itemid=167&layout =default.

84. Rousseau, DM, s.v. "Musique," OC, 5:923. Béatrice Didier notes that Rousseau's understanding of Greek music is very advanced. Béatrice Didier, *La Musique des lumières: Diderot, l'Encyclopédie, Rousseau* (Paris: PUF, 1985), 43.

85. The paragraph paraphrases and quotes Rousseau, *Essai sur l'origine des langues* 20, OC, 5:429.

86. Jean Starobinski (in *Jean Jacques Rousseau: Transparency and Obstruction* [Chicago: University of Chicago Press, 1988]) sees this as a dream, an impossibility. Rousseau rather thinks of it, I argue, as a signpost along a path that perhaps has no final end.

87. See here my "Is the Political Realm More Encompassing than the Economic Realm?," *Public Choice* 137 (2008): 439–50, esp. 448–50.

LISTENING TO MUSIC
Lawrence M. Zbikowski

1. Edmund Husserl, *On the Phenomenology of the Consciousness of Internal Time (1893–1917)*, trans. John Barnett Brough, Edmund Husserl Collected Works, vol. 4 (Dordrecht: Kluwer, 1991), 156.

2. Jean-Luc Nancy, *Listening*, trans. Charlotte Mandell (New York: Fordham University Press, 2007), 20.

3. Ibid.

4. Ibid., 66.

5. Ibid., 17.

6. Lawrence M. Zbikowski, "Musical Gesture and Musical Grammar: A Cognitive Approach," in *New Perspectives on Music and Gesture*, ed. Anthony Gritten and Elaine King (Burlington, VT: Ashgate, 2011).

7. In this connection see Carolyn Abbate, "Music—Drastic or Gnostic?," *Critical Inquiry* 30 (2004): 505–36.

8. Nancy, *Listening*, 64.

9. "Der Leiermann" is the concluding song of Schubert's song cycle *Winterreise*; "Fairytale" was Norway's winning entry in the 2009 Eurovision song contest.

10. Victor Kofi Agawu, "Music in the Funeral Traditions of the Akpafu," *Ethnomusicology* 32 (1988): 87.

11. Ibid., 90.

12. Ibid.

13. I give a summary of research on categorization in chapter 1 of *Conceptualizing Music: Cognitive Structure, Theory, and Analysis* (New York: Oxford University Press, 2002).

14. Eleanor Rosch, "On the Internal Structure of Perceptual and Semantic Categories," in *Cognitive Development and the Acquisition of Language*, ed.

Timothy E. Moore (New York: Academic Press, 1973), 111–44; Eleanor Rosch, "Cognitive Representations of Semantic Categories," *Journal of Experimental Psychology: General* 104 (1975): 192–233.

15. I discuss conceptual models in greater depth in chapters 3 and 5 of *Conceptualizing Music* and give practical examples of how musicians employ them in "Modelling the Groove: Conceptual Structure and Popular Music," *Journal of the Royal Musical Association* 129 (2004): 272–97.

16. Lawrence W. Barsalou, "Deriving Categories to Achieve Goals," *Psychology of Learning and Motivation* 27 (1991): 1–64; Lawrence W. Barsalou et al., "Concepts and Meaning," in *Chicago Linguistics Society 29: Papers from the Parasession on the Correspondence of Conceptual, Semantic and Grammatical Representations*, ed. Katharine Beals et al. (Chicago: University of Chicago, Chicago Linguistics Society, 1993), 23–61.

17. The notion of a "musical work" that I use here is not very heavily freighted and serves simply as a shorthand for the articulations of musical practice acknowledged by the members of a given musical culture. For a fuller discussion of the "work concept" and its place in Western musical traditions see Lydia Goehr, *The Imaginary Museum of Musical Works: An Essay in the Philosophy of Music* (Oxford, UK: Clarendon, 1992).

18. Paul Connerton, *How Societies Remember* (Cambridge: Cambridge University Press, 1989), 102.

19. Although Nancy speaks of incorporation in just this way—"transcendental resonance is also incorporated—even, strictly speaking, it is nothing but that incorporation (which it would be better to call: the opening up of a body)" (*Listening*, 29)—incorporation remains rather abstract: the body is again a receptacle or submissive vessel rather than an agent.

20. Umberto Eco, *A Theory of Semiotics* (Bloomington: Indiana University Press, 1976), 88.

21. Nancy, *Listening*, 34.

22. Terrence W. Deacon, *The Symbolic Species: The Co-evolution of Language and the Brain* (New York: Norton, 1997), chap. 3.

23. Michael Tomasello, *The Cultural Origins of Human Cognition* (Cambridge, MA: Harvard University Press, 1999); Michael Tomasello, *Origins of Human Communication* (Cambridge, MA: MIT Press, 2008).

24. Charles Sanders Peirce, *Collected Papers of Charles Sanders Peirce*, vol. 2, ed. Charles Hartshorne and Paul Weiss (Cambridge, MA: Belknap Press of Harvard University Press, 1960), 157.

25. For a research review that contrasts similarity and analogy see Dedre Gentner and Arthur B. Markman, "Structure Mapping in Analogy and Similarity," *American Psychologist* 52 (1997): 45–56. As Gentner and Markman acknowledge, similarity and analogy are perhaps best viewed as points along

a continuum, although they also make a strong argument for ways to distinguish between judgments guided by these two cognitive strategies.

26. Further, we could say that the *shape* embodied by this icon correlates with the sensations we would feel were a hand to be placed on our bare back, a translation from the visual to the tactile perfectly in keeping with current work on embodied experience.

27. Eco, *A Theory of Semiotics*, 191–220, 245–58.

28. Keith J. Holyoak and Paul Thagard, *Mental Leaps: Analogy in Creative Thought* (Cambridge, MA: MIT Press, 1995), chap. 1; Douglas L. Medin, Robert L. Goldstone, and Dedre Gentner, "Respects for Similarity," *Psychological Review* 100 (1993): 254–78.

29. Lawrence M. Zbikowski, "Dance Topoi, Sonic Analogues, and Musical Grammar: Communicating with Music in the Eighteenth Century," in *Communication in Eighteenth-Century Music*, ed. V. Kofi Agawu and Danuta Mirka (Cambridge: Cambridge University Press, 2008), 283–309.

30. Nancy, *Listening*, 35.

31. As a further reflection on cognitive categories and the conceptual models relative to which they are organized, Rybak's "Fairytale"—Norway's entry into the 2009 Eurovision song contest—would not fit easily into the category *Norwegian songs*, not the least because it was sung in English.

32. Although it is common to characterize timbres with a significant degree of low-frequency disturbance as "dark," this suggests a further cross-domain mapping between sound and the color spectrum. It should also be noted that funeral practices in the Western tradition are not monolithic: the final movement of Johann Sebastian Bach's mourning ode "Lass, Fürstin, lass noch einen Strahl" (BWV 198), for instance, is in moderate tempo and makes use of rhythmic figuration that is decidedly dance-like.

33. Nancy, *Listening*, 67.

MI MANCA LA VOCE: HOW BALZAC TALKS MUSIC—OR
HOW MUSIC TAKES PLACE—IN *MASSIMILLA DONI*
John T. Hamilton

1. "J'ai lu Hoffmann en entier, il est au-dessous de sa réputation, il y a quelque chose, mais pas grand-chose; il parle bien musique." Honoré de Balzac, letter of 2 November 1833, in *Lettres à Madame Hanska*, ed. R. Pierrot, 4 vols. (Paris: Laffront, 1990), 1:84. Unless otherwise noted, all translations are mine.

2. Balzac, letter of 7 November 1837, in ibid., 1:419.

3. Graham Robb affirms that the opera plot was indeed Balzac's first purely literary undertaking, after postponing his "philosophical investigations." Graham Robb, *Balzac: A Biography* (New York: Norton, 1994), 58.

4. Honoré de Balzac to Laure Surville, née Balzac, 6 September 1819, in *Correspondance*, ed. R. Pierrot, 5 vols. (Paris: Garnier, 1960–69), 1:36.

5. "Nous parlâmes musique, nous étions plusieurs: quoique je fusse musicien comme on était autrefois actionnaire de la lotterie royale de France, quand on y prenait un billet, c'est-à-dire pour le prix d'un coupon de loge, j'exprimai timidement mes idées sur *Mosè*. Ah! il retentira longtemps dans mes oreilles, ce mot d'initiation: 'Vous devriez écrire ce que vous venez de dire!'" Honoré de Balzac to Maurice Schlesinger, 29 May 1837, quoted in Pierre Brunel, "*Mosè* dans *Massimilla Doni*," *L'Année balzacienne* 15 (1994): 39–54.

6. In *Vie de Rossini*, Stendhal employs the same turn of phrase ("parler musique") to introduce his brief chapter on *Mosè in Egitto*: "Notre âme était admirablement disposée *à parler musique* et à reproduire ses miracles." Stendhal, *Vie de Rossini*, ed. Pierre Brunel (Paris: Gallimard, 1992), 339.

7. Balzac first published this analysis separately in the journal *La France musicale* on 25 August 1839.

8. "Cette langue [sc. de la musique], mille fois plus riche que celle des mots, est au langage ce que la pensée est à la parole; elle réveille les sensations et les idées sous leur forme même, là où chez nous naissent les idées et les sensations, mais en les laissant ce qu'elles sont chez chacun. Cette puissance sur notre intérieur est une des grandeurs de la musique. Les autres arts imposent à l'esprit des créations définies, la musique est infine dans les siennes. Nous sommes obligés d'accepter les idées du poète, le tableau du peintre, la statue du sculpteur; mais chacun de nous interprète la musique au gré de sa douleur ou de sa joie, de ses espérances ou de son désespoir. Là où les autres arts cerclent nos pensées en les fixant sur une chose déterminée, la musique les déchaine sur la nature entière au'elle a le pouvoir de nous exprimer." Honoré de Balzac, "Massimilla Doni," ed. René Guise, in *Études philosophiques, La Comédie humaine*, vol. 10, Bibliothèque de la Pléiade (Paris: Gallimard, 1979), 587–88; English: *Massimilla Doni*, trans. Clara Bell and James Waring (Whitefish, MT: Kessinger, 2004), 45–46. Subsequent references are to these editions, cited in the text as "MD" with page numbers to both editions. Throughout, the English translation has been slightly modified.

9. For Balzac's familiarity with this aesthetic program, see the many citations gathered by Marc Eigeldinger in *La Philosophie de l'art chez Balzac* (Geneva: Cailler, 1957), 79–95.

10. Theodor Adorno, *Notes to Literature*, trans. Shierry W. Nicholsen, vol. 1 (New York: Columbia University Press), 124.

11. I am referring, of course, to Bloch's *Geist der Utopie* (2nd ed., 1923), whose central section consists in a "Philosophie der Musik." English: *The*

Spirit of Utopia, trans. Anthony Nassar (Stanford, CA: Stanford University Press, 2000), 34–164.

12. For an analysis of *Gambara* and *Massimilla Doni,* together with *Sarrasine,* see Béatrice Didier, "Le Temps de la musique: Trois nouvelles de Balzac," *L'Année balzacienne* 8 (2007): 49–58. See also Klaus Ley's extensive readings in *Die Oper im Roman: Erzählkunst und Musik bei Stendhal, Balzac und Flaubert* (Heidelberg: Winter, 1995).

13. For a general overview of Balzac's relation to music and musicians, see D. C. Parker, "Balzac, the Musician," *Musical Quarterly* 5 (1919): 160–68.

14. Balzac to Maurice Schlesinger (undated), in *Correspondance,* 3:285–87; Balzac to Mme. Hanska, 24 May 1837, in *Lettres à Mme Hanska,* 1:505–6.

15. A similar temporal and geographical dislocation is evident in Balzac's "Vendetta," written in the key year of 1830 and evoking the long lost France of 1814. I am grateful to Andrew H. Clark for pointing this out.

16. John Ruskin, writing in 1849, famously evokes Venice's "perfection of beauty . . . still left for our beholding in the final period of decline: a ghost upon the sands of the sea, so weak—so quiet,—so bereft of all but her loveliness, that we might well doubt, as we watched her faint reflection in the mirage of the lagoon, which was the City, and which the Shadow." John Ruskin, *The Stones of Venice,* ed. Jan Morris (London: Folio Society, 2001), 3–4.

17. "Le Vénitien se sentit comme foudroyé; tandis qu'une voix cria: *le voilà !* dans les oreilles de la duchesse" (MD 547/5).

18. "Par quel phénomène moral l'âme s'emparait-elle si bien de son corps qu'il ne se sentait plus en lui-même, mais tout en cette femme à la moindre parole qu'elle disait d'une voix qui troublait en lui les sources de la vie?" (MD 547/4).

19. Balzac published the tale of *Facino Cane* in 1836. It opens with a strong evocation of the writer's garret in the Rue de Lesdiguières. Balzac, *Etudes de mœurs: Scènes de la vie parisienne,* ed. Pierre-Georges Castex et al., *La Comédie humaine,* vol. 6, Bibliothèque de la Pléiade (Paris: Gallimard, 1977).

20. "Peuple occupé de théories philosophiques, d'analyse, de discussions, et toujours troublé par des divisions intestines" (MD 587/45).

21. "La musique moderne, qui veut une paix profonde, est la langue des âmes tendres, amoureuses, enclines à une noble exaltation intérieure" (587/45).

22. "Moïse est le libérateur d'un peuple esclave! . . . souvenez-vous de cette pensée, et vous verrez avec quel religieux espoir la Fenice tout entière écoutera la prière des Hébreux délivrés, et par quel tonnerre d'applaudissements elle y répondra!" (MD 588/46).

23. See Matthias Brzoska, "Mosè und Massimilla: Rossinis *Mosè in Egitto* und Balzacs politische Deutung," in *Oper als Text: Romantische Beiträge zur Libretto-Forschung* (Heidelberg: Winter, 1986), 125–45.

24. "[Genovese est] le premier chanteur qui m'ait satisfait. Je ne mourrai donc pas sans avoir entendu des roulades exécutées comme j'en ai souvent écouté dans certains songes au réveil desquels il me semblait voir voltiger les sons dans les airs. La roulade est la plus haute expression de l'art" (MD 581/39).

25. "Jamais la musique ne mérita mieux son épithète de divine" (MD 612/68).

26. "Quand un artiste a le malheur d'être plein de la passion qu'il veut exprimer, il ne saurait la peindre, car il est la chose même au lieu d'en être l'image. L'art procède du cerveau et non du cœur. Quand votre sujet vous domine, vous en êtes l'esclave et non le maître. Vous êtes comme un roi assiégé par son peuple. Sentir trop vivement au moment où il s'agit d'exécuter, c'est l'insurrection des sens contre la faculté!" (MD 613).

27. See Ley, *Die Oper im Roman*, 189–95.

28. Roland Barthes, *S/Z* (Paris: Editions du Seuil, 1970); English: *S/Z: An Essay*, trans. Richard Miller (New York: Hill and Wang, 1974).

29. The theatrical potential of Balzac's narrative was entertained by Oskar Schoeckh, who composed an opera, *Massimilla Doni*, in 1935.

30. "Ce *Mi manca la voce* est un de ces chefs-d'œuvre qui résisteront à tout, même au temps" (MD 603/60).

31. "Elle me verse des flots de pourpre dans l'âme" (MD 604/61).

32. "Que le ciel épuise ses grâces sur ta tête!" (MD 604/61).

33. "Il devenait le plus mauvais de tous les choristes" (MD 604/60).

34. See Georg Lukács, *German Realists in the Nineteenth Century*, trans. Jeremy Gaines and Paul Keast (Cambridge, MA: MIT Press, 1993), xxv–xxvi.

35. The novella *Gambara* is found in the same volume of the Pléiade edition cited earlier (ed. R. Guise, vol. 10), 478.

36. "Dans cinq ans, *Massimilla Doni* sera comprise comme une belle explication des plus intimes procédés de l'art. Aux yeux des lecteurs du 1er jour, ce sera ce que ça est en apparence, un amoureux qui ne peut posséder la femme qu'il adore parce qu'il la desire trop et qui possède une miserable fille. Faites-les donc conclure de là à l'enfantement des oeuvres d'art!" Balzac to Mme. Hanska, 22 January 1838, in *Lettres à Madame Hanska*, 1:580.

SPEAKING OF MUSIC IN THE ROMANTIC ERA: DYNAMIC
AND RESISTANT ASPECTS OF MUSICAL GENRE
Matthew Gelbart

1. Franz Liszt, *Life of Chopin*, trans. Martha Walker Cook (Philadelphia: Leypoldt, 1863; reset and repaginated reprint, Mineola, NY: Dover, 2005), 6. Page numbers refer to the reprint edition.

2. On habitus, see Pierre Bourdieu, *Outline of a Theory of Practice* (Cambridge: Cambridge University Press 1977), chapter 2.

3. Johann Joachim Quantz "From *Essay on a Method for Playing the Transverse Flute*," trans. Oliver Strunk, rev. Wye J. Allanbrook, in *Strunk's Source Readings in Music History*, ed. Leo Treitler, rev. ed. (New York: Norton, 1998), 803.

4. Hans Robert Jauss, "Theory of Genres and Medieval Literature," in *Modern Genre Theory*, ed. David Duff (Harlow, UK: Longman, 2000), 133. Here, Jauss discusses the medieval conception of *genera dicendi* as including the type of elocution used and the social class of the characters depicted.

5. "Die modernen Dichtarten sind nur Eine oder unendlich viele. Jedes Gedicht eine Gattung für sich." Friedrich Schlegel, *Literary Notebooks, 1797– 1801*, ed. with an introduction and commentary by Hans Eichner (Toronto: University of Toronto Press, 1957), 116.

6. See, particularly, Peter Szondi, "Friedrich Schlegel's Theory of Poetical Genres: A Reconstruction from the Posthumous Fragments," in *On Textual Understanding and Other Essays*, ed. Peter Szondi, trans. Harvey Mendelsohn (Manchester: Manchester University Press, 1986), 75–94; Cyrus Hamlin, "The Origins of a Philosophical Genre Theory in German Romanticism," *European Romantic Review* 5 (1994): 3–14; Tilottama Rajan, "Theories of Genre," in *The Cambridge History of Literary Criticism, Volume 5: Romanticism*, ed. Marshall Brown (Cambridge: Cambridge University Press, 2000), 226–49.

7. Carl Dahlhaus, "Zur Problematik der musikalischen Gattungen im 19. Jahrhundert," in *Gattungen der Musik in Einzeldarstellungen: Gedenkschrift Leo Schrade*, ed. Wulf Arlt, Ernst Lichtenhahn, and Hans Oesch (Bern: Francke, 1973), 840–95; Dahlhaus, *Foundations of Music History*, trans. J. B. Robinson (Cambridge: Cambridge University Press, 1983); Dahlhaus, *Esthetics of Music*, trans. William W. Austin (Cambridge: Cambridge University Press, 1982), esp. 14–15; and Dahlhaus, "New Music and the Problem of Musical Genre," in *Schoenberg and the New Music*, trans. Derrick Puffett and Alfred Clayton (Cambridge: Cambridge University Press, 1987), 32–44.

8. Dahlhaus's work on genre is full of sharp observations and arresting examples. Taken as a whole, however, its ideological thrust is clear. For

example, Dahlhaus opens his article on the "problematics" of genre in the nineteenth century with loaded wording indicating that music might "emancipate" itself from genre. ("Zur Problematik," 840). Rajan and Julia Wright argue that the Romantics became increasingly aware that genre was linked to ideology. In Rajan and Wright's case, they continue to open up this discussion, to consider what ideologies were inherent in the Romantics' own awareness and in our modern awareness of genre. But Dahlhaus stops short of this metacriticism of Romantic ideology. Tilottama Rajan and Julia Wright, introduction to *Romanticism, History, and the Possibilities of Genre: Re-forming Literature, 1789–1837*, ed. Tilottama Rajan and Julia Wright (Cambridge: Cambridge University Press, 2006), esp. 1–2.

9. Deconstructing the assumption of "musical autonomy" is one of the guiding principles, for example, behind Richard Taruksin's *Oxford History of Western Music* (New York: Oxford University Press, 2005). On Dahlhaus's investment in autonomy, see James Hepokoski, "The Dahlhaus Project and its Extra-Musical Sources," *19th-Century Music* 14 (1991): 221–46; and Anne C. Shreffler, "Berlin Walls: Dahlhaus, Knepler, and Ideologies of Music History," *Journal of Musicology* 20 (2003): 498–525.

10. See Jeffrey Kallberg, "The Rhetoric of Genre: Chopin's Nocturne in G Minor," *19th-Century Music* 11 (1988): 238–61, esp. 242.

11. This claim comes in Goethe's famous essay "Shakespear und kein Ende!," in *Ästhetische Schriften 1806–1815*, Johann Wolfgang Goethe Sämtliche Werke, Abt. 1, vol. 19, ed. Friedmar Apel (Frankfurt: Deutscher Klassiker Verlag, 1998), 650; see also 638. Goethe in fact distinguishes subtly between "drama" and "theater piece" (*Theaterstück*) here (646), and in a larger context, the same work may often be treated in two very different ways: with the emphasis on the dramatic as a type of literature or with the emphasis on the corporeal and physical presence in the playhouse.

12. Among the most influential formulations of the tripartition of literature into fundamentally lyric, epic, and dramatic types was Goethe's discussion of the "Naturformen" of poetry in his *West-östlicher Divan*, Johann Wolfgang Goethe Sämtliche Werke, Abt. 1, vol. 3/1, ed. Hendrik Birus (Frankfurt: Deutscher Klassiker Verlag, 1994), 206–8.

13. Robert Schumann, *Gesammelte Schriften über Musik und Musiker*, 5th ed. (Leipzig: Breitkopf & Härtel, 1914), 1:27. Translation amended from Schumann, *On Music and Musicians*, ed. Konrad Wolff, trans. Paul Rosenfeld (Berkeley: University of California Press, 1946), 45.

14. Richard Leppert, *The Sight of Sound: Music, Representation, and the History of the Body* (Berkeley: University of California Press, 1995), xx–xxi.

15. Arthur Schopenhauer, *The World as Will and Representation*, trans. E. F. J. Payne, 2 vols. (New York: Dover, 1966), 2:450.

16. Georg Wilhelm Friedrich Hegel, *Hegel's Aesthetics: Lectures on Fine Art*, trans. T. M. Knox, 2 vols. (Oxford, UK: Clarendon, 1975), 2:888–92, 2:955–58.

17. Recent musical scholarship has picked up on the place of the body and its movement in musical praxis in a series of important studies on musical iconography (Leppert, *The Sight of Sound*), opera (e.g., Mary Ann Smart, *Mimomania: Music and Gesture in Nineteenth-Century Opera* [Berkeley: University of California Press, 2004]) and instrumental music (esp. Elisabeth Le Guin, *Boccherini's Body: An Essay in Carnal Musicology* [Berkeley: University of California Press, 2006]). However, the interrelationships between the body (or groups of bodies) and musical categories, labels, and the changing settings and communicative aims of different genre systems is a line that remains to be taken much further.

18. A good quick summary of Schlegel's rhetoric on the novel can be found in Rajan, "Theories of Genre," 235.

19. As Dahlhaus has outlined, music theorists were relatively late to embrace a "mixed" genre ("Zur Problematik," 874–78). John Daverio has considered the introduction of Schlegelian literary ideas of generic combination in the music of Schumann and Brahms, among others. See John Daverio, "Schumann's 'Im Legendenton' and Friedrich Schlegel's 'Arabeske,'" *19th-Century Music* 11 (1987): 150–63; and Daverio, "Brahms's Magelone Romanzen and the Romantic Imperative," *Journal of Musicology* 7 (1989): 343–65.

20. See Rajan, "Theories of Genre," 243. For further discussion of Romantic reconceptions, conflations, and distortions of ancient ideas about genre and mode, see Gérard Genette, *The Architext: An Introduction*, trans. Jane E. Lewin (Berkeley: University of California Press, 1992), esp. 62–63 on Goethe.

21. Heinrich Christoph Koch, *Musikalisches Lexikon* (Frankfurt: Hermann, 1802), 820. Translations are mine unless otherwise noted.

22. Ibid.

23. Koch himself struggled to balance various elements across his different descriptions of "style." See Keith Chapin, "Strict and Free Reversed: The Law of Counterpoint in Koch's *Musikalisches Lexikon* and Mozart's *Zauberflöte*," *Eighteenth-Century Music* 3 (2006): esp. 98–99.

24. Richard Wagner, "Das Kunstwerk der Zukunft," in *Gesammelte Schriften und Dichtungen*, 3rd ed., 10 vols. (Leipzig: E. W. Fritsch, 1898), 3:97–98. Translation amended from *Richard Wagner's Prose Works*, trans. William Ashton Ellis, 2nd ed., 8 vols. (London: Kegan Paul, Trench, Trübner, 1895–1912), 1:127–28.

25. Richard Wagner, *Opera and Drama*, in *Richard Wagner's Prose Works*, vol. 2, trans. William Ashton Ellis, 2nd ed. (London: Kegan Paul, Trench,

Trübner, 1900), 38–39. German original in *Gesammelte Schriften und Dichtungen,* 3:248.

26. *Neues Universal-Lexikon der Tonkunst,* 3 vols., ed. Eduard Bernsdorf (Dresden: Robert Schaefer, 1856–61), 2:561–62.

27. Ibid.

28. "Kammer-Concert, Kammermusik: Hierunder versteht man a.) die zur Privatunterhaltung der Fürsten bestimmte Musik, zu der Niemand ungeladen Zutritt hat; b.) Compositionen klassischen Genres für eine kleine Anzahl von Instrumenten, als Trios, Quartette, Quintette, etc. zur Aufführung in Privatzirkeln." Julius Schuberth, *Kleines musikalisches Conversations-Lexikon: Ein encyklopaedisches Handbuch enthaltend das Wichtigste aus der Musikwissenschaft, die Biographien . . . etc.* (Leipzig: Schuberth, 1871), 193. There were several previous editions of this reference work with a slightly different title, but the earlier ones I have been able to consult were not yet expanded to include this entry.

29. "Kammerstyl: Compositionen im strengen Satz; der Kammermusik entsprechend." Ibid.

30. Wagner, from "Über die Anwendung der Musik auf das Drama" ("On the Application of Music to the Drama"), in *Gesammelte Schriften und Dichtungen,* 10:182–83.

31. See Walter Frisch, *Brahms: The Four Symphonies,* 2nd ed. (New Haven, CT: Yale University Press, 2003), 147–52.

32. In *Opera and Drama,* for example, his concern is with *drama* (in action) more than with Goethe's *"dramatic"*—and the composer's attempts to infuse the world of instrumental music with the *dramatic* run into contradiction more readily. See also Anette Ingenhoff, *Drama oder Epos? Richard Wagners Gattungstheorie des musikalischen Dramas* (Tübingen: Niemeyer, 1987).

33. The terms "micro-genre" and "super-genre" have been used by the Russian scholar Marina Lobanova, though the way she uses the terms is quite different from mine. In addition, she addresses almost exclusively compositional and structural concerns. See Marina Lobanova, *Musical Style and Genre: History and Modernity,* trans. Kate Cook (Amsterdam: Harwood, 2000), esp. 182–83.

34. Thus, for example, Hermann Danuser in his article on genre (*Gattung*) for the second edition of the *Musik in Geschichte und Gegenwart* suggests that *Gattung* is a kind of middle ground between *Oberbegriff* and the narrower *Art,* related to *Art* somewhat as genus to species (in *Die Musik in Geschichte und Gegenwart,* 2nd ed., 26 vols. in two parts, ed. Ludwig Finscher (Kassel: Bärenreiter, 1994–2007), Sachteil 3:1042–43). However, any claims that *Gattung* or "genre" can be universally limited to one level of discourse, however consistently one author setting up a framework may maintain

such separation, are belied by the fact that most writers not formulating a full system interchange words such as *Gattung* and *Art* (and several others) in a much more fluid way. To take an example from the period at hand, E. T. A. Hoffmann, in various reviews, uses *Gattung* to refer to the symphony (*Allgemeine musikalische Zeitung* 13, no. 48 [1811]: 797) and to "ernsten, heroischen Opern" (ibid., 13, no. 11 [1811]: 185), but when approving of the allegretto movement of Beethoven's Piano Trio op. 70, no. 2, because the concept of the whole movement is only grasped by the interlacing of all three instrumental parts, he says Beethoven has thus stayed true to the type (*Art*) of composition at hand (ibid., 15, no. 9 [1813]: 151). If anything, *Art* here suggests a classification broader rather than narrower than a single *Gattung*— perhaps the idea of intimate chamber music in general, derived from the ideal of the string quartet. (This very sort of slippage makes it entirely fitting, in my opinion, that all these three examples are translated as "genre" by Martyn Clarke in *E. T. A. Hoffmann's Musical Writings*, ed. David Charlton [Cambridge: Cambridge University Press, 1989], 264, 272, and 317.)

35. Johann Nikolaus Forkel, *Allgemeine Geschichte der Musik*, 2 vols. (Leipzig: Schwickert, 1788 and 1801), 1:45. For another, similar example, see the extended discussion of musical genres in Ferdinand Hand, *Aesthetik der Tonkunst* (Leipzig: Hochhausen und Fournes, 1837; Jena: Carl Hochhausen, 1841).

36. Translation modified from Schumann, *On Music and Musicians*, 116. Original in Schumann, *Gesammelte Schriften über Musik und Musiker*, 1:329.

37. I thank Lawrence Kramer for stressing this in his comments on an earlier version of this chapter. Indeed, as Kallberg's and Jim Samson's work on Chopin has shown, genre could become flexible in new ways in the nineteenth century even as it maintained a strong influence over composition and reception. As Samson has put it, "Old genres survived and were recontextualised in the later nineteenth century, but tended ultimately towards fragmentation. . . . New genres emerged but remained fragile, the consensus about them often tentative." Jim Samson, "Chopin and Genre," *Music Analysis* 8 (1989): 229.

38. Wulf Arlt, "Gattung: Probleme mit einem Interpretationsmodel der Musikgeschtichtsschreibung," in *Gattung und Werk in der Musikgeschichte Norddeutschlands und Skandinaviens: Referate der Kieler Tagung 1980*, ed. Friedhelm Krummacher and Heinrich W. Schwab (Kassel: Bärenreiter, 1982), 11.

39. I have addressed this issue at greater length in my book *The Invention of "Folk Music" and "Art Music": Emerging Categories from Ossian to Wagner* (Cambridge: Cambridge University Press, 2007).

40. See Alastair Fowler, *Kinds of Literature: An Introduction to the Theory of Genres and Modes* (Oxford, UK: Clarendon, 1982), chapter 1; Susan Stewart,

Crimes of Writing: Problems in the Containment of Representation (New York: Oxford University Press, 1991), chapter 4, esp. 102–3.

41. Dahlhaus, "New Music and the Problem of Musical Genre," 40.

42. See Max Horkheimer and Theodor W. Adorno, *Dialectic of Enlightenment*, trans. Edmund Jephcott, ed. Gunzelin Schmid Norr (Stanford, CA: Stanford University Press, 2002), 94–136, esp. 127. Note that Horkheimer and Adorno try to recover even Mozart and earlier musicians from the "taint" of uniform styles or genres by arguing that they worked against these (103).

43. Dahlhaus, "New Music and the Problem of Musical Genre," 40. A similar argument is presented in Siegfried Mauser, "Auflösung und Zerfall des Gattungsgefüges im 20. Jahrhundert," in *Die Geschichte der musikalischen Gattungen*, ed. Matthias Brzoska (Laaber: Laaber-Verlag, 2006), 352–57.

44. Danuser makes a thoughtful concession to this type of argument at the end of his *Musik in Geschichte und Gegenwart* article on *Gattung* (1066).

45. Liszt, *Life of Chopin*, 90–92.

46. Indeed, later in the book, Liszt more or less defines Classicism as attachment to moribund *forms* and Romanticism as a desire to escape these. Ibid., 73. Subsequent references to the English translation of this book are cited parenthetically in the text.

47. Original French in Franz Liszt, *F. Chopin* (Paris: Escudier; Leipzig: Breitkopf und Härtel; and Brussels: Schott, 1852), 4.

48. This is akin in some ways to Schumann's description (even as he got interested in counterpoint itself) of Bach's fugues as "character pieces of the highest type" (Schumann, *On Music and Musicians*, 89). The point that formal considerations only became a central part of genre discussion in the seventeenth and eighteenth centuries is made by Dahlhaus in "New Music and the Problem of Musical Genre," 34.

49. See René Wellek and Austin Warren, *Theory of Literature* (New York: Harcourt, Brace, 1949), 241.

WEATHER REPORTS: DISCOURSE AND MUSICAL COGNITION
Per Aage Brandt

1. Charles Rosen, *Beethoven's Piano Sonatas: A Short Companion* (New Haven, CT: Yale University Press, 2002). Charles Rosen, who is skeptical about musical imagery and who bluntly dismisses commentary that reports it as "pseudo-poetry" and "philosophical speculation," admits that Beethoven's sonata op. 31, no. 2, may be inspired by Shakespeare's *Tempest* but that he probably did not read much more of the drama than the title. In Rosen's great study *The Classical Style: Haydn, Mozart, Beethoven* (New York: Norton,

1997), 375, he writes that the "Credo" of Beethoven's *Missa Solemnis,* with its crossing scales, "must be accepted as Beethoven's audible *image of eternity,* and they [the scales] are the equivalents of the words, "I believe in the life to come, *world without end,* amen" (my italics). The Cleveland Baroque Orchestra Apollo's Fire recently offered concerts featuring Rebel, Vivaldi, Rameau, and Duchiffre (the latter a contemporary postmodern baroque composer) under the title "Earth, Wind, and Fire."

2. But as the French poet, poetician, and mathematician Jacques Roubaud ironically remarks, when a poem says that it rains, it means that it rains in the poem, nowhere else. Jacques Roubaud, *Poésie, etcetera, ménage* (Paris: Stock, 1995). My question: how are we to understand this statement?

3. The Russian linguist Roman Jakobson's famous "poetic function" lets the "message" of a text be focused on in itself, which it has to be, when the text is dereferentialized. If the poem is not internally dereferentialized—if, for example, it looks like a private letter—it can be dereferentialized externally by appearing in a context of undetermined addressees, e.g., a book of poetry (as such addressing everybody and nobody). Roman Jakobson, "Closing Statements: Linguistics and Poetics," in *Style in Language,* ed. T. A. Sebeok (Cambridge, MA: MIT Press, 1960).

4. The only exception (example of music not being nonreferential) I can think of is the phenomenon we call a *jingle:* musical signals and short, stereotypical phrases informing us of the imminence or the presence of a generic entity in the space of performance: it is deictic—it does say *here, now, this.* Jingles are signatures, equivalents of proper names. Jingles are regarded as degenerate, rudimentary musical expressions, but they may alternatively have been at the origin, in the evolution of human symbolization, of what we now consider autonomous and "genuine" music. We still use a particularly tonal prosody when we *call* on someone by a name, in the vocative mode. As Steven Brown has suggested, music and language may have a common ancestor. Steven Brown, "The 'Musilanguage' Model of Music Evolution," in *The Origins of Music,* ed. Nils L. Wallin, Björn Merker, and Steven Brown (Cambridge, MA: MIT Press, 2000), 271–300.

5. Igor Stravinsky, "Quelques confidences sur la musique" (1935), in Eric Walter White, *Stravinsky: The Composer and His Works* (Berkeley: University of California Press, 1966), 539.

6. Igor Stravinsky and Robert Craft, *Conversations with Igor Stravinsky* (New York: Doubleday, 1959), 15. For an excellent account, see Richard Taruskin, "Stravinsky and the Subhuman—A Myth of the Twentieth Century: *The Rite of Spring,* the Tradition of the New, and 'the Music Itself,'" in *Defining Russia Musically: Historical and Hermeneutical Essays* (Princeton, NJ: Princeton University Press, 1997), 360–89.

7. Nicholas Cook, "Imagining Things: Mind into Music (and Back Again)," in *Imaginative Minds*, ed. Ilona Roth (Oxford: Oxford University Press, 2007), 123–46. Roger Reynolds describes his method in *Form and Method: Composing Music* (New York: Routledge, 2002).

8. Even in newer theory of metaphor as a prelinguistic, semantic, conceptual process, the distinction between "source" and "target" or between constituent "input spaces" maintains the corresponding distinction between the object of attention—the reference, or "target"—and the way in which it is grasped *extrinsically*, through a "source" theme that does not have to be part of the experience itself. However, this question of the *extrinsic or intrinsic* status of a metaphoric description is not easy to answer. In the scene of the ringing cell phone quoted in the epigraph, is the "poking holes in a silken fabric" an extrinsic or a intrinsic description—is the metaphor part of the phenomenon itself as experienced by the attentively listening critic, or is it an a posteriori part of its recall in the writing mind of the critic?

9. Some disturbing "noise" in the debate may stem from the modernist routine declaring that art is about itself insofar as it is "pure" (an idea prolonging the Parnassian *l'art pour l'art* of the nineteenth century).

10. Donald Rosenberg, music review, *Cleveland Plain Dealer*, 30 September 2008, my italics.

11. Cf. Gilles Fauconnier, *Mental Spaces* (Cambridge, MA: MIT Press, 1985), and newer accounts of mental space theory in Per Aage Brandt, "Music and the Private Dancer," in *Spaces, Domains, and Meaning: Essays in Cognitive Semiotics* (Bern: Peter Lang, 2004). See note 21.

12. Cognitive aesthetics is a branch of cognitive science and deals with art: why is there art at all? How do we perceive and understand it? What are the social functions of art? What is going on in the brain when we perform or are exposed to art? A good musicological example of cognitive aesthetics that draws on the subbranch of cognitive semiotics is Ole Kühl, *Musical Semantics* (Bern: Peter Lang, 2008).

13. Zachary Lewis, music review, *Cleveland Plain Dealer*, 16 December 2008, my italics.

14. My claim is that music experienced as bad or uninteresting does not trigger the space-building that critics report and most listeners are likely to recognize; the better the music, according to listeners, the more they will mobilize spatial imagination and attribute it to the music. My evidence? The critical response occurs rarely in negative reviews of music and frequently in positive reviews. Alex Ross reports that Stockhausen excitedly wrote to Goeyvaerts, one of the coinventors of the "total serialist language," about the new technique and its application to the electronic medium: "This music sounds indescribably pure and beautiful!" He then likened it to "raindrops in

the sun." Xenakis, talking about his *Metastaseis,* likened the effect of the glissandos to the sound of hail drumming on a hard surface or millions of cicadas singing in a field on a summer night. Alex Ross, *The Rest Is Noise: Listening to the Twentieth Century* (New York: Farrar, Straus and Giroux, 2007), 395, 398. These are comparisons; the composers use them to qualify something they feel to be beautiful, and the means of doing so are clearly forms of spatial imagination.

15. Strong codes characterize institutionalized symbols; weak codes characterize interpersonal icons. Symbols typically express obligations, and icons express facultative ideas. (Although formulated in a different way, this modal observation was originally made by C. S. Pierce in his semiotic papers.)

16. As mentioned in note 4, jingles are referential, whereas pure music is not. Jingles are also strongly coded. If music is the result of code weakening—"dejingling," so to speak—it is easy to understand its lack of semantic referentiality. The code weakening discussed here is not intended as a theory of art. It does characterize playful behavior in general, I think. Playfulness, however, is closely related to artfulness.

17. So, in a sense, art generically seems to be socially negative: playful where religion as an institution needs to be serious and socially affirmative. Church music may be useful for creating feelings of awe and sacredness, but it is also reportedly dangerous, because it is playful, hence possibly diabolic.

18. In language, this could be a definition of rhetoric.

19. Cf. Duke Ellington's beautiful "Mood Indigo."

20. Peter Szendy begins his book *Listen: A History of Our Ears* (New York: Fordham University Press, 2008) by mentioning the lost moment when he "began to *listen to music as music.* With the keen awareness that it was *to be understood* (entendre) [*sic*], deciphered, pierced rather than perceived": "If this moment . . . can't be situated in my immemorial past, what I know or think I know, on the other hand, is that musical listening that is *aware of itself* has always been accompanied in me with the feeling of a *duty.* Of an imperative: you *have* to listen, one *must* listen" (1). Listening to music is different from hearing a noise, because it is a form of paying attention, because someone is "saying" or intending something, and the listener is ethically involved. Szendy's development of this overture goes slightly more in the direction of the listener's self, whereas my analysis goes through the Other and beyond the attention shared to what the music is felt to be "about." (Szendy seems to react to the word itself, "listen," from an old Indo-European verb that means "obey"; cf. Ancient Greek *klúo.*)

21. Simply put, the meaning of something heard must be something happening in space, even if we hear it in the dark or with our eyes closed.

Auditive perception is per se space-creating, whatever be the causal, physical source of the sound. But if what we hear is *produced* (*intended*) *for hearing*, it creates a *mental* space—namely, an idea of a space in the Other's mind, to be shared as we share emotions.

22. Arnold Schoenberg's string sextet *Verklärte Nacht*, op. 4 (1899), uses Richard Dehmel's poetry, telling a story of a passionate nightly conversation ending in the line, "O sieh, wie klar das Weltall schimmert! Es ist ein Glanz um Alles her" (See how bright the universe gleams! There is a shine around all things).

23. In *Spaces, Domains, and Meaning*, I critically discuss the notion of *mental spaces*, a category developed in cognitive semantics to account for the possibility of meaning in language altogether. If an event is thought to "take place," according to some sentence, we have to understand the event as happening in some imaginable surrounding. So how does the mind do this? That is of course an empirical question; all data suggest that we are using inner vision, provided by the occipital visual cortex. How, if so, did we develop such a forceful inner vision? I ask. Music, or protomusic, as Steven Brown suggests in "The 'Musilanguage' Model of Music Evolution," may have paved the way. This is what I am claiming here: the mental operation we use when imagining a story, for example, unfolding in a fictive universe, may have been developed through the phenomenology attached to playful, intentional performance and interpretation of sounds (including dancing), produced by the body and some instrumental extensions of it. In short, music may have shaped the capacity of the human mind to unfold a world-independent semantic dimension in language. On cognitive semantics and mental spaces, see Gilles Fauconnier and Mark Turner, *The Way We Think: Conceptual Blending and the Mind's Hidden Complexities* (New York: Basic Books, 2002).

MESSIAEN, DELEUZE, AND THE BIRDS OF PROCLAMATION
Sander van Maas

1. Olivier Messiaen, *Music and Color: Conversations with Claude Samuel* (Portland, OR: Amadeus, 1994), 238.

2. Jean-Luc Nancy, "La Déconstruction du christianisme," *Les Études philosophiques* 4 (1998): 513.

3. See in particular Raymond Murray Schafer, *The Music of the Environment* (Vienna: Universal Edition, 1973). Ecocritical awareness of a more political kind becomes apparent in Messiaen's concerns over the nuclear threat in the 1950s. See Robert Fallon, "Birds, Beasts, and Bombs in Messiaen's Cold War Mass," *Journal of Musicology* 26, no. 2 (2009): 175–204.

4. Peter Hill and Nigel Simeone, *Olivier Messiaen: "Oiseaux exotiques"* (Aldershot, UK: Ashgate, 2007). Robert Fallon, "Messiaen's Mimesis: The

Language and Culture of the Birds Styles" (Ph.D. diss., University of California, 2006); and idem, "The Record of Realism in Messiaen's Bird Style," in *Olivier Messiaen: Music, Art and Literature*, ed. Christopher Dingle and Nigel Simeone (Aldershot, UK: Ashgate, 2007). Other relevant publications on Messiaen and birdsong are mentioned in subsequent notes. See also Vincent Benitez, *Olivier Messiaen: A Research and Information Guide* (New York: Routledge, 2008).

5. François-Bernard Mâche, "Messiaen and Birdsong," typescript of an unpublished lecture delivered at the University of Athens, Messiaen Conference, December 2008. As will become clear later in the chapter, Mâche soon revised his opinion.

6. Pascal Ide: "The anecdote is well-known: the conductor Charles Münch complained with Messiaen about the difficulties posed by the extreme slowness of the final piece of *L'Ascension* (orchestral version): 'They are human beings, he said about the musicians.—But I compose for the angels,' the maestro answered." Pascal Ide, "Une rencontre décisive," in *Olivier Messiaen homme de foi: Regard sur son oeuvre d'orgue* (Paris: Trinité Média Communication, 1995), 79.

7. Recently we have witnessed a steady expansion of the ecocritical study of music. Still searching for a enduring label, ecocritical musicology, or ecomusicology, aims to bring together, formalize, and institutionalize the wide variety of research that addresses the relation between music and nature. The Ecocriticism Study Group of the American Musicological Society, which was founded in 2007, defines its task as "exploring the intellectual and practical connections between the studies of music, culture and nature. In particular, the ESG seeks to integrate the study of music with the well-developed field of literature scholarship known as ecocriticism, which highlights the manifold roles of nature and environment in the creation and interpretation of culture." See http://www.ams-esg.org (accessed 5 May 2011).

8. This reference to Derrida's notion of the *à-venir* (the "to-come") should be understood as an oblique one. The key idea is that the "to-come" is irreducible to the future. See Jacques Derrida, "Hospitality," *Angelaki: Journal of the Theoretical Humanities* 5, no. 3 (2000): 14.

9. For an overview see Bernd Herzogenrath, ed., *Deleuze/Guattari & Ecology* (Basingstoke, UK: Palgrave Macmillan, 2009).

10. Ronald Bogue, "Rhizomusicosmology," *SubStance* 66 (1991): 85–101.

11. Olivier Messiaen, *Technique of My Musical Language* (Paris: Leduc, 1956), 1:34. Hill and Simeone, *"Oiseaux,"* 22.

12. Hill and Simeone, *"Oiseaux,"* 27.

13. Ibid., 43.

14. Ibid., 45.

15. See also his later remarks on the syncretistic character of the bird style in *Faith in Music* (1986), a documentary film directed by Alan Benson (Princeton, NJ: Films for the Humanities & Sciences, 2004).

16. Hill and Simeone, *"Oiseaux,"* 109.

17. Given the static nature of the work, these motif should be regarded as attributes rather than as leitmotifs, in analogy with the iconography of the saints (cf. Augustine's eagle).

18. Mâche remarks that for Messiaen birdsong was "deeply imbued by an emotional imagery." Mâche, "Messiaen and Birdsong."

19. Ibid.

20. The American composer James Fassett (1904–86) used the Cornell recordings (or recordings very similar to them) at the same time as Messiaen was making his transcriptions. Fassett did not make the detour via notation and instrumental or vocal performance but worked directly from record to tape to compose his 1955 three-movement tape composition *Symphony of the Birds* (reissued on CD in 2005 by EM Records, EM144CD). See also Hill and Simeone, *"Oiseaux,"* 89.

21. François-Bernard Mâche, *Musique, mythe, nature, ou, les dauphins d'Arion*, Collection d'esthétique 40 (Paris: Klincksieck, 1983); published in English as *Music, Myth, Nature, or the Dolphins of Arion*, trans. Catherine Dale (Chur, Switzerland: Harwood, 1992).

22. This approach is outlined in François-Bernard Mâche, *Musique au singulier* (Paris: Odile Jacob, 2001).

23. Frans de Waal, *The Ape and Sushimaster: Cultural Reflections of a Primatologist* (New York: Basic Books, 2001), 153.

24. Mâche, quoted in Márta Grabócz, "The Demiurge of Sounds and the Poeta Doctus: François-Bernard Mâche's Poetics and Music," *Contemporary Music Review*, 8, no. 1 (1993): 135.

25. J. Hall-Craggs, quoted in Mâche, *Music, Myth, Nature*, 124.

26. This scheme would run from vocality back to orality and ultimately to *buccality:* "songs" from the back of one's throat. See also Kiene Brillenburg Wurth's essay in this volume.

27. To this register also belong those cases (*Zauberflöte, Siegfried*) in which humans and animals communicate through a common language.

28. See *Les Cours et conférences de Gilles Deleuze*, at http://www.le-terrier .net/deleuze (accessed 5 May 2011).

29. Although Deleuze coauthored the book with Guattari, judging by the courses mentioned, it is reasonable to state that he may be held responsible for the sections on music.

30. Gilles Deleuze and Félix Guattari, *A Thousand Plateaus: Capitalism and Schizophrenia* (Minneapolis: University of Minnesota Press, 1987), 300.

31. "Block" was a notion that Deleuze developed on the basis of Pierre Boulez's thinking in *Penser la musique aujourd'hui*. See Timothy S. Murphy, "Boulez, Proust and Time: 'Occupying without Counting,'" *Angelaki: Journal of the Theoretical Humanities* 3, no. 2 (1998): 69–74.

32. Deleuze and Guattari, *A Thousand Plateaus*, 299.

33. "Sur la musique I," March 8, 1977, at Vincennes, in *Les Cours et conférences de Gilles Deleuze*.

34. Deleuze and Guattari, *A Thousand Plateaus*, 300. Bogue (see later in the chapter) typically does not mention this element of resistance in his discussion of the refrain. Ronald Bogue, "Minority, Territory, Music," in *Deleuze's Way: Essays in Transverse Ethics and Aesthetics* (Aldershot, UK: Ashgate, 2007), 27–31.

35. Deleuze and Guattari, *A Thousand Plateaus*, 300.

36. The reference here is to the "hurdy-gurdy song" in the passage on the Eternal Return in the third part of Nietzsche's *Thus Spoke Zarathustra*. This song is sung by Zarathustra's animals, which both summarize and enact the logic of the Eternal Return by singing, according to Zarathustra, in the manner of a barrel organ. Friedrich Nietzsche, *Thus Spoke Zarathustra*, trans. Adrian Del Caro (Cambridge: Cambridge University Press, 2006), 175–76.

37. Deleuze and Guattari, *A Thousand Plateaus*, 309.

38. Ibid., 347. For the development of the "cosmic refrain" Deleuze makes extensive use of Jean Barraqué's comments on the third part of Debussy's *La Mer*, "Dialogue du vent et de la mer."

39. Deleuze and Guattari, *A Thousand Plateaus*, 333.

40. Ibid., 478.

41. Ibid., 342.

42. Ibid.

43. Ibid., 308–9.

44. Olivier Messiaen, *Traité de rythme, de couleur, et d'ornithologie*, vol. 1 (Paris: Leduc, 1994–2002), 37–68.

45. Deleuze and Guattari, *A Thousand Plateaus*, 309.

46. Ibid.

47. Ronald Bogue, "Violence in Three Shades of Metal: Death, Doom and Black," in *Deleuze and Music*, ed. Ian Buchanan and Marcel Swiboda (Edinburgh: Edinburgh University Press, 2004), 97. Incidentally, to my knowledge Deleuze does not use the notion of the virtual in his writings on music.

48. Ibid., 99.

49. See in particular Fallon, "Messiaen's Mimesis."

50. On the productive aspects of mimesis see Philippe Lacoue-Labarthe, *Typography: Mimesis, Philosophy, Politics* (Stanford, CA: Stanford University Press, 1998), 255.

51. Since the latter pieces often develop against a sonorous background rather than in the void of montage, I prefer to call them collages. The principle of juxtaposition, though applied differently, is similar.

52. Hill and Simeone, *"Oiseaux,"* 35 (example 2.8).

53. Tracy Strong, *Jean-Jacques Rousseau: The Politics of the Ordinary* (Lanham, MD: Rowman and Littlefield, 2002), 52. On denaturing see also Jean-Luc Nancy, *The Creation of the World or Globalization,* trans. François Raffoul and David Pettigrew (Albany: SUNY Press, 2007), 87.

54. See C. K. Catchpole and P. J .B. Slater, *Bird Song: Biological Themes and Variations* (Cambridge: Cambridge University Press, 2008), for more details about recent findings regarding the structure of birdsong.

55. Richard Steinitz, "Des canyons aux étoiles . . . ," in *The Messiaen Companion,* ed. Peter Hill (London: Faber and Faber, 1995), 479.

56. For a historical overview see Linda Kalof and Brigitte Resl, *A Cultural History of Animals,* 6 vols. (London: Berg, 2007). See also Sonia Roberts, *Birdkeeping and Birdcages: A History* (New York: Drake, 1973).

57. Messiaen never refers to Eden as either the originary form of nature or the model for his own transformation of nature. On the relation with technicity in Messiaen see chapter 5 of my *The Reinvention of Religious Music: Olivier Messiaen's Breakthrough toward the Beyond* (New York: Fordham University Press, 2009), 125–57.

58. Messiaen, *Music and Color,* 239. For an introduction to the subject see Andrew Linzey, *Animal Theology* (Urbana: University of Illinois Press, 1994).

59. "Et l'avenir?," audio recording on *Olivier Messiaen: Les Couleurs du temps; Trente ans d'entretiens avec Claude Samuel,* CD, INA/Radio France, 211814 (2000), track 7.

60. Jeremy Thurlow, "Messiaen's *Catalogue d'oiseaux:* A Musical Dumbshow?," in *Messiaen Studies,* ed. Robert Sholl (Cambridge: Cambridge University Press, 2007), 119–44.

61. Rainer Maria Rilke, letter of February 25, 1926, quoted in Heidegger, *Off the Beaten Track* (Cambridge: Cambridge University Press, 2002), 213–14. On the importance of Rilke's thinking for Messiaen see Julius Christoph Tölle, *Olivier Messiaen: Éclairs sur l'Au-delà . . . Die christlich-eschatologische Dimension des Opus ultimum* (Frankfurt am Main: Peter Lang, 1999), 192.

62. Messiaen, *Music and Color,* 238–39.

63. Jean-Luc Nancy, "The Deconstruction of Christianity," in *Dis-Enclosure: The Deconstruction of Christianity* (New York: Fordham University Press, 2008), 150.

64. One could also think here of the analogy seen by Messiaen between his bird music and the tapestry of Jean Lurçat which features many flowers artfully juxtaposed with animals, minerals, and vegetables and organized thematically with occasional birdlike constellations. See Messiaen, "The Life and Works of Jean Lurçat (1892–1966)," in Dingle and Simeone, *Olivier Messiaen: Music, Art and Literature*, 279–88.

65. Bogue, "Rhizomusicosmology," 95.

66. Constantin V. Boundas, "Deleuze-Bergson: An Ontology of the Virtual," in *Deleuze: A Critical Reader*, ed. Paul Patton (Oxford, UK: Blackwell, 1996), 81–106.

67. Ibid., 102.

68. Quoted in Almut Rößler, *Beiträge zur geistigen Welt Olivier Messiaens* (Duisburg: Gilles und Francke, 1984), 103, my translation.

69. Olivier Messiaen, *Conférence de Notre-Dame* (Paris: Leduc, 1978); Deleuze and Guattari, *A Thousand Plateaus*, 337.

70. Discontinuous form is only the most obvious manifestation of this problematic. I refer to Nicholas Cook's discussion of the musical montage and collage to underscore the irreducibility of absence in music. Nicholas Cook, "Uncanny Moments: Juxtaposition and the Collage Principle in Music," in *Approaches to Meaning in Music*, ed. Byron Almén and Edward Pearsall (Bloomington: Indiana University Press, 2006), 107–34.

71. Other examples being the sixth movement from the oratorio *La Transfiguration de Notre-Seigneur Jésus-Christ* and the sixth scene, "Le prêche aux oiseaux" (The Sermon to the Birds), from the opera *Saint François d'Assise*.

72. On the intensification of life through music and its mysterious ontological status see Lawrence Kramer, "Mysteries of Animation: History, Analysis, and Musical Subjectivity," *Music Analysis* 20, no. 2 (2001): 153–78.

73. For Messiaen, the birds may be said to have represented *telotypes* rather than archetypes: images of the ultimate destiny of life rather than of its origin.

74. Rodolphe Gasché, *The Wild Card of Reading: On Paul de Man* (Cambridge, MA: Harvard University Press, 1998), 30–31.

75. A typical occurrence of this "shall" is found in the Apocalypse of John 21:4, to which Messiaen frequently refers: "And God shall wipe away all tears from their eyes; and there shall be no more death, neither sorrow, nor crying, neither shall there be any more pain: for the former things are passed

away." The first part of this verse was used in the title of the seventh move-ment of his orchestral *Éclairs sur l'Au-delà* . . .

76. Jacques Derrida, *The Work of Mourning* (Chicago: University of Chi-cago Press, 2001), 217.

1. Marguerite Duras, *India Song*, trans. Barbara Bray (New York: Grove, 1989), 11.

2. "À vrai dire, je ne sais pas trop d'où il vient Carlos d'Alessio, on dit du pays argentin, mais lorsque j'ai entendu sa musique pour la première fois, j'ai vu qu'il venait du pays de partout." Marguerite Duras, liner notes to *India Song et autres musiques de films* (Le Chant du Monde, 1991).

3. Before Schelling borrowed the term for his *Philosophy of Mythology*, Coleridge, in an "essay" read at the Royal Society of Literature, coined it: "symbol fades away into allegory, but yet in reference to the working cause . . . , and thus never ceases wholly to be a symbol or tautegory." Samuel Taylor Coleridge, "On the Prometheus of Aeschylus" (address, Royal Society of Literature, 18 May 1825); cf. Jean-Luc Nancy, *The Inoperative Community*, trans. Peter Connor, Lisa Garbus, Michael Holland, and Simona Sawhney (Minneapolis: University of Minnesota Press, 1991).

4. Nancy, *The Inoperative Community*, 49–53. While I was preparing this chapter, Laura Odello reminded me of the fact that Vladimir Jankélévitch already mentions the Schellingian tautegory in his *La Musique et l'ineffable*: "Music is simultaneously 'allegorical' and (as Schelling said) 'tautegorical.' It is an allegory to the extent that, through its reticence [*par pudeur*], it ex-presses by hinting [*à demi-mot*], obliquely. But if allegory is a detour taken by an express intention, or by intentional expressionism, a system of ciphers or hieroglyphs or ideograms, then music is, to the contrary, a 'tautegory.' To the extent that music signifies something other, it is as suspect as a painting done by numbers, as didactic poetry or symbolic art: it is no longer music but ide-ology, a sermon meant to edify. Considering its naïve and immediate truth, music does not signify anything other than what it is." Vladimir Jankélévitch, *Music and the Ineffable*, trans. Carolyn Abbate (Princeton, NJ: Princeton Uni-versity Press, 2003), 66. Nancy does not mention Jankélévitch either in *The Inoperative Community* or, to my knowledge, in his more recent writings on music and listening.

5. See Nancy, *The Inoperative Community*, 45–46.

6. Friedrich Nietzsche, *The Birth of Tragedy and Other Writings*, trans. Ronald Speirs (Cambridge: Cambridge University Press, 1999), 33 (§6), emphasis mine.

7. Ibid., 34, original emphasis.

8. Carl Dahlhaus, *The Idea of Absolute Music*, trans. Roger Lustig (Chicago: University of Chicago Press, 1989), 63. I have quoted and commented on these lines in *Listen: A History of Our Ears*, trans. Charlotte Mandell (New York: Fordham University Press, 2008), 18. Elsewhere, Dahlhaus writes that, "historically, it is not the 'extramusical' that is added to absolute music, but on the contrary absolute music that constitutes a form of abstraction or reduction of types of instrumental music." Dahlhaus, "Thesen über Programmusik," in *Klassische und romantische Musikästhetik* (Laaber: Laaber-Verlag, 1988), 365.

9. These songs are discussed in Peter Szendy, *Tubes: La Philosophie dans le juke-box* (Paris: Minuit, 2008) and in a series of articles published in the French review *Vacarme*, between 2007 and 2008 (http://www.vacarme.org); the book has been translated into English and published as *Hits: Philosophy in the Juke-Box and Other Essays*, trans. Will Bishop (New York: Fordham University Press, 2012).

10. *Divertimento teatrale* in one act set to a libretto by Giovanni Battista Casti, commissioned by Emperor Joseph II to be performed in Vienna at the Schönbrunn Orangerie, 7 February 1786 (at the other end of the Orangerie, members of the German troupe presented Mozart's *Der Schauspieldirektor*, also commissioned for the occasion). Richard Strauss borrowed the argument of *Prima la musica* for his *Capriccio* in 1942.

11. "POETA.—Dunque credete che parole e musica/si possa in quattro dì . . . MAESTRO.—Circa a la musica/non ve ne date pena, ella è già pronta ;/ e voi sol vi dovete/le parole adattar. POETA.— Questo è l'istesso/che far l'abito, e poi/far l'uomo a cui s'adatti. MAESTRO.—Voi, signori poeti, siete matti./Amico, persuadetevi ; chi mai/credete che dar voglia attenzione/alle vostre parole?/Musica in oggi, musica ci vuole. POETA.—Ma pure questa musica conviene/ch'esprima il sentimento, o male, o bene. MAESTRO.—La mia musica ha questo d'eccellente,/che può adattarsi a tutto egregiamente."

SPEAKING OF MICROSOUND: THE BODIES OF HENRI CHOPIN
Kiene Brillenburg Wurth

1. All archived files of the series have been released as a podcast series at *Speaking of Music—Rewind*, at http://www.exploratorium.edu/40th/podcasts .php (accessed 11 January 2011).

2. John Cage on *Speaking of Music*, 1987 (at the very end of the conversation), at http://www.exploratorium.edu/tv/index.php?project=92&program= 1092 (accessed 11 January 2011).

3. It is a descendant of the "professional" approach to music sketched by Keith Chapin in his chapter in this volume. However, musicology is a

profession that has learned to speak. In just the same way, literary studies have focused on literature that lends itself to formalist, structuralist, and poststructuralist theories. See Jonathan Culler, *Literary Theory: A Very Short Introduction* (Oxford: Oxford University Press, 2000); and Culler, *The Literary in Theory* (Stanford, CA: Stanford University Press, 2007).

4. Lawrence Kramer, *Interpreting Music* (Berkeley: University of California Press, 2010), chapter 1. As Kramer states succinctly, "Music uncovers the movement from emptiness to fullness that constitutes meaning as the outcome of interpretation. Music both provokes this movement and enacts it" (7).

5. As the Swedish sound poet Sten Hanson remarks, sonorous poetry should not be regarded as a consequence of the Futurists, Dadaists, or Lettrists. Rather, it "is one of the consequences of new machine tools and new media—the tape recorder, the electronic music studio, the long-playing record, radiophony—that were available to poets and musicians. Sonorous poetry was born in Paris at the beginning of the 1950s. Chopin was not the first to use the tape recorder as a poetic instrument, but he certainly was the first to realize the possibilities fundamentally different from those he discovered in all oral poets, and he was the first to render this phenomenon clear theoretically." Sten Hanson, "Henri Chopin, poète sonore," in *Poésie sonore internationale*, by Henri Chopin (Paris: Jean-Michel Place, 1979), 123. All translations are my own unless otherwise noted.

6. Steve McCaffery, "Voice in Extremis," in *Close Listening: Poetry and the Performed Word*, ed. Charles Bernstein (Oxford: Oxford University Press, 1998), 166.

7. Michael Lenz, "A Short Outline of Sound Poetry/Music After 1945," in *"GLUKHOMANIA.RU": An Electronic Museum of Lingua-Acoustic Space*, curated by Dmitry Bulatov, at http://glukhomania.ncca-kaliningrad.ru/pr_sonorus.php3?blang=eng&t=0&p=9 (accessed 11 January 2011).

8. Mirella Bandini, *Pour une histoire du lettrisme* (Paris: Jean-Paul Rocher, 2003); Bernard Girard, *Lettrisme: l'ultime avant-garde* (Dijon: Les Presses du Réel, 2010). In *Poésie sonore internationale*, Chopin remarks that the great error of Lettrism was its doctrinal development (84).

9. Douglas Kahn, *Noise, Water, Meat: A History of Sound in the Arts* (Cambridge, MA: MIT Press, 1999), 291.

10. Michael Lenz, "A Short Outline of Sound Poetry/Music After 1945," at http://glukhomania.ncca-kaliningrad.ru/pr_sonorus.php3?blang=eng&t=0&p=9 (accessed 11 January 2011).

11. See in particular "Köchel que j'aime" (1969), along with the other works collected in François Dufrêne, *Crirhythms, Osmose-Art and Various Works, on Ubuweb Sound*, at http://www.ubu.com/sound/dufrene.html (ac-

cessed 11 January 2011). For examples of ad-buster activities, see https://www.adbusters.org/ (accessed 9 January 2013).

12. Chopin, *Poésie sonore internationale*, 43.

13. Greil Marcus, *Lipstick Traces: A Secret History of the Twentieth Century* (Cambridge, MA: Harvard University Press, 1990), 275.

14 Isidore Isou, *Introduction à une nouvelle poésie et à une nouvelle musique* (Paris: Gallimard, 1947).

15. Frédéric Acquaviva, "Henri Chopin: Avant-Garde Pioneer of Sound Poetry," *Guardian*, 5 February 2008. See also Hanson, "Henri Chopin, poète sonore," 122; Henri Chopin, "Conférence" (no date), in *Erratum# Noise.Art. Poetry*, at http://www.erratum.org/old/chopin/conferencechopin2.html (accessed 11 January 2011).

16. Herman Sabbe, *Cinquième Saison*, 17, quoted in Chopin, *Poésie sonore internationale*, 119.

17. See Henri Chopin's overview of the history of sound poetry in *Poesie internationale sonore*, 13–45.

18. Audiography involves the process of inscribing in sound. Hence, it is a mode of writing.

19. Gerald Bruns makes the same observation in his *The Material of Poetry: Sketches for a Philosophical Poetics* (Athens: University of Georgia Press, 2005), 63. Words, Chopin says, are in the service of profit, submission, and imposition—and therefore useless to him: "The Word has created profit, it has justified work, it has made obligatory the confusion of occupation (to be doing something), it has permitted life to lie. The Word . . . creates the inaccurate SIGNIFICATION, which signifies differently for each of us unless one accepts and obeys, if, often, it imposes multiple points of view which never adhere to the life of a single person and which one accepts by default, in what way can it be useful to us? I answer: in no way." Chopin imagines the absence of the Word as follows: "Because it is not useful that anyone should understand me, it is not useful that anyone should be able to order me to do this or that thing. It is not useful to have a cult that all can understand and that is there for all, it is not necessary that I should know myself to be imposed upon in my life by an all-powerful Word which was created for past epochs that will never return: that adequate to tribes, to small nations, to small ethnic groups which were disseminated around the globe into places whose origins escape us." Henri Chopin, "Why I Am the Author of Sound Poetry and Free Poetry" (1967), on *Ubuweb*, at http://www.ubu.com/papers/chopin.html.

20. Gilles Deleuze and Felix Guattari, *A Thousand Plateaus: Capitalism and Schizophrenia*, trans. Brian Massumi (London: Continuum, 2004), 88.

21. Charles Bernstein has rightfully complicated the notion of a "before language" in his introduction to *Close Listening*. As he puts it, "Writing does

not eclipse orality nor does the symbolic law supersede the amorphousness of the 'semiotic,' any more than objectivity replaces subjectivity (or vice versa). . . . Better than to speak of the preverbal, we might speak of the omniverbal. Rather than the presymbolic, we might say *asymbolic* or *heterosymbolic.*" Clearly this is a critical note with respect to the idealization of orality among sound poets/artists such as Chopin. Bernstein, introduction to *Close Listening*, 20.

22. Jean-Luc Nancy, *Ego Sum* (Paris: Flammarion, 1979), 162, quoted in Sara Emily Guyer, "Buccal Reading," *New Centennial Review* 1 (2007): 71–87.

23. Chopin, "Why I Am the Author of Sound Poetry and Free Poetry."

24. Ian James, "The Persistence of the Subject: Jean-Luc Nancy," *Paragraph* 25 (2002): 125–41.

25. Bruns, *The Material of Poetry*, 49.

26. Thomas Twining, *Aristotle's Treatise on Poetry, Translated, with Notes on the Translation, and on the Original; and Two Dissertations on Poetical, and Musical, Imitation* (1789; reprint, Westmead, UK: Gregg, 1972), 49.

27. Sander van Maas, *Wat is een luisteraar? Reflectie, dorsaliteit en interpellatie in hedendaagse muziek* (Utrecht: Universiteit Utrecht, 2009), 12.

28. Lawrence Kramer, *Why Classical Music Still Matters* (Berkeley: University of California Press, 2009), 21.

29. Lawrence Kramer, "The Devoted Ear: Music as Contemplation," in *Musical Meaning and Human Values*, ed. Keith Chapin and Lawrence Kramer (New York: Fordham University Press, 2009), 69.

30. Marshall Brown, "Music and Fantasy," in ibid., 99.

31. Mieke Bal, *Traveling Concepts in the Humanities* (Toronto: University of Toronto Press, 2002).

32. Wilhelm von Humboldt, *On Language*, ed. Michael Losonsky (Cambridge: Cambridge University Press, 1999).

33. Jean-Luc Nancy, *The Fall of Sleep* [*Tombe de sommeil*], trans. Charlotte Mandell (New York: Fordham University Press, 2009), 7.

34. Ibid., 6.

35. Quoted in Andrew Norris, "Projections of the Pulseless Body: Don Van Vliet and Henri Chopin," *Chapter and Verse* (2005), http://www.popmatters.com/chapter/Issue3/beefheart.html#19#19.

36. Jean-Luc Nancy, "On the Soul," in *Corpus*, trans. Richard A. Rand (New York: Fordham University Press, 2008), 124.

37. Ibid., 125.

38. Roland Barthes, "Rasch," in *The Responsibility of Forms*, trans. Richard Howard (Berkeley: University of California Press, 1991), 299.

39. Ibid., 307; Charles Rosen, *The Romantic Generation* (Cambridge, MA: Harvard University Press, 1995), 108.

40. Henri Chopin, text published in *Les Cahiers de l'Ircam—Recherche et musique* no. 6, trans. Andrea Cernotto (Paris: Centre Georges Pompidou, 1994), withdrawn from http://ubu.clc.wvu.edu/sound/chopin.html. Writing on *Le Corpsbis & co* in 1995, Emanuele Carcano reinforces this impression of an initial raw and untouched bodily material when observing that Chopin "creates a dense texture in which the relations among the sounds are free from the forgery caused by man's inclination to give the aspect of a conscious intuition to the prelinguistic message." The poem, Carcano decides, is a "microscopic biological reality." Emanuele Carcano, "Le Corpsbis & co," 1995, at http://ubu.clc.wvu.edu/sound/chopin.html. I do not trust these statements of an absence of difference, of a naïve immediacy that—furthermore—do not do justice to Chopin's complex techniques, working with echoes, delays, and audio feedback to create the body as a space outside of itself: in its difference to itself. I return to this issue of the body in relation/in its difference to itself later, with reference to Jean-Luc Nancy.

41. Jean-Luc Nancy, "Corpus," in *Corpus*, 19.

42. Yet there is also something very "natural" about this superimposition, if we think of the continuous or circular breathing in musicians and singers.

43. Henri Chopin, "Short Extract about My Working Method Using My Voice, without Any Words or Letters; Only My Voice and Of Course My Mouth Are Used," n.d., at http://ubu.clc.wvu.edu/sound/chopin.html.

44. Serge Brindeau, "La Poésie contemporaine depuis 1945," in Chopin, *Poésie sonore internationale*, 121.

45. Steven Connor, "Windbags and Skinsongs," http://www.stevenconnor.com/windbags/ (accessed 9 January 2013).

46. Michel Serres, *The Five Senses: A Philosophy of Mingled Bodies*, trans. Margaret Sankey and Peter Cowley (1985; reprint, New York: Continuum, 2008), 141.

47. As far as I know, Sander van Maas has been the first to analyze Nancy's philosophy of "the" body and/as soul in relation to the sound body. I am heavily indebted to his work on the self as vibration here. See: Sander van Maas, "Klanklichaam," in *Intermediale Reflecties*, ed. Henk Oosterling and Renée van de Vall (Rotterdam: DAF Cahiers, 2002), 50–57; Sander van Maas, "Lyrical Bodies: Music and the Extension of the Soul," in *Chrono-Topologies*, ed. Leslie Kavanaugh (Amsterdam: Rodopi, 2010), 159–177.

48. Nancy, "On the Soul," 126.

49. Ibid., 128.

50. Van Maas, "Lyrical Bodies," 170.

51. Nancy, "On the Soul," 123.

52. Ibid., 124.

53. Ibid., 123.

54. I refer readers to Chopin's performance videos available on Ubuweb, for instance, this amazing, undated performance: http://ubu.clc.wvu.edu/ film/chopin_undated.html.

55. Dick Higgins, "The Golem in the Text," 1992, quoted in Nicholas Zurbrugg, "Technological Performance and Techno-Aura," n.d., at http:// www.cyberpoem.com/text/zurbrugg_en.html; see also Nicholas Zurbrugg, "Marinetti, Chopin, Stelarc, and the Auratic Intensities of Postmodern Techno-Bodies," n.d., National Centre for Contemporary Art, http://glukho mania.ncca-kaliningrad.ru/pr_sonorus.php3?blang=eng&t=0&p=28.

56. Steve McCaffery, *Prior to Meaning: The Protosemantic and Poetics* (Evanston, IL: Northwestern University Press, 2001), 179.

57. Steven Connor, "Michel Serres' Five Senses," 1999, at http: //www.stevenconnor.com/5senses.htm.

58. Jean-Luc Nancy, *Listening*, trans. Charlotte Mandell (New York: Fordham University Press, 2007), 21.

59. I again refer the reader to this undated performance by Chopin on Ubuweb: http://www.ubu.com/film/chopin_undated.html.

60. Peter Szendy, *Listen: A History of Our Ears*, trans. Charlotte Mandell (New York: Fordham University Press, 2008), 143.

61. Ibid., 142.

62. Ibid.

63. David Toop, "Sound Body: The Ghost of a Program," *Leonardo Music Journal* 15 (2005): 28–35.

64. Jean-François Lyotard, *Postmodern Fables*, trans. Georges van den Abbeele (Minneapolis: University of Minnesota Press, 1997), 243. See my *Musically Sublime* (New York: Fordham University Press, 2009), 105.

ON THE ETHICS OF THE UNSPEAKABLE
Jairo Moreno

I wish to thank Amy Cimini, Stephan Hammel, Ana María Ochoa, Steve D. Smith, and the anonymous reviewers for their helpful comments on drafts of this chapter, and the editors, Andrew H. Clark and Keith Chapin, for their critiques and most of all for their care for the question of music and speech.

1. Georg Picht, *Erinnerung an Martin Heidegger*, ed. Günther Neske (Pfullingen: Neske, 1977), 244; cited, along with the Schumann example, in Paul van Dijk, *Anthropology in the Age of Technology: The Philosophical Contribution of Günther Anders*, trans. Frans Kooymans (Amsterdam: Rodopi By, 2000), 90–91. Heidegger came to differentiate philosophy from thinking; hence, the distinction here cannot be between music and thought but between music and language as it does philosophical work. This functional

take on language is in turn different from the poetic sense of language that he valued most in his own late thought.

2. John Hamilton, *Music, Madness, and the Unworking of Language* (New York: Columbia University Press, 2008), xiv (italics in the original).

3. Vladimir Jankélévitch, *Music and the Ineffable*, trans. Carolyn Abbate (Princeton, NJ: Princeton University Press, 2003). For Jankélévitch, this particularity does not render music unspeakable; instead, words are said never to exhaust the infinite multiplicity of musical meaning.

4. Giorgio Agamben, *Infancy and History*, trans. Liz Heron (London: Verso, 1993), 4.

5. Roland Barthes, "The Grain of the Voice," in *Image-Music-Text*, trans. Stephen Heath (New York: Hill and Wang, 1988), 179–89.

6. Christopher Small, *Musicking: The Meanings of Performing and Listening* (Middletown, CT: Wesleyan University Press, 1998).

7. Emmanuel Levinas, *Otherwise than Being, or, Beyond Essence*, trans. Alfonso Lingis (Boston: Kluwer, 1981), 41. He gives as an example Xenakis's *Nomos Alpha* for unaccompanied cello.

8. Ludwig Wittgenstein, *Philosophical Investigations*, trans. G. E. M. Anscombe (Oxford, UK: Blackwell, 2001), §373.

9. Ludwig Wittgenstein, *Tractatus Logico-Philosophicus*, trans. C. K. Ogden (Mineola, NY: Dover, 1998), Proposition 7.

10. Maurice O'Connor Drury, *The Danger of Words and Writings on Wittgenstein*, ed. David Berman, Michael Fitzgerald, and John Hayes (London: Routledge, 1973), ix, xiv.

11 W. J. T. Mitchell, "The Unspeakable and the Unimaginable: Word and Image in a Time of Terror," *English Literary History* 72 (2005): 295.

12. On the distinction between norm and decision, see Carl Schmitt, *Political Theology*, trans. George Schwab (Chicago: University of Chicago Press, 1996), chapters 1 and 2.

13. Here, it is worth mentioning Peter Szendy's observation that listening carries, in addition to a certain injunction (to listen is always "listen to!"), a potential to being shared. This sharing takes the form of talking or speaking and constitutes a passage toward a social life of listening different from listening as a form of sociability. See Peter Szendy, *Listen: A History of Our Ears*, trans. Charlotte Mandell (New York: Fordham University Press, 2008).

14. This summarizes Ernesto Laclau's analysis in "Why Do Empty Signifiers Matter to Politics?," in *Emancipation(s)* (London: Verso, 1996), 37. The models of the limit I present in the text address Laclau's work in, among others, *Emancipations*; Ernesto Laclau and Chantal Mouffe, *Hegemony and Socialist Strategy: Towards a Radical Democratic Politics* (London: Verso, 1985), esp. chapter 3; Judith Butler, Ernesto Laclau, and Slavoj Žižek, *Contingency,*

Hegemony, Universality: Contemporary Dialogues on the Left (London: Verso, 2000); and Laclau, *On Populist Reason* (London: Verso, 2005). I also draw from a three-part seminar Laclau taught at New York University in spring 2007 and a short interview I conducted with him at the time. A useful critical review of Laclau's thought appears in Oliver Marchart, *Post-Foundational Political Thought: Political Difference in Nancy, Lefort, Badiou and Laclau* (Edinburgh: Edinburgh University Press, 2007).

15. Parmenides, *Parmenides of Elea: Fragments, a Text and Translation with an Introduction*, trans. and ed. David Gallop (Toronto: University of Toronto Press, 1984), 55.

16. Immanuel Kant, *Critique of Pure Reason*, trans. Norman Kemp Smith (Boston: Bedford / St. Martin's, 1965), B 111.

17. Ibid., A 515 = B 543; italics in the original.

18. Immanuel Kant, *Prolegomena to Any Future Metaphysics (with Selections from the Critique of Pure Reason)*, trans. and ed. Gary Hatfield (New York: Cambridge University Press, 1997), §57.

19. Ibid.

20. Michael Inwood, *A Hegel Dictionary* (London: Blackwell, 1992), s.v. "Limit, Restriction, and Finitude," 177–78.

21. Kant, *Critique of Pure Reason*, B 191. Note that this opposition is maintained even in occasions when human activity mobilizes the two domains. Keith Chapin (in an editorial communication) reminds me of the fact that for "Kant a decision involves a (phenomenal) reaction to a cause and is also a (noumenal) instantiation of free will." But the domains remain as discrete parts of an opposition, even and particularly when seemingly coming together.

22. Ibid., A 255.

23. Ibid.

24. Herbert James Paton, *Kant's Metaphysics of Experience: A Commentary on the First Half of the Kritik der reinen vernunft*, vol. 2 (London: Allen & Unwin, 1936), 457–58. For an opposite interpretation, see Henry Allison, *Kant's Transcendental Idealism: An Interpretation and Defense*, rev. and enlarged ed. (New Haven, CT: Yale University Press, 2004). Thanks to Stephan Hammel for bringing this text to my attention.

25. Judith P. Butler, Ernesto Laclau, and Reinaldo José Laddaga, "The Uses of Equality," *Diacritics* 27 (1997): 9.

26. See the incisive analysis of Kant's appeal to sovereignty in Martin Hägglund, *Radical Atheism: Derrida and the Time of Life* (Stanford, CA: Stanford University Press, 2008), 20–30.

27. "By saying 'the Thing *is* non-phenomenal,' we do *not* say the same as 'the Thing *is not* phenomenal.'" Slavoj Žižek, *Tarrying with the Negative:*

Kant, Hegel, and the Critique of Ideology (Durham, NC: Duke University Press, 1993), 111. See Kant, *Critique of Pure Reason*, B 307.

28. Georg Wilhelm Friedrich Hegel, *Science of Logic*, trans. A. V. Miller (1812; reprint, London: Allen and Unwin, 1969), 127.

29. Inwood, *A Hegel Dictionary*, s.v. "Limit, Restriction, and Finitude," 179.

30. For a similar but alternative approach to difference, see Gregory Batteson's notion of "complementary differentiation," in *Steps to an Ecology of Mind: Collected Essays in Anthropology, Psychiatry, Evolution, and Epistemology* (Chicago: University of Chicago Press, 1972), §61.

31. Jacques Derrida, "Signature Event Context," in *Margins of Philosophy*, trans. Alan Bass (Chicago: University of Chicago Press, 1985), 308–30.

32. I should note that I am not suggesting here an understanding of difference such as Deleuze's, in which "difference itself" stands in a constitutive antagonistic relation (and only antagonistic) to all representation. See Gilles Deleuze, *Difference and Repetition*, trans. Paul Patton (New York: Columbia University Press, 1995).

33. We are reminded how in Roman Jakobson's influential development of Saussure all systems of meaning are rendered as languages.

34. Laclau makes this point about the simultaneous impossibility and necessity of the limit explicitly in Butler, Laclau, and Laddaga, "Uses of Equality," 9.

35. Giorgio Agamben, *Homo Sacer: Sovereign Power and Bare Life*, trans. Daniel Heller-Roazen (Stanford, CA: Stanford University Press, 1998), 21.

36. At the conference that initially inspired this collection, I illustrated this torsion by means of a Möbius strip, whose topology disallows not only a limit between inside or outside but also their coming together. Žižek makes use of this figure to describe the subject-object relation in Hegelian subjectivity in *The Fragile Absolute, or Why Is the Christian Legacy Worth Fighting For?* (London: Verso, 2000), 28. Žižek himself borrows from Lacan's use in Seminar IX ("L'Identification," 1961–62) and its elaboration in "L'Étourdit" (1973).

37. Butler, Laclau, and Laddaga, "Uses of Equality," 8.

38. Translation by John Hamilton (personal communication). Hamilton offers this grammatically correct version: "It is necessary to speak and think that a being is: for Being is, and nothing is not." The use of neuter definite article (Gr. *to*) turns the infinitives "to speak" (*legein*) and "to think" (*noein*) into the English gerundial forms "speaking" and "thinking." Compare with this recent rendering: "It must be that what is there for speaking and thinking of is; for [it] is there to be, Whereas nothing is not" (Parmenides, *Parmenides of Elea*, 6.1–2; see also 8.34–36).

39. References to "Being" here are not to "*a* being" but to the raw possibility of being at all, following the classic Heideggerian distinction between ontology (Being) and the ontic (being in its manifold expressions).

40. Jacques Derrida, "The Supplement of the Copula: Philosophy *before* Linguistics," in *Textual Strategies: Perspectives in Post-Structuralist Criticism*, ed. Josué V. Harari (Ithaca, NY: Cornell University Press, 1980), 90.

41. Jean-Luc Nancy, "Abandoned Being," in *The Birth to Presence*, trans. Brian Holmes (Stanford, CA: Stanford University Press, 1993), 38.

42. Martin Heidegger, *Being and Time: A Translation of Sein und Zeit*, trans. Joan Stambaugh (Albany: State University of New York Press, 1996), 29–30. For a useful discussion of the bind between voice and Being in Heidegger, see Mladen Dolar, *A Voice and Nothing More* (Cambridge, MA: MIT Press, 2006), 95–97.

43. Aristotle, *Metaphysics*, E2, 1026 a34–1026 b4. A similar position is elaborated throughout Aristotle's *Topics*, book 1. References to Aristotle are from the *Complete Works of Aristotle, the Revised Oxford Edition*, ed. Jonathan Barnes, 2 vols. (Princeton, NJ: Princeton University Press, 1995). To be sure, the expressions "of X, it is said in multiple ways" or "of X, it is multiply spoken" are characteristic of Aristotle's argumentative style in his natural philosophical and psychological writings, his aim being to constantly clarify a term before moving on to another. However, here I wish to point out the multiplicity of a term—*logos*—as it enters the political, a realm not entirely subsumable under Aristotle's natural philosophy or his psychology.

44. Nancy, "Abandoned Being," 44–45.

45. Aristotle, *Politics*, I:1253a 7–8.

46. Ibid.

47. This analysis is indebted to Agamben's account of this distinction in *Homo Sacer*, 1–8.

48. This argument lies at the core of the notion of biopolitics, the historically constituted conjunction of life and the political in which the former, taken as "biological processes of man as a species," becomes the focus of the latter. Foucault, whose definition is partly cited here, is a key figure. See Michel Foucault, *History of Sexuality, Vol. 1: An Introduction* (New York: Random House, 1978); Foucault, *"Society Must Be Defended": Lectures at the Collège de France, 1975–1976*, ed. Mauro Bertani and Alessandro Fontana, trans. David Macey (New York: Picador, 2003); Foucault, *The Birth of Biopolitics: Lectures at the Collège de France, 1978–1979*, ed. Michel Senellart, trans. Graham Burchell (New York: Palgrave Macmillan, 2008). Besides Agamben, others have worked on the subject, including Michael Hardt and Antonio Negri, in *Empire* (Cambridge, MA: Harvard University Press, 2000), *Multitude: War*

and Democracy in the Age of Empire (New York: Penguin, 2004), and *Commonwealth* (Cambridge, MA: Belknap Press of Harvard University Press, 2009); Judith Butler, in *Precarious Life: The Powers of Mourning and Violence* (London: Verso, 2004) and *Giving an Account of Oneself: A Critique of Ethical Violence* (New York: Fordham University Press, 2005); and Roberto Esposito, in *Bíos: Biopolitics and Philosophy*, trans. (Minneapolis: University of Minnesota Press, 2008). For Agamben, see also *Remnants of Auschwitz: The Witness and the Archive*, trans. Daniel Heller-Roazen (New York: Zone Books, 2002), and *The Open: Man and Animal*, trans. Kevin Attell (Stanford, CA: Stanford University Press, 2003).

49. Jacques Rancière, *Disagreement: Politics and Philosophy*, trans. Julie Rose (Minneapolis: University of Minnesota Press, 1999), 14 (see also 15, 30, 65, 66, 88, 123, and 137).

50. Aristotle, *Politics*, I:1254 b24–25.

51. Rancière, *Disagreement*, 24, and 22–23 (see also 26–27).

52. The focus on the sonorous and the acoustic here is not meant to reinscribe an uncomplicated version and well-known critique of phonocentrism but simply to present the frame in which Agamben, Nancy, and Rancière elaborate their analyses.

53. Georg Wilhelm Friedrich Hegel, *Hegel's Phenomenology of Spirit*, trans. A. V. Miller (Oxford: Oxford University Press, 1977), 439 (¶ 726).

54. Agamben, *Homo Sacer*, 21.

55. The marches brought large numbers of other-than-Hispanic or Latino demonstrators, including citizens, but public discourse and media coverage amplified the unexamined association of illegal immigrants and migrants with Hispanics.

56. Cristina Beltrán, "Achieving the Extraordinary: Hannah Arendt, Immigrant Action and the Space of Appearance," unpublished manuscript. A published and revised version of this manuscript, "Going Public: Hannah Arendt, Immigrant Action and the Space of Appearance," *Political Theory: An International Journal of Political Philosophy* 37, no. 5 (2009): 595–622, does not alter the basic points I borrow here. My thanks to Professor Beltrán for sharing her essay in advance of publication. The reference to Arendt is to Hannah Arendt, *The Human Condition*, 2nd ed., with an introduction by Margaret Canovan (Chicago: University of Chicago Press, 1998). We are reminded that for Arendt the vita activa is "unquiet" (*askholia*) and that, as Davide Panagia notes, "there has never been a quiet democratic movement." Davide Panagia, *The Political Life of Sensation* (Durham, NC: Duke University Press, 2009), 52.

For a more historical analysis of the 2006 marches, one centered on Chicano politics in Southern California, see Alfonso Gonzales, "The 2006 Mega

Marchas in Greater Los Angeles: Counter-Hegemonic Moment and the Future of El Migrante Struggle," *Latino Studies* 7 (2009): 30–59.

57. "Right" is here used in a narrow sense, from the perspective of U.S. law; by that narrow logic, having no right to be on U.S. soil in the first place, illegal immigrants have no right to express themselves.

"Sonorization" is used here in Deleuze's sense, denoting, in this case, the power of places and spaces to be expressive of sound, not solely as an expression of people's sonic being. Although I do not pursue the consequences of this notion here with regard to place, I adopt the position that during the marches, place, sound, and people were equivalent. Thanks to Amy Cimini for reminding me of Deleuze's use of the term. See Gilles Deleuze and Félix Guattari, "On the Refrain," in *A Thousand Plateaus: Capitalism and Schizophrenia*, trans. and foreword by Brian Massumi (Minneapolis: University of Minnesota Press, 1987); and Gilles Deleuze, *Francis Bacon: The Logic of Sensation*, trans. Daniel W. Smith (London: Continuum, 2003). The term is used in a negative sense by Paul Virilio to refer to pollution caused by a relentless "artistic production of resonant and noisy sound-scapes," as John Armitage describes it; see Armitage, "Art and Fear: An Introduction," in *Art and Fear*, by Paul Virilio, trans. Julie Rose (London: Continuum, 2003), 1.

58. The connection between Spinoza and Barthes is of course historical, given Barthes's deep investment in Henri Bergson and relation to Vladimir Jankélévitch, both heirs to a Spinozist tradition. A key distinction, again, is that Spinoza does not restrict his thinking of the body to the human body and does not abrogate the potential of thought to interact with bodies.

59. My reference to a field of the sensate adapts Rancière's notion of the "distribution of the sensible" or "the system of self-evident facts of sense perception that simultaneously discloses the existence of something in common and the delimitations that define the respective parts and positions within it." Jacques Rancière, "The Distribution of the Sensible: Politics and Aesthetics," in *The Politics of Aesthetics*, trans. and with an introduction by Gabriel Rockhill (London: Continuum, 2004), 12.

60. The expression "surrogate terrain" is George Yúdice's: *The Expediency of Culture: Uses of Culture in the Global Era* (Durham, NC: Duke University Press, 2003), 55. The literature on English-Spanish bilingualism is extensive. A good introduction to the legal issues and debates appears in the dedicated essays in *The Latino/a Condition: A Critical Reader*, ed. Richard Delgado and Jean Stefancic (New York: NYU Press, 1998).

61. Here too might belong the idea that music holds no place of privilege vis-à-vis the sonic, an argument heard made most often by sound studies scholars. See, for instance, Douglas Kahn, *Noise, Water, Meat: A History of Sound in the Arts* (Cambridge, MA: MIT Press, 2001); and Jonathan Sterne,

The Audible Past: Cultural Origins of Sound Reproduction (Durham, NC: Duke University Press, 2003).

62. Nancy, "Abandoned Being," 44.

63. The expression "poverty of trace" originated in conversation with Laura Odello and Peter Szendy and refers to the equivocal condition of music such that its ephemeral materiality is felt to leave no trace or else to leave a trace as delicate as it is rich, such that what can be said of it is thought to be never enough.

64. Judith Butler and Gayatri Chakravorty Spivak, *Who Sings the Nation State? Language, Politics, Belonging* (London: Seagull Books, 2007), 57, 59, 62–63. Susan Bickford, a political theorist, elaborates the dimension of listening in Arendt in *The Dissonance of Democracy: Listening, Conflict, and Citizenship* (Ithaca, NY: Cornell University Press, 1996). For a more conventional examination of specifically musical dimensions of politics in the United States, see Nancy S. Love, *Musical Democracy* (Albany: State University of New York Press, 2006).

65. Adriana Cavarero, *For More than One Voice: Toward a Philosophy of Vocal Expression*, trans. Paul Kottman (Stanford, CA: Stanford University Press, 2005), 179, 180 (italics in original).

66. Ibid., 182.

67. Butler ties the anthem to the marches in Los Angeles and other California cities (Butler and Spivak, *Who Sings the Nation State?*, 58). It needs to be noted that each single Spanish citation in these pages contains a misspelling, remarkable in light of the well-publicized polyglot virtuosity of Butler's coauthor (the book is in the form of a dialogue) and Butler's longstanding residence in California, but perhaps telling of the lingering disengagement in certain critical circles with Hispanic and Latino politics in general.

68. The producer, Adam Kidron, stated, "I want the anthem to be more easily understood by Spanish-speakers and it is a mark of solidarity by Latin immigrants that they are prepared to share in this America and we all appreciate it." Joanna Walters, "Come Sing Along, Señor Bush," *Guardian Online*, 30 April 2006, http://www.guardian.co.uk/world/2006/apr/30/usa.joanna walters (accessed 1 February 2011).

69. John Holusha, "Bush Says Anthem Should Be in English," *New York Times*, 28 April 2006, http://www.nytimes.com/2006/04/28/us/28cnd-anthem.html?ex=1303876800&en=08c47125f97ce6ea&ei=5090&partner=rssuserland&emc=rss (accessed 22 June 2009). A comprehensive overview of the debates surrounding "Nuestro Himno" appears in Barbara Lynn Speicher and JC. Bruno Teboul, "Nuestro Himno: Discursive Indignation and Moral Panic over the Translation of a National Symbol," *International Journal of Diversity in Organisations, Communities and Nations* 8, no. 4 (2008): 177–85.

70. CBS News, *Face the Nation*, with Bob Schieffer, 30 April 2006, transcript at http://www.cbsnews.com/htdocs/pdf/face_043006.pdf, 5–6.

71. The argument is Rancière's and has recently been elaborated by Panagia, in *The Political Life of Sensation*, 40. The literature on the politics of recognition under multicultural regimes is extensive. A classic text is Charles Taylor, *Multiculturalism: Examining the Politics of Recognition*, ed. Amy Gutmann (Princeton, NJ: Princeton University Press, 1994). A robust anthropological critique focused on a settler nation but with a wider analytical reach appears in Elizabeth A. Povinelli, *The Cunning of Recognition: Indigenous Alterities and the Making of Australian Multiculturalism* (Durham, NC: Duke University Press, 2002).

72. Under the Obama administration, "immigration authorities have backed away from the Bush administration's frequent mass factory round-ups of illegal immigrant workers. But federal criminal prosecutions for immigration violations have actually increased this year." Julia Preston, "Firm Stance on Illegal Immigrants Remains Policy," *New York Times*, 3 August 2009, http://www.nytimes.com/2009/08/04/us/politics/04immig.html?scp=35&sq=&st=nyt (accessed 7 September 2009). Much of the debate has been stirred by news of deaths of illegal immigrants while in detention. A 31 July 2009 editorial in the *New York Times* reported the existence of a secretive system whereby in a year, as many as three hundred thousand illegal immigrants were detainees without access to lawyers or their families. "President Obama's Department of Homeland Security rejected a petition in federal court to enact legally enforceable standards for the treatment of immigrant detainees. Instead, the administration is sticking with a Bush-era system that relies in part on private contractors for quality control, even though those outside monitors are often former federal immigration agents." "Detained and Abused," *New York Times*, 31 July 2009, http://www.nytimes.com/2009/08/01/opinion/01sat2.html?scp=38&sq=&st=nyt (accessed 7 September 2009).

73. Cavarero, *For More than One Voice*, 200–201.

74. Ibid., 201.

75. Steven Feld and Aaron Fox, "Music and Language," *Annual Review of Anthropology* 23 (1994): 35.

76. Butler and Spivak, *Who Sings the Nation State?*, 113.

77. Elizabeth A. Povinelli, "The Child in the Broom Closet: States of Killing and Letting Die," *South Atlantic Quarterly* 107, no. 3 (2008): 511. Povinelli's statement refers to a short story by Ursula Le Guin in which "the happiness and well-being" of the inhabitants of a fictional city depend "on a small child being constrained to and humiliated in a small, putrid broom closet" (509). She goes on to analyze indigenous life in late liberal Australia.

78. Butler, *Precarious Life*, 48, paraphrasing from Adriana Cavarero, *Relating Narratives: Storytelling and Selfhood*, trans. P. Kottman (New York: Routledge, 2000).

RÉCIT RECITATION RECITATIVE
Jean-Luc Nancy

1. Philippe Lacoue-Labarthe, *Portrait de l'artiste, en général* (Paris: Christian Bourgois, 1979), 90. I will speak here of the *récit* and of Philippe Lacoue-Labarthe. One by the other, and one for the other. Of the story he made of his life; of the life—the thought—he drew from stories.

2. Philippe Lacoue-Labarthe, *L'Allégorie* (Paris: Galilée, 2005), 19.

3. *Récit* can mean "narrative," "story," or "tale." In music, it can mean "recitative" or "solo."

4. *"Il arrive que."* [*Il arrive* can mean either "it occurs, it happens" or "he arrives." —Trans.] Philippe Lacoue-Labarthe, *Poetry as Experience*, trans. Andrea Tarnowski (Stanford, CA: Stanford University Press, 1999), 89.

5. Georg Wilhelm Friedrich Hegel, *Enzyklopädie der philosophischen Wissenschaften im Grundrisse*, 3rd ed., ed. Friedhelm Nicolin and Otto Pöggeler (Heidelberg: Osswald, 1830; reprint, Hamburg: Meiner, 1991), 50 (§17). Page numbers refer to the reprint edition.

6. Ibid.

7. At the same time, philosophy also supposes its own narrative: it too has already begun before beginning. Either there have been preliminary, imperfect forms of *logos*, or *mythos* must be regarded both as illusory knowledge and as raw knowledge, waiting for the arising of "logic." In one way or another, there has been antecedence, either of philosophy to itself, or of something else. More generally, no philosophical text is in fact exempt from narrative. We can easily demonstrate this. Hence, it is both inexact and yet enlightening to simplify as I do here, by reducing philosophers' texts to their intentions.

8. Cf. Philippe Lacoue-Labarthe, *Musica Ficta*, trans. Felicia McCarren (Stanford, CA: Stanford University Press, 1994), 93–94, where this failure is imputed to art that wants to be "itself": the fault of the subject thus turns out to be to form the intimate motivation of art (as well as of religion, according to the passage in question—but that is another matter, if art is itself "caesura of religion," as the conclusion of the same book asserts).

9. Philippe Lacoue-Labarthe, *Phrase* (Paris: Christian Bourgois, 2000), 45.

10. Philippe Lacoue-Labarthe, "The Echo of the Subject," in *Typography: Mimesis, Philosophy, Politics*, ed. Christopher Fynsk (Cambridge, MA: Harvard University Press, 1989), 175.

11. Italo Calvino, *If on a Winter's Night a Traveler*, trans. William Weaver (New York: Everyman's Library, 1993), 149.

12. This is from the French translation of *As I Lay Dying*, which differs from the original "Meet Mrs. Bundren, he says."—Trans.

13. Malcolm Lowry, *Under the Volcano* (New York: Lippincott, 1965), 375.

14. Philippe Lacoue-Labarthe, *Le Chant des Muses* (Paris: Bayard, 2005), 29–30.

15. Lacoue-Labarthe, "The Echo of the Subject," 145.

16. About musical romanticism, it would be apt here to begin an examination of the *lied*—a beloved form for Lacoue-Labarthe, as well as for a whole contemporary taste whose deep motive must stem from this: the *lied*, often a small narrative, attempts a delicate equilibrium between melody and rhythm or else, to anticipate what will come later, between *aria* and *recitativo*. It allows singing effusion as well as speaking pulsation, one aligned with the other. When it is successful, that is what can be heard.

17. Of the upper-case Subject as distinct from the lower-case subject, see Lacoue-Labarthe, *Musica Ficta*, 77.

18. Nor is it easy to separate rhythm from melody without some overlap. But that is another question.

19. There should be some analysis of how in the contemporary fate of music, ever since Wagner and Debussy and including Schoenberg and Berio and the blues, Miles Davis, certain aspects of pop and rock, and even electronic music and rap, something of the recitative has penetrated into where there used to be only an "air [tune, aria]" and perhaps even a "pretty air." Far from being at the service of action to give more prominence to arias, as was the case in classical opera, recitative is once again, unlike the ornamental aria, finding a value less linked to language than to the pulsation of speech, to psalmody, to threnody, to antiphon—to response too, and thus, through another form of echo, to the religious past of the recitative. Probably the narrative precedes and follows us. "Caesura of religion," said Lacoue-Labarthe.

20. Lacoue-Labarthe, *Phrase*, 130.

21. Lacoue-Labarthe, *L'Allégorie* (Paris: Galilée, 2006), 17, "Récitatif."

PER AAGE BRANDT, originally from Denmark, is Adjunct Professor of Cognitive Science at Case Western Reserve University. He specializes in structural semantics and cognitive semiotics. His thesis, *La Charpente modale du sens* (1992), introduced catastrophe topology as a way to describe dynamic schematizations in discourse. His latest book, *Spaces, Domains, and Meaning* (2004), develops the concepts of mental space and blending theory within a semiotic framework. He is also active as a jazz pianist, poet, and translator. His latest book of poems is *These Hands* (2011).

KIENE BRILLENBURG WURTH is Associate Professor of Comparative Literature at Utrecht University and project leader of the VIDI-project "Back to the Book" (2011–2016), funded by the Dutch Research Council. She is the author of *Musically Sublime: Infinity, Indeterminacy, Irresolvability* (2009) and editor of *Between Page and Screen: Remaking Literature through Cinema and Cyberspace* (2012). She has published widely in peer-reviewed journals and volumes and is preparing a new monograph on "analogue" literature in a "digital" age.

KEITH CHAPIN is Lecturer in Music at Cardiff University. He has taught at Fordham University (New York) and at the New Zealand School of Music (Wellington). He specializes in issues of critical theory, music aesthetics, and music theory in the seventeenth through twentieth centuries and in particular on issues of counterpoint. He has been Coeditor of *Eighteenth-Century Music* and Associate Editor of *19th-Century Music* and sits on the editorial boards of these journals. He was coeditor (with Lawrence Kramer) of *Musical Meaning and Human Values* (2009). Recent articles have appeared in *Music & Letters*, *19th-Century Music*, and the *International Review of the Aesthetics and Sociology of Music*.

ANDREW H. CLARK is Associate Professor of French and Comparative Literature at Fordham University. He is the author of *Diderot's Part* (2008).

He works and writes on literature, aesthetics, and science in the early modern period.

MATTHEW GELBART is Assistant Professor in the Department of Art History and Music at Fordham University. He is the author of *The Invention of "Folk Music" and "Art Music": Emerging Categories from Ossian to Wagner* (2007) and has also published articles in several journals, including *JRMA*, *Ethnomusicology*, *Eighteenth-Century Music*, and *Music and Letters*. His research interests include late eighteenth- and nineteenth-century music; musical labels, identities, and genres; Scottish music; and rock music. He is currently working on a new book project titled *Listening to Novelty: Musical Genre and Romantic Ideologies*, for which he was the recipient of the 2010–2011 American Philosophical Society Sabbatical Fellowship.

JOHN T. HAMILTON is Professor of Comparative Literature at Harvard University and has held visiting positions at the University of California–Santa Cruz, New York University, and the University of Bristol. Publications include *Soliciting Darkness: Pindar, Obscurity and the Classical Tradition* (2004), *Music, Madness, and the Unworking of Language* (2008), and *Security: Politics, Humanity, and the Philology of Care* (2013).

LAWRENCE KRAMER is Distinguished Professor of English and Music at Fordham University, Editor of the journal *19th-Century Music*, and a composer whose works have been performed internationally. His many books include, most recently, *Interpreting Music* (2010) and *Expression and Truth: On the Music of Knowledge* (2012), both from the University of California Press. Recent premieres include *Another Time* for voice, violin, and cello and *A Short History (of the 20th Century)* for voice and percussion.

SANDER VAN MAAS is Professor of Musicology at Utrecht University and teaches musicology at the University of Amsterdam. He authored *The Reinvention of Religious Music: Olivier Messiaen's Breakthrough toward the Beyond* (2009) and coedited the volumes *Liminal Auralities: Music, Language and Listening* (forthcoming) and *Contemporary Music and Spirituality* (forthcoming).

JAIRO MORENO teaches at the University of Pennsylvania and is the author of *Musical Representations, Subjects, Objects: The Construction of Musical Thought in Zarlino, Descartes, Rameau, and Weber* (2004).

JEAN-LUC NANCY is Professor Emeritus at the Université Marc Bloch, Strasbourg. He has been a visiting professor at the University of California–San Diego, the University of California–Berkeley, and the Freie Universität in Berlin, among other institutions. He is the author of numerous works, including, most recently, *Adoration: The Deconstruction of Christianity II* (2013) and *L'Equivalence des catastrophes* (2012). Among the most recent of his many books to be published in English are *Corpus; The Ground of the Image; Dis-Enclosure: The Deconstruction of Christianity; Noli me tangere: On the Raising of the Body; On the Commerce of Thinking: Of Books and Bookstores;* and *The Truth of Democracy*. On the subject of the sonorous and its perception, he has published *A l'écoute* (*Listening*, 2002).

LAURA ODELLO is director of a research program at the Collège international de philosophie, where she runs a seminar on the theme of appropriation. She has translated Derrida, Nancy, and Virilio, among others, into Italian and collaborates on the Italian journal of philosophy *aut aut*. She is currently finishing a book on Jacques Derrida and the deconstruction of sovereignty. Recent publications include "'Tout se joue à la limite . . . ': Derrida et l'espace cryptique," in *Limite-illimité, questions au present* (2012), and "L'Image infectée," in *Penser au cinéma* (forthcoming).

TRACY B. STRONG is Distinguished Professor of Political Science at the University of California, San Diego. He is the author of several books, including *Friedrich Nietzsche and the Politics of Transfiguration* (3rd ed., 2000), *Jean-Jacques Rousseau and the Politics of the Ordinary* (2nd ed., 2001), and, most recently, *Politics without Vision: Thinking without a Banister in the Twentieth Century* (2012). From 1990 to 2000, he was Editor of *Political Theory: An International Journal of Political Philosophy*.

PETER SZENDY is Professor of Philosophy at Paris Ouest Nanterre and musicological adviser for the concert programs at the Cité de la musique. He also taught in the Music Department at the Université Marc Bloch, Strasbourg, from 1998 to 2005 and was Visiting Fellow in the Council of Humanities at Princeton University. He has been the senior editor of a journal and book series published by IRCAM. He is the author of *Hits: Philosophy in the Jukebox* (2012), *Sur écoute: esthétique de l'espionnage* (2007), *Membres fantômes: Des corps musiciens* (2002), and *Listen: A History of Our Ears* (2007).

LAWRENCE M. ZBIKOWSKI is Associate Professor and Chair of the Department of Music at the University of Chicago. He is the author of *Conceptualizing Music: Cognitive Structure, Theory, and Analysis* (Oxford, 2002). He has contributed chapters to *The Cambridge Handbook of Metaphor and Thought* (2008), *Communication in Eighteenth Century Music* (2008), *New Perspectives on Music and Gesture* (2011), *Music and Consciousness* (2011), and *Bewegungen zwischen Hören und Sehen* (2012) and has also published in the *Dutch Journal of Music Theory*, *Music Analysis*, *Music Humana*, *Musicæ Scientiæ*, *Music Theory Spectrum*, *Ethnomusicology*, and the *Journal of Musicological Research*. During the 2010–11 academic year, he held a fellowship from the American Council of Learned Societies and was also Fulbright Visiting Research Chair at McGill University.